INVISIBLE POLITICS

Hanes Walton, Jr.

INVISIBLE

POLITICS

Black Political Behavior

STATE UNIVERSITY OF NEW YORK PRESS   ALBANY

SUNY Series in Afro-American Society
John Howard and Robert C. Smith, Editors

PUBLISHED BY

STATE UNIVERSITY OF NEW YORK PRESS, ALBANY

© 1985 STATE UNIVERSITY OF NEW YORK

ALL RIGHTS RESERVED

PRINTED IN THE UNITED STATES OF AMERICA

NO PART OF THIS BOOK MAY BE USED OR REPRODUCED IN ANY MANNER WHATSOEVER WITHOUT WRITTEN PERMISSION EXCEPT IN THE CASE OF BRIEF QUOTATIONS EMBODIED IN CRITICAL ARTICLES AND REVIEWS.

FOR INFORMATION, ADDRESS STATE UNIVERSITY OF NEW YORK PRESS, STATE UNIVERSITY PLAZA, ALBANY, N.Y., 12246

LIBRARY OF CONGRESS CATALOGING IN PUBLICATION DATA

WALTON, HANES, 1941-
  INVISIBLE POLITICS.
  (SUNY SERIES IN AFRO-AMERICAN SOCIETY)
  BIBLIOGRAPHY: P.
  INCLUDES INDEX.
  1. AFRO-AMERICANS — POLITICS AND GOVERNMENT.
2. AFRO-AMERICANS — SUFFRAGE. I. TITLE. II. SERIES.
E185.615.W32 1985   320'.08996073   85-4647
ISBN 0-87395-966-3
ISBN 0-87395-991-4 (pbk.)

10 9 8 7 6 5 4 3 2

To
Dr. Prince A. Jackson, Jr., a
college president who understood the two great traditions of Black
colleges, teaching and research, and enriched them both

Contents

List of Tables

Foreword

This essay addresses itself first to the goals and standards of the series of books on Afro-American Society to be published by the State University of New York Press and then to the character of Hanes Walton's *Invisible Politics: A Multidimensional Analysis of Black Political Behavior,* the inaugural work in the series.

The scholarly literature on black culture and society in the United States is vast. From their inception in the nineteenth century, all of the social science disciplines have devoted an enormous amount of attention to the country's shifting race relations. Indeed, the first two sociological works published in the United States, Henry Hughes's *Treatise on Sociology, Theoretical and Practical* and George Fitzhugh's *Sociology of the South,* as defenses of slavery, dealt with race.

In this vast literature by an enormous number of scholars, there are a number of classics, still vital today, which made major contributions to the body of empirical information on black culture and society or presented fundamentally new and insightful theoretical models for the analysis of the dynamics of race in America. Some of the classics contributed in both dimensions.

Among the works that have been pivotol in the study of black America are W.E.B. Du Bois's *The Philadelphia Negro: A Social Study* (1899), Gunnar Myrdal's *An American Dilemma: The Negro Problem and American Democracy* (1944), and Stokely Carmichael and Charles Hamilton's *Black Power: Politics of Liberation in America* (1967).

These and other classics set the standards to which this series aspires. Each of them at the time of publication was at the cutting edge of research and analysis rather than being merely a synthesis of existing knowledge. It may be instructive to briefly review the contributions of each of these works, inasmuch as the sum of their unique contributions constitutes the goal of this series.

W.E.B. Du Bois's *The Philadelphia Negro* was published at a time when empirical work on black society was weak. George Washington Williams's, *The History of the Negro in the United States* had been published in 1883, but had largely fallen into limbo. Social science thought of that era reflected the influence of social Darwinism. Major figures within sociology, such as W.E. Thomas and Charles Horton Cooley, subscribed in varying degrees to the notion that racial stratification—the subordination of blacks within an atmosphere of racial antagonism—was inevitable. Empirical data on blacks that was found in the social science literature at all tended to be for the purposes of illustrating, rather than testing, social Darwinist ideas. In *The Philadelphia Negro* Du Bois marshalled empirical data on black life. The book is a landmark, both substantively—in the fidelity with which it conveyed certain dimensions of black life—and in terms of what it indicated about the purposes of empiricism in the social sciences—the data test rather than illustrate ideas.

From *The Philadelphia Negro* we draw as a standard for the works in this series that, to the extent that they are empirically oriented, they make a strong substantive contribution, presenting a body of information that in its own right becomes an important resource for scholars.

Gunnar Myrdal's *An American Dilemma*, published more than 40 years after Du Bois's work, came at a time when the study of black life in the United States was in a *cul-de-sac*. The race relations cycle theory of Robert Park had dominated much of social science thinking for the preceding twenty years. A generation of scholars had been trained by Park at the University of Chicago and had used his analytic methods in the study of race. Briefly, Park had posited that race relations go through a cycle of contact between racial groups; conflict between them leads to assimilation, presumably of the minority group into the society of the majority. Ostensibly the United States was in the second stage of conflict and the subordination of blacks. There were a number of problems with Park's theory: among them, of course, was that it was not correct.

An American Dilemma made two major contributions to the study of blacks. First, it assembled an enormous body of data. It went to the realities of black life. It portrayed what *was* and what people *believed*. Second, it did not fit its data into a preconceived scheme or theory but used them to illuminate the tension between American ideals and the reality of racial subordination. An appreciation of the reality of that tension has informed much of the social science literature on blacks and configurations of race in the United States ever since.

A second goal of this series, drawn from reflection on this classic, is the publication of works that are not only of major significance in terms of data but that also articulate frameworks and vocabularies that provide greater insight into black life and culture.

Finally, *Black Power* by Stokely Carmichael and Charles Hamilton, published in 1969 made a signal contribution to the literature on blacks and the dynamics of racial change. In effect, this work articulated a new perspective for analyzing race issues. In the several years preceding its publication, a number of civil rights laws had been passed in response to massive black and white protests against segregation and legalized racism. Both the civil rights movements of that period and the scholarly literature on race relations conceptualized racism as psychological traits of individuals, which translated into a set of collective practices, which yielded the systematic denial of opportunities and rights to blacks. Given this conceptualization of the "causes" of race problems in the United States, the Civil Rights laws of the 1960's, insofar as they proscribed acts that were clearly discriminatory in racial terms, should have moved the society far toward "solving" its race problem.

The concept of "institutionalized racism" as articulated in *Black Power*, provided part of the explanation as to why this did not occur. This multidimensional concept suggested that racially invidious consequences might not reflect consciously malicious intent, but might stem from institutional practices, seemingly neutral in character, which result in systematically negative outcomes for blacks and other minorities.

This is a complex concept. Its policy implications provide the axis of bitter debate between those who believe that the civil rights laws of the 1960s represent the extent to which the society can or should seek racial melioration and those who believe that affirmative steps are necessary, overt racism aside, to achieve just ends.

The premises of *Black Power* have been integrated into the vocabulary used by policy-makers as they debate alternatives.

A third goal of this series then is to produce works that contribute to policy debate in terms of issues crucial to Blacks and thereby crucial to the entire society.

The classic literature therefore provides both the inspiration for this series and the standards it seeks to meet. Given these goals it is appropriate that Hanes Walton's work be the first published in the series. Many of the best works on black life and culture came at a time when existing analytic frameworks proved inadequate to describe or accout for new realities. Black politics as an academic subfield has needed a work combining both empirical sweep and theoretical sophistication. New realities in terms of the relationship of blacks to the political system have called for a work providing a theoretical method and an analytic vocabulary sufficient to move the study of black politics forward. In those terms Professor Walton's *Invisible Politics* is an exciting first work in the series.

Let us comment briefly on its contemporary meaning and then on its place in terms of the goals of this series. To understand the contemporary importance of Walton's book it is necessary to appreciate three propositions.

First, the civil rights movement of the 1960s effected significant change in the status of blacks. Its successes in terms of ending restrictions on voting rights and gaining access to public accomodations, in effect, brought blacks full *legal* rights of citizenship. The marches and public demonstrations of that period appealed to the conscience of the nation, playing on the tension between humane ideals and grim racial realities that Myrdal had identified a generation earlier.

Second, in the wake of the successes of the civil rights movement of the 1960s two opposing trends are found in the black community. On the one hand the size of the black middle class has expanded—there are more black college graduates, more blacks in professional and white-collar jobs, more blacks in responsible positions in various public bureaucracies—yet at the same time the size of the black underclass has also expanded enormously. More than half of all black children are born to unwed mothers, unemployment among blacks continues to run two to three times that of whites, the rate of welfare dependency continues to be high. In short, there is a tangled set of problems involving the black underclass, not subject to solution via the passage of more civil rights laws. Policy with regard to these problems requires the shifting of public priorities and the reallocation of societal resources.

Third it is clear that the kind of coalition of conscience that provided the impetus for passage of the civil rights legislation of the 1960s is no longer likely to be assembled. But on the other hand, the dramatic rise in the number of black elected officials since the passage of the Voting Rights Acts, the increasing participation of blacks in the political process and the strength shown by the Reverend Jesse Jackson in the primary elections for the 1984 Democratic presidential nomination suggest the importance of black politics as the fulcrum of change for of black life and futures. In these terms, it is also particularly appropriate that Professor Walton's book be the inaugral publication in this series.

Invisible Politics as the inaugural work also exemplifies the standards we set. It is enormously rich in the data on black politics, marshalling information from a variety of sources to describe the many complex dimensions of Black political behavior. It provides both a critique of older analytic frameworks and lays the foundation for a new perspective. As Professor William Nelson of The Ohio State University writes in a prepublication review:

> Professor Walton has made a valiant, and largely successful effort to meticulously analyze the basic assumptions of the traditional behavioral approach, and to reformulate behavioral assumptions in a fashion more suitable for a realistic understanding of the position of Blacks in the political system. This is a highly ambitious undertaking. Professor Walton has pulled it off with remarkable skill. This book will fill a critical void in the analysis and interpretation of Black politics. Students will be especially impressed with Professor Walton's encyclopedic and adroit coverage of the literature in the field and the manner in which he illuminates in an interesting and profound way the major theoretical flaws in traditional behaviorism as regards the analysis of Black political behavior. *Invisible Politics* will require that many scholars wedded to the traditional approach rethink their assumptions and restructure their methodological instruments.

We expect the book will define the terms of theory and research in black politics for a long time to come.

We do not expect every publication in this series to be a classic. In any event, only time determines the ultimate status of a work. However, we have set high standards and the probability of the series making a lasting contribution to the literature is increased thereby. *Invisible Politics* makes a major contribution to the important field of black politics. As editors we are proud to inaugurate the series with its publication.

John R. Howard, Mount Vernon, New York
Robert C. Smith, Burtonsville, Maryland

Preface

My Personal Journey to the Behavioral Approach to Black Politics

The behavioral approach to black politics is the prime concern of this book, which is based upon empirical data gathered from (1) a national survey conducted especially for the study, (2) interviews, (3) case studies, (4) participant observations, (5) aggregate data, and (6) statistical inferences. Although this book is the outgrowth of more than eight years of intensive analysis of black political behavior, the journey to this particular methodological approach began long ago.[1]

Morehouse College Professor Robert Brisbane, in his American government course, introduced me to numerous factors affecting black political behavior that were omitted in the text we used. Brisbane tried to explain black political behavior in meaningful terms, making clear the realities under which they both labored.[2]

The next year I was formally introduced to the behavioral movement sweeping the discipline when Professor Arthur Banks taught a course on the governmental process using David Truman's book *The Governmental Process,* as the text. We analyzed the group approach to the American political process, discussing its relationship to human nature. During the second semester Banks used Eulau's *Reader in Political Behavior.* Later Professor Tobe Johnson provided insight into administrative behavior using the heuristic models of Herbert Simon, Dwight Waldo, and other behaviorally oriented scholars in public administration.

Johnson and Banks indicated the possible usefulness of the behavioral approach; nevertheless, this new scholarly movement was making only small, if any, advances into the study of black political activities. Outside the college walls, the student sit-in movement had begun, and the need to plan strategies was becoming increasingly clear. Sound strategies based upon a precise analysis of group needs and resources were hotly debated throughout the sixties, only heightening our concern for scientific and rigorous analysis. But the discrepancies we confronted were great. In the classroom the behavioral studies on voting told us that the evils and problems were alienation, cynicism, and apathy, while outside, in order to vote, blacks were fighting archaic registration systems, literacy tests, economic reprisals, unfriendly registrars, poll taxes, and just plain old racism.

I began my graduate work in political science under a brilliant black political scientist, Professor Samuel Dubois Cook. In his methodology course, he addressed one of the crucial problems raging around this new movement: the fact-value conflict. Not only did Cook reveal the strengths and weaknesses of both sides of the controversy, but he also revealed how the debate touched upon the black political predicament. He took issue with the value neutralism of the behavioral movement and stressed the continuum between fact and value.

In courses on the American Political Process, Cook moved from the philosophical and normative realm to reveal the influences of regionalism on politics, especially the political culture of the South and its concomitant influence on national politics. He turned to the V.O. Key classic, *Southern Politics,* to illustrate his point, also using it to demonstrate how the techniques of behavioralism could help expand one's knowledge of politics. Finally, he described how much of black political activity, then as now, marched to a different tune than did white political activity. Overall, Cook, Brisbane, Banks, and Johnson revealed to me the lack of insights which the new movement had garnered out of black political activity and the discontinuities in the political realms of whites and blacks.

When I began the long trek for the advanced degree at Howard University, I met Professor Harold Gosnell, one of the pioneer behavioralists and author of a classic work on black politics.[3] He provided me with scholarly insights into the behavioral movement, the conflicts in the field, black politics, and the key books and personalities in both areas. For two years, I was fortunate to have Professor Gosnell's individual instruction and guidance. In session after session we would discuss the leading works in the areas of parties, elections, political communication, and political leadership, and he would point out weaknesses in the works, methodologies, and findings, noting the vast amount of research needed in each field.

Other Howard professors were important to the growth of my political understanding. Professor Bernard Fall in his international politics classes spoke of the ways quantitative techniques could be used to study international conflict and make policy programs more incisive. In a course on political philosophy, the late Professor Emmett Dorsey probed the question of facts and values while simultaeously noting how the civil rights movement and black political activity continued to be stifled by systemic barriers. Then, as the research assistant of Professor, now President, Nathaniel Tillman, Jr., I had to read numerous legal and political articles on judicial behavior. Our discussions led to my greater understanding of the interplay between legal rules and rights and individual actors within the criminal justice system.

Just as I was ending my doctoral studies, the first full-length book on black political behavior appeared—Matthews and Prothro's *Negro and the New Southern Politics.* Although hailed as a landmark work, the book, using Blalock's causal model, concluded that individual factors instead of structural variables were responsible for black political behavior, a finding in direct opposition to conclusions presented to the U.S. Civil Rights Commission's Hearing on Voting.[4] The concern in the testimony for the Civil Rights Commission was for structural changes and presented again the disparity, between scholarship and political action.

As I completed my doctoral studies, I concluded that several things had come to the forefront about the behavioral approach to black politics. This new movement revealed that black political behavior in its individualistic causal basis ran counter to what those working in the civil rights movement were trying to achieve, especially in terms of the Voting Rights Act. Behavioralistic political literature was at best incomplete, unsystematic, noncumulative, and, in some cases, contradictory. Moreover, this new movement had, for the most part, bypassed black political activity; there was nothing on black parties, black judicial behavior, and the like. Thus, in 1961, when Robert Dahl penned an epitaph for the behavioral approach in political science in the *American Political Science Review* (Dec, 1961), the data on black political activity either needed clarification or were invisible altogether. Cook puts it this way:

> The categories and presuppositions in Political Science generally speaking contain built-in filters that automatically block-off significant sectors of experience, selecting certain phenomena, to the exclusion of others. They are self-feeding and self-perpetuating—paralleling and reinforcing the racist character of political life. Thus, the empiricism and realism of American political science are not empirical and realistic enough; the idealism of the discipline is not sufficiently idealistic and the behavioral school fails to come to grips with the total behavior and workings of political system.[5]

In Cook's estimation, "to the extent that blacks are made invisible and ignored, to that degree the political system is not functioning properly."

However, the tendency to make blacks invisible was not a new phenomenon. W.E.B. Du Bois wrote,

> It is as though one, looking out from a dark cave in a side of an impending mountain sees the world passing and speaks to it; speaks couteously and persuasively, showing them how these entombed souls are hindered in their natural movement, expression and development, and how their loosening from prison would be a matter not of simply coutesy, sympathy and help to them, but aid to the world.... It gradually permeates the minds of the prisoners that the people passing do not hear; that some thick sheet of invisible...plate glass is between them and the world.[6]

Richard Wright declared, "American whites and blacks both possess deep-seated resistance against the Negro problem being presented even verbally in all of its hideous fullness, in all of the totality of its meaning.... This fact is as true of the churches as of the trade unions; as true of Negro organizations as of whites; as true of the political left as of the political right, as true of white individuals as of blacks."[7] Ralph Ellison explains it in his classic *Invisible Man*, saying,

' I am invisible, understand, simply because people refuse
to see me. Like the bodiless heads you see sometimes in
circus sideshows, it is as though I have been surrounded
by mirrors of hard distorting glass. When they approach
me they see only my surroundings, themselves or
judgments of their imagination, indeed, everything and
anything except me. '[8]

In sum, the behavioralists' tendency to render blacks invisible is
part of a broader pattern in race relations, and must be seen and
understood in that larger context. But the crux of the problem is their
tendecy to base all potitical behavior on sociopsychological and
intrapsychic causes, even for a group that has faced overwhelming
systemic influences and forces.

I would like to thank those who toiled with me in exploring the
political behavior of the invisible and plotting the impact of both
external and internal forces. First, the survey had to be conducted
without foundation funds, and numerous individuals helped me
tabulate the results. A former political science graduate student and
lawyer gave unlimited time, day and night. This individual, Vernon
Neely, was aided from time to time by Norman Young, an undergraduate who gave also unlimited time. Two brilliant mathema-
ticians, Geanelvin Walton and Johnny L. Houston, helped with
difficult computations, while Calvin Riley and Jerry Wilson drew the
graphs, figures, and diagrams with a fine hand and discerning eye. As
for secretarial help, Lillie Mae Key and Shirly Brown started the
project, Betty Lawton worked her way through four drafts, and my
wife, Alice Walton, typed through more than two additional drafts.
All of these people have done more than I can hope to pay them for.

Students in my graduate political science class in Research
Methods at Savannah State College-Armstrong State College who
helped with local interviews and tabulations. Are: Jeffrey Jenkins,
Dan Stevenson, Catherine Thomas, Joyce Manker, and Josh Harris.
In addition to my graduate students, a number of scholars conducted
special case-study projects on particular problems. Among them were
Professors Willie T. Yancey, Otis Johnson, and Delacy Sanford of
Savannah State College. The works of Marguerite Barnett, Joseph
Bernd, Dan Bowen, Robert Brisbane, Carolyn Cabe, Samuel Cook,
Johnnie Daniels, Harold Gosnell, C. Vernon Gray, Charles Hamil-
ton, William Harvard, James Harvey, Matthew Holden, Robert
Holmes, Perry Howard, Clint Jones, Mack Jones, Leslie McLemore,

Milton Morris, Jewel Prestage, Donald Strong, Gilbert Ware, and Fredrick Wirts proved to be lights in a dark and tangled jungle and made a clear path in the forest.

Numerous other individuals, political leaders, politicians, and organizational men gave time for interviews and political discourses. In many instances, their insights proved invaluable. The people at the Georgia Archives and in the Fulton County Office of Registration were of great assistance.

Generous thanks are further extended to the Past President of Savannah State College, Dr. Prince Jackson, Jr.; the Past Dean, Dr. Thomas H. Byers; and my Past Chairman, Dr. Elmer J. Eean, who helped in a variety of ways to make this research possible at a small black college. The staff at the library, Miss Margaret Mitchell, Miss Vivian Chandler, Miss Francena Johnson, Miss Evelyn Richardson, Mrs. Magdeline Allen, Mr. Andrew McLemore, made a great contribution to my work effort. I truly appreciate this.

Finally, I thank my wife Alice; my parents, Mr. and Mrs. Thomas H. Walton; and Mr. and Mrs. James Williams, my in-laws, who provided inspiration from moment to moment. Any errors of judgment and fact are due to my inability to listen to all of the excellent counsel I got from colleagues, family, and friends.

Hanes Walton, Jr.
Savannah State College

Chapter 1

Introduction

Political behavioralism is much more than mere statistical and sociopsychological technique. It is a specific philosophy about the good life and the *summum bonum* (the highest good). In political thought, philosophers have sought the summum bonum by restructuring political institutions or political society or reshaping man's political nature. Political behavioralism cast its lot with the latter category: Find political man, then reshape him in the image of the political good and the good life will follow. Failure to understand this basic thesis is a failure to understand the works of the political behavioralists.

The Quest for 'Inner Man'

Political behavioralism has placed man at the center of the political universe. In the political behavioralist's world, as concentric as the Copernican cosmos, all political things revolve around "political man." Heinz Eulau writes, "Behavioralism...(is) unequivocal in its choice of the individual as the empirical unit of analysis." In fact, throughout his many works on this approach, he has been consistent in describing its focus.[1]

But Eulau is only one of the many spokesmen. Another political behavioralist puts it this way: "The behavioral focus is in essence a focus on action or the acts of individuals or groups in various social settings." He continues: "The political behavior approach *does*, after all, *focus* on the behavior and the psychological and sociological variables which affect it."[2] Lester W. Milbrath agrees: "The major concern," he argues, "is to explain individual human behavior as it relates to the political system. Therefore, the human organism, rather than groups or the political system, usually is taken as the unit of analysis."[3]

In methodology, the word is the same. "Behavioral theory," write David Apter and Charles Andrain, "is concerned with motivation and perception, learning and adaptation.... Thus in behavioral research, analysis of both individuals and small groups has been central."[4] William Welsh adds: "The behavioral perspective...means emphasizing the political behavior of individuals rather than the characteristics of institutions such as legislatures, executives, and judiciaries."[5] Lawrence C. Mayer puts it another way. "Political psychology is strictly micro-analytical. Political psychology refers to data and generalizations about individuals."[6]

Advancing Mayer's idea that psychoanalytic theory is a form of political methodology, G. David Garson explains the political behavioralist focus. "Regarding the unit of social or political action, the psychoanalytic approach tends to emphasize primarily the individual in isolation...and his peers in collective relations."[7]

However, not all behavioralists have explained their focus this way. One group, searching for uniqueness, explained the same reality in a different fashion. "Among the determinants of political behavior are one's early childhood, one's sex, occupation, religion, income, education, institutional role, geographic location and race, the values of one's primary and reference groups, and the organizations to which one belongs, the strength of one's affiliations with various of these, the congruence and incogruities among their political values."[8]

The chief focus of the political behavioralist is the individual: both the unit and level of analysis from the behavioralist perspective is "political man." *Perceiving the political world from the vantage point of the individual however, forces the political behavioralist to emphasize the individual at the expense of the political system.* In the political behavioralists' writings the political system goes out of view. Focusing solely on man, the political behavioralist fails to note the propensity of the political system for prevention of justice,[9] for institutional racism;[10] for corruption;[11] for oppression;[12] and for deceit and the misuse of political power. *A focus on the individual leads inevitiably and logically to the weaknesses and imperfections inherent in man and away from the imperfections and weaknesses of the political system.* Moreover, those behavioralists who are desirous of attaining the good political life have structured numerous public policy proposals and compensatory programs to improve the individual and not the system. Further, the focus on the individual implies that institutional arrangements, structural devices, organizational types and legal rules do not affect political behavior as much as intrapsychic and sociopsychological forces do. In other words, their assumption is that laws and organizations that prohibit voting would not affect an individual's voting behavior as much as his sex, income, occupation, social status, political values, and primary and secondary reference groups.

The individualistic focus of the behavioralists affects their use of such techniques and methods as probability statistics, survey research, correlation, and causal modeling, which they use to find *primary* intrapsychic and sociopsychological determinants of individual motivations and perceptions. But to use such techniques *only* in such a fashion is, in a sense, to misuse them.

Finally, the individual-centered behavioral approach in black political behavior has produced a vast literature that proposes that the individual weaknesses and imperfections it uncovers are a result of blacks' individual shortcomings and not the result of any systemic factors under which they have labored. In the words of Malcolm X, *the victim becomes responsible for his own victimization.* The political good in the context of this literature , therefore, rests with improving the individual and not the environment in which he exists.

Few, if any, political behavioralists have insisted that an individual-centered political universe needs rethinking. Eulau wrote, "The focus on individual political behavior has increased the range and reach of political research. But as yet it has not contributed as much as we might hope to the analysis of the behavior of collectives (which are as real as individual human actors)"[13] But then he hastened to add that "the reluctance of students of individual behavior to be concerned with the behavior of the units to which individuals invariably belong is understandable."[14] Others besides Eulau point out the limitations of the behavioral focus. Stephen Wasby noted, "It is now recognized that the focus of the behavioral approach on the individual is not sufficient; how individual decisions are aggregated is also vital, because individual preferences cannot by themselves explain collective decisions."[15] Milbrath agrees: "The behavior of the two system (Micro and Macro) is often interrelated; individual (micro) political behavior affects the behavior of the larger political system (macro); Macro characteristics, in turn, affect micro behavior"[16] Garson adds: "the research should be aware, however, that there are other possible levels of causation that may be operating instead of or in addition" to individual psychological ones.[17] But these critics go no further than to point out this particular weakness, and those who have taken up behavioralism have been forced down one of two paths in their quest for the inner political man and the good political life. These alternate paths are logical and natural outgrowths of the failure to see the intrinsic weaknesses of this methodological focus.

The first path has led to the rationalization and justification of elit rule (some have called it elitist democracy) and numerous systemic imperfections, a consequence of finding political man to be irrational, antidemocratic, and pathological.[18] Eugene Burdick noted in an analysis of the behavioralistic voting studies, that "the voter who emerges...has little of the rationality of the 'citizen' of democratic theory" and "the voting studies etch a portrait of the contemporary voter as a person who votes with relatively high frequency, but... with very little interest and...information...and with very low emotional involvement in the entire process. The act of voting seems divorced from any coherent set of principles."[19] In fact, the weight (or burden) of the evidence found by the political behavioralists led some to argue that the electorate was composed primarily of "fools." In response, the late V.O. Key cried, "the perverse and unorthodox argument of this little book is that voters are not fools."[20] But Key's last volume was criticized as being out of hand.[21]

To those critics who say that political man is not irrational or pathological but that the behavioralists' conclusion is a result of faulty methodology, the behavioralists repeat that the empirical evidence show man to be suffering from numerous complex social pathologies. In fact, throughout the writings of behavioralists like Dahl, Lane, Lipset, and numerous others, political man comes up short; he is both anti-liberatarian and anti-democratic. Many, in contemplating such evidence, have concluded, like Thomas Dye, that "mass governance is neither feasible nor desirable. Widespread popular participation in national political decisions is not only impossible...it is incompatible with the liberal values of individual dignity, personal liberty and social justice. Efforts to encourage mass participation in American politics are completely misdirected...It is the irony of democracy that masses not elites, pose the greatest threat to the survival of democratic values."[22] Behavioralist models of American politics therefore seem to justify elite rule.

The second path taken by some political behavioralists has ended in their calling for a resocialization of "political man" to attain a better society. In short, change man and then the political system will become perfect. The behavioral psychologists are close behind. B. F. Skinner has argued that all of the neurotic pathologies inherent in man can, with the aid of technology, be programmed out, the result will be a truly perfect social order.[23]

Looking at the vast problems in the black ghetto, two white sociologists made this prescription:

> Our own experience convinced us that most Negroes are unable to build their own institutions because of this sick deficiency of power, this culturally induced psychological, physiological and mental instability. Only the infants, cared for and loved from as young as three months of age, hold promise of possibilities of helping any significant proportion of the ghetto population in a relatively short period of time. It is necessary that the infants spend twelve hours a day away from their pathological family and cultural enviroment if long-range social change is to be initiated.[24]

The crucial question is whether changing solely the ghetto inhabitant's personality will have any impact on the individuals who control, enforce, and maintain the ghetto. In short, does modifying the individual really modify the weaknesses in the system?

An even more important and basic question is to ask why this individual focus prevails.In political science, Richard Dawson has sought to shed some light on the reasons for the individual focus. "Since the end of World War II," he writes, "the world has witnessed a great increase in the amount and rapidity of political and social change. New nation-states have been created. Old empires and coalitions have disintegrated. In a period of only two decades the number of independent nation-states in the world has more than doubled. Professional observers of politics consequently have come to give more attention to questions of political change, political stability, political development, and poltical disintegration."[25]

The literature is replete with such words and phrases as "saliency," "linkage," "transference," "revolution," "homeostasis," "equilibrium," and "contingencies," to name a few. The presuppostitions of this political vocabulary are that the individual should be remade and that this is how systemic continuity is to be maintained. The preservation of man, of civilization, and of political society are clearly fundamental to the writers of this school.

But, in the final analysis, the individual-centered behavioral approach has led either to the justification of placing power in the hands of a few or to establishing a utopia through personality modification. Each alternative leaves systemic imperfection as a dependent variable of human nature.

Human Nature as a Framework

The theoretical framework of behavioralism is responsible for the logical conclusions and orientations of behavioralists. Paramount to the behavioral thrust is the concern with human nature. In fact, the theoretical wellspring of the political behavioralism movement is the quest for the essence of human nature. Graham Wallas and Arthur Bentley, at the turn of the century, refocused the attention of political scientists on the role of human nature in political life.[26] Both men were reacting to the traditional, institutional, and legal approaches in political science. However, it was not until Charles Merriam and his students at the University of Chicago, especially Harold D. Lasswell, picked up where Wallas and Bentley had left off," that political behavioralism" came into its own." "Merriam re-asserted the desirability and propriety of applying psychological and sociological insights and techniques to political investigation, and he insisted on the need for minute inquiry and microscopic studies of the political process carried on by scientific methods."[27] The focus of the behavioralists is on the "inner man," the sociopsychological sources of human motives. Don Bowen writes, "most of what today is called 'political behavior' continues to speak of motives, emotional states, goals, and calculations of political actors. Indeed, some of the most fruitful of all concepts in political science rest on the nonobervable attitudes and psychic structures which cannot in any sense be called hard data. The ghosts then have not been entirely exorcised."[28] This quest for "psycho-politics" is in the eyes of critics a search for phantoms rather than hard facts. The political behavioralists, following Machiavelli, Hobbes, Rousseau, Locke, and Madison, have employed human nature as a basic theoretical framework to structure government and society.

One wonders how a search for the "inner man" will fully reveal the meaning of human political enterprise. Surely a political universe with both man and the political system as the twin suns will grant new insights into the true meaning of the human political enterprise. Political behavioralism, however, emphasizes only the individual, constructing a political theory based on unprovable assumptions about human nature.

Political Behavioralism and the Political Good

To equate the political good with determinants at the individual level involves a significant amount of reductionism and an equally significant amount of intrapsychic over-determinism. Herein lies the problem. The methodology is weak because it relies on one mode of discovery. It is more logical to assume that the political good emanates not only from a restructuring of the individual but of the system as well. Certainly such an assumption deserves a hearing in the academic arena.

But first, what the behavioralists have found about black political activity needs reassessment. And to do the reassessment a review of the literature on black political behavior of recent decades is in order. However, before we review the literature, we must examine the nature and scope of black political behavior.

A Definition

Black political behavior is a function of individual and systemic forces, of "inner" and "outer" forces, of intrapsychic and societal realities, of things seen and unseen, of sociopsychological and material forces, of micro and macro influences. To be sure, the weight of the "inner" forces may not be equal to the weight of the "outer" forces. Moreover, one or the other might not be readily discernable in some situations.

Those studies of black political behavior that have generated theories and stratagems based on single, deterministic factors are bound to be of limited use because they have caught only a portion of black political reality, and many, as we shall see, have mistaken the shadow for reality. Second, those studies with single motivating factors have generated proposals for public policy that have enhanced an ideology of victimism and helped to preserve the social system built upon it.[29]

Besides the factors that determine all political behavior in America, black political behavior is informed by unique forces. It is a variant form of American political behavior. It is inspired and shaped *by some features and currents that do not form the basis of all American political behavior because it is rooted in the black experience in America.* And this experience is radically different from the experience of other immigrant groups.

In fact, to fully understand black political behavior one must know the context from which it sprang and the factors that influenced and nurtured that context. To fail in this most elemental task is to misunderstand black political activity.

Black political behavior is a variety of political patterns, experiences, and activities. It is heterogenous, at times and in some places more factionalized than unified, more conflictive than cooperative, and more discordant than harmonious. These differences arise from the numerous divisions in the black community, divisions of class, ideology, politics, and culture. Moreover, black political behavior is not monistic, static, or time-bound. It undergoes cycles of stagnation, deviation, and regeneration. The flux of social growth and decay affects the black political milieu as it does any sociopolitical milieu. In short, the current realities of black political patterns might not be the same tomorrow.

Black political behavior is *not* ethnic political behavior. Despite the similarities, it is different. Edgar Litt writes, "The 'older' theories of ethnic politics were based on the examination of European immigrant groups adapting to the urban industrial order. The 'newer' ethnic politics, however, involves non-caucasians dealing with a highly complex urban enviroment."[30] Leslie McLemore, in a seminal essay, agrees, noting, "The very foundations...of black politics rest on the clear understanding that Afro-Americans are a *racial* group and not an ethnic group."[31] Louis Wirth concurs: "The Melting Pot philosophy in the United States...applies to the ethnic minorities but exludes the racial minorities, notably the Negro."[32]

Despite these differences, "It has become academically fashionable to lump black politics in some category called ethnic politics and claim that they are synonymous."[33] But a distinction must be made. An ethnic group differs culturally from the majority while a racial group differs not only culturally but also phenotypically from the majority. These differences have been crucial in the Afro-American's political experience and behavior.

The failure to note the differences can cause both methodological and substantive problems. The problem arises, argues Mack Jones, with "the establishment of a linear model of ethnic group or out group politics and a Procrustean forcing of the black political experience in the contrived model, and in the process, obfuscating, if not eliminating outright the crucial variables in the black political experience."[34]

The Limitations of the Literature

Most of the studies on black political behavior, ignoring systemic external influences, identify individual black pathologies and black deviation from the "norm" as the crux of the problem. This is true of both white and black political scientists, of political science and other social sciences. For instance, two white political scientists note, "Low participation by blacks contributes to continued deprivation which in turn leads to lower levels of efficacy and trust. The process, in other words, is circular and nasty."[35] A black political scientist reflects, "when viewed against the pattern of politics within the society as a whole, black politics is to an extent 'pathological.'"[36] Elsewhere he has commented, "one also senses among blacks an unfortunate gullibility not uncommon to people who are desperate. Blacks yielded to the blandishment of every seemingly progressive party or politician yet had little to show for their vacilliation."[37] In both statements, the victim and not the system is portrayed as responsible somehow for his own desperate plight. The individual victim suffers from some dreaded disease or maladjustment, and his behavior is never described as the consequence of systemic or external influences. These are only two examples, but the literature on black political behavior is replete with such "scientific" findings.

In discussions of black voting behavior, blacks' failure to vote is alway listed as "apathy," "alienation," "fear," "cynicism," or ascribed to low socioeconomic status. Such systemic forces as poll taxes, white primaries, racial gerrymandering, reading and interpretation tests, boss and machine manipulation, and reregistration are rarely considered as significant. In studies of black political socialization, the problems listed are disorganized and dysfunctional black families and

similarly handicapped black peer groups and schools, rarely unemployment, blocked career goals, and slum housing. With behavioralism, the individual forces always take precedence over systemic ones.

However, even when it is clear that individual forces do not fully
explain black political behavior, "scholars" press the matter anyway.
For example, Matthews and Prothro, in *Negroes and the New
Southern Politics*, the only full-length study on black political
behavior, concluded: "The overall explanatory power of our model is
sufficient to account for about 40 percent of the variance in the
political activities of Negroes throughout the South . . . (yet) to account
for 40 percent of the variance in a form of political behavior does not
take all the mystery out of that aspect of human life; but it does
significantly reduce the area of mystery."[38] *This book—described as a
"monumental study," "a classic in southern politics," and "one of the
most sophisticated behavioral studies to be performed on black
politics"—admits that an individual explanatory approach will not
explain 60 percent of black political activity.* The authors are to be
commended for their own insight, not characteristic of the other
literature in the field.

A few scholars challenged the individual explanatory thesis, but
they did not prevail. Margaret Callcott, in a quantitiative analysis of
black political participation, found: "The high level of Negro voting
participation in post-civil war Maryland is contrary to the findings of
most studies of present-day voting behavior, which repeatedly show
that Negros participate at much lower rates than whites."[39] She
continues: "These studies also show that participation is a function of
low income, low occupation and educational levels, and of residing in
rural rather than urban areas."[40] Having made these findings, Callcott
states: "The high Negro participation which characterized the Maryland political scene from 1870 to 1900 suggest that there is nothing
inevitable about such present-day relationships. Mass Negro participation occurred despite a socio-economic position that was more
peripheral in the past than it is at present; participation of rural
Negroes tended to exceed that of urban Negroes."[41]

Frederick Wirt concurs. He found that neither community
character nor psychological explanation sufficiently explains the
variations of compliance outcomes in Panola County, Mississippi.
"Instead," he writes, "what we do see is that regardless of community
characteristics, where the federal registrar went in, more blacks were
registered in proportion to whites than in counties without federal
intervention."[42]

In step with Callcott and Wirt's challenge to the individual explanatory variable is the work of black political sociologist Johnnie Daniel. In one of the most innovative but rarely noted behavioral studies of black political activities to appear, Daniel found that "The counties that have the highest levels of Negro political mobilization are those counties that had both Negro candidates and federal examiners, and the counties that have the lowest levels of Negro political mobilization are those counties that had neither Negro candidates nor federal examiners."[43] Daniel continues, "These findings indicate that the previously low levels of Negro voter registration cannot be explained simply by Negro apathy; for attention must be given to the prohibitive social system in which they lived."[44] Further, "These findings suggest that the generalizations of Matthews and Prothro and their model of Negro political behavior must be seriously questioned."[45]

However, long before Callcott, Wirt, and Daniel's specific findings had shown that individual variables and intrapsychic components were not enough to explain black political behavior and shortly after Matthew and Prothro had admitted to a 40 percent effectiveness, Don Bowen said, "Most of the research on political behavior in America has concentrated on explaining political behavior as a consequence of apolitical or nonpolitcal factor."[46] He suggested that attention be turned to "an examination of the ways in which the structures and processes of politics itself may influence the individual's political actions," It should be found out, he argued "what difference it makes to political behavior whether there are competitive party systems, single member districts, council manager plans, or any of a host of other possible questions which may arise with variations on political structure."[47]

The findings of Callcott, Wirt, Daniel, and Bowen are buttressed, in part, by some of the original studies of black political behavior. The earliest studies of black political behavior began at those schools where the behavioral movement took off: in the thirties and later, Chicago, Columbia, Pennsylvania, and down South, Atlanta and Emory universities, were the places where the first behavioral studies of black politics were carried out.[48] The findings often ran counter to the popular generalization that were creeping into the literature, but these "unusual" findings did not prevail or have much impact on the behavioral revolution.

Another problem evolving from the individual focus of the literature on black political behavior is the heavy emphasis on comparison. Behaviorally oriented researchers, in setting up experimental and control groups mandated by the scientific method, invariably developed black and white samples that were equal on demographic variables. Each sample has similar educational, economic, age, regional, housing, and social status levels. This pairing of demographic realities leads one to assume that the two groups are equal, politically and socially. Then, when the comparisons between the two groups are drawn and vast gaps inevitably emerge, explanations are sought only in terms of individual variables, which are inherent in the very nature of the behavioral approach. But the disparities might be due to the differences in the two groups themselves. On this point, the literature is silent.

Similar demographics do not make groups equal—politically or socially. The politics of race, which expresses itself in poll taxes, white primaries, racial gerrymandering, racial poverty, and numerous discriminatory institutional political arrangements does not permit both groups to have equal access, resources participation, representation, and finally, rewards. In fact, the politics of race (systemic variables) are the determinants accounting for the differences and must be included with the individual ones.

Last, this constant comparison of black and white political behavior in the literature created certain ideological pespectives. The comparisons either imply or clearly state that white political behavior is superior, correct, or normal political activity, while black political behavior, with one or two exceptions, is unusual, unconventional, incorrect, inadequate, abnormal, or inferior. Are the comparisons done to reassure one group and confirm the other group's supposed backwardness? The literature certainly goes beyond the concern for the scientific method of experimental and control-group apparatus.

Another limitation stemming from comparison is that most studies are really studies of white political behavior with small or moderate samples of blacks included as an afterthought, as a curious exception, or to fulfill the dictates of the scientific method. This has created a vast behavioral literature, yielding complex interpretations and generalizations about black political behavior, based on extremely small samples of the black population. These samples never reached the magnitude of the samples on which the theories about white political behavior are based. Nor did the limited size of the samples cause any of the behavioralists to qualify their findings. Knowledge of black political behavior rests on some of the most tenuous empirical evidence possible. But nowhere in the literature will one find discussion of this almost scandalous practice, which is below the standard accepted by the profession.

Since few studies exist with black political activity as the central element in the empirical research, and some samples of black individuals remain small, the literature on black political behavior, to say the least, is not holistic. Literature on black political behavor is in bits and pieces, imbedded in other studies. Thus, the literature on black political behavior is unrelated unconnected, noncumulative, often contradictory, and unsystematic. The literature is like a vast jigsaw puzzle that is still only partly solved.

Closely related to this lack of organization and coherence is the tendency toward a "phenomenon" approach. As newer and different forms of political expressions manifest themselves in the black community and, therefore, in the white community, more behavioral research is generated. For instance, if we group the behavioral literature on black politics into two categories electoral or conventional participation and nonelectoral or unconventional participation, a cursory examination of the literature will reveal the second category as having received the greatest amount of attention, especially riot behavior.

However, the new literature regarding the recent "phenomenon" of black office-holding, which is in the first category, threatens soon to surpass the literature on the unconventional area.[49] The current fascination with black elected officials, like the older fascination with black protest politics, is a clear example of this phenomena-cycle, an approach to black politics that leaves too much undone and too much unknown. Some studies seek to explain black politics from studying black elected officials alone. Surely black political activity is more than the efforts of black elected officials, and the two are not synonymous. The problem is similar to the problem that arose in the "protest politics" literature: it failed to show the link between politics and public policy and the link between protest politics and regular political activity. The literature tended to bifurcate protest politics and political participation into artificial categories. The new approach combines the two categories, black elected officials and their politics, making them represent all of black politics. In sum, poor distribution abounds in the unconventional literature as well as in the new, emerging literature in the conventional area.

When all the literature on black political behavior is considered, several crucial weaknesses emerge. It tends to (1) suggest curious comparisons, (2) be narrowly confined to a few areas, (3) stress individual determinism, (4) be phenomenally oriented, (5) remain unsystematic and noncumulative. These only compound the problems of *black invisibility* and limited notions of the political good, with their policy implications flowing from the behavioral findings.

A Multidimensional Approach

To transcend the problems inherent in the behavioralist approach to the study of black politics, one must follow certain basic and fundamental research paths. First, black political behavior must be defined differently, as the result of at *least* two forces, not one. Second, methodological techniques currently employed must be reshaped to discover multifaceted forces in a diverse political reality.

With redefinition comes reconceptualization. The behavioralist approach, in an effort to enhance its scientific character, generated a wide array of new concepts and terms to explicate the internal determinants of political action, the single force it chose. Thus were born such concepts as "political culture," "political socialization," "political personality typologies," "models of voting behavior," "empirical political theories," and numerous categories of political participation. The list is long, but they are alike in that all would speak to and explain individual sociopsychological variables. One example: The creator of the concept of "political culture" sees it as a "particular pattern of orientation to political action." Then he describes "orientation to political action" as a "set of meanings and purposes" which included "attitudes toward politics," "political values," "ideologies," "national character," and "cultural ethos," all of which are, indeed, psychological variables.[50]

The simple question is: can a political culture be made up *only* of mental variables, attitudes and orientations? Or is it made up of both mental and institutional realities: Second, can a culture have more than three dimensions—cognitive, affective, and evaluative? For instance, can it be instructive, reformist, supportive, and antagonistic, indeed, all of these things simultaneously? And finally, can a concept which did not consider the black subculture in its genesis or implementation be usefully applied to blacks without some modification? A new work has found the concept to be woefully deficient in a number of areas and raises significant questions about its applicability.[51] Such key considerations must be raised, if many of the current concepts are to prove useful in explicating political behavior.

Beyond the stage of redefinition and reconceptualization, there is the hurdle of methodological technique. Several research tools are employed by behavioralists, but their prime tool is the survey, which seeks to gather and analyze the values, attitudes, and beliefs of individuals. "Omnipresent and omnipotent," writes Herbert Hyman, "if it were not idolatrous, might be apt description of the survey method in political psychology." He continues, "surveys are indeed powerful weapons. They are omnipresent because their feasibility and desirability make them attractive to many scholars....Survey research seems to rule the realm of political psychology."[52]

The concept of "political culture" provides an example. Having described the concept as mentalistic, Almond then uses the survey as the primary tool for his exploration of "political culture." Questionnaires are *the* methodological tool for gathering data on the concept. This was true of most other concepts developed by this approach in political science.

In fact, in the handbooks on ways to develop questionnaires for survey research, one is constantly told how to reduce all concerns to psychological questions and indices.[53] But if one studies these instruments carefully, he will notice that while they do indeed probe many psychological dimensions, they all begin with demographic or sociological questions about age, sex, education, income, and the like. Such questions suggest that questionnaires can ask about other variables, particularly institutional, systemic, and contextual ones. These concerns do not have to be reduced to psychological terms or be correlated with them. They can reveal insights in and of themselves.

This study, with its new basic presuppositions and definition tries to move beyond the traditional unidimensional portrait of black political behavior. It is a multidimensional analysis and seeks to indicate the possible existence of alternate views of behavioral concepts, methodological techniques, findings and patterns, and research paths. However, an alternate perspective is not the only feature of this approach.

In order to see the interaction of both internal and external forces in political behavior in general and black political behavior in particular, this study combines the data gathered by survey-research sources with data gathered from aggregate data analysis. These sources are supplemented, where possible with case studies, interviews, content analysis, historical accounts, and institutional and legal descriptions.

First a study of the black electorate initiated by C. Vernon Gray, then the director of research at the Joint Center for Political Studies, permitted the calculation of the total number of blacks of voting age in each county in the United States for both 1960 and 1970. A national survey based upon these findings was conducted during 1972, 1973, and 1974.[54] To avoid the problems inherent in the comparison syndrome, the researchers conducted the national survey among *black voters* and *black nonvoters* and not among blacks and whites.

A word should be said at this point about the division of the respondents into black voters and black nonvoters, as opposed to the standard techniques of having nearly equal black and white groups. First, the latter technique does permit in-depth intragroup analysis because of the heavy intergroup comparisons. Second, if one is pursuing black political participation, benchmarks should be established from either the group or at least with other similarly located minority groups and not with the dominant majority if a more valid picture is to be constructed. Few in the majority have experienced the full impact of systemic forces that the black minority has. Third, nonvoting blacks may participate politically in many ways, excepting only voting. Therefore, they influence and help shape some of the activities of those who do vote. Moreover, their individual perceptions are sometimes different from those who do vote. Finally, because many individuals move back and forth between the two groups, it is essential to collect information from both. This approach permitted a snapshot and episodic national perspective of individual participants. Moreover, to update and supplement this single national survey, similar data were taken from the nearly annual General Social Surveys conducted by the National Opinion Research Center (hereafter NORC) of the University of Chicago. But since these nearly annual surveys (they were conducted from 1972-1978, 1980, 1982 for a total of nine) contained only a very few blacks per survey (mean 171), all nine of the surveys were pooled and used in a cumulative fashion, except where indicated in the text.

But more than these data were needed. Angus Campbell writes: "Survey analysts have typically paid little attention to the institutional structure within which political behavior occurs. That is to say, they have seemd to assure that political institutions were the same for everyone and could, therefore, be ignored. It is not difficult to demonstrate that this assumption is quite improper... the different states differ a great deal in the obstacles they create for the would-be voter."[55] He continues, "Negroes are undoubtedly subject to many devised impediments" to their participation in politics.[56] To get beyond the national sweep of the survey and look at subnational obstacles, aggregate election data were compiled and analyzed from the northern black congressional districts of the late Congressmen William Dawson and Adam Clayton Powell from the mid 1940s until the beginning of the 1970s.

To look at state and local politics and to avoid at the same time the estimating that generally occurs when housing and census tracts are reduced to political units, we needed to find a state that kept black aggregate election data by *race*. Louisiana is such a state, having kept track of black registration statistics and blacks of voting age for more than three-quarters of a century. Aggregate data like these provided a very accurate view of the fluctuation in black political participation for nearly a century.

The new portrait of black political participation emerging from this study is unprecedented in its comprehensiveness, as it includes black individual political participants, black organizational political participants, black political decision makers, the forces of black international awareness, and all on the national, state, and local levels. However, it nevertheless is not the final portrait of black political behavior, for black political life responds to the continuing shifts in the American political process.

Moreover, this approach avoids falling into either of the two basic strategies of political inquiry, i.e., exploratory or verificatory (causal) studies.[57] It is not wholly exploratory as it does not start from "scratch," and it is not wholly causal as it does not intend to verify current propositions. Such is not possible, given the techniques for data gathering, the data available, and the continual changes in and around the black community. At best, this new strategy of inquiry is inferential. From the data it surmises the tendencies, trends, and prevalent characteristics.

Still, the survey data, the aggregate data from northern black congressional districts, and the data from Louisiana did not cover the local scene at all. Hence, it was necessary to find a city that could provide accurate aggregate election data. Atlanta (Fulton County), Georgia, was chosen because the city kept not only voter registration by race but also kept voting returns by precinct since the early 1960s on computer printouts. Analysis of these aggregate data permitted one not only to see black voting age population, black voter registration, and black voter turnout in city, county, state, and national elections with an accuracy heretofore unknown, but gave researchers a definite advantage over speculative estimates of the past.

In the areas of black organizational behavior and international political behavior, there exists no storehouse of aggregate data. For this reason, content analysis, historical accounts, and black elite activities and pronouncements were used. To obtain facts about role behavior by legislators, judges, and political leaders, cases for which we have little aggregate data, we conducted interviews, performed content analysis, and tabulated socioeconomic backgrounds, taking past studies into account.

In sum, a multidimensional approach includes both internal and external factors and permits both a vertical and a longitudinal view. Its findings are not conclusive and inflexible; they are tentative, inferential, and subject to future change. However, before concluding about the nature of a multidimensional perspective and a systemic-structural approach, the words of Kenneth Hoover are strikingly apt: "Western culture," he writes, "has for a long time viewed social problems as a matter of the weakness of human nature." He continues: "This approach invites introspection and the examination of personal intentions, motives, and dispositions. Social science, by and large, encourages a different approach: Look around you. Before deciding that the individual is totally responsible for his or her actions, consider the environmental factors, the structures of power, the forces of conditioning, the real dimensions of choice that face people in social situations, and the material possibilities people actually have of solving their own problems. These circumstances are sometimes more susceptible to change than are inward dispositions that grow out of a conscious and unconscious history of individual development."[58]

Therefore, in order to enable academics and scholars to "look around" in black political behavior and black politics, a systemic-structural approach is encouraged. And such an approach requires certain basic things. First of all, the past and current external forces shaping the black political experience *must* be included in any explanatory model. Without involving these variables, the explanations renered by the model are not rooted in the unique experience of the people that the model is supposed to explain. Secondly, this approach requires that all of the crucial variables in a situation be identified in order to explain the resultant behavior. For instance, the systemic variables, defined here as those governmental factors on the federal, state, and local levels, like laws, public policies, and governmental actions, or the lack of these things, must be carefully identified. The structural variables (defined here as those institutional arrangements in organizations like Congress, legislatures, political parties, conventions, pressure groups, committees, and other political bodies, and in the political process such as electoral systems) that may be barriers and hindrances in the attainment of full participation must be noted and indicated.

Connected to the structural and systemic variable are the contextual ones that exist in the local environment like the KKK, bosses and machines, economic reprisals, the presence or absence of leadership, recalcitrant registrars, etc., also affect and shape behavior. These too must be placed into the explanatory model if sound, valid, and balanced explanations are to result.

These variables, systemic, structural, and contextual, are not a part of the explanatory features of an individualistic-psychological approach. The unidimensionality of the latter approach is in many instances designed to exclude these other crucial variables. Thus, a multidimensional perspective, one which attempts to place the variables of the systemic-structural approach in the explanatory model, has to probe for external and internal influences by design.

In each of the following chapters, the literature overview will present the individual variables that are said to be controlling political behavior. Then, the rest of each chapter will probe for some of the systemic and structural variables that are also shaping and affecting black political behavior. To find these variables it is necessary to move beyond a study of attitudes and intentions and employ other political science methodologies to see other dominant variables in action. The new findings that emerge here, and hopefully in the years ahead, will provide better, more holistic, and viable explanations about the black political experience and black political behavior.

Chapter 2

Black Political Culture

Gabriel Almond is the father of the concept of political culture, which he defines "as consisting of cognitive, affective and evaluative orientations to political phenomena, distributed in national populations or in subgroups."[1] Later Almond added to his earlier definition, elaborating three different "directions: (1) substantive content, (2) varieities of orientations, and (3) the systemic relations among these components."[2] However, the fundamental psychological character of the concept remains. In the words of Lucian Pye, "all of these definitions stress the psychological or subjective aspects of behavior."[3]

In his writings, Almond reveals that he developed the concept with an eye toward the use of survey research methodology.[4] Recently, he has written that the development of that methodology "was the catalytic agent in the political culture conceptualization and research that took place in the 1960s.[5] Thus, curiously, "the nature of the definition predetermined the methodology and the findings arising from the survey technique preordained the definitional attitudes of the concept."[6]

The point is whether the definition of the concept can be broadened and if a different methodology can be used to grasp the concept in a different context. But first, it will be helpful to see how Almond's concept has been used to analyze the political activities of the black community.

We can begin with Almond himself. "Our American sample" for *The Civic Culture* included fewer than "a hundred black respondents, hardly representative of the black population. Hence, we failed to deal with the political attitudes of American blacks."[7] One of the critics of the book said, "One of the major omissions from the description of American political culture in *The Civic Culture* which seems rather glaring in retrospect, is the absence of any separate treatment of the political culture of America's black minority."[8] Almond then reveals that data from the approximately one hundred blacks in the sample were the subject of a secondary analysis by Dwaine Marvick.[9] But what we are not told is that Marvick treated the black responses not under the aegis of political culture but under political socialization. Are the two concepts similar? Can such a transfer take place without much difficulty, and how useful are the findings under such circumstances? These questions have never been adequately handled by critics of Marvick's findings. *The Civic Culture* refers only to *one* southern black's attempt to register to vote. There is no other discussion of the small black sample.

Three years after the publication of the book, another group of scholars exploring black political behavior in the South declared that the Almond concept was too vague, ill defined, and difficult to apply to the southern black political situation in the 1960s.[10] They indicated that the situational variables (external factors) when "taken together ...(with the psychological variables) provide a reasonably clear and specific meaning to the ordinary vague concept of political culture."[11] "Black political activity," they indicate, "has been discouraged for generations; the benefits they have derived from government have been few. To maintain a personal sense of civic competence would seem difficult when attempts to influence government are doomed to failure."[12] As Matthews and Prothro see it, one must take into account both the internal and external factors in the South to grasp the black political culture.

Following Matthews and Prothro's book was a work by Harry Holloway, published three years later. Looking at the same southern black political culture but without the cautiousness of Matthews and Prothro, Holloway took the three aspects of the political culture from *The Civic Culture* (which had not used its black sample) and applied then uncritically to an analysis of black political activity in the South. Since he did not add the external or situational factors to the psychological ones, the results, to say the least, were inadequate.[13] Psychological explanations and not the laws of segregation were advanced for low levels of black political participation.

Does a Black Political Culture Exist?

The major problem, ignored by the scant literature on the subject, is whether a black political culture even exists. The controversy cannot be ignored. The historical and sociological literature abounds with the idea that the black community is deprived of a distinct culture. Daniel P. Moynihan and Nathan Glazer write, "the Negro is only an American, and nothing else. He has no values and culture to guard and protect."[14] They also are moved to say, "without a special language and culture, and without the historical experiences that create an elan and a morale, what is there to lead them to build a life, to patronize their own?"[15]

This thesis, which holds "that racism and poverty are the sources of much of what has been called Afro-American culture, black ghetto culture, or even the culture of poverty," is held not only by Glazer and Moynihan, but by a diverse group of academicians, psychologists, social workers, and educators, including blacks as well as whites.[16] Acceptance of this thesis means acceptance of the notion that since no black political culture exists, no system of black political beliefs, symbols, values, institutions, and expressions exist. Blacks would be the most volatile and unattached elements within the polity. In fact, studies of black adult and white attitudes have shown that blacks' confidence and trust in American government is much lower than whites'. These studies further aver that the transmission of political values in the black community does not take place as it does in the white community.

However, the thesis that black culture and political culture is nothing but ignorance, poverty, and social pathologies reflects only a part of reality. Moreover, the thesis suffers from conceptual omissions and a poor understanding of the nature of culture. "Any people," Ralph Ellison opines, "who could endure all of that brutalization and keep together, who could undergo such dismemberment and resuscitate itself, and endure until it could take the initiative in achieving its own freedom is obviously more than the sum of its brutalization."[17]

Finally, there is the matter of bias and ethnocentrism. Booker T. Washington succinctly captures the reason that the dominant culture inveights against the black culture: "no white American ever thinks that any other race is wholly civilized until he wears the white man's clothes, eats the white man's food, speaks the white man's language, and professes the white man's religion."[18] Any other viewpoint has difficulty getting its hearing. The reason lies with one of the main roots of the current debate: the field of sociology.

The debate between E. Franklin Frazier and Melville Herskovits over the survival of traditional and indigenous African cultural institutions in contemporary black American communities created a dilemma for many scholars[19] and had a serious effect upon the study of black life and politics in America.

Herskovits, in his now-classic study *The Myth of the Negro Past,* did a thorough debunking of the widely accepted myth that "the Negro is a man without a past." On the basis of comparative study of African-derived cultures in the new world, he generalized that there existed in black communities significant traces of African political, economic, familial, religous, and aesthetic institutions. For him, the African past had survived.[20] However, despite his painstaking research, he overstated his case in several areas, notably that of the family.

Frazier, then the leading scholar on the black family, easily refuted Herskovits's theories. Once the flank was weakened, Frazier moved to attack Herskovits broadside, declaring his entire effort to be fruitless. He wrote, "These scraps of memories which form only an insignificant part of the growing body of traditions in Negro families, are what remains of the African heritage. Probably never before in history has a people been so nearly completely stripped of its social heritage as the Negroes who were brought to America."[21] In Frazier's view, the African heritage died by the second generation: "old men and women might have brooded over memories of their African homeland, but they could not change the world about them. . . . Their children who knew only the American environment soon forgot the few memories that had been passed on to them and developed motivation and modes of behavior in harmony with the new world."[22] For Frazier the African cultural heritage was at best "forgotten memories" in black communities. In his estimation Herskovits, though well meaning, had erred completely.

Frazier's most valid criticisms concerned Herskovits's handling of the family, but when he asserted that these weaknesses were representative of the whole study, he overstated his case. Few observers saw the flaw. Frazier later modified his earlier position as he ridiculed the "Black Bougeoisie" and bemoaned the fleeting effects of an African cultural heritage, but scholars, journalists, and laymen, writing about blacks, have since usually accepted Frazier's refutation of Herskovits, labeling blacks as traditionless, cultureless, and "made in America." They grounded their explanations in the "culture of poverty" thesis.

However, this thesis, always under at least mild attack, came under increasing pressure. The most curious thing about the new criticisms is their location of the *major source* of black culture. Charles Keil, an ethnomusicologist, looked among nothern urban blacks and found the black culture located in the urban blues.[23] Ulf Hannerz, a Swedish anthropologist, who studied a Washington, D.C., black community, located black culture among lower class blacks.[24] Roger Abrahams found it in contemporary folklore, oral expression, and lifestyles in urban America.[25] All these analysts found the black culture located in some aspect of the black urban community, making their defense not quite persuasive. But their studies only signaled more to come.

Historian Eugene Genovese said that the black culture grew out of white paternalism in the slavery era.[26] Peter Woods, another historian, implied that it arose during slavery in black majoritarian areas with many African-born blacks.[27] Historian Gerald Mullin arrived at just the opposite conclusion, suggesting that it was rooted in slavery among highly acculturated and skilled urban blacks.[28] Each of these proponents of a black culture fitted it into some special niche, adding little force to the concept of a general black culture. These authors base the black culture in no less than six different frames of reference and thereby create something of a scholarly impasse. Like Frazier and Herskovits, they became concerned with the locus of the culture rather than its existence and influence.

Some scholars did get beyond the "made in America" syndrome. Black sociologists St. Clair Drake and Horace R. Cayton, in their classic *Black Metropolis,* noted that blacks had indeed created a "world within a world." "The people of Bronzeville have, through the years crystallized certain distinctive patterns of thought and behavior.... The customs and habits of Bronzeville's people are essentially American but carry overtones of subtle differences."[29] Summarizing, they noted that "Bronzeville's culture is but a part of a larger national Negro culture, its people being tied to...other Negroes by innumerable bonds of kinship, associational and church membership and a community minority status. The customs inherited by Bronzeville have been slowly growing up among American Negroes in the eighty years since slavery."[30]

Writing in 1966, some twenty one years after the official publication date of the book in 1945, St. Clair Drake, reflecting on the black experience in America, wrote: "A Negro 'subculture' gradually emerged, national in scope, with distinctive variations upon the general American culture in the field of literature, art, music, and dance, as well as in religious rituals and church polity."[31] He reasons that "The spatial isolation of Negroes from whites created Negro

'communities,' and increased consciousness of their separate subordinate positions.''[32] This, in turn, gave rise to black institutions, black
politics, and black folkways and classways behind the dark curtain.
This complex of forces led to the rise of the black culture. "The
'ghettoization' of the Negro," noted Drake, "has resulted in the
emergence of a ghetto subculture with a distincitive ethos...recogni-
zable in all Negro neighborhoods."

White sociologist W. Lloyd Warner agreed. Blacks and other
deviant cultural groups develop subsystems of their own, he indicated, which order their community lives and relate them to the
dominant white group.[33] Basically, Drake and Cayton argue only that
spatial isolation is necessary for the emergence of a culture, and not
that this isolation is in itself a culture.

Margaret Walker Alexander, a new force in black *belles lettres,*
has moved the Drake and Cayton thesis even further. "Black Culture,"
she writes, "is as old as mankind's earliest recorded literature, art, and
religion for black culture began in black Africa more than five
thousand years ago with Egyptian and Ethiopian civilizations." She
adds that the "Black Culture has two main streams—a sociological
stream...and an artistic stream."[34] The artistic stream, she continues,
"has five branches: language, religion, art, music, and literature."[35]
And she goes on to explain the influence of each branch from the past
to the present.

To Cayton's, Drake's, and Walker's insights, Daniel Thompson
adds: "From the very beginning of this nation until the present,
blacks have undergone a whole set of personal and sociocultural
experiences entirely their own."[36] Hence, in his view, blacks "have
been subject to a unique range of experiences endemic to the special
substatuses they occupy within all major social categories.... This
means then even when they are performing common social roles they
usually have uncommon experiences."[37]

Although numerous scholars have argued for the existence of a
black culture, the forces set in motion by the Frazier—Herskovits
debate simply overshadowed them. Thompson's work, however,
began with the thesis that a black culture does exist and that it has
had continuous meaning for black political activity and behavior.
Throughout this chapter, I will offer further proof to support that
thesis. My definition of black political culture is that it is composed
of both intrapsychic and external systemic factors that originate from
elements both inside and outside of the black community. This
chapter will explore some of the ideological and institutional features
of these factors.

The Elements of the Black Culture

Two early black scholars, W.E.B. Du Bois and Ralph Bunche, addressed the question of what the separate black political culture entails. Du Bois, writing in 1915 indicated that the election of black "governors" in some early New England towns was rooted in African tradition: "there early began to be some internal developments and growth of self-consciousness among Negroes. For instance, in New England towns Negro 'governors' were elected. This was partly an African custom transplanted and partly an endeavor to put the regulations of slaves into their own hands."[38]

Bunche saw the same kind of political consciousness among blacks when they elected their "own" mayors or held straw elections. In 1941 he wrote, "throughout the South there is a tendency to elect 'bronze mayors' and to work up regular campaigns with posters and meetings in connection with their elections."[39] This type of activity also occurred in northern cities. Drake and Cayton describe the custom: "The annual elections of the 'mayor of Bronzeville' grew into a community event.... Each year a Board of Directors composed of outstanding citizens of the Black Belt took charge of the mock election. Ballots are cast at corner stores and in barbershops and poolrooms. The 'mayor', usually a businessman, is inaugurated with a colorful cermony and a ball. Throughout his tenure he is expected to serve as a symbol of the community's aspirations. He visits churches, files protests with the mayor of the city, and acts as official greeter of visitors to Bronzeville. Tens of thousands of people participate in the annual election of the 'mayor.'"[40]

In the 1960s blacks continued this tradition by holding "Freedom Elections" in Mississippi, organizing black political parties and leagues, running independent political candidates, and holding state, local, and national political conventions.[41] In short, black political consciousness goes deep, imbedded in the black political experience and is an essential part of the black political culture. Evaluating this false and futile black political activity, Bunche argued "that the Negro is very much a political animal and that his political urges will find expressions in other channels whenever he is deprived of participation in the usual political processes."[42]

The insights of Du Bois and Bunche, that black political consciousness (i.e., the running and supporting of black leaders and officials who symbolize black needs and aspirations) is a prime element of the black political culture, have been expanded by those of Charles Hamilton and Matthew Holden.

Both scholars have used their own research as well as the data provided by the social anthropologists and psychologists who have been exploring black life in the urban centers and rural areas of the North and South. In addition, Jewel Prestage, Milton Morris, and Dwaine Marvick have argued the existence of a black political culture, but they have not discussed the details of this reality.

Hamilton argues that the black community has undergone several abrupt cultural transformations (political traumatization) making for constant cultural adaptative and survival mechanisms (improvisations), which work against longterm political planning and protracted political actions. To overcome these problems, Hamilton argues, black political leaders use the spoken word as opposed to verbal or written words, and appeal to emotions to articulate a situation of crisis, "rapping" hard on the man to get concerted political action.

Essentially, Holden agrees but adds some important points. He sees in the black community a great desire to get out of the black predicament (hope for deliverance), a great urge to get back at the oppressor (wish for defiance), and a strong notion that the group is right (moralism). While these things work for black political unity, in Holden's view, other factors work against it: cynicism about one's predicament, fear of trying to get out and failing, as well as self-assertive individualism (Dionysian) and authoritarian leadership leading to separatism.

Both men point out factionalizing forces operating in the black political culture. However, only Holden strives to identify the basic political motivating and unifying factors in the black political culture. Hamilton, on the other hand, mostly stresses those elements that involve the implementation of the motivating forces. He is concerned with how the community responds to its subordinate position. Both men identify what can be called the *expressive* elements of the black political culture, i.e., those forces within the black culture that tend to divide it.

Having outlined the essential elements in the black political culture, our focus can turn to a more detailed look at its dimensions for a clearer view. However, first we must examine the nature of black political ideologies to fully understand the interplay of forces within the black political cultural system.

Black Political Ideologies: A Cultural Force

Traditionally, political ideologies in the black community have been looked at as curious or as perhaps historically interesting but not as motivating forces.[43] Many social scientists study black political ideologies to see why people adhere to them rather than to see how they affect and shape black political action. The fascination among social scientists with the Black Muslim sect (now the Bilalian) is a prime example.[44] Yet none of the studies on the sect delves into its political behavior. Even fewer scholars have bothered to analyze the role that black nationalism plays in black politics or how it translates itself into political action in the black community.[45] In fact, most scholars have argued that black nationalism is *apolitical*. They fail to see the different manifestations of black nationalism as both a force for separation and a politically motivating vehicle.

Even when a few scholars inquire into the driving force of a black political ideology, they generally conclude that such ideologies are illogical, inconsistent, and without intellectual distinciton.[46] But these ideologies and value belief systems, though far from sophisticated, have motivated blacks to herculean political efforts. There is no denying the wide range and depth of political beliefs within the black community.

Before we look at specific ideologies and value systems prevalent in the black culture, we should reflect upon their common features. Reduced to their essentials, all black political ideologies have four elements: (1) race, (2) humanism, (3) economics, and (4) empowerment. Because of the systemic realities in which blacks find themselves, their ideological perspective includes some vision of race. Extreme black political ideologies centralize all their myths and key forces around black people. At the other extreme, some blacks hold that this is not a consideration at all and should be excluded. They see society and political participation as functioning around other criteria such as merit, issues, and political preferences. And between these two extremes are those ideologies that seek a mixture of racial and nonracial criteria.

Attached to the notion of race in black political ideologies are those values about man and the human family. Extreme racial political ideologies of any kind, black or white, carry values that emphasize color: goodness, evil, purity, equality—all values derived on the basis of racial features.

Another element concerns economic participation and well-being. In extreme black political ideologies, the distribution of goods and services and scarce resources are made on the basis of race or sometimes such variables as equality. Racial participation in the distribution system is specified to ensure a fair distribution of goods and services. For instance, in black Marxian or socialist ideologies, economic distribution is determined by nonracial criteria to ensure justice.

Finally, there is the ideological concern with power and how to get and use it for the community. Views range from a demand for full control of a few southern states like the Republic of New Africa (RNA) to a belief that power should be shared and ultimately the faith that only the best man, because of his skill, training, and past performance, should wield power.

Some black political ideologies emphasize the economic element and seek to politicize blacks around economic concerns. Here the emphasis of the Black Panthers comes to mind. They desire black political mobilization to achieve economic equality first, which will be essential to the black race and humanistic in its outlook, leading to ultimate empowerment.[47] Black integrationism first seeks black political mobilization around social acceptance and assimilation basing political empowerment on merit. Pan Africanism, as developed by black activist Stokely Carmichael, means political mobilization around race; humanistic concerns and economic matters will follow providing the basis for future black empowerment.[48]

Responding to the impact of these various ideological forces, black political behavior becomes (1) *supportive* in an innovative reformist fashion, (2) *reactive* in an effort to maintain preferred positions, or (3) *creative* in the development of new black political devices and techniques.

In the electoral area, the supportive ideologies seek changes and improvements in the position and economy of the black community through the major political institutions. Despite their use of existing institutional vehicles, these are new ways for improving the black situation in America.

The reactive ideologies are the efforts of conservatives seeking to maintain preferred positions and the status quo. They operate within the mainstream of political institutions, not so much to inhibit all black progress as to enhance the benefits of the privileged few. With the election of a conservative Republican President in 1980 and 1984, the reactive ideologists received a chance to expand, attract more recruits and shift their focus and thrust. Many of the conservative black spokesmen elevated by this administration, the dominant mood of the country, and sectors of the intellectual and commercial media, came to argue for a reduced and restricted role of the federal government in the black community, particularly in the area of social programs. Several of these black conservatives even argued for this posture in the area of civil rights. By pitching their arguments and suggestions *only* and *constantly* to the black community and by continually justifying to whites and blacks reduced governmental efforts in the black community, when such reductions increased misery and problems, they became little more than apologists for the white conservative power structure. With these blacks as point men and as respondents to black demands that these reductions enhanced and created new problems rather than eliminating old ones, the white conservative power structure needed only to reduce, cut back, eliminate, shut down and *then promise* that things would get better.

In the *creative* realm, the emergent black political activity *might* have been supportive had it not been for closed systemic channels, organizational inertia, and institutional racism. This behavior is exemplified by sit-in activity, protest, and direct action, i.e., unconventional forms of political participation, and racial political entities such as black political parties, independent black political candidates, black pressure groups, and exotic black political socializing devices and agencies. Eventually, some of these creative forms of black political behavior which arose as a result of systemic dysfunctions were abused by the system as in the case of the Mississippi Freedom Democratic Party. Or they might have chosen to enter the regular systems and become supportive, as in the case of several members of the Black Panthers in the early seventies. Some remained outside the system and continued in their innovative efforts until they disappeared.

A Survey of Black Ideologies

According to the theorists, there are three key dimensions of a political culture. They are (1) the cognitive orientations, i.e., an individual's knowledge of the political system; (2) the affective orientations, i.e., an individual's feelings about the political institutions and their manager; and (3) an evaluative process, i.e., individual judgements of the political system.

Given the invisibility of blacks in the traditional conceptual schemes, it is obvious why the behavioral studies on blacks reveal so little useful information about the black political culture. Blacks' absence, moreover, renders the *key* elements of this concept suspect. At best, these concepts can be used only as starting points for the study of black politics. In fact, a word of caution should be added about the labels "liberal," "moderate," and "conservative." Blacks certainly understand how the concepts are used in the American political process, but such terms are relatively meaningless in the black community. Originally these labels referred to basic philosophical positions on government and its use of power, but today the labels are used by political candidates as code words for attracting voters. When this occurred in the 1972 and 1976 presidential primaries, as professed liberal Democratic candidates did not automatically receive black support, there was much amazement. As the survey for this study was conducted, it was apparent time and time again that these labels had little attraction in the black community.

The crucial question, then, is what cultural forces in the black community shape the black world view about political legitimacy, the political good, and politically acceptable governmental acts? Obviously, there must be some forces and cultural institutions that do this, but current literature gives us few answers.

Since it has been noted that black political ideology plays a significant role in the black political culture, it would be well to see what linking this variable with black attitude structures reveals.

In developing a political analysis like this, we found the old liberal-conservative continuum to be a powerful summary tool, useful in determining the patterns in black political culture. Table 2.1 shows the self-designated divisions in the black community. Blacks were asked to classify themselves on the liberal-conservative scale, excluding racial concerns. A near majority of blacks, voters and nonvoters,

TABLE 2.1. Self-Identified Ideological Positions in the Black Community: On Nonracial Matters

Ideological Position	Black Voters	Black Nonvoters
Liberals	43% (216)	50% (123)
Moderates	38% (190)	37% (90)
Conservatives	19% (96)	13% (33)
Total	100% (502)	100% (246)

SOURCE: National Black Survey, 1972-74.

classified themselves ideologically as liberals. However, on racial matters with all other concerns excluded, we found (Table 2.2) that blacks in both categories are overwhelmingly liberal, with only a very small segment labeling themselves as conservative.

TABLE 2.2. Self-Identified Ideological Positions in the Black Community: On Racial Matters

Ideological Position	Black Voters	Black Nonvoters
Liberals	85% (428)	90% (222)
Moderates	10% (51)	7% (18)
Conservatives	5% (23)	3% (6)
Total	100% (502)	100% (246)

SOURCE: National Black Survey, 1972-74.

These data reveal blacks not only have ideological positions on political issues, but these ideological viewpoints are strongly affected by one element of the black political culture: *racial consciousness.* In sum, on general political matter a majority of blacks take liberal positions but not on matters of race where they take overwhelmingly liberal positions. The findings are parallel to those of Bartley, who, using aggregate data, found blacks in one state to be the most consistent liberal voters on all matters for two decades 1948-1968.[49]

Using recent survey data and analyzing them by sex, it is possible to see that nearly three-fourths of black men and women see themselves as liberals and moderates. Slightly less than one-fourth see themselves as conservatives. But since this survey didn't permit its results to be analyzed by a factor or feature of the black political cutlure, it can be assumed that these self-identifications in Table 2.3 are on nonracial matters. The inclusion of an element of the black political culture like racial consciousness would have provided greater survey insight. For instance, the data in Table 2.3 and 2.1 closely parallel each other in terms of black voters. Thus, ideologies can take

TABLE 2.3. Self-Identified Ideological Positions in the Black Community by Sex: 1972-1982*

Ideological Position	Black Men %	Black Women %
Liberals†	44% (179)	39% (225)
Moderates	32% (132)	39% (221)
Conservatives†	24% (97)	22% (125)
Total	100% (408)	100% (571)

*In order to get fairly representative cell entries, the numbers for each year were pooled and treated in a cumulative fashion.

†The NORC Survey questionnaire used a seven-point scale, three liberal and three conservative positions. Each of these three positions has been merged to present a more simplified table.

SOURCE: National Opinion Research Center's, *General Social Surveys, 1972-82.*

on an importance in the black community if they are related to features and facets of life that are important in that community and its interest. But differently, when racial issues become involved with political matters, then the ideological situation changes dramatically and it becomes a real force in shaping black political behavior.

If black political ideologies are factors in shaping black political behavior, can they become the bases for evaluating governmental policies and programs? Can blacks determine which political programs and actions are in their best interest? Again using recent survey data, several insights into the patterns of black political cognition and evaluation can be seen. The data in Table 2.4, drawn from the NORC survey, show how blacks (by sex) perceived governmental expenditures on eleven different governmental programs. The highest percentage of black men and women in the table notes that too *little* is being spent to "improve the conditions of blacks" as a group. The next largest percentage notes that too *little* is being spent in "halting the crime rate," "protecting the environment," "dealing with drug addiction," "improving the nation's education and health systems," and "solving the problems of the big cities,"—all elements that are closely related to the needs and interest of the black community. But in terms of "welfare programs," the lowest percentages are recorded in terms of too *little* support. Put differently, increased governmental expenditures in the area of welfare is not nearly as high a priority as governmental expenditures that will affect the race, and its community.

In two areas of the eleven presented, "space exploration" and "foreign aid," blacks attitudes reflected that too much was being spent by the government. However, in one other area, expenditures on "military, armament and defense," blacks felt that such expenditures were about right or sufficient. Thus, black attitudes in this one continuous national survey indicate that blacks can and did evaluate governmental spending in terms of their own self interest and that of the nation-state. Blacks, in this survey at least, saw the government as spending too little to help the group and its community. They supported the present levels of expenditures for the defense of the county but opposed external expenditures that left in the form of foreign aid and space exploration.[50]

In sum, black political cultural elements such as race consciousness and moralism can clearly be seen as forces operating upon black political knowledge, feelings, and value judgements. Moreover, blacks discriminate well among those institutions, individuals, and policies

TABLE 2.4. Black Evaluation of Governmental Expenditures on Foreign and Domestic Programs by Sex. 1972-82*

Types of Programs	*% Black Men*	*% Black Women*
Space Exploration		
Too Much	73 (369)	83 (576)
Too Little	6 (29)	2 (16)
(Polled Sample Size - 1200)	(505)	(695)
Improving and Protecting the Environment		
Too Much	8 (39)	9 (58)
Too Little	69 (339)	64 (440)
(Polled Sample Size - 1179)	(494)	(685)
Improving and Protecting the Nation's Health		
Too Much	3 (17)	4 (26)
Too Little	77 (393)	72 (518)
(Polled Sample Size - 1225)	(509)	(716)
Solving the Problems of the Big Cities		
Too Much	10 (50)	10 (64)
Too Little	72 (352)	65 (433)
(Polled Sample Size - 1150)	(487)	(663)
Halting the Rising Crime Rate		
Too Much	7 (36)	6 (43)
Too Little	75 (378)	74 (515)
(Polled Sample Size - 1204)	(507)	(697)
Dealing with Drug Addiction		
Too Much	9 (36)	9 (59)
Too Little	72 (361)	70 (485)
Polled Sample Size - 1191)	(502)	(689)
Improving the Nation's Education System		
Too Much	2 (10)	3 (19)
Too Little	74 (384)	69 (492)
(Polled Sample Size - 1232)	(516)	(716)
The Military, Armaments and Defense		
Too Much	35 (171)	32 (203)
Too Little	21 (104)	24 (154)
(Polled Sample Size - 1134)	(490)	(644)
Improving the Conditions of Blacks		
Too Much	1 (5)	2 (12)
Too Little	84 (432)	83 (599)
(Polled Sample Size - 1239)	(516)	(723)

Foreign Aid

Too Much	72 (354)	68 (469)
Too Little	10 (47)	12 (80)
(Polled Sample Size - 1184)	(494)	(690)

Welfare

Too Much	23 (117)	24 (171)
Too Little	47 (239)	48 (337)
(Polled Sample Size - 1209)	(506)	(703)

*These expenditure questions had six possible responses but only the two most extreme answers were used to construct the table, therefore, the percentages do not total 100.

SOURCE: National Opinion Research Center's General Social Surveys, 1972-1982.

of the political system that work for or against their best interest as a race; they do not condemn wholesale the entire system. Overall, this limited data base indicates that black knowledge of the political system reflects their experience with the realities of the political system; their trust and distrust stem from the system's responsiveness to their needs.

Portrait of a Black Political Cultural Institution: National Scene

Having viewed some of the psychological dimensions of black political culture, we can turn to some of the institutional features of the political culture. Political behavioralists emphasize values and beliefs as the prime or only elements of a political culture. In the final analysis, values beliefs, and ideas must be transmitted from one generation to the next and this transmission process requires the existence of institutions and political mentors. John Kincaid writes "Political culture would seem to be transmitted from generation to generation through political socialization, *political mentoring* (especially of activists), and engagement in political action."[61] An example of such an institution and political mentors in the black community is the *National Scene Magazine*, and its founder L.H. Stanton, and editor C.L. Holte.

The emergence of L.H. Stanton as a black political mentor came in steps and then in waves. He was born in 1906 and graduated from Marquette University in Milwaukee, Wisconsin, in 1928 with a degree in accounting and membership in Alpha Phi Alpha fraternity.[52] Stanton moved to New York City and found that he had to set up his own business because no white firm would hire black accountants. However, before he launched his own firm on Fifth Avenue, he worked during the depression on several black newspapers as a reporter and subscription seller, learning the business from bottom up. Once he launched his accounting firm, he discovered that a number of black clients in the midst of a depression were not enough to sustain the firm. He therefore branched out, forming a mail order business, a wholesale grocery business, and an advertising and publishing business. The latter issued *Continental Features,* a black editorial cartoon feature, and *National Scene,* a monthly black newspaper magazine supplement.

But the tasks of raising revenue, getting the articles, editing the material, supervising the printing, checking the proofs, and seeing to the distribution of the supplement, as well as attracting advertising revenue, proved too much. Moreover, now Stanton had competition from such magazines as *Dawn Magazine* and *New Black Monitor.* Stanton turned to a personal friend, C. L. Holte, a black political-culture "institution" in his own right. This proved to be the right match. Over the next six years, *National Scene* became a black political-cultural force to be reckoned with by the black masses.

Clarence Holte was a man committed to the resurrection and preservation of his people's literary roots. When Stanton called upon Holte, he found a reservoir of black history, which could be communicated in all of its variations to the black masses. He also got Holte's vast and unsurpassed book collection of African and Afro-American History. First, Holte wrote a series of articles on all facets of the black experience in the New World; in all, twenty-two articles for the supplement.[53] This was not all, for Holte was also to conceive, develop, nourish, and edit his Global series. The series, with Holte as a supervisory editor, propelled the supplement to unprecedented heights

Letters of praise from readers, organizations, groups, and school districts poured in. Holte saved random samples for later reference. Before, such letters had been used simply as keepsakes and to impress potential advertisers, only to be destroyed to save space. However, Holte saved many for posterity, and they give us important insight into black political culture.

Political letter writing is an old form of political expression. It can provide fresh and unmistakable evidence about public impact.[54] Usually, political letters are written to editors or political representatives. It is rare that people write with enthusiasm to a magazine supplement of a local newspaper. Letters to this type of publication generally cannot be printed, nor are they likely to be answered.

The letters praise Stanton and Holte for bringing the material out and for the high quality of the articles. All of the letter asked for more articles like these and expressed pride and satisfaction with what they read. Many sought permission to use the materials either in their high school or college and university classes.

Analysis of the letters' origins indicates that the greatest number of letters came from New York, Ohio, and New Jersey, with the nidwest and far west accounting for a second large grouping. Washington, D. C., Puerto Rico, and four southern states were each represented by one letter. Table 2.5 reveals that people from some twelve different categories sent letters to the *National Scene*. The largest single group (44 percent) came from unaffiliated individuals as determined by the stationary letterhead and signature. The next largest froup were college and university professors, followed by black cultural organizations and local public school officials.

From the standpoint of communication to a mass audience, the letters from the schools and colleges, book publishers, newspapers, black culture groups, and libraries suggest that the articles in *National Scene* could reach a much larger audience than the magazine's own circulation indicates. These data can be compared with the circulation data for *National Scene* to see how representative the sample is to the overall readership of *National Scene*.

TABLE 2.5. Affiliation of Letters to the *National Scene*

Group Affiliation	Number of Letters	Percentage
None	14	44
Universities and College	5	16
Black Cultural Groups and Organizations	2	6
Newspapers	2	6
Public Schools	2	6
Book Publishers	1	3
University Libraries	1	3
Law Firms	1	3
Congress	1	3
Foreign Nationality	1	3
Ministry	1	3
Banker	1	3
Total	32	99

The magazine was sent to 23 states and Washington, D. C. The 32 letters came from 13 different states, or about one half of all those reached by *National Scene*. Two letters came from Oregon and New Jersey, where no black paper carries the magazine; another letter came from Puerto Rico, which also does not have a paper carrying the magazine. The magazine and its ideas were affecting people outside its normal sphere of influence. Although this data base suggests that the spillover effect of the magazine is small, it also suggests that it has good impact inside its sphere of influence.

Moreover, it is interesting to note that in areas like New Jersey, Ohio, and Minnesota, where the circulation figures are comparatively small or nonexistent, the impact seems disportionately large.If cultural values are to circulate within the political community, culture-bearing institutions must be present and operative. In addition, these institutions must absorb and reject certain features out of the social milieu from which they emerge, to develop their own version of the mix of cultural values for transmission. Finally, these institutions need not be permanent or strong institutions to have an impact. They can be fragile, transient, and inconsistent.[55] And men like Stanton and Holte can play political mentoring roles.

External Values as Systemic Forces

So far, this analysis has focused on black ideologies and value-bearing institutions in order to further explicate the nature and scope of the black political culture. But this culture exists in a larger cultural system and matrix. At times, this culture, dubbed a sub-culture when it is seen from the standpoint of the larger system, inevitably confronts and conflicts with the larger cultural system of the dominant majority. When this happens, the larger system will attempt to alter, remove, or transcend the values, the belief structure, and the institutions in the black community.

This has happened and has been a frequent and recurrent feature of the black political experience. A prime contemporary example occurred after Jesse Jackson announced on November 3, 1983, that he would be a candidate for the Democratic Party's nomination for president. Once this happened, the editors of one of the leading national liberal magazines, *The New Republican* attempted to set into motion an entire new set of values and beliefs for the black community through the influence of its journal. Of Jackson's candicacy they argued: "Since it is clear that Mr. Jackson won't be the presidential nominee, his campaign based as it is on the proffered notion that mobilizing hitherto unmobilized masses can put one of their own in the Oval Office—must necessarily be an exercise in false hopes."[56] Their *first* value judgement is: *He won't win.*

Then they wrote: "___the failure of [the other Democratic contenders] candidacies will dash no one's hopes. In any case, they are plausible candidates for Vice-President. Mr. Jackson is not. Nor is he experienced in public life. His opponents are, without exception; no shadow, moreover, has been cast on their management of public funds."[57] Their *second* value judgement is : *He is not qualified and possibly is a crook.*

They continued: "The Jackson campaign—its aims, its slogans, its cynical maneuvers about designating a woman for Vice-President—is riddled with fakery, the kind of fakery that will disillusion and disillusion cruelly."[58] How will the Jackson candidacy do this? According to the Editors "such manifestly able political leaders as...Charles Rangel or Tom Bradley—for whom we [meaning liberal whites] could without any embarrassment stretch and push the political system finally to fulfill its promise of color blindness-..."will not get their chance now because Jackson's failed effort might suggest that it cannot be done.[59] And perhaps most importantly, in the Editors' view, this effort will destroy the hopes of the black masses and increase their misery and desperation. They wrote, "Too often the country's racial minorities have been promised imminent redemption—only to have the expectation crushed in a fashion that has intensified and validated their experience of helplessness, depression and social disintegration."[60] Their *third* value judgement is: *He will destroy the chances of promising black leaders and crush what little hope that still remains among the black masses.*

They continued: "Mr Jackson would take his people and those many whites who feel normative common cause with them down a path that leads out of the national consensus. This consensus is fundamentally generous and conscientious, which is why Martin Luther King, Jr., applied his genius to...[it]....Mr. Jackson's instincts run the other way."[61] Their *fourth* value judgement is: *He is a former disciple of King, but is no longer following in his footsteps.* Jackson for them, particularly if he runs, is now an anti-hero destroying King's legacy.

They continue: "Obviously Mr. Jackson is not a Communist or anything like one, but the presence of such people [Jack O'Dell] in key foreign policy roles in his entourage is evidence, at the very least, of very bad political and moral judgement."[62] In addition, the Editors found that "...the Jackson campaign—and Mr. Jackson himself— recall nothing so much as the Henry Wallace campaign of 1948. Given those who don't really want Mr. Jackson to win but will vote for him anyway, it also evokes the George Wallace campaign of 1968 and 1972..."[63]Their *fifth* value judgement is: *He is led by leftwingers and is, in a sense, a black Wallace, i.e., an individual making clear racist appeals and attracting only black racists. In short, it is a left-led right-wing movement.*

Finally, they write: "Perhaps Mr. Jackson will miraculously transcend himself in the course of his campaign; but at the outset, that campaign is not worthy of the people it purports to represent and lead."[64] Their *sixth* value judgement is: *He is to be avoided by blacks until he changes to suit these writers.*

In the beginning of their editoral, these Editors reflected: "To the 'political community,'...the meaning of this black man's candidacy is measured mostly by what it will do to the hopes of the various white candidates." Thus, all of their observations and value judgements simply show how his candidacy will hurt and harm the black community and some of its selected leaders. This is a very clever technique and the question can be raised: what does it all mean?

It means that a new set of value judgements have been created specifically for the black community, particularly for its political culture. And it also means that this white cultural institution will do all in its power to reshape and remold values in the black community.[65] The editorial stand represented in this editorial should alert black leaders who are liberally disposed and allied with this element to begin working through black institutions to try and usher in new values and beliefs or at least to stymie the old ones. In addition, value-projecting essays like this one provide opposition black leaders with reasons for their actions and clearly tell them what whites desire. And finally, value-projection efforts or systems like this print media organization provide, in many instances, a supportive network for those blacks who will follow this lead in fashioning white values and beliefs for black consumption.

As an example of the rationale technique, the black mayor of Birmingham, Richard Arlington, used the slogan "He Can't Win" to rally opposition to Jackson in the Alabama primary. This was effective in the city in reducing the turnout for Jackson. Georgia State Senator Julian Bond's speech to the Association for the Study of Afro-

American Life and History, a black historical organization, was designed to accomplish the same end: reduce support for the Jackson candidacy.[66] An example of the supportive network technique can be clearly seen in the emergence of the conservative Reagan administration. Conservative black spokesmen who espoused and offered justification for the Reagan policies got great support for the propogation of their ideas and proposals.

The external values that the *New Republic* created for the Jackson candidacy are just one of many examples that white liberal and conservative media organizations and political leaders (who might quietly speak to "responsible" black leaders) and other political entities put into place to restructure internal belief systems in the black political subculture. Each external value judgement developed by either the "liberal" or "conservative" establishment is usually carefully crafted to appeal to someone of influence in the black community (or the white community who has influence there) to help change and reshape its values and beliefs. And when these appeals are made, black culture-bearing institutions and political mentors will have to struggle to counteract them. In the case of the Jackson candidacy, usually it was the black church that fought these external values and their black spokesperson.

A Concluding Note

Many factors have led to a poor understanding of the black culture in general and the black political culture in particular. Nevertheless, throughout the long black odyssey in America, a black culture had both the necessary and sufficient conditions to grow and to transmit itself from generation to generation. The culture has to be seen from two perspectives, one emphasizing the psychological factors and the other, the external (systemic) factors and forces that provide the enviroment in which the culture must develop, grow and interact with the main culture. Finally, to see the culture, one must first assume it exists. By assuming otherwise, one permits invisibility to take over research direction and dictate the results.

Chapter 3

Black Political Socialization

Herbert Hyman, originator of the concept of political socialization, merged it in intrapsychic concerns. The concept addressed the nature, scope, and significance of individual political learning and, ultimately, how that learning would affect the political system.[1] How individuals internalized political attitudes and norms and what could be done if such attitudes and norms were not supportive became a major thrust of this kind of research. In short, the individual became the center of attention.

However, about a decade after the concept had been developed, Jewel Prestage found that "even though there has been a great volume of writing and research on political socialization, very little has been directed to political socialization of American Blacks."[2] All this would change greatly immediately after the black riots of the late sixties and early seventies. Studies of blacks' political socialization would multiply—at least until the riots slowly faded from the scene. What were the basic findings of this extensive literature?

The weight of the conclusions "suggest that black people tend to relate rather differently to the political system and have a far greater sense of personal alienation and political futility than do similarly located whites."[3] The reason we are told, lies in the dysfunctional agents of socialization in the black community. Having accepted as valid Moynihan's thesis about the black family and the omnipresent "culture of poverty" thesis, the literature says that the black family has broken down, the schools are stifled by ignorance and lack of discipline, and the peer groups simply mirror this tangle of pathology. Hence, no transmission of political values, attitudes, and norms can take place. And since there is supposed to be direct linkage between the political culture and political socialization, the lack of one means the absence of the other. The explanations, of course, are rooted in individual, not systemic, forces and factors.

However, Leslie McLemore tells us that not only does socialization go on in the black community, but that the literature itself is narrow and myopic in regard to the socializing agents in the black community.[4] (At best, only three or four agents are commonly accepted.) Erik Erikson concurs, "One of you asked me yesterday how I would put into my terms the role of a Black Panther at this time in history and in this place." Well, "For every group to be liberated, it is essential to realize sooner or later that they themselves absorbed the dominant values that enslaved them and in fact, based their identities in them." These negative values, Erikson asserted, must be destroyed, "and by sheer impact, you (the Black Panthers) are probably the most effective on the domestic scene for shaking up the old self-image."[5]

To the insight and findings of McLemore and Erikson, journalists Pat Watters and Reese Cleghoen add strong supporting evidence, simultaneously bringing to the fore the creative aspect of black political behavior. They write:

> "Can the adaptive ability of Negroes, which sprang
> out of their historic position of disadvantage, not be
> applied to political opportunity? In the past, Negroes
> adapted to limited opportunity, to segregation, to
> complete exclusion: they adapted by means healthy
> and unhealthy, desirable and undesirable. But when
> the chance came, they often climbed up rapidly, and
> this repeatedly has surprised people who had thought
> Negro 'Traits' were unchangeable rather than
> temporary adaptations to brutal situations."[6]

They note how rural whites, politicians, and sheriffs accustomed to seeing blacks "in their place" were startled "when thousands arrived at the courthouse to prove they really did want to vote." These defenders of the old order, and much of the current literature on black

political socialization, "had mistaken necessary adaption for acceptance and their nature."[7] Black ingenuity and creative political
behavior, despite systemic impositions, have gotten the political
message across.

The Literature

"Political Socialization," writes Kenneth P. Langton, "refers to the
way society transmits its political culture from generation to generation."[8] It may serve to preserve traditional political norms and
institutions or can become a vehicle of political and social change.

Milton Morris and Carolyn Cabe have reviewed the literature of
political socialization and find that out of a "total of 281 articles and
monographs and 39 dissertations dealing with political socialization
done prior to 1967, 6 articles and 4 dissertations dealt specifically with
blacks. Eighteen of 101 articles and books and 19 of the 208
dissertations done since 1967 deal with black political socialization."[9]
Morris and Cabe summarize: "The research clearly suggests that in
three attitudinal dimensions which are considered relevant for politics, black youth lag behind whites. Blacks are found to be less
knowledgeable about politics, less efficacious, and less trusting in
attitudes toward the political system. In attitudes toward political
authority, black respondents seem more supportive of authority than
whites."[10] And most of the research findings since the Morris and
Cabe study "have not significantly altered their summation."[11]

The important thing about the findings and research here is not
so much what they found as the time in which they found it. Political
socialization research on blacks commenced during the black social
revolution, at at time when governmental responses to blacks' needs
in terms of policies and programs were unequalled in American
history. Blacks' appearing nonsupportive and distrustful seemed un-
appreciative. Bullock and Rogers analyzed the findings of socialization research and concluded, in discussing the implications of black
support for the political system, that blacks were more prone to riots
and no longer "tolerant of failures in alleviating black inequality."[12]
Their remarks convinced many scholars and laymen that the government had done its part, that blacks just could not be satisfied. It was a
conclusion with an Alice-in-Wonderland quality about it.

A second summation of political socialization research on blacks
came five years after the Morris and Cabe study. This work looked

specifically at the literature on political efficacy and trust, examining
four explanations for the noticeable differences between blacks and
whites in these two areas, and testing by comparative analysis to see
which explanation offers the best insights. The author, Paul Abramson, concluded that the *"political-reality explanation,"* i.e., that racial
differences result from differences in the political enviroment in
which blacks and whites live, tended to have the greatest support in
the literature, to be the most "parsimonious," and to deserve further
"serious research consideration."[13] He found that the "intelligence
explanation," i.e., that racial differences result form differences in
political education with American schools, had limited scope and
rested on some questionable assumptions: while the "social-depriva-
tion explanaton," i.e., that racial differences result from social-
structural conditions contributing to low feelings of self-confidence
among blacks, was only a "valid partial explanation" with some
major limitations.[14]

Abramson did suggest that a fifth explanation, i.e., that a black
political subculture is operative, an idea of black political scientists
Jewel Prestage and Milton Morris, made a lot of sense and needed
"greater development."[15] Ultimately, however, he dropped the notion
in favor of the political reality explanation. "The subcultural
socialization thesis" he avers, "is fully compatible with the political
reality explanation."[16]

Overall, Abramson's book provides a solid review of the literature
assessment of the representativeness of the findings, evaluation of the
reliability and validity of the measures use to study political attitudes
among pre-adults. The book's four appendixes contain a wealth of
information, ranging from the places (sites) where the various studies
have taken place to the items used in each of the indexes by every
researcher. But the book is limited by its emphasis on individual
psychological variables as explanations for the black socialization
process, a limitation that creates severe problems.

First, the focus is on black children and pre-adults. Second,
concern centers on ways that external factors can be reduced to
psychological variables. And third, both the book and the literature
assume that the same questions used for whites could work for
blacks.[17] However, all of these concerns, though major, are insignificant when compared with the fact that the author ignored the structure
and nature of black political socialization. Black political socialization cannot be identified with white political socialization. The
process has at least three steps, including *resocialization* as well as

counter socialization. In the black community, political socializaton occurs differently and leads to different results.

Second, it is essential to move beyond mere individual concerns to look at the systemic factors, the structural, social, political, and economic differences that exist between the two racial groups. One must see how these differences affect "political learning and teaching." Several black scholars have found that simply by using different kinds of questions, they could find different learning and teaching processes./[18]

Finally, this chapter looks at how black institutions and other agents of socialization, permanent and nonpermanent, can act not only upon children but adults as well. During the sixties, black leaders like Martin Luther King, Jr., taught blacks through mass demonstrations and movements, using single galvanizing events instead of long-term formal processes to overcome centuries of powerlessness so that blacks would become social and political forces acting for their own betterment. Such single, once-in-a-lifetime phenomena must be viewed against long-term processes to see how they affect both children and adults in the black community.

The Agents

The agents responsible for counter socializaton and resocialization are the family, the press, the church, the schools—all of them termed dysfunctional by the literature that accepted the culture-of-poverty thesis. These are the key agents responsible for overcoming discontiuties and incongruencies in black political learning and teaching. Blacks identify the church, family, and schools as having the most significant influence on their political learning (see Table 3.1).

TABLE 3.1. Agents of Political Socialization of Black Voters and Nonvoters

Agents	*Black Voter*		*Black Nonvoter*	
Black Church	24%	(154)	25%	(66)
Black Minister	6%	(40)	5%	(12)
Black Family	22%	(144)	22%	(57)
School	20%	(131)	17%	(44)
PeerGroups/Friends	20%	(126)	14%	(35)
Media	8%	(51)	17%	(45)
Total	100%	(646)	100%	(259)

SOURCE: National Black Survey: 1972-74

Moreover, blacks see a vast difference between the church as a socializing agent and the minister as an agent. In their view, the church is much more significant than the minister. In fact, in the black community, in sharp contrast to the white, the church plays the dominant role in the socialization process. The family, the school, and peer groups in that order, are the next significant agents.[19]

Several factors can explain not only the major role played by the church but the reason that the institution rather than the leaders are seen as crucial education agents. First, since two of the main elements of the black political culture are its oral tradition and its moralism, an institution built around these two features would play a significant role. Second, the black church, one of the oldest of black institutions, has always combined religion with social activity. In short, much more is discussed in the black church than simply religion and the soul's salvation. Politics, economics, gossip, social status, education, and numerous other topics have importance in church, too. Put another way, the black church reflects the black community, so among its major concerns are the problems faced by that community.

Members of the black church in their various auxiliaries debate their political views and problems with one another to arrive at a political position to act upon. Political scientist Charles V. Hamilton has noted that even if a church and minister are not specifically concerned with electoral or pressure group politics, they are nonetheless working to help black individuals and the black community.[20] Normally, church concern leads to significant action. A recent example is the Reverend Leon Sullivan in Philadelphia and his OIC training centers. The latest example is the black church's role in Jesse Jackson's candidacy and race for the presidency.

Not only is the church a place where political ideas and responses can be learned and matured, it is the place where many of the leading black political figures, nationally and locally, have developed. One can point to the Reverend Jesse Jackson, or the late Reverend Adam Clayton Powell, or the Reverend Andrew Young, Mayor of Atlanta. Hamilton shows that such a pattern has existed since Reconstruction.[21] Black preachers helped to bring the politics of the day into the Lord's house, as did the black masses. And surely they have discussed from time to time the politics of their leadership. Moreover, the black community has had many churches with ministers who have developed numerous political positions in their dealings with each other. The black community, it has been noted, is over-churched.[22]

The net result for the black community is a startling richness and variety in its political culture.

Another reason why the church plays such a significant role in black political socialization is the protest nature of its ideology. Many scholars have noted the patience, humility, and docility with which black religion has endowed its adherents. Yet few have noted that black religion has also formed the basis for the early slavery revolts and the modern civil rights movement.[23] Black religion has been a spur to political action and changes.

The next most important politicizing agent in the black community is the family. Again contrary to popular wisdom, blacks feel that the family unit is quite useful in shaping and transmitting political values. Most scholars have noted only the "pathology" of the black family and have refused to note its many herculean feats to survive.[24] Recent scholars have revealed that the black family transmits oral knowledge of American presidents, their party affiliation, and their significance for the black community. In short, values regarding political partisanship are transmitted via the black family. Second, the family in numerous instances acts to counter the negative political symbols focused on the black community by maintaining the "legacy of slavery." And the family usually transmits the basic elements of the black political culture.

The third and fourth important agents among blacks are the schools and peer groups. Normally, one could expect more of the schools, but, basically, the schools have, passed on negative, through textbooks or at best limited images about black political participation. Hence, the schools' place is relatively low; their role is reduced because they have normally been controlled by forces outside of the black community.

Finally, other significant agents are the media. Table 3.2 reveals that, when the media are examined on racial basis, blacks prefer to rely on black-directed media for their political cues, values, and orientations. Few blacks rely solely on the white media as a basis for their political judgements. The pattern of resorting to black institutions instead of white ones is a common one in black political culture.

Recently popular "black films" are an excellent example of the kinds of media sources for blacks' role models and political orientations. As Robert Brisbane notes, the black revolution had its most dramatic impact in motion pictures. "Gone from the scene were such black-mouthed versions of Uncle Tom as Stepin Fetchit, Mantan

Moreland, and Eddiew 'Rochester' Anderson. The so-called black film made its debut, and it presented black audiences with such new characters as 'Shaft', 'Nigger Charlie', and 'Super Fly'. The new films were popular...but in the view of many observers they were producing new black stereotypes."[25] However, these new stereotypes were black folk heroes with whom blacks could also relate.

In the final analysis, contrary to the evidence in the literature, blacks *do* see certain institutions as being focal in shaping and transmitting their political values and outlooks. In fact, blacks choose black institutions over white institutions as the major agents in directing their political orientations. And given the recent tide of black nationalism, this seems normal and natural. But even without such a mood, blacks' attachment to their own institutions seems no different from other ethnic groups' attachments to their institutions.

TABLE 3.2. Use of Media Sources by Black Voters and Nonvoters

Media	Black Voter	Black Nonvoter
Black Newspapers	88% (516)	73% (178)
White Newspapers	12% (72)	27% (67)
Total	100% (588)	100% (245)
Black Radio/TV	79% (521)	88% (198)
White Radio/TV	21% (141)	12% (26)
Total	100 (662)	100% (224)

SOURCE: National Black Survey: 1972-1974

The Structural Flow

Within the black community a twofold socialization process is under way. First, the white community is constantly seeking to socialize the black community toward certain goals it defines. From time to time these goals have changed, from slavery to segregation to integration to isolation. At the same time, black political socialization is trying to filter out, negate, or reorganize this white outlook and to politicize and socialize the black community toward goals, and political patterns desired by the black community. These are drawn both from some of the *constant* and some of the *fluctuating* features of the black experience in America.

This entire structural process is graphically described in Figure 3.1. It notes that the political socialization process in the black community has three steps.

First, whites try to socialize blacks through their media and agents. In Step 2, the black community circumvents or redefines the white political orientation to match the needs and realities of the black community. And on the basis of this redefinition, blacks act politically. Step 3 indicates the result of the redefinition. Some black political behavior reflects the needs and decisions of the black community, i.e., it is in tune with the black political outlooks and values inherent in the black political culture. However, some black political behavior goes untouched or unmoved by the reconversion process. This behavior, though not the dominant black political behavior, is in most cases the behavior desired by whites. The old label for these black individuals was "Uncle Toms." Currently, they are referred to as "Oreo Cookies," as blacks with processed minds, or as hustlers. On the other hand, some blacks emerge from the reconversion process overly converted. Their behavior is labeled ultra-black nationalist, extremist, and the like.

The behavior of writers for black newspapers provides an excellent example of the ways this process works. A close analysis of black newspapers will reveal that in any major crisis period in black-white relations in America, when white political socialization is negative and asserts that blacks are inferior, subhuman, and the like, black newspapers sometimes report this, but always provide numerous examples to refute the negative image projected by whites.[26]

During the era of disfranchisement the black editor-owner of the *Richmond Planet* of Richmond, Virginia, waged an unceasing war against the arguments offered for the restriction of black voting rights in that state.[27] In Pittsburg, Pennsylvania, Robert Vann of the *Pittsburgh Courier,* used his paper to fight the racist doctrines and policies of the fascists, and their invasion of Ethiopia. He sent a reporter to Ethiopia to cover the war and to report on the heroic efforts of the Ethiopians in face of the Italian invasion. *Savannah Tribune,* which lasted from 1874 to 1961, fought vainly against not only local racist propaganda, but national propaganda as well.[28] Even prior to the twentieth century the black press constantly challenged the myth of white supremacy propounded by the agents of white socialization.[29]

A Concluding Note

Political behavioralists writing about political socialization have accepted the individualistic learning theories advanced by psycholo-

Fig. 3.1.   The Structural Flow of Black Political Socialization

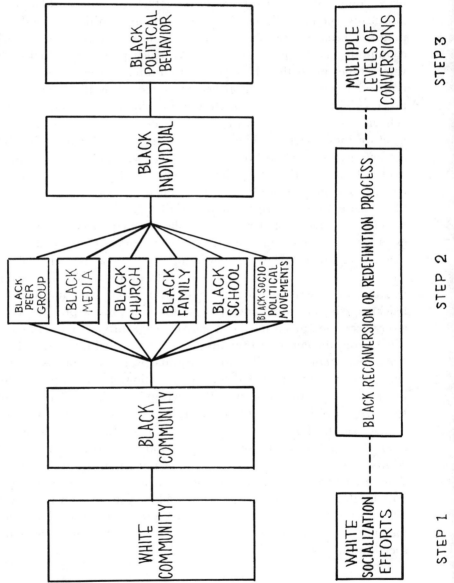

gists and have said that only three factors socialize the individual politically: the family, the school, and the peer group. But in reality the government itself socializes people. Further, it can enforce its socialization by resorting to force and the exercise of its legal power. For instance, a major feature of southern, and to a lesser extent northern, society after Reconstruction was to socialize blacks into accepting an inferior and subordinate status in American life.[30] Hence, black political socialization and its various processes must be seen as operating inside this nexus, which includes both internal and external forces.[31]

Chapter 4

Black Political Opinion

The study of black political opinion focuses on the political issues confronting blacks and on their impact on members of the black community. Past studies have explored black political opinion to determine if blacks are anti-or pro-civil rights, anti-or pro-Semitic, anti- or pro-white, and anti- or pro-democratic. Seldom is attention paid to much else. Such an approach has created numerous problems, as we shall see.

Public opinion was a concern of classical political philosophy. Philosophers like Rousseau who wrote on the body politic called it the "general will." Others labeled it "the will of the people."[1] Recently, theorists of political democracy have designated it the voice of "John Q. Public." Walter Lippmann, in his classic *Public Opinion,* shifted attention in the study of public opinion from the "body politic" to the individual.[2] By describing it as the "picture in our heads" that affects our attitudes and behavior, Lippmann showed that public opinion was an individual thing. But political opinion, while individually held, is not individually derived. It emerges from systemic and individual factors.

In part, political opinion may be manipulated. Various groups have structured political ideas and engineered public opinion since the beginning of political democracy in government and are likely to continue in this role long into the future. The manipulators of political opinion include the government itself, public relations firms, and majority and minority groups and their leaders.

Students of political opinion are concerned not only with its formation and manipulation but also with its distribution in a polity. Generally speaking, distribution deals first with the "direction of opinion" and second with its incidence among persons differently situated in the social structure.[3]

In the first, researchers are concerned with whether political opinions are positive, negative, or neutral. A closely related concern is whether or not people's attitudes cluster around a particular issue. Statisticians call this *unimodality*. The political scientists call it *consensus*, denoting "widespread popular agreement on a question." If the public is divided into pro and con clusters, there is then what political scientists call *conflict* and statisticians call *bimodality*. Finally, variations in the intensity of public opinion is called *concentration* by political scientists or *multi-modality* by statisticians. In short, opinion can be moving in the direction of consensus, conflict, or concentration, positively or negatively.

Research concerning the second pattern of distribution concerns itself with the formation and distribution of opinions among different social and geographical segments in society;[4] such groups, for example, as the John Birch Society, Americans for Democratic Action, American Medical Association, Baptists, Catholics, Black Panthers, Southerners, and others. Of course, "this is not to say that every member of a given group shares the same viewpoint; in fact, group cohesion may sometimes be minimal. It is to say, however, that group leaders take stands on political issues, endeavor to identify their members with these opinions and exert group influence in politics.[5] Researchers are interested also in the linkage and impact of public opinion, especially their effect on parties, pressure groups, and individual behavior. V.O. Key writes, "Public (and political) opinion...may simply be taken to mean those opinions held by private persons which governments find prudent to heed. Governments may be compelled toward action or inaction by such opinions; in other instances they may ignore it, perhaps at their peril; they may attempt to alter it; or they divert or pacify it.... (But), whatever the character or distribution of opinion, governments may need to estimate its nature as an incident to many of their actions."[6] In short, political opinion can be decisive in the success and failure of public policies and governments themselves. With this in mind, most of the modern texts on public opinion argue that it fulfills three major functions in the political system, the (1) *supportive,* (2) *permissive,* and (3) *demand* functions.

Basically, black political opinion oscillates between supportive and demand positions on most issues facing the black community. Only in a few cases is black political opinion permissive. To gain a hearing for their demands, blacks have developed instruments and institutions not found in the constitutional apparatus.

The key functions of public (and political) opinion are its (1) *formation,* (2) *distribution and direction,* and (3) *impact and linkage.*

The Literature

Given the key features of the study of political opinion, it is clear that the serious study of black political opinion is yet to begin. None of the major works on public opinion devote as much as a chapter to black public opinion.[7] What is even more crucial is that the little work that does appear is concerned primarily with the distribution and direction of black political opinions and attitudes.

Most of the early data on black political opinion was collected by pollsters, to ascertain the direction of black opinion on certain key social issues.[8] The social psychologists, who sometimes led but mostly followed the pollsters, continued in the same vein, only adding a few more key issues such as how blacks felt about civil rights, violence, black leadership, protest, prejudice, segregation laws, the integration of schools, and the role of government.[9] Political scientists, at first following in the paths blazed by the pollsters and social psychologists, later shifted their focus to the perceptions held by black rioters.[10]

In the midst of the riot studies, political scientists began an analysis of the formation of black opinions at the pre-adult and adult levels. These inquiries helped political scientists to refocus the study of black political opinions, transforming it into political socialization and unconventional political behavior and labeling it protest, alienation, anomie, powerlessness, and the like.[11]

Social scientists have been concerned only with the distribution and direction of black opinion on a few key issues facing society. Currently, they have redirected interests toward the formation and consequences of public opinion, i.e., political socialization and contemporary unconventional political reactions. However, their preoccupations have obfuscated and misinterpreted reality, creating, in effect, illusions.

The focus on distribution and direction alone makes black political opinion seem baseless. Research of this type tells us that x number of blacks favor riots, want better housing, desire better job opportunities, as opposed to y—data that give us a feeling for the mood in black America but no insight into the reasons blacks feel this way or the circumstances that motivate their opinions. Without a base, or reason, black political opinions seem hortatory, polemical, rhetorical, if not unjustified sounds of fury. In addition, the literature on the riots implies that failure to deal with these angry frustrations and feelings might lead to a time of burning.

Moreover, when the direction of black attitudes is contrasted with white attitudes on key issues like civil rights, violence, or black power, whites and blacks seem in opposition to each other. Each group appears to be at the other's throat,[12] two separate societies moving in different directions. Although this may be the case, it nonetheless offers no help to the segments within each community trying to work with the other. Voices from the white community ask, "when are they going to be satisfied?" "What are they angry about now?" The implication is that blacks have no legitimate grievances. Richard Bardolph puts it thus:

> Whites including not a few liberals, were hurt and angered when blacks continued to raise their demands after a decade and a half of civil rights victories in courts and legislatures had made concessions after concessions. They failed to understand that the concessions should not have been necessary in the first place, and that they had not, after all was said, made very much difference. The ultimate reason for seeking admission to unsegregated schools and buses and theaters had been the imputation of racial inferiority which segregation so clearly proclaimed. But after the courts decreed an end to segregation the implication was still there...in private and personal ostracisms; in shabby employment opportunities; in inferior schools; in ghetto stores where shoddy merchandise was sold at inflated prices to a trapped clientele...."[13]

Hence, a black basis for demands remained.

In addition to portraying blacks' demands as baseless, researchers' emphasis on distribution and direction creates the impression that black public opinion should act in tandem with white opinion. Such a normative assumption fails to acknowledge the fact that black public opinion emerges from separate and distinct conditions that do not exist in the white community. Real black opinion becomes *invisible*. Political scientists' shift of attention to political socialization only maintains this invisibility.

Finally, this emphasis on direction and distribution results in a widespread preoccupation with the reasons why black opinions are not in line with white opinions. In the literature, this is called "implications for system support." It ends inevitably with the partial explanation of alienation, anomie, despair, powerlessness, and frustration; in a word, with black pathology.[14] It is the black man's fault that his opinions are not in line with white opinions.

Ultimately, this approach leads to the conclusion that black political opinions have no impact or make no linkages with government and its agencies or public policy. The literature reveals black public opinion to be impotent. Black ideas, we are told, are not weapons. If this were true, slavery and segregation would still be social forms, and blacks would still be waiting for whites to give them freedom.

Eric Hoffer writes, "Mass movements do not usually rise until the prevailing order had been discredited. The discrediting is not an automatic result of the blunders and abuses of those in power, but the deliberate work of *men of words with a grievance.*"[15] He continues, "Thus imperceptibly the man of words undermines established institutions, discredits those in power, weakens prevailing beliefs and loyalties, and sets the stage for the rise of mass movement."[16] In politics, social movements created and sustained by political ideas and opinions do affect government and public policy.[17]

Black political opinion did exist. When it was manipulated, shaped, and structured by symbols and myths wielded by its leaders and opinion-making agencies, it did alter the political structure in America. Whether it was the myth of nonviolence of Martin Luther King, Jr.,[18] or the myth of black power, black Americans have responded with action to affect public policy.

The Nature of Black Political Opinion

Black political opinion is not a phantom. It exists and it is effective. Moreover, black political opinion is rooted in the black experience and black political culture in America. It is part and parcel of the black political community and it is as much shaped and structured by the black community as it is affected by the white community.

Black political opinions arise in part from the wretched conditions in the black community and the knowledge that the white community condones and permits them to exist. Blacks see certain issues differently than whites.

Take the matter of welfare. The black community's political opinions differ in both distribution and direction, buty they also differ in their concern about improving public policy on this matter. Table 4.1 reveals that blacks do not see welfare in the same negative fashion that whites see it. In listing their priorities in public policy, they rank it last but poverty first (Table 4.2). The black community sees a strong difference between the two. They do not see welfare as a tool to alleviate poverty or as a negative device. Yet welfare is the lowest of their public policy concerns, as shown in Table 4.2.

TABLE 4.1.   Black Views of Appropriate Welfare Payment Levels

	Black Voters	Black Nonvoters
Welfare payments should be		
Increased	69% (451)	68% (196)
Decreased	20% (134)	22% (64)
No Opinion	11% (73)	10% (29)
Total	100% (658)	100% (289)

SOURCE: National Black Survey: 1972-74.

TABLE 4.2 Rank Order of Public Policy Concerns: Black Voters and Nonvoters

Black Voters		Black Non Voters	
Poverty	63% (355)	Poverty	39% (89)
Civil Rights	20% (111)	Civil Rights	24% (55)
Education	12% (70)	Education	24% (55)
Welfare	5% (31)	Welfare	13% (29)
Other	0% (1)	Other	0% (3)
Total	100% (568)	Total	100% (231)

SOURCE: National Black Survey: 1972-74.

While these examples serve to suggest that the socioeconomic environment in the black community helps to shape black political opinions, they do not reveal the role of some additional actors.

Black Sense of Community:

Coupled with the existential conditions in the socioeconomic environment in the black community is the emergence of a sense of community among blacks, a feeling of unity. Political scientists studying "developing" societies call this sense of community "political integration."[19] It is, in effect, the creation of common political structures or orientations, which produce a climate of opinion conductive to high levels of integration among otherwise mutually disinterested or even antagonistic individuals or groups. This can occur gradually, intentionally, or because of a single dramatic event or crisis.

Since colonial America blacks have sought consciously through communication to produce not only a group awareness but also an internalization or active sharing of interests within the group strong enough to encourage them to coordinate their behavior in pursuit of common interests. For an interesting parallel, let's look for a moment at whites in colonial America. Richard L. Merritt, in his pioneering study of the integrative processes that led to the rise of an American community during colonial America, has shown that these processes were slow but steady.[20] He writes, "The shifts of attention and symbolic identification came neither overnight nor as a result of slow, steady and virtually automatic processes. Judging from the use of symbols in their newspapers, the colonists had to learn to think in a purely American rather than in an imperial context. The learning process seemed to progress rapidly at some stages, to hold relatively steady in others, and in some cases even to decline."[21] He concludes that from 1735 to 1775, the trend was straight upward.

In many ways, what Merritt saw parallels the rise of a black community in America. Slowly and gradually, blacks have come to see themselves as a coherent and functioning political community that was separate and distinct, apart from the majority community— despite the white community's arguments to the contrary.

Merritt used as one of his indices the number of times the colonists referred to themselves as "Americans" helped create the sense of community. Using a similar index, Martin Dann notes that from its inception, the black press has tried to create a sense of community among blacks in America. He writes, "The black press provided one of the most potent arenas in which the battle for self-definition could be fought and won. By stressing the primacy of racial pride and thus forming ethnic solidarity, the black press becomes along with the church, a central institution in the black community. Black editors and their correspondents, as leaders in the community, not only were able to communicate information vital to the community and necessary for its cohesion, but also were often the only

educational resources available."[22] It was the early black press that
began proclaiming "a national identity for free blacks and slaves," an
identity which proclaimed "a nation within a nation."[23] The black
press became a prime force in creating a sense of community among
free blacks in early America.

Dorothy Porter, in her analysis of early black writing, prior to
1820, has observed the same trend toward the creation of a sense of
community long before the advent of the press. Commencing in 1760,
these writings, including "constitutions and laws of beneficial societies; speeches before mutual aid and educational societies; the
report of the earliest annual conventions for the improvement of the
free people of color; arguments for and against colonization; printed
letters, sermons, petitions, orations, lectures, essays, religious and
moral treatises, and such creative manifestations as poems, prose
narratives, and short essays," articulated some form of social and
racial consciousness.[24] Many led to the creation of mutual benefit
organizations or flowed from them. In some of these tracts, blacks
referred to themselves as "Sons of Africans," "Africans," or "members
of the African race." Even the black protest pamphlets, Porter argues,
flowed from the sense of community and fostered it, because they
addressed grievances perpetrated upon blacks by whites.[25] In addition,
she notes the central role of the church in fostering these pamphlets,
"as one might suppose." Porter indicates that protest gatherings were
usually held in church buildings, "which afforded the incumbent
pastor or church leader an opportunity to express himself fully in
opposition to the oppressive social conditions that were the subject of
the occasion. The publication of actions taken or issues discussed in
such meetings helped to swell the trade of pamphlet literature in
those early times.[26]

Robert Kerlin has found that the black press since the 1890s has
continued this tradition of building a sense of community. After an
extensive analysis of the black press, Kerlin counseled, "To know the
Negro, read his papers extensively.... Read their editorials, their
sermons and addresses, and their news items; read their reports of the
proceeding of their congresses, conventions, and conferences, their
petitions and resolutions; read their poems and stories and dramatic
sketches; look at their cartoons."[27] Kerlin wrote in 1919, but Maxwell
Brooks arrived at the same conclusion in 1959 after an extensive
qualitative analysis of the black press. As Table 4.3 shows, Brooks
found that far more positive than negative symbols appeared in the

black press. "One may infer,...." wrote Brooks, "that Negro journalists'.... writings are more constructive, their views more positive, and
that they are less inclined to be neutral or to compromise."[28]
Following Brooks, Roland Wolseley, in a comprehensive study,
concludes that the black press builds a sense of community only on
the racial matters but is conservative on all other positions.[29] In sum,
the black press has always endeavored to create a sense of community
among black Americans; it is bolstered by the works of black authors.
Today, many writers are developing a *black aesthetic* ("a corrective, a
means of helping black people out of the polluted mainstream of
Americanism").[30] Robert Brisbane notes that "many are only marginal writers and non-poets whose sole objective is the politicization
of the black masses. The output of these writers is never above the
level of militant rhetoric and crude propaganda."[31]

TABLE 4.3.   Positive and Negative Symbols of Black Life in the Black Press

Papers	*Total*	*Positive*	*Negative*	*Neutral*
Courier	24.85	48.99	40.96	10.04
Afro-American	22.35	54.46	35.80	9.73
Journal & Guide	18.88	57.93	33.39	8.66
Amsterdam News	9.48	49.36	42.82	7.80
Defender	24.43	55.47	37.41	7.10
Total	99.99	53.52	37.69	8.78

SOURCE: Maxwell R. Brooks, *The Negro Press Reexamined*, (Boston: Christopher
Publishing House, 1959), p. 38.

In addition, black social and political organizations have worked
to create community feelings. Porter writes: "Mutual benefit organizations were among the first organized expressions of social consciousness by blacks residing in cities of the North.... Adherents rallied to
accomplish a variety of purposes, to provide not just for a particular
class of blacks but for all those in need of financial help, protection or
enlightened leadership."[32] Moreover, black leaders articulated the needs
and concerns of that community and so added impetus to the cause.
Some even spoke of "some type of manifestation, either in person or
process, capable of alleviating black suffering, thereby bringing in the
millennium."[33] From various nooks and crannies within the black
community came many forces to create a widely shared sense of
community.

Sanction and the Sense of Community

At the same time, there arose the desire to defend the sense of community. In fact, a device emerged for insuring everyone's allegiance to that community. The sanctions blacks imposed on each other to maintain their sense of community were public ridicule and stereotyping. Stereotyping was done publicly by black leaders, the black press, and black writers, as well as privately by individuals. It took the form of parody, satire, burlesque, and derision. The stereotypes simplified, overgeneralized and exaggerated the characteristics of a person who is perceived to be acting against the black community and its self-interests.

Two of the best known books of this type are E. Franklin Frazier's *Black Bourgeoisie* and Nathan Hare's *Black Anglo Saxons*. Both works are biting satires of black middle class people and their phony imitations of white behavior. Both works poke fun at and assert clear values about black middle class behavior. Each justifies hostility toward these blacks because they deny their black culture and cultural heritage.

Today this technique is especially popular among new black writers and poets. When poet Don L. Lee wrote that he came to "integrate Negroes with black folk," he signaled a new effort to promote the concept of community. These black writers have seriously ridiculed those not acting in the black community's best interest.[34]

But not only scholars, writers, and poets have ridiculed and criticized those blacks perceived as not acting in the best interest of the community; so, too, have black newspaper editors. Many speak of "race traitors." Few studies have been made of the history of these editorial statements. Research among archives of old papers yields comments like the following: "The old Negro and his futile methods must go. After fifty years of him and his methods the race still suffers from lynching, disfranchisement, Jim Crowism, segregation and a hundred other ills. His abject crawling and pleading have availed the cause nothing. He has sold his life and his people for vapid promises tinged with traitor gold. His race is done. Let him go."[35] This editorial was from the *Crusader* in New York, October 6, 1919.

The Fort Worth Hornet, on October 25, 1919, editorialized in a similar fashion. In an editorial entitled "Beggar Leaders" the editor wrote: "The time will come in the South when men, white men, will refuse to encourage thse so-called and self-appointed Negro beggars to work and play a game of deception. Most of these miserable hypocrites threw around them an orphan home cloak, or a church cloak, or a purposed industrial Negro school cloak, where girls are to be taught cooking and the boys farming."[36] In fact, during this era of emergent black consciousness such titles as "False Leadership," "Colored Traitors," "Goodbye, Black Mammy" are representative. They strained the language of anathema to "the limit for the adequate castigation of tale bearers and lick spittles, the cringing, hat-in-hand tribe, the Brutuses and Benedict Arnolds."[37] In sum, the black press has always poured out its contempt for acts of race betrayal, race disloyalty, and cowardice.

Political cartoons have employed stereotypes to attack those operating against racial unity. For example, one widely used cartoon of the NAACP showed a small skinny man (labeled "those who contribute") carrying a large fat man smoking a cigar (labeled "those blacks who fail to give") across a deep canyon on a small creaky plank. Black political cartooning is a rich art, but no studies of it comparable to those made of Herblock and Thomas Nast have yet been done.[38]

The rhetoric of black leaders and the slogans of black movements have sought to identify black enemies within the community. These labels include "Uncle Tom," "Black Mammie," "Oreo Cookie," "hustlers," and others. Such techniques will be explored further in the section on black political symbols, below.

The black community has developed many techniques to enforce and enhance a sense of community among blacks. These sanctions seem to increase significantly during periods of heightened racial consciousness.

Divergencies and the Sense of Community

The black sense of community has never gone unchallenged. Not only have internal forces disrupted it, the white community has sought constantly to destroy it. With its use of the symbol of the "melting pot" and its plea for homogeneity and integration, the white community has tried to destroy a sense of community among blacks. Abolitionists of yesterday and liberals of today have urged blacks to seek assimilation with the larger white society. Even without such action by whites, the great documents speaking of "equality" and "the freedom of all men" serve as a constant beacon attracting blacks to assimilate.

However, in nearly every period of her history, America has denied, refused, and suppressed black assimilation. Blacks are both drawn toward and forced away from an "American community." These conflicting forces ultimately lead to the creation of a black community. The black community develops institutions and ideas that create a sense of belonging based on racial consciousness and a common cultural heritage. Some blacks came to think of themselves as "African All."

Racial consciousness preceded black nationalism, which is a culmination of a complex of forces rather than an abrupt act or decision. It is an action as well as a reaction to the black man's American odyssey. Its intensity is a result of the oscillation of the divergent tendecies in society; it recoils and expands in response to the forces acting upon it. Kenneth Clark, noting this tendency, argued that the creation of new black power slogans during the sixties to enhance the sense of community was harmful. "Black Power," he argued, "is the contemporary form of the Booker T. Washington accommodation to white America's resistance to making democracy real for Negro America. While Booker T. made his adjustment to and acceptance of white racism under the guise of conservatism, many if not all of the 'Black Power' advocates are seeking to sell the same shoddy moral product disguised in the gaudy package of racial militancy."[39] Clark himself was caught up in the oscillation process. Even he, while attacking black-power advocates, defended a rather vague alternative view of the black community as a physical reality in nearly every American community. In fact, it's physical reality sometimes makes discussion of its symbolic value difficult. this has been it's Achilles heel; while it may or may not exist as a "state of mind," it certainly does exist as a "state of being," and so remains a half-formed reality in the black mind. But even half-formed it can be called up.

Symbols: Imagery and Drama

Black political symbols are evocative. They call forth that half-formed sense of community inherent in some black political opinions and the complete or even inflated images of other blacks.

Private black opinion inherits and internalizes the contradicitons inherent in black political realities and environment. Blacks hold these perceptions in store on both the conscious and unconscious levels.[40] The private attitudes can become motivating forces for political action because of the effect of symbols manipulated either by the black or the white community. Pranger writes: "Depending on particular situations, however, different weight will be given to different meanings. Meaning varies with its placement and the clientele in that situation."[41] Put another way, "personal, private motivation has two sources: the will to power (potential) manifesting itself in public action, and fear of the risk involved in such a quest, typified by shrinkage of individual interests to orientation and security."[42] In short, sociopolitical events are assimilated into the black personality, "with its objective background of heredity, environment, and development, its present subjective strivings, and its future aspirations."[43] Blacks will respond to black political symbols in varying ways because of the unresolved tensions in their personality. That black political symbols, in sum, can elicit only so much response has been the concern of numerous black consciousness-building movements. Today such a movement is called cultural nationalism.

Black political symbols fall basically into two categories: the referential and the condensed. Referential black symbols evoke a cognitive and/or affective response: displays of the black flag (red, green, and black), the clenched black fists, the African decals, the Black Panther symbols, or the wearing of the afro hair-styles and dress. Moreover, behavior itself becomes symbolic. Acting black, thinking black, reading black, dressing black, eating black, and having African names are examples of this form.

Summarizing, then, black political opinion is presently treated in the literature under the rubic of political socialization. In most cases, researchers fail to see it as being rooted in the black experience in America. Numerous segments of the black community seek to create a sense of community, but that sense is never pervasive because the white community continues to counter with appeals for itegration and promises of equality. Meantime, the black community seeks to maintain a modicum of community by using sanctions. Moreover, black political symbols are developed during crisis and periods of intense tension to promote black unity.

A sense of community is always *a latent opinion* in the black community. It can become a *manifest* opinion in times of crisis and great tension. Normally, racial consciousness does not manifest itself, for not all issues facing the black community are racial. In short the main function of black political symbolism is to bring forth latent

TABLE 4.4. Black Newspapers and the Concentration of Blacks at County Level

State	No of Newspapers	Distribution by Counties with Black Populations of:		
		50%	49-30%	29-0%
Alabama	7		3	4
Arizona	2			2
Arkansas	1			1
California	23			23
Colorado	2			2
Connecticut	2			2
Delaware	1			1
District of Co.	3	3		0
Florida	14		1	13
Georgia	13		5	8
Illinois	12			12
Indiana	3			3
Iowa	1			1
Kansas	1			1
Kentucky	2			2
Louisiana	7		2	5
Maryland	1			1
Massachusetts	2			2
Michigan	5			5
Minnesota	5			5
Mississippi	4		2	2
Missouri	8			8
Nebraska	1			1
Nevada	1			1
New Jersey	4			4
New York	11			11
North Carolina	6		1	5
Ohio	8			8
Oklahoma	3			3
Oregon	1			1
Pennsylvania	7			7
South Carolina	1			1
Tennessee	2		1	1
Texas	17			17
Virginia	4			4
Washington	4			4
Wisconsin	3			3
Total	192	3	15	174

SOURCE: This table is based on data from Harry Ploski and Warren Marr, *The Negro Almanac*, revised edition (New York: Bellwether, 1976), pp. 925-927 and additional information acquired by the author.

features of black political opinion, racial consciousness, and so to enable unified racial action.

The Black Opinion Makers: Black Media and White Media

Black political opinions are shaped by certain institutions and agencies of the news media. One of the leading molders of black political opinion is the black press. Allan Morrison wrote in 1966: "Since the first Negro journatistic experiement of 1827, some 2,700 Negro newspapers have appeared in America, of which 153 survive today." Moreover, Morrison notes that these publications, despite poorer facilities and resources and stiff competition from the white press, have "continued to voice the aspirations, articulate the demands and protest, and mirror the progress and problems of 20 million Negro Americans...."[44] Since 1966, the black press had continued to grow, developing political positions as well as recording the political news for the black community.

Table 4.4 further reveals the geographic distribution of black papers in relation to the percentage of blacks located in each community. We find the highest number of black newspapers in counties where the black population is 30 percent or below. Only one black newspaper is found in countries where the black populaton is over 50 percent.

Table 4.5 shows that the South and the North lead in the total number of black newspapers. Yet overall most of the black population is to be found in the South and Northern part of the nation. However, further probing reveals that less than five of the papers would fall in cities not considered standard metropolitan statistical areas. In short, most black newspapers are concentrated in urban centers and very few are located in the rural areas.

The same is true for black radio stations. The majority (see Table 4.6) are located in and around large urban centers. And although there is only one black television station, black-oriented programs such as "Soul Train" and "Black Journal" are syndicated mainly in the large urban communities. In fact, even the concerns over black access to cable television have been focused on the urban complex.[45]

In a word, the black media are located in urban areas where blacks may constitute a majority in central city, but only one third of the population county-wide. Few black-opinion media-making or-

TABLE 4.5. Black Newspaper by Region

Regions	Number of Newspapers	Percentage
South	87	45.3
North	47	24.4
West	32	16.6
East	26	13.5
Total	192	99.8

SOURCE: Ploski and Marr (ed.) *The Negro Almanac*, rev. ed., (New York: Bellwether, 1976), pp. 925-927.

South = Alabama, Florida, Georgia, Louisiana, Mississippi, North Carolina, Tennessee, Texas, Virginia.

North = Illinois, Michigan, New Jersey, New York, Ohio and Pennsylvania.

gans exist in the rural areas, or in the counties where blacks are the dominant population majority.

Yet, especially in the south, major movements for social justice, equality, and freedom began in places where the black media were lacking. For example, the Montgomery bus boycott began in a city where only one black newspaper existed, and its total weekly circulation was not over 1,500. (In 1956, the black population in that city was roughly 38 percent [51,680] of the total population.) Nevertheless, the city mobilized, literally through the church and by word of mouth.[46] The SNCC effort led by Stokely Carmichael in rural Lowdnes County, Alabama with the formation of the Lowdnes County Freedom Organization (the Black Panther Party) used word-of-mouth and mass meetings to replace the usual media found in urban settings.

A poll of twenty-five black rural candidates concerning their campaign techniques where media were not available revealed that twenty-four thought that mass meetings, leaflets, and face-to-face contact were the most effective tools.[47] Where the black media were available, the majority of candidates listed the black media as their first choice and the white media as a second choice.

The key point is that black radio and newspapers are not the most significant opinion shapers in the rural black community, where word-of-mouth channels, mass meetings, and always the "talk" at the black church are far more important. The word, "nommo," passed via informal channels, plays a major role, especially where electronic gadgetry does not exist.

TABLE 4.6. Black Radio Stations or Black Programming

States	Number of Stations
Alabama	14
Arkansas	3
California	10
Colorado	1
Connecticut	2
Florida	18
Georgia	15
Hawaii	2
Illinois	7
Indiana	5
Iowa	2
Kansas	1
Kentucky	6
Louisiana	15
Maryland	4
Massachusetts	1
Michigan	6
Minnesota	2
Mississippi	13
Missouri	4
Nebraska	1
New Jersey	6
New Mexico	2
New York	8
North Carolina	18
Tennessee	9
Texas	9
Ohio	7
Oklahoma	4
Pennsylvania	3
South Carolina	5
District of Columbia	3
Utah	1
Virginia	7
West Virginia	2
Washington	3
Wisconsin	3
Total	222

SOURCE: Ploski and Marr (eds.), *The Negro Almanac,* revised edition (New York: Bellwether, 1976), pp. 939-944.

In sum, although black opinion makers are concetrated in the urban centers, black opinion-making apparatus consists of more than the media. The oral tradition in the black political culture is strong;

the word, passed informally, helps to shape opinions. Furthermore, negative impact of the white media must also be taken into account.

The Communication Flow Theory Revisited

Since the advent of the behavioral revolution in political science, several theoriests have tried to develop a complete explanation of the political system on the basis of a theory of communication or information flow.[48] However, a crucial obstacle to the completion of that theory is the incomplete understanding of the role of internal communication-flow structures in the various political subcultures of the nation-state.

Second, the control of the opinion-shaping apparatus by the majority leaves the determination of truth and reality up to them. Carl T. Rowan writes, "This country's rulers are using the media to obscure truths about racism, poverty, injustice, and economic and political repression."[49] With the majority determining reality, minority sub-communities must accept the picture presented, reshape it to their concepts, or do a little of both. And it is in this shadow world that the shapers of black opinion must work. Hence, black political opinion finds itself subject to two pictures of reality, making the task of researchers on the subject quite complex. The perennial problem confronting black political opinion is that it cannot stop one sphere of society from creating its picture of reality but it must constantly reshape the distortions it creates to fit its own perceptions.

Any refined communication theory or model or government must address itself to the existence of various information-flow systems inherent in numerous political subcultures and to the complexities that result because these subsystems are subject to the distorting efforts of the majority systems. For example, the information flow system in the Mexican-American political subculture is vastly different from that of the black subculture or the Indian subculture.[50] Any communication model that does not incorporate these is a very limited model indeed.

Chapter 5

Black Voting Behavior

In 1940 black political scientist Ralph Bunche made a very incisive comment: "The vote has become a fetish with many Negroes, but there is little evidence that social problems anywhere in the world are solved by fetishism."[1] By 1975, a contrary position was emerging, as academicians were developing the idea that blacks could solve their social problems through voting.[2] But Bunche's view was farsighted. "The great masses of whites," he wrote, "throughout the country, who have long been enfranchised, have been able to make but little progress toward solutions of many of their own problems with the ballot."[3]

Bunche's comments are still instructive. First, he suggests the difficulties in using the vote as the sole solution to black social problems. Second, he focuses on the concern blacks have long had with voting, even though that simple act for most blacks in the forties was an impossible dream. Few writers have surpassed Bunche's insights about voting behavior as a fetish and the vote as a black political resource.

Some Beginning Notes

The major explanations of black voting behavior are: (1) socio-economic status index (SES), (2) fear and apathy index and (3) group consciousness. The first explanation dominates the literature and has withstood nearly all challenges. The third arose from the Verba and Nie volume in 1972, while the fear and apathy explanation emerged in 1973 under heavy fire from the proponents of the SES index. All three are based in individualistic rather than systemic factors.

The hunt for the inner man led to explanations of black voting behavior on the basis of socioeconomic status, (SES) index. Conventional wisdom put it thus: the higher a black person's SES, the more likely he or she is to vote and participate in politics. The lower his or her SES, the lower his or her level of voting and participation. Matthews and Prothro concluded, "Most Negroes have low social status, relatively small incomes and limited education received in inferior schools.... The low voting rates of Negroes in the South are, to perhaps a large extent, a result of these factors rather than of direct political discrimination by the white community."[4] They argue that political and legal rights will not give rise to a large and effective black electorate, which will "have to avail substantial social and economic change."[5]

Recently, Lester Salamon challenged this explanation of black voting.[6] He argued that fear and apathy might be a better guide to explaining voting behavior than the SES index. However, Salamon's new departure was seriously challenged, primarily on the basis of statistical measurement.[7]

Prior to the rise and decline of Salamon's explanatory thesis, Verba and Nie had ventured a new one. They argued that blacks are an exception to the standard SES model of political participation and that black deviation from it could be accounted for by their group-consciousness model. "The key variable in the group consciousness model," they wrote, is "group consciousness itself."[8] The statement is a perfect tautology. They developed their argument in a similar fashion. "If a deprived group," they argued, "is to use political participation to its advantage...it must somehow bypass the processes that lead those with higher social status to participate more and those with lower status to participate less...there are a variety of ways of bypassing this process...in relation to American blacks, (it) is the development of self-conscious awareness of one's group membership."[9] And after several sophisticated measures and controls, they substantiate their group-consciousness model. Using this model and their modes of participation, Verba and Nie discerned that when some variables are controlled, there were areas of political participation in which blacks vote or participated at higher rates than whites. This new explanatory thesis was greeted with enthusiasm in some quarters, for it had shown in a comparative way blacks being equal to whites in political participation rates. But a look beyond the surface reveals some heavy difficulties inherent in this new thesis.

For instance, is black self-awareness, or group-consciousness just a recent phenomenon? What about black group conscousness during the Garvey Era? The Depression era? The New Deal Era? And during the forties under A. Philip Randolph's leadership? Or during Reconstruction? Is it not true that some blacks have always demonstrated a great deal of group consciousness? If the answer to any of these questions is positive, then just how effective and explanatory *is* the group-consciousness model? Second, is not group consciousness a sociopsychological variable, like fear and apathy and social status? Since, the 1965 Voting Rights Act eliminated certain systemic political obstacles and did not elevate black socioeconomic conditions, would Verba and Nie's thesis be an attempt to save the SES model itself and the generalizations it had generated about blacks in light of a new reality, i.e., large-scale black political participation but with still low socioeconomic levels? Some students of black voting behavior, long before the Verba and Nie thesis, had found the "base line" SES model to be deficient and of limited use.

Generally speaking, the SES index, the fear-and-apathy index, and the group-consciousness model all collapse before the realities of systemic and structural factors. In fact, they are limited, if not poor, explanatory tools of black voting behavior.

Since the era of disfranchisement, the black voter was politically neutralized, legally and illegally, both in the South and the North. And in such a system where political neutralization was and is the *norm,* the explanatory indices formulated by the political behavioralists obfuscate, rather than illuminate, reality. Study of internal sociopsychological factors could shed little light on the near insuperable external factors like the political structure. For a better insight, let us briefly examine these highly acclaimed and often-employed explanations of black voting and political participation.

For instance, in Mississippi a black attorney, Perry Howard, was an active political participant. He attended every Republican National Convention from 1924 to 1960 as the national committeeman from the state of Mississippi and was honored in 1960 as the oldest continuous delegate to the Republican National Convention.[10] Likewise, he was active in the Republican party and patronage politics in the state. But after 1928, he could not vote in *Mississippi politics.* As a lawyer he had status, he was well educated, and he acquired a small fortune in Republican patronage politics. According to the behavioral SES index he should have been a key voter. Howard, however, is just one of the many black Republicans who resided in the South who found voting to be impossible.[11] Many black Democrats did not cast ballots during this period for the same reason.

This is a historical example; we can also turn to a statistical one. Henry J. Abraham pointed out: "On the first surpervised registration day under the new statute (Voting Right Act of 1965), Negro voter lists in nine counties with a history of rampant discrimination in Alabama, Louisiana, and Mississippi increased by 65 percent...Extending their work to four other counties, the federal voting examiners had registered almost 20,000 Negroes with ten days."[12] By the May 1966 primaries, more than 150,000 voted in Alabama alone. In fact the dramatic change in the political involvement of blacks since the 1965 Voting Rights Act is "far more rapid than any change in the level of education and income among blacks."[13] The correlation technique will not readily explain this rapid increase in voting. In short, the standard indices will not *satisfactorily* explain it.

Noting the vast limitations of the SES index, Johnnie Daniel notes that the key to the black political mobilization since 1965 was not the SES index, but a change in the political structure.[14] His findings clearly indicate that the "counties that have the highest levels of Negro political mobilization are those counties that had both Negro candidates and federal registrars, and the counties that have the lowest levels of Negro political mobilization are those counties that had neither Negro candidates nor federal registrars."[15] Frederick Wirt, in one of the best works on Southern politics since V. O. Key's book, agreed with Daniel. Looking at the motivation for black political activism, he sees "national laws" as the force that changed "the basis of old South politics by dealing a new set of players into the game..."[16]

Bowen agreed. "In the United States," he writes, "Negro political participation in the South has risen dramatically since the 1965 Voting Rights Act overrode state barriers to voting." However, Daniel, Wirt, and Bowen limit their insights to the year 1965 and since. But what we shall show shortly is that with any major positive change in the political structure, black political mobilization increased. It did so in 1944 after *Smith* v. *Allright* and after many other key legal decisions that changed the political structure.

There are still other challenging data. Douglas Rae has pointed out that electoral laws (structural forces) have serious political consequences and can affect individual and group political participation. "Any law has some consequences, whether good or ill, for all of the groups which enter the sphere of life which it applies...These *electoral laws* are of special importance for every group and individual in the society, because they help to decide who write other laws."[17] He concludes, "If a single pattern emerges from this study with status approaching a 'law' it is the persistent bias of electoral laws in favor of strong parties as against their weaker competitors."[18] In sum, a key variable in blacks' voting behavior is their political neutralization and not so much their purported behavioral problems.

A second closely related matter should be noted. The tendency is to combine the black electorate with the black voter. Political behavioralists tend to see these groups as synonymous, which is only one small step from concluding that blacks are apolitical, apathetic or politically alienated. "Blacks don't vote," "blacks don't participate in large numbers in politics as whites do," "blacks must become aware of the power of the ballot," "blacks must be educated politically," and "basically blacks are the largest group of non-voters," and similar statements abound in the leading scholarly journals and major studies.

However, by definition the black electorate is composed of all blacks in the voting age population (VAP), but black voters are those of the VAP that actually register and cast ballots. Clearly, if the black electorate is neutralized, only a small number of blacks would be voters.

Confusion in definitions leads to further blurring, which causes a masking effect. For instance, the drive to restore suffrage rights to blacks seemed to be a liberal undertaking, and once the ballot was restored, it seemed that blacks had lost nothing except the right to vote for a few years. But the reality is much more complex than that.

The political neutralization of blacks led to the loss of not only significant political power, but of all those factors associated with political power in a democracy. For instance, the number of counties with a black majority was much higher in 1900 than in 1980. In political representation alone, neutralization cost the black electorate far more than it can now hope to attain. What black representatives from these counties could have achieved in terms of socioeconomic benefits for the black community is staggering. No one will ever know the cost in human lives, human suffering, and human cruelty. In a word, there is no such thing as catching up. What was lost remains lost.

The Black Voter: The Portrait in the Literature

To examine black voting behavior, we must first delineate the dominant characteristics of the scholarly literature on black voting. The numerous theories that abound in the literature evolved primarily from four "landmark" voting studies.[19] We shall also look at recent works on voting behavior and cull from them key notions about black voting.

Three theories emerge from the literature: (1) theories about black party affiliations, (2) theories about black group and individual voting characteristics, and (3) theories comparing black and white voting characteristics. Most in the first category present findings about black attachment to the Democratic and Republican parties, but some focus also on independent voting and third-party affiliation. The second catagory focuses primarily on how blacks vote as a group in each election as well as how they act individually. In this category we commonly find the SES index being used to describe black voter participation levels. Some works discuss income, residential parameters, and time-bound thesis, but they represent a minor thread among the major ideas of the last three decades.

The first book on voting behavior, *The People's Choice,* researched primarily by political sociologists, contained no picture of black voting, in either the 1944 or 1948 election. The reason is that in the area selected for the study, Erie County, Ohio, "none of the ethnic groups, Negroes, Germans, or other formed an organized voting unit."[20] This "model" research work omitted race and ethnicity, rendering blacks (and other) voters invisible. Invisible, that is academically. Blacks did vote, North and South, in the 1944 and 1948 presidential campaign.

The second "landmark" study entitled, *Voting,* focused on Elmira, New York. In Elmira, blacks comprised "about 3 percent of the population."[21] The original sample included 17 blacks, while the post election sample had 150 supplemental blacks included.[22] The number of blacks in the original sample, as shown in Table 5.1, is so small that it is statistically insignificant.

The Voter Decides, which was based upon a nationwide sample conducted by the Survey Research Center (SRC), had 61 blacks or 9.21

percent of the total in its 1948 sample. In the 1952 sample, there were 157 blacks or 9.72 percent.

The fourth "landmark" study, *The American Voter,* which was also based upon SRC survey data, revealed a different black sample number in nearly each table. For example, there were four tables in the book that listed the total number of blacks in each case (see Table 5.1), and the number of black respondents varies with each question.

TABLE 5.1. The Black Presence in the "Landmark" and Major Voting Studies*

Name of Study	No. of Whites	No. of Blacks	Black %
1. *People's Choice*	600	0	0
2. *Voting*			
1st Survey	1,012	17	1.62
2nd Survey	1,012	150*	12.72
3. *The Voter Decides*			
1st Survey	601	61	9.21
2nd Survey	1,457	157	9.72
4. *The American Voter*			
Table 11.4	754	184	19.61
Table 11.5	754	184	19.61
Table 11.6	2,268	111	4.66
Table 16.3	0	310	100.00
5. *Negroes and New Southern Politics*			
1st Survey	694	618	47.10
6. *Elections and Political Order*			
Table 12.3	207	81	28.12
Table 12.5	0	88	100.00
7. *Participation in America*			
Raw Sample	2,260 whites & 28 other	261	10.23
Weighted	2,653 whites	406	13.11
8. *The Changing American Voter*	19,775 (p. 360)	(Doesn't specify)	

*Supplemental Sample.

*In many of the SRC studies, the black sample was so small that it could only be analyzed in a selected fashion and yield statistically significant results. Thus, the results could only be reported in a few tables. In sum, small samples yield only partial data and a limited perspective.

Only in the book's Table 16.3 are black respondents not compared with white. In short, this book used blacks only in a selective and partial fashion. Blacks were not in the overall thrust of the work. They appeared on four occasions, three in comparison with whites (see Table 5.1).

In 1966, two new "landmark" voting studies appeared. *Elections and the Political Order* was a continuation of the SCR studies and included only one article on the South. It had three tables noting the black presence. The total number of blacks in each table is less than one hundred. The second book, *Negroes and the New Southern Politics,* is the only one of the landmark studies devoted to black political participants, though black political actions were contrasted with those of white southerners. The number of blacks in the sample was 618, compared with 694 whites in the sample. Even in this much lauded volume, whites outnumber blacks. Blacks were 47 percent of this study on themselves.

By 1972, *Participation in America* appeared. Its raw sample included 2,260 whites, 28 others, and 261 blacks, or 10.2 percent. The weighted sample had a few more blacks, raising the black percentage to 13.1. The authors felt that this percentage was larger than the census estimates of blacks in the national population at that time.[23]

The truth of the matter is that numerically, blacks, in this study and the others, are too few in number to generate meaningful data about voting behavior. The underlying reason is that blacks are an afterthought. It was assumed that they deserved minority share. *But no one raised the question as to whether a minority share is enough to expose political reality.*

The most recent volume, *The Changing American Voter,* hasn't solved this essential problem. Blacks still have a minority share. In this book, based upon all of the SRC and National Opinion Research Center data, no new surveys on blacks were included, leaving the supposedly new interpretations to be based on the few blacks that had been included in the old surveys. Second, only two figures (13.8 and 14.5) in the book are devoted entirely to blacks. Most of the other eighteen tables that mention blacks are devoted to the examination of the issue of black welfare.[24] The tables looking at this "new issue" show blacks' party identification as being heavily Democratic and blacks as being the most liberal group in America. All eighteen compare black positions with other American groups.

Lyman Kellstedt, examining the SRC data from 1952 to 1972, found that the national surveys included very few blacks. Numbers range from a low of 87 to a high of 382, for an average of 211. The mean percentage was 14.5.[25] The small number of blacks in the books and surveys creates a major problem that researchers have failed to deal with: the question of accuracy and sampling error. Richard Niemi and Herbert Weisberg write, "With common sampling procedures, a sample of size 1,500 generally leads to a 'sampling error' of about 3 percent, which means that most of the time (95 percent of the time, actually), the result from the sample will not be more than 3 percent off the true results. A survey may find 74 percent of the public favoring some policy, but it should be read as saying that from 71 to 77 percent of the public favor the policy when the 3 percent margin for error is taken into account."[26] But then, in a note they add, "A national sample of 1,500 would contain only about 150 blacks and an estimate of their responses would be subject to much more than 3 percent error."[27] Many survey researchers believe that oversampling and weighing will overcome this problem, but the mere doubling or tripling of the black percentage in the population would not resolve the error. [28] All of the works on blacks relying on small numbers in the sample subset are subject to large sampling error, and their findings are subject to much more than a 3 percent error. All the major voting studies as well as the SRC surveys are susceptible to this statistical error.

Articles on black voting behavior on the other hand, sometimes used aggregated instead of survey data. The wide range of the subjects of these articles makes summary difficult. Some cover registration, others voter turnout, some party support and identification, and some the influence of special factors. Some look at national problems, some at congressional, or state, or local ones.[29] They are alike only in their use of explanatory indices. They stray little from the standard SES explanation, which is nearly universal in the literature. Generalizations developed in these works reflect this heavy emphasis on sociopsychological variables. Herein lie the problems.

Weaknesses in the Literature

The literature on black voting behavior suffers from serious methodological problems. First and foremost are the exceedingly small data bases upon which the generalizations were formulated. As Table 5.1 reveals, the black presence is indeed startlingly small. Their numbers are so sometimes so small as to be statistically insignificant.

The second weakness is that the literature gives us little data on the black political independents or black third-party voting. In fact, one can almost conclude from the volumes that such does not exist. The researcher have failed to probe for these questions.

The third weakness is the variety of geographical regions that are surveyed in the "landmark" studies. The first two studies in Table 5.1 focused on northern suburban areas. The second two based their findings on SRC national surveys, and one was a secondary analysis of earlier surveys. Overall, the southern region gets favored along with northern suburbia. No urban area is included, and the use of southern areas before 1965 serves primarily to depress black participation rates. This raise the question as to whether the southern samples were used intentionally to depress black participation rates.

Fourth, these books and articles show blacks with a bias for the Democratic party. But in fact, most of the studies were researched during the era when blacks were strongly supporting the Democratic party either because of its New Deal or civil right policies. Yet, none of them attempt to compensate for this "peculiar" historic bias. Would the generalizations that result hold equally in the case of an era of high Republican responsiveness to the black community? If the answer is negative, then all that these books and articles are saying is that blacks have had to choose between the lesser of the two evils. In short, black support for the Democratic party would be significant only if both parties were equally responsive.

Another crucial deficiency in the literature is its time frame. Most of the studies discussed concern the period before 1965, long before massive black political involvement and voting occured. The adequacy of their insights for the post-1965 period must be thoroughly reexamined.

Underlying all these weaknesses is the notion that what drove and motivated whites to vote and participate also drove blacks. The literature tells us that black voting is merely white voting in blackface. The literature flounders when it so misrepresents realities of the system.

Structural and Systemic Influences

In order to clearly understand black voting behavior, its genesis, its frame of reference, and its points of departure, one must begin with a careful analysis of the impact of white efforts to neutralize blacks politically; the external and systemic realities.

The net black political loss has been high indeed. Blacks in 1880 formed the majority in nearly 311 counties. By 1970, nearly one-hundred years later, blacks are that proportion of the population in only 102 counties. The loss as indicated in Figure 5.1, has been rapid and unrelenting. To arrive at the consequent loss in potential black poltical representation, one needs only to count the total political offices available in each county then and now. It becomes evident how very staggering the loss in political power has been, when one sees that the loss leads inevitably to loss in political outputs from government. How many improvements of schools, streets, employment opportunities, and social services never occurred in the black community because of white political neutralization? The word then, is not "disenfranchisement"; it is "political neutralization" because blacks lost much more than the right to vote, they lost all the political benefits which accure from suffrage rights.

The black shift to cities and their rising political control there have not offset the loss in the counties. Only about ten or fifteen cities in this decade have a 50 percent or higher black population. Yet the total loss in counties just in the recent decade was more the 30 percent. Moreover, the city is a much smaller political base than the county and is subject to more political control than is the county. In fact, some counties have control over city governments and their political officials.

The effects of neutralization upon voting have been cumulative and restrictive, showing that black voter participation is not just a simple matter of low or high SES indices. At the national level, black voting was directly affected by systemic forces, most notably, by the passage of the Fifteenth Amendment in March, 1870. Black voting in national and state elections has risen or declined in response to such systemic factors as disenfranchisement in the 1890-1901 era, the destruction of the white primary in 1944, and the passage of various laws affecting voting in 1957, 1960, 1965, 1970, and 1975. Clearly changes in black voter participation show a much stronger relationship to the rise and fall of structural barriers than to shifts in socioeconomic forces. In fact, if there were enough accurate aggregate data on the national level about black voting for the period 1870 to 1972, the very low correlation between SES index and black voting would be apparent, as would the much stronger one between structural barriers and voting behavior. The SES index cannot effectively explain the wide flunctuations.

Louisiana provides a valuable case, as it is one of the few states which has kept voter registration by race for the last century. Figure

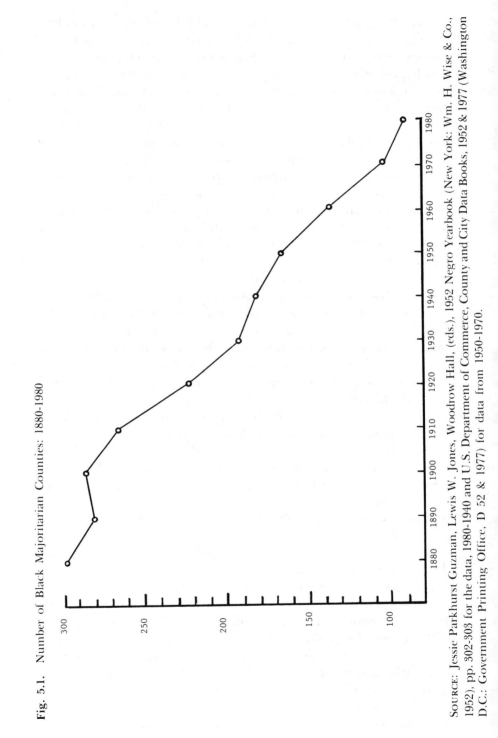

Fig. 5.1.   Number of Black Majoritarian Counties: 1880-1980

SOURCE: Jessie Parkhurst Guzman, Lewis W. Jones, Woodrow Hall, (eds.), 1952 Negro Yearbook (New York: Wm. H. Wise & Co., 1952), pp. 302-303 for the data, 1980-1940 and U.S. Department of Commerce, County and City Data Books, 1952 & 1977 (Washington D.C.: Government Printing Office, D 52 & 1977) for data from 1950-1970.

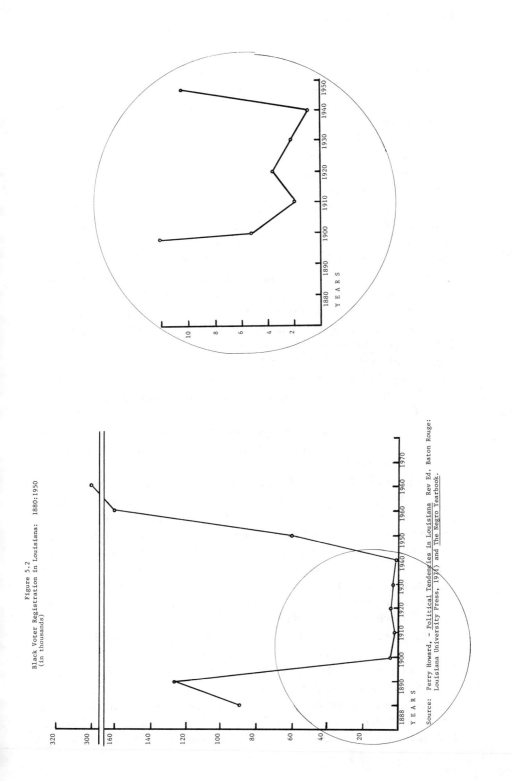

Figure 5.2

Black Voter Registration in Louisiana: 1880:1950
(in thousands)

Source: Perry Howard, - Political Tendencies in Louisiana Rev Ed. Baton Rouge:
Louisiana University Press, 1971) and The Negro Yearbook.

5.2 gives the vital aggregate data on black registration, revealing the impact of political neutralization. Education and income data go back only to 1940, making a complete picture impossible without some form of estimation or manipulation. We well return to this matter later.

Louisiana first neutralized (disfranchised) blacks at the State Constitutional Convention of 1898. On January 1, 1897, 130,444 blacks were registered. This number was approximately 44 percent of the total electorate. By March 17, 1900, only 5,320 blacks were registered, 3.59 percent of the black voting age population. Overall, this made blacks only 4.1 percent of the total electorate. From 1900 to 1940, there was a steady decline, until in 1940 less than one half of one percent of black voting age population was registered. In 1944, after the *Smith* v. *Alright* decision, black registration began moving slowly upward, taking a massive leap after 1964. However, in the meantime the irrecoverable loss of political units (counties) has occured. In 1880, were thirty-six black majoritarian counties, but in 1970 the number had dropped to nine, a loss totaling three-fourths over a century, larger than in the nation as a whole. In Figure 5.3, which juxtaposes data concerning the black voting age population, black registration, and black majoritarian counties, the pattern of loss and fluctuation becomes clear.

If the data were available, we could correlate black registration with median black education and income over the ninety-year span. We can calculate the levels of decline in median education and income on the basis of an average of the data we do have (the result would not be entirely correct, because of the depression era and the rise of black public education). The growth or decline in the black education and income levels would be linear, often inversely related to black voter registration. The cause-and-effect relationship between SES and registration would seem, at numerous points, rather tenuous. The Louisiana data call into serious question the sociopsychological explanations of black voting patterns. Systemic, structural, and legal factors provide better explanations.

To move from the state to the local level, the same kind of trend can be seen in Atlanta, where registration figures by race have been kept over the years. In Figure 5.4, based on black registration data, there is a slow move upward after political neutralization had occurred statewide in 1908. But the jump in black registration from 6,876 in February, 1946, to 21,137 in June, 1946, or the rise to 91,000 in 1969 from 63,000 in 1965, cannot be accounted for by sociopsycho-

Fig. 5.3. Black-Voting-Age-Population, Black-Registration-and-Black-Majoritarian-Counties In Louisiana: 1880-1970

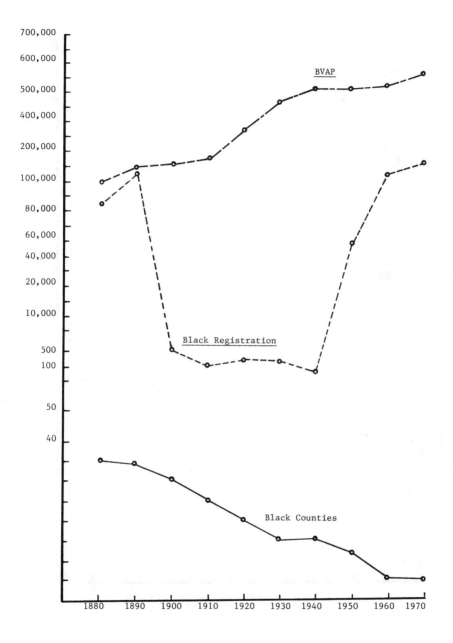

SOURCE: Perry Howard, *Political Tendencies in Louisiana* Rev Ed. Baton Route: Louisiana University Press, 1971) and *The Negro Yearbook*.

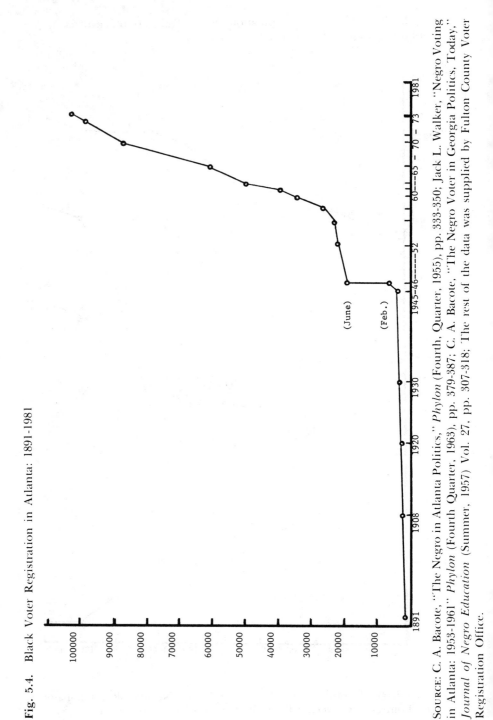

Fig. 5.4. Black Voter Registration in Atlanta: 1891-1981

SOURCE: C. A. Bacote, "The Negro in Atlanta Politics," *Phylon* (Fourth, Quarter, 1955), pp. 333-350; Jack L. Walker, "Negro Voting in Atlanta: 1953-1961" *Phylon* (Fourth Quarter, 1963), pp. 379-387; C. A. Bacote, "The Negro Voter in Georgia Politics, Today," *Journal of Negro Education* (Summer, 1957) Vol. 27, pp. 307-318; The rest of the data was supplied by Fulton County Voter Registration Office.

logical variables alone.[30] On April 18, 1946, the federal courts in *Chapman* v. *King* invalidated the white primary in the state.

If accurate income and education data were available for Atlanta for the 1891-1981 period, there would likely be a stronger positive correlation because of the linear nature of black registration rates and the linear nature of black income and education levels. As noted earlier, however, the surges in registration cannot be accounted for completely by the SES index. And in this instance, the possible positive correlation would be hiding more than it revealed.

In the case of Atlanta, black registration, voting, and voter turnout have been carefully analyzed in terms of their relationships to the socioeconomic status of citizens of the different black wards and precincts. Nearly every scholar arrives at the same conclusion: the SES index differentiates the various precincts and wards from each other, but it is of little help in explaining the casual motivations of black voters.[31] For instance, Margaret Dobbins, after analyzing eleven pre-dominantly black precincts by SES levels in the 1957 and 1961 majoral elections, discovered that while the middle-income black precincts outregistered the upper and lower income black precincts, black voter turnout in the primary and run-off elections was about the same in each precinct, regardless of its SES levels. She writes, "On voter participation there is little or no distinction between persons from the different socioeconomic precincts. The people in the lower class precincts voted as much and as often as those in upper and middle class precincts. Thus, once the different class groups are registered, voter intent and behavior are essentially the same."[32]

Earlier, Bacote analyzed black political participation in Atlanta and came to similar conclusions.[33] Jack Walker, writing at the same time of the Dobbins Study, states, "Negro voters act with greater unity and vote in larger percentages than registrants in either of the blocks within the white community."[34] Walker drew his conclusions from the analysis of black political units in Atlanta that contained both working class and middle income neighborhoods.

Charles Rooks studied the 1969 Atlanta mayoral election. He found: "When precincts of high and low socioeconomic status within the black community are compared, there is little difference in their voting behavior."[35] A year after Rook's study, Bartley arrived at the same conclusion. "The discovery that socioeconomic characteristics made little apparent difference in the voting tendencies of Negro 'citizens' was confirmed in presidential, congressional, mayoralty, and aldermanic electoral contests in both Atlanta and Macon, Georgia."[36]

The clear indication is that the sociopsychological indices generally are different for black voting behavior.

But let us shift briefly from the analysis of aggregate data to look at the survey data. Although there are little reliable data available, the Census Bureau's study based on population samples reveals sharp rises and declines in black voting trends in a relatively short time frame (see Table 5.2). The changes in black voter turnout, even in this limited survey, closely parallel the findings in the aggregate data regarding the fluctuation in black voting behavior.

TABLE 5.2. Black Voter Participation in Presidential and Congressional Election

Years	% Participation	% Change
1964	58.5	
1968	57.6	−0.9
1970	43.5	−14.1
1972	52.1	+8.6
1974	33.8	−18.3
1976	48.7	+14.9
1978	37.2	−11.5
1980	50.5	+13.3
Mean	47.7	

SOURCE: Bureau of Census, *Statistical Abstract of the United States*, 1970, 1972, 1981, (Washington, D.C.: U.S. Government Printing Office, 1981), pp. 369, 374, and 499, respectively.

Moving outside the South, beyond the neutralizing efforts of both laws and social customs, to the North and Midwest, one finds the politcal machines. Although both survey and aggregate data are scarce, it is fairly well known that the majority of the machines and bosses were dependent on a high turnout of lower income blacks.[37] In some areas, even upper income blacks were included. What is the role of the structural and systemic variables here, as opposed to the SES index? Obviously, the power of the machine had more sway than the sociopsychological variables. Moreover, in many ways, machine control neutralized the black voter.

Black Voters and Primary Elections: Presidential, State Congressional, and Local

The literature of the political behavioralist, with its over-emphasis on the SES index, reveals little if anything on black voting in primary elections. To be sure, the literature talks about black voter turnout and participation, but without specifying to what degree in different types of elections and on the sundry levels of government. The voting studies were primarily concerned with national elections. Readers are left to extrapolate from them or infer from the findings that turnout and participation in national elections would be the same as those in state and local elections. Few scholars bothered to analyze turnout in primary and general elections on the state and local levels. This failure led to some very weak generalizations about black voting.

Prior to the 1972 presidential election year, black presidential hopefuls had not competed in the presidential preference primaries with major party contenders. They avoided these primaries and offered themselves for president on the tickets of third or minor parties.[38] The data in Table 5.3 reveal that this effort began more than a hundred years ago with more than twenty men and women running for the Oval Office. These candidates have amassed nearly a million votes with some thirteen seeking the Vice-presidency and eleven seeking the Presidency. The mean vote for twenty-one candidates stands at more than 40,000 votes. By any standards, these results would be considered miniscule, but the key reality here is technique,. i.e., the instrumental use of political alternatives to affect presidential elections, rather than the level of electoral support.

Along with this third party technique, black politicians have employed another strategy. In the South, black Rebublicans put up their own slate of presidential electors in various states between 1920 and 1956. In 1964 and 1968, black Democrats in Mississippi and Alabama followed a similar pattern. The actions of the earlier group were precipitated by a lily-white Republican party which placed its own electors in the field; the later group's actions arose out of the fact that the state Democratic legislators and politicians eliminated the names of the national party candidates entirely. Both examples are for the most part exceptions to the general rule. Out of this strategy techniques evolved a third one. At the national political conventions, black individual's names have been put in nomination. Frederick Douglass's name was put forth in the Republican Convention of 1888 and he received one and one-half votes. Nearly eighty years later at the Democratic Convention, Reverend Channing Phillips and Georgia State Representative Julian Bond received 46 and 87½ votes respectively. All of the nominees eventually withdrew their names.

Having tried all of these techniques and others besides with only limited results, it was obvious that the next logical and evolutionary step would be for a black to run in either the democratic or republican presidential primaries. And when the structural barriers surrounding the black electorate began to fall with the Voting Rights Act of 1965, it was simply a matter of time.

TABLE 5.3. Black Presidential Candidates of Minor Parties: 1856-1980

Candidates	Party	Position	Year	Votes
1. Frederick Douglass	Political Abolitionist	V.P.	1856	
2. Frederick Douglass	Equal Rights Party	V.P.	1872	
3. Simon P. Drew	Interracial Independent Party	V.P.	1928	
4. George Edwin Taylor	National Liberty Party	P.	1904	
5. James Ford	Communist	V.P.	1932	102,991
6. James Ford	Communist	V.P.	1936	80,160
7. James Ford	Communist	V.P.	1940	46,251
8. Charlotta Bass	Progressive Party	V.P.	1952	140.023
9. Rev. Clennon King	Afro-American Party	P.	1960	1,485
10. Reginald Carter	Afro-American Party	V.P.	1960	1,485
11. Clifton DeBerry	Socialist Worker	P.	1964	43,720
12. Charlene Mitchell	Communist	P.	1968	1,076
13. Eldridge Cleaver	Peace & Freedom Party	P.	1968	36,563
14. Dick Gregory	Freedom & Peace Party	P.	1968	47,133
15. Paul Boutelle	Socialist Worker Party	V.P.	1968	41,388
16. Jarvis Tyner	Communist	V.P.	1972	25,595
17. Andrew Pulley	(C.DeBerry in some states)			
	Socialist Worker Party	P.	1972	66,667
18. Julius Hopkins	People's Party	V.P.	1972	78,756
19. Willie Mae Reid	Socialist Worker Party	V.P.	1976	91,314
20. Margaret Reid	People's Party	P.	1976	49,024
21. Jarvis Tyner	Communist	V.P.	1976	58,002
22. Angela Davis	Communist	V.P.	1980	45,023
23. Andrew Pulley	Socialist Worker Party	P.	1980	6,272
24. Clifton DeBerry	Socialist Worker Party	P.	1980	38,737
25. Larry Holmes	Workers World Party	V.P.	1980	13,330
Total (does not include the vote for R. Carter)				962,122
Mean (calculated with only 21 of the above candidates)				45,815

SOURCE: Adopted and Revised from Hanes Walton, Jr. and Ronald Clark, "Black Presidential Candidates: Past and Present," *New South* Vol. 27 (Spring, 1972), pp. 14-22. the data for the first three candidates were taken from Herbert Aptheker, (ed.) *A Documentary History of the Negro People in the United States* (New York: Citadel Press, 1951). The data for the next three candidates came from Svend Petersen, *A Statistical History of the American Presidential Elections* (New York: Frederick Ungar, 1968). The remaining candidate data came from: Richard Scammon (ed), *The American Vote Series Vol. 1-15. The data for Simon P. Drew came from the Negro Yearbook 1931-32.*

Congresswoman Shirley Chisholm (D.-N.Y.) broke with past established techniques, entering ten of the 1972 presidential primaries as a Democratic hopeful. As Table 5.4 shows, the vote for Chisholm was low, averaging a little over 35,000 votes in each state. Chisholm received nearly 3 percent of the votes in each state and so acquired before the first-ballot nomination 35 delegates. This was exactly 7.2 percent of the total black delegates present. However, in the ten states where Chisholm ran, the total number of black delegates were 138, or 28.5 percent of the total at the convention.

In comparison with the size of black electorates in the states where the primaries were held, Chisholm's total vote was indeed low. Only in New Mexico did the percentage of votes received exceed the black percentage of the electorate. In New Mexico, Chisholm received 2.2

TABLE 5.4. Black Voting in Presidential Preference Primaries: 1972

State	Black VAP	Black % of Total Electorate	Votes for Chisholm	% of Votes Received	Black Delegates to Convention
New Hampshire	2,000	11.4	d.p.	d.p.	0
West Virginia	39,000	3.4	d.p.	d.p.	0
Nebraska	25,000	2.5	1,645	0.9	1
New Mexico	11,000	1.8	3,186	2.2	1
Oregon	18,000	1.2	2,905	0.7	2
Rhode Island	17,000	2.6	d.p.	d.p.	2
Wisconsin	77,000	2.6	9,119	0.8	5
Maryland	441,000	19.7	12,279	2.2	9
Florida	621,000	13.9	44,786	3.6	11
Massachusetts	115,000	3.0	d.p.	d.p.	11
Indiana	244,000	6.8	d.p.	d.p.	12
North Carolina	665,000	23.6	61,359	7.5	13
Tennessee	373,000	15.9	18,630	3.8	16
Pennsylvania	664,000	8.8	d.p.	d.p.	22
Ohio	623,000	9.5	d.p.	d.p.	27
Michigan	647,000	12.4	43,746	2.8	30
California	922,000	7.0	155,009	4.6	50
Mean			35,226	2.91	

SOURCES: *Congressional Quarterly Weekly Reports*, July 1, 1972, p. 1577; July 8, 1972, pp. 1642 & 1655. *Here votes were taken from the same sources but as the primary results were reported.* Black VAP and percentages: *The World Almanac, 1973* (New York: Newspaper Enterprise, 1972), p. 147.

NOTE: In all, Chisholm received 35 delegates (from the different states and territories) out of a grand total of 483 black delegates. d.p. = Chisholm did not participate or enter the primary.

percent of the votes cast, while blacks make up 1.8 percent of the total electorate.

If one took the votes that Chisholm received in each state as black votes and determined the percentage for each state, it could be said that on the average for the ten states she received a little more than 11 percent of the black vote. But a much more conservative figure would be the average of the two percentages to arrive at a working index. In this instance, the 3 percent turnout and the 11 percent hypothetical turnout would yield an overall 7 percent index.

Therefore, it could be concluded that the average black turnout for a black presidential hopeful in presidential preference primaries without major financial backing and strong endorsement by the black political leaders would be in the neighborhood of 7 percent. However, the black turnout for a black candidate having financing and the support of the black community might be considerably higher.

The crucial handicaps of the Chisholm campaign were lack of funds, a small and untrained voluntary organization that received no direction from a national headquarters, and her failure to receive the endorsement of such major black organizations as the Congressional Black Caucus, the National Black Political Assembly, the NAACP, and the National Conference of Black Elected Officials. Few black leaders of any significance bothered to endorse her efforts,[39] nor did she receive much support from any national feminist organization. Nonetheless, she captured support of women, young people, blacks, and other minorities. She explains, "My potential support went far beyond the black community. It could come from the women's movement, from young voters, and even from a growing number of older white voters, who had reached the end of their patience with the programs and candidates of the two major parties."[40] Chisholm went on to assert that she alone had the potential to forge these groups into a winning coalition. The aggregate data in Table 5.4 do not support her evaluation. In fact, she failed in nearly every state to develop these groups into a significant force in the primaries, receiving only low levels of support from any group. Her amateurish and impoverised campaign needed more than optimism to sustain it.

The black turnout and participation in the Chisholm campaign is only part of the story on black voting in presidential preference primaries. The 1976 and 1980 presidential preference primaries in Georgia provide additional insights on black participation. In Table 5.5 the aggregate data reveal that blacks in their first opportunity to participate in a state presidential primary strongly supported their native-son candidate, Jimmy Carter over well-known national liberal democrats. However, by the 1980 primary, the situation had significantly altered. The liberal democratic candidate, Edward Kennedy, who did not personally campaign in the state, got one-fifth of the black vote and Carter's vote dropped by nearly one-third—at least in the urban centers of the state.

TABLE 5.5. Black Voting in the Democratic Presidential Primaries in Georgia: 1976 and 1980

		Urban	Rural
Candidate *Years*			
	Atlanta	*Savannah*	*Hancock County*
	1976 Election Year		
Carter	92.4%	89.5%	74.5%
Udall	4.1%	0.7%	2.0%
Others	3.5%	9.8%	23.5%
	1980 Election Year		
Carter	64.6%	77.6%	80.2%
Kennedy	20.4%	18.7%	10.9%
Others	15.0%	3.7%	8.9%

SOURCE: Adapted from Hanes Walton, Jr., *The Carter Vote in Georgia: An Election Data Analysis* (Forthcoming).

The story in the rural sector of the state was quite different. The black vote for Carter increased over the 1976 percentage as well as the vote for the liberal candidate, Kennedy, but not nearly as much as in the urban centers. Black rural voters seemingly perceived Carter as being more attuned to their needs and interests than did the urban black voters who seemed upset with his past presidential performance.

Outside of Georgia, the black vote in 1976 was strongly pro-Carter in the primaries and less inclined toward the traditional liberal Democratic candidates.[41] In four years that changed considerably, but not enough to cause Carter to lose his bid for a second nomination. And while the data are spotty, what data there are suggested that blacks turned out in the 1976 primaries from 30-to-40 percent of their voting strength.[42] By the 1980 presidential primaries, this had declined to below 20-to-30 percent. Much of the large turnout in 1976 was aided in part by the appearance of the black civil rights leadership from Atlanta, like Andrew Young and the King family, which supported Carter. But this support in 1980 could not overcome a perceived bad performance record on Carter's part.

The Jesse Jackson Presidential Bid

Black presidential primary voting changed dramatically in 1984 and one of the major catalysts in this change was the role played by civil rights leader Jesse Jackson. On November 3, 1983, he announced his candidacy for the democratic presidential nomination. That act sent tremors through the black and white political establishments.

The question of an appropriate political strategy in presidential elections had *always* troubled black political leadership. In each national election year, scores of influence-making strategies would be proposed and consensus would be difficult to achieve because some leaders would argue for the support of the Democrats, others for the support of the Republicans, other for favorite son, a coalition, or third-party alternatives. And in different presidential years, depending on events and circumstances, several strategic techniques would be employed. But as the techniques escalated, there emerged the question of who would head the new strategy. In the early days when only a few civil rights organizations and black elected officials existed, the selection problem remained in minor key. But with the increase in both civil rights organizations and elected officials, the selection problem became actue. And it reached major proportions in 1972 when Congresswoman Shirley Chisholm selected herself.

This is not just a problem in national black politics, it is also one in local and state politics as well. For with many politically ambitious blacks and the reality of only a single political base, success depends on who will be selected. To deal with this problem, some local black communities have used black political conventions, while others like the supporters of Harold Washington, employed some different tactics.[43] On the national level black leaders developed an *ad hoc* coalition for a 1984 Election Strategy Group but couldn't decide whom to run or back.[44] Thus, both prior to Jesse's announcing and after, the problem of selection came forth in various forms of opposition by both black and white observers.

Before he announced, black journalist Barbara Reynolds, who had written a critical biography of Jackson thought out loud: "I for one, don't think Jesse will run.... To often he would say he was running and squeeze the public relations value from it and then change his mind. Secondly, I think Jackson would rather remain a kingmaker than try to be a king. And lastly,...Can Jesse stand the same type of financial scrutiny that is going to be applied to the other candidates? Will he finally have to explain why approximately $1

million of money funded to him through the Department of
Education is messed up and give a clear accounting of his other
funding sources? Nope, I don't think Jesse will run." A white
journalist wrote: "...the Presidency seems...an odd job for a man of
his qualifications. He has never held public office...whether elective
or appointive. He has no experience in some important areas, such as
foreign policy. In fact, the whole notion of making a Presidential bid
would appear to be frivolous if Jackson and his supporters weren't so
serious about it."[45]

After his announcement, the problem of selection shifted, though
not completely, to one of influence. Simply put, would he advance or
hinder black interest in the election? Black political scientist
Marguerite Ross Barnett has written: "The most vocal core group of
opponents of a black presidential candidacy work mainly within, nationwide organizations with heterogenous constituencies....
These individuals and organizations operate mainly on the federal
level, often with considerable sophistication and ...are looking,
in most cases to make an early commitment to a major Democratic party candidate in hopes of gaining an influential part in
the campaign."[46] Thus, there is the ticklish problem of Jesse's
influence eventually being greater than theirs. To maintain their
power and influence, they had to oppose such a candidacy.

Who then would support such a candidacy? In a profound way,
Barnett saw this group of supporters better than anyone else.
"Advocating a black presidential bid," she writes, "are mainly more
locally-based politicans; the more peripheral, less well known, less
well supported national civic leaders; and a variety of individuals,
politicized by Reagan administration policies and encouraged by
recent victories in Chicago and by the mood of political awareness in
numbers of black communities across the country."[47] In many ways,
Jesse's run was underneath a struggle between these two black
political confederations. And at least halfway through the primary
season, the group which supported Jesse was the clear-out winner.
They had only lost to Mayor Richard Arrington in Birmingham. He
strongly opposed Jesse and won. The other leaders who did so either
lost outright by whopping margins or came out so badly scarred that
they lost in principle. In Table 5.6 the data show that at the end in
the 1984 presidential primaries (not the caucuses), Jackson had
captured almost 2.7 million votes for nearly sixteen 15.6 percent of the
national primary vote. He had won two caucus states (at least in the
first round, Virginia and South Carolina), won ten congressional

districts, qualified for matching federal campaign funds, captured a sizable number of delegates to the convention and proved himself extremely capable in the debates with other candidates. Moreover, almost all of his vote came from the black community. One political analyst at midpoint noted: "Give Jackson credit for one important insight: he realized that a black run for President in 1984 suited the mood and needs of black America to a T." He continued. "Most prominent black politicans thought Jackson was wrong (or that he was the wrong candidate), and tried to convince him not to run. But Jackson saw the pride and enthusiasm set off by the election of black mayors in Philadelphia and Chicago. He sensed that blacks felt it was time to move their cause to a new plateau."[48] In reflection upon Table 5.6. Jackson gathered little support in the New England states or the "media Fishbowl." But in the sourthern primaries (Alabama, Florida, Georgia) which occurred on "Super Tuesday," Jackson came into his own and moved to real prominence during the "foundry period" (March 20-April 10) in the northern urban states of Illinois, New York, and Pennsylvania. In fact, in Chicago, New York, and Philadelphia alone he captured nearly half of his total votes by the midpoint of the campaign. Although, most of the states in the second half of the primary season had fewer black voters, Jackson was still able to maintain his momentum and score major successes.

TABLE 5.6. Black Voting in the Presidential Preference Primaries: 1984

States	Black VAP-1982	Black % of the Electorate	Votes for Jackson	% of votes Received	No. of delegates won
New Hampshire	2,000	0.4	5.311	5.2	0
Vermont	800	0.2	5,761	7.8	0
Alabama	644,000	22.9	83,787	19.6	9
Florida	923,000	11.3	144,263	12.2	1
Georgia	982,000	24.3	143,622	21.0	17
Massachusetts	143,000	3.4	31,824	5.0	0
Rhode Island	18,000	2.5	3,875	8.7	0
Puerto Rico		didn't			
			participate		
Illinois	1,077,000	12.9	348,843	19.7	2
Connecticut	143,000	6.0	26,395	12.0	1
New York	1,631,000	12.4	355,541	25.6	51
Wisconsin	111,000	3.2	62,524	9.8	5
Pennsylvania	720,000	8.1	264,463	16.0	18
District of Columbia	320,000	65.8	67,091	67.4	13

Tennessee	479,000	14.2	80,847	25.2	15
Louisiana	813,000	26.6	136,707	42.9	24
Indiana	265,000	6.8	98,190	13.7	7
Maryland	664,000	20.8	129,387	25.0	17
North Carolina	897,000	20.3	243,945	25.4	15
Ohio	717,000	9.2	237,133	16.4	10
Nebraska	30,000	2.6	13,495	8.8	1
Oregon	23,000	1.2	37,106	9.3	1
Idaho	2,000	0.3	3,104	5.1	0
California	1,298,000	7.1	non-preference		30
New Jersey	610,000	11.0	159,788	23.6	9
New Mexico	16,000	1.7	22.168	11.8	1
South Dakota	1,400	0.3	2,738	5.2	0
West Virginia	45,000	3.2	24,697	6.7	0
North Dakota	1,900	0.4	didn't enter		0
Montana	1,700		388 (write in)	1.1	0
Totals		299.3	2,732,993	450.2	247
Mean		10.3		16.7	

SOURCE: All of the election—votes for Jackson and % of votes received—came from the various Secretary of States Offices, except New Hampshire, District of Columbia, and Tennessee. The election returns for these states were taken from the *Congressional Quarterly Weekly Reports.* The Black VAP (Voting-Age Population) and the Black % of the electorate was taken from Thomas E. Cavanagh, *The Impact of the Black Electorate* (Washington, D.C.: Joint Center for Political Studies: 1984) pp. 8-9. And the number of Delegates won in each of the primary states was taken from: "State-by-State Democratic Delegate Count," *Congressional Quarterly Weekly Report* (July 7, 1984), p. 1629.

But this was the score in the primaries. In the caucus states, Jackson was equally impressive. Rhodes Cook writes: "Jackson's strength in the Southern caucus states has been one of the surprises of the campaign. Conventional wisdom holds that success in the low-turnout world of the caucuses is based on organization, which the late-starting Jackson campaign largely lacked." Yet Jackson overcame this obstacle "by barnstorming the Sourthern caucus states, he won at least 25 percent of the delegates elected at first-tier caucuses in South Carolina, Mississippi and Virginia."[49]

Thus, this macro perspective of Jackson's efforts reveals it to be quite impressive across the board. But even a micro view yields the same type of results. For instance in Georgia, the southern state where he received his greatest support, the data in Table 5.7 indicate that while Jackson was being opposed by such black political luminaries as State Senator Julian Bond, Daddy King, Coretta Scott King and

Mayor Andrew Young, he carried their hometown of Atlanta and Fulton County and won two congressional districts in the state. His lead over the white candidate whom the luminaries supported was nearly two-to-one or greater in certain parts of the state.

TABLE 5.7. Black Urban and Rural Voting in the Democratic Presidential Primaries in Georgia: 1984

Candidates	Atlanta*	Urban Savannah	Rural Hancock County
Jesse Jackson	58.4	71.5	66.5
Walter Mondale	34.9	20.3	15.7
Gary Hart	5.4	4.7	7.0
Others	1.3	3.4	10.8
	100	99.9	100

*The Atlanta data were calculated from black percents where blacks were 90% more of the registered voters. The Savannah data were calculated from the two black commission districts which are over 80% black.

SOURCE: Data supplied by Fulton and Chatham County Voter Registration Offices and the Georgia Secretary of State. Calculations prepared by the author.

Turning from aggregate data to survey data, the type of support that Jackson garnered had already been shown and predicted in a series of surveys conducted annually by the National Opinion Research Center (hereafter NORC at the University of Chicago. This survey had asked the following question: "If your party nominated a (Negro/Black) for President, would you vote for him if he were qualified for the job." Because for some years the question was only asked of whites and due to the fact that only a few blacks were in the sample in the years that the question was asked of blacks, we have pooled the survey and the results are in Table 5.8. They indicate that blacks are strongly supportive of the idea and by far the strongest supporters. This is followed by the "others," i.e., Indian, Asian, and Latin Americans. The smallest percentage group of supporters would be whites. But the high percentage of support indicated by whites does not square with reality as in the Jackson campaign nor with political reality. For instance, the wording of the question helped to get this very high

TABLE 5.8. Who Would Vote For Black President by Race: 1972-82

Race of Respondent	Yes	No
Black	96.2 (459)	3.8 (18)
Others	85.1 (57)	14.9 (10)
White	80.6 (6105)	19.4 (466)

SOURCE: NORC General Social Surveys, 1972-82.

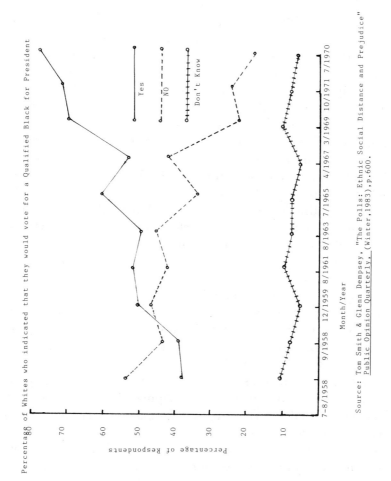

positive response with its qualifiers: "If your party nominated" and "if he were qualified for the job." Many researchers and analysts found similar high responses in the sixties when whites were asked if they were in favor of equality. There would be a sharp drop off of support when equalty for Negroes was asked. This is known as the "abstract question syndrome." By posing the question in the abstract and with qualifiers, support among white will remain high. But if qualifiers were removed and the question specifically asked about support for Jesse Jackson, then there would be a sharp drop off.

The data in graph 5.8 reveal the percentage of whites from 1958 until 1970 who indicated that they would or would not vote for a black for president, and those who didn't know. Basically speaking, the graph shows a steadily increasing trend in the percentage of whites who would support a qualified black for the presidency. But the data as indicated earlier are somewhat ideal. For when asked by pollsters if they (whites) would also support an Atheist, Jew, Catholic, Baptist, Quaker and a Mormon for the presidency, whites indicated even stronger support for each and every ethnic and religious group than for blacks, except the Atheist. Tom Smith, who conducted this research, writes that blacks, "have ranked at the bottom in the presidential preference questions, except for the atheists."[58] He goes on to indicate that in every poll dealing with social standing, social distance, disloyalty, and not being family oriented, blacks have been ranked by whites continually near the bottom of the scales. Thus, the high percentage of whites who indicate support for a qualified black presidential candidate must be seen with a very critical eye because that support, as the Jackson candidacy proved, cannot always be had or found.

However, the data also provide insights into the fact that a historical antecedent existed for the Jackson candidacy beyond what happened in Chicago and Philadelphia. And many analysts have made the mistake of alluding to black mayoral victories in these cities as the factor that set off or made possible the jackson candidacy. The Gallup organization began asking this type of question in the fifties and has continued in sporadic fashion until the NORC surveys began. Black indication of support for the idea has been strong and consistent, due in part to the fact that it is a feature of the black political culture, i.e., racial consciousness in voting behavior, and it is rooted in the black political experience.

The second reality which the data in the table indicate is that Jackson's discussion of a "Rainbow Coalition" is not completely baseless, because other groups have indicated strong support for the idea and some support has occurred during Jackson's race for the democratic nomination.

However, unaware of a historical and cultural basis for the very strong support that Jackson has received in the black community, many observers, black and white, have come to consider it to be a fluke, a contemporary phenomenon, or that Jackson simply capitalized on an emerging trend. Using these types of explanations many white opinion makers have then made the quantum leap in reasoning that due to this type of support—which has reached movement proportions (Robert Brisbane has indicated that every twenty years another black movement takes place and this is at the end of another twenty-year cycle)[51] Jackson will be able to destroy the Democratic party at its 1984 national convention.[52] In fact, so many essays, editorials, commentaries and comments on this point arose near the middle of the primary season that the frontrunner, Walter Mondale, suggested to his black supporters that they hold a series of meetings to develop a convention strategy which, if it didn't "Stop Jackson," would at least counterbalance his political influence at the convention.[53] The first "Blacks for Mondale" meeting took place in Birmingham and it was co-convened by Mayor Richard Arrington and Coretta Scott King. However, other key Mondale supporters like Mayor Andrew Young, Rep. Mickey Leland, Julian Bond, and Mayor Coleman Young, reading the political winds in the black community, found ways not to attend the meeting. And while the convention discussed various issues, it came to no conclusion about Jackson's demand for an end to "run-off primaries."[54]

In sum, "the former Vice President (who) is described as convinced that he cannot make any large public concessions to Jackson," because he wants the southern white vote (which is problematical)—decided as a strategy to get other black leaders to try to overshadow and outshine Jackson at the national convention.[55] Matthew Holden calls this type of leaders "clientage" politicans, i.e., black politicans who work for the white political establishment.[56] At times they have been successful, but in the long run the black community have prevailed.

The crucial question, beyond the historial bases and cultural factors, then is what made the Jackson primary effort so much more successful than Chisholm's? Otis Johnson the Jackson campaign director for the 1st Congressional District in Georgia and Chatham County (areas that Jackson won despite the fact that the white Congressman Lindsay Thomas (D. GA) had walked through the district with Senator John Glenn, and Senator Sam Nunn had endorsed Glenn, while Mondale had the support of Andrew Young and Julian Bond in the district) says very vividly that it was "a carefully designed organization—one which developed strategies to maintain the momentum which Jesse generated during his two visits to the areas. There were weekly rallies, for workers, excellent field coordination and constant communication with the district leaders through a steering committee that was kept fired up."[57] In fact, Johnson feels that although the issues that Jackson raised were helped by his charisma, it was ultimately the organization. And "if Jackson's state coordinator, State Rep. Tyrone Brooks, hadn't been so lax in his job, Jackson would have had an even greater showing in the state."

Attorney Clarence Martin, a local organizer of several black political campaigns in the district, agrees but "quickly adds that Jesse's charisma helped a great deal. Having run campaigns for candidates with and without charisma," Martin argues persuasively that on "balance Jackson's dynamic appeal enhanced his impressive showing and record win in the area."[58]

The comments made by these astute observers not only add insights to the question but when they are compared with the initial effort made by Shirley Chisholm, they stand out. For according to Chisholm's own recollections, the lack of organization and organizational skills accounts for the limited showing despite her charisma. Thus, at midpoint, Jesse had more that three times as many votes as she had captured in the entire race and nearly four times the delegates.

In the presidential primaries, and maybe beyond, the Jackson candidacy demonstrated another feature of black voting, the worth of black political endorsements. One writer put it this way: "Some of the most popular black elected officials have been unable to deliver their constitutiences to Walter Mondale...and they have tried to accept the popular verdict gracefully rather then fight it. These politicans must have been shaken by the realization that Jackson can go over their heads to reach the mass of black voters."[59] Jackson out-fought Young in Detroit, Congressman Rangel in Harlem, Goode in Philadelphia, and Bond, Young and the Kings in Georgia. For instance, in State

Senator Julian Bond's district in Atlanta, Georgia, Table 5.9 reveals that Jesse nearly steamrolled Bond and his candidate Mondale— winning almost twice the votes and support. To put it lightly, this was a political embrassment for Bond. But this wasn't the first time that Bond had been unable to deliver. In 1976, when he endorsed Rep. Morris Udall over Carter, who had Andrew Young's backing, Bond's district went overwhelming for Carter. So much for black political endorsements. The key point here is the question of political sovereignty. Many popular black elected officials, because of their educational, political, organizational, and charismatic skills, have come to think that they control their black districts and voters. Thus, they think nothing of telling black folks how to vote in all types of elections. This type of arrogance and false thinking smacks of the days of segregation when the black community relied on cues from black leaders who coalesced with white progressives. It was also a time when educational levels and information about politics was low in the black community. But that day is past in some places and may soon be in other. The ability to tell black voters for whom they should vote is obviously eroding and has been for some time. The Jackson candidacy again demonstrated the fact that the black voters are in many instances their own political sovereigns—not the popular black elected officials who have local control. Andrew Young also demon- trated this is 1976 when he went over the heads of black leaders to the masses to get support for Carter.

TABLE 5.9. The Vote for Democratic Presidential Candidates in State Senator Julian Bond's 39th District: 1984*

Name of Candidates	Percentage	Votes
Jackson	56%	12,274
Mondale	34%	7,512
Hart	5.1%	1,135
Others	4.9%	1,190
Total	100%	22,111

*Black registered voters in Senator Bond's district are 78.5 percent of the total voters.

SOURCE: Data supplied by the Fulton County Voter Registration Office.

What then can be said about the impact of the Jackson campaign? First and foremost, it has altered the black political behavioral options at national political conventions. Added to the old strategies of (1) increasing black delegates to the conventions, (2) questioning presidential candidates to get a commitment on black issues, (3) working to get specific platform planks, can now be a black balance-of-power strategy—possibly determining whom the president can be and getting a potential black vice presidential candidate. For instance, on this balance-of-power strategy, in Northern Virginia, during the state political caucuses, when blacks saw that Jackson couldn't win the necessary number, they switched to the Hart forces and one of them declared that "Jesse Jackson can't do beans if there's no horse race."[1] *(Washington Post* March 25, 1984, p. A5).

The second impact of a black running in the primaries for the black community is that it can: (1) socialize young blacks to understand that the presidency is a possible goal, (2) bring new black participants into the political process, (3) increase black political participation in the primaries (4) elevate black concerns to a major place in the process and counteract other strategies in the party, such as the southern strategy, which have dominated the party's perspective for awhile. Finally it can become a vehicle to articulate and achieve new civil and economic rights for the black community. In addition, a black running in the primaries can train, and leave at the local and national level, a cadre of skilled organizers and campaign workers with political experience in presidential elections. In Liberty County, Georgia, the black woman who ran the Jackson campaign had never worked in a political campaign or organization before, yet she won the county for Jackson. And as the campaign moved on, it left this woman and many like her with political skills and abilities that they might have never gotten otherwise.

In terms of political parties and the Democratic Party in particular, a black running in the primaries, as Jackson has, can demonstrate conclusively the power, size, and turnout ability of the black vote. Before, the power and turnout strength of the black voter was nearly invisible, and analysts always made "estimates." But since the Jackson race, even the Republican party, seeing the black strength, has had some second thoughts.

Finally, a black running in the primaries, and Jackson in particular, has revealed to the white community that many political issues were not being addressed by the other candidates and that any complete candidates for the presidency, as Columnist David Broder noted, needed to address themselves to these abandoned issues if Americans were to have a balanced and humane governmental system.[60] Also, such a candidacy provides the white community with a picture of several black political scenarios for the future.

In the final analysis, as the data in Table 5.6 indicate, Jackson participated in 27 of the 30 democratic primaries and won in two of them. He didn't enter the Puerto Rico, North Dakota or Montana primaries, yet he received some write-in votes from Montana. How ever, in the primary states, the mean black electorate stood at 10.3 percent, running from a high of 65.8 percent in Washington, D.C. to a low of .2 percent in Vermont and Montana. Jackson's highest vote totals came in New York and the lowest in Montana. By the same token Jackson won his greatest number of delegates in New York and the smallest number in Florida, Connecticut, Nebraska, Oregon and New Mexico. And in terms of the percentages of votes received, Jackson got his highest percentage in New York and lowest in Montana. Basically speaking, in the states and urban areas, where the black populations were the largest, Jackson ran the strongest.

Overall, when all the primary and caucus states are taken into account, Jackson won more than three million votes and some 384.2 delegates. To say the least, it is a record for a black democratic candidate and a record turn out for black voters in presidential primaries. Jackson averaged from 30 to 95 percent of the black vote in his presidential bid.

Black Primary Voting: Additional Insights

Overall, from the Chisholm and Jackson candidacies, it has been shown that black voters in the democratic primaries can respond to liberal democratic candidates, the endorsement of civil rights leaders, the existence of a black candidate, and the past performance of presidential candidates. And these things can affect black voter turnout and the degree of candidate support in the primaries. The data also suggest that urban and rural black voters might respond with different degrees of support for the same political candidate. And black voters can switch from supporting native-son candidates in one election year to black and liberal candidates the next election year if the circumstances are correct.

In the Republican presidential primaries where the data are even more tenuous and spotty and where there are even fewer black Republicans than there are black Democrats, it is hazardous to venture any suggestions. Much more data needs to surface before any accurate insights can be made about the factors affecting and shaping black Republican voters in presidential primaries.

Beyond presidential primaries; Table 5.10 reveals that about one-third of black voters turn out in congressional races, and that this turnout increases for local-level primaries. The mean black turnout at all three levels for all candidates is 40 percent.

However, when primaries include black candidates, the turnout on the congressional and local levels tends to rise, but it drops slightly for statewide candidates. The overall mean for the three levels is 45.8 percent. Even among black nonvoters, there is a significant rise, as shown in Table 5.11. Seemingly, black voters prefer to turn out for candidates closer to them at the grassroots level. The tendency among blacks to turn out in relatively large numbers for contests involving black congresspersons might have something to do with the increasing number of blacks running for Congress and the rising visibility of blacks in Congress.

TABLE 5.10. Black Political Participation in Primary Elections: All Candidates

Type of Elections	Percentage of Black Voters	Percentage of Black Nonvoters Had they Voted
Congressional	33.3 (247)	10.8 (33)
House	35.3 (247)	10.8 (33)
Senate	33.0 (231)	8.1 (25)
State	41.2 (288)	11.4 (35)
Gubernatorial	39.8 (278)	10.8 (33)
Lt. Governor	35.5 (348)	6.8 (21)
House	40.5 (283)	9.1 (28)
Senate	32.0 (224)	6.5 (20)
Local	43.5 (304)	13.4 (41)
Mayoralty	43.5 (304)	13.4 (41)
Aldermanic	42.8 (299)	10.8 (33)
County Commissions	39.6 (277)	5.9 (18)
Mean Three Levels	40.0	11.8
Total Number of Cases	698	305

SOURCE: National Survey Data, 1972-1974.

Turning now to historical aggregate data shown in Table 5.12, we can see that black voters in 1920 turned out in large enough numbers to elect blacks to the state legislature in nine states, to elect at least six to aldermanic seats, and to support a minimum of eight candidates for Congress. Of this number, the most successful black candidates were Republicans and Farmer-Laborers, a reversal of the present-day tendency. Black Democrats in this era had poor support in nearly every type of election. Today, black Republicans face the same situation.

Table 5.11. Black Political Participation in Primary Elections: Black Candidates

Type of Elections	Percentage of Black Voters	Percentage of Black Nonvoters Had they Voted
Congressional	39.1 (343)	18.3 (56)
House	49.1 (343)	18.3 (56)
Senate	44.6 (312)	16.7 (51)
State	38.3 (268)	16.3 (50)
Gubernatorial	38.3 (268)	16.0 (49)
Lt. Governor	28.6 (200)	7.8 (24)
House	38.3 (268)	16.3 (31)
Senate	30.2 (211)	10.1 (31)
Local	50.2 (351)	25.9 (79)
Mayoralty	50.2 (351)	23.9 (73)
Aldermanic	49.2 (344)	25.5 (78)
County Commissions	43.1 (301)	19.6 (60)
Mean Three Levels	45.8	17.9
Total Number of Cases	698	305

Source: National Survey Data, 1972-1974.

The point is that the historical data reveal the tendency of black voters to support black candidates, a feature of the black political culture noted in Chapter 2. In addition, it suggests that the turnout rate is similar. The major difference is a reversal of black party affiliation, suggesting the "softness" of contemporary party affiliation.

Moreover, contemporary aggregate data corroborate the historical and survey data noted earlier. Taking the five original blacks elected to the Georgia legislature as a result of systemic change—in this case, court-enforced reappointment—and looking at the black voter turnout in these black districts as well as in black senatorial districts over about a decade, one gains a wholly new perspective. Figure 5.5 shows that the black voter turnout is lower than the level of support given by the survey respondents. The highest consistent level of black voter turnout is in the old legislative districts represented by Julian Bond (now State Senator)(line 4). The turnout in the 1974 primary was not for Bond, but for the state representative who succeeded him when Bond moved to the Georgia Senate. The mean turnout in the Bond district for the four elections in which he participated was 30.9 percent.

TABLE 5.12. Black Political Candidates in the 1920 Primaries and General Elections

Candidates	Office and Location	Party	Outcome
	State Legislature		
A. H. Roberts	Illinois	Rep.	Won
Warren B. Douglas	Illinois	Rep.	Won
Sheadrick B. Turner	Illinois	Rep.	Won
John C. Asbury	Pennsylvania	Rep.	Won
Andrew T. Stevens	Pennsylvania	Rep.	Won
Harry J. Capehat	West Virginia	Rep.	Won
T. Gillis Nutler	West Virginia	Rep.	Won
Harry E. Davis	Ohio	Rep.	Won
John C. Hawkins	New York	Rep.	Won
Walter C. Alexander	New Jersey	Rep.	Won
J. H. Ryan	Washington	Farmer-Labor	Won
Frederick M. Roberts	California	Rep.	Won
	Alderman*		
W. M. Moore	Mississippi	Rep.	Won
George Combs	Nicholasville, KY	Rep.	Won
B. Jackson	Chicago, IL	Rep.	Won
T. E. Stevens	Cleveland, TN	Rep.	Won
George W. Harris	New York, NY	Rep.	Won
Charles H. Robert	New York, NY	Rep.	Won
T. W. Fleming	Cleveland, OH	Rep.	Won
	Congressional-House*		
Harry E. Davis	Ohio	Rep.	Lost
S. E. Woods	Ohio	Rep.	Lost
B. T. Hughes	Ohio	Rep.	Lost
G. L. Davis	Ohio	Rep.	Lost
Henry M. Higgins	Ohio	Rep.	Lost
Mary Seymour	Hartford, CT	Farmer-Labor	Lost
	Congressional-Senate*		
W. R. Green	Ohio	Rep.	Lost
W. Ashbie Hawkins	Maryland	Rep.	Lost

*Denotes a partial listing.

Rep. = Republican.

SOURCES: "Negro Legislators," *Crisis*, Vol. 21 (January, 1921), pp. 120-21; and Normal Andrews, "The Negro in Politics," *Journal of Negro History*, Vol. 5 (October, 1920), p. 436.

Figure 5.6 gives the black voter turnout for black senatorial candidates Horace Ward and Leroy Johnson in the six primary elections between 1964 and 1974. One candidate received more black voter support than respondents expressed in the survey analysis, while the other candidate received considerably less support. Johnson was finally defeated in the 1974 primary, after he had in 1973 made a disastrous run for mayor of Atlanta, getting less than 4 percent of the total vote.[61] Ward stayed in office until Governor Jimmy Carter appointed him to a judgeship, permitting Bond to run for the Georgia Senate in 1974.[62]

Most of the state representatives continued to stay in office through 1976. In 1975, State Representative Ben Brown became Governor Carter's presidential campaign manager and continued in that capacity through the 1976 election, at which time he won his state legislative seat again. Later, he resigned to accept a high office with the National Democratic Party.

Despite the ability of all these candidates to retain their seats over more that a decade, black voting in these primaries and for each candidate fluctuated, suggesting the role that opposition might have had in the turnout. In fact, between 1964 and 1974 each candidate had opposition in one or more of the primaries. In the 1972 election, four members of the House group and Senator Ward all faced and defeated opposition. In the other years, only one or maybe two members of the group faced opposition in the primary. But in the years of opposition, black voter turnout for black candidates was higher than that for white and Rupublican candidates.

In sum then, black support in congressional, state, and local primaries is strong enough to elect black candidates. Aggregate data suggest lower levels of support in house races but higher levels in senate races, although in all races the support stays between one-fourth to one-third of the black voting community.

In presidential primaries, black voters show a strong turnout in response to the efforts of popular black candidates and organizations. Lower responses come when only one of these factors is working. In Georgia, black urban support was higher than rural support in the primaries, a trend that reversed itself in Carter's second primary, where black rural support was greater than black urban support.

These sundry examples suggest that variations in levels of black support in primaries are responses to systemic and structural factors found in the nature of the campaigns, personalities, black political

Fig. 5.5 Black Voter Primary Turnout: An Aggregate (State Legislative Districts) and National Survey Picture.

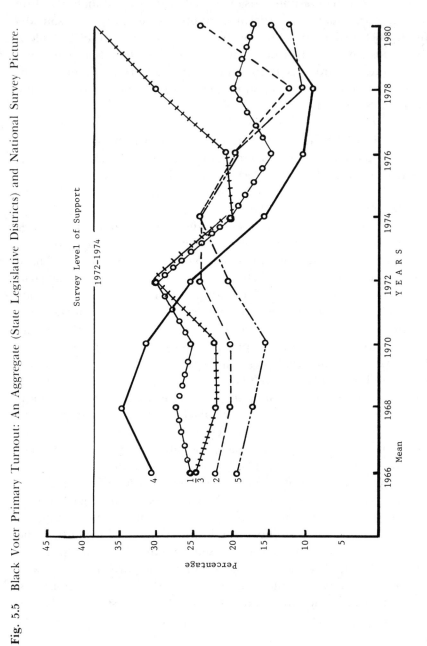

SOURCE: See Appendix: The Atlanta Aggregate Data (Figure 5.5)

Fig. 5.6. Black Voter Primary Turnout: An Aggregate (State Senate Districts) and National Survey Picture.

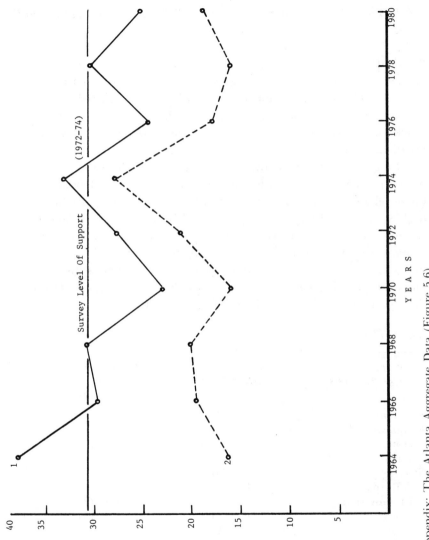

Y E A R S

SOURCE: See Appendix: The Atlanta Aggregate Data (Figure 5.6)

candidates, and organizational efforts. The changes, which are
notable especially in the aggregate data, do not seem to be determined
by SES or racial consciousness.

Black Voting and General Elections: Presidential, Congressional, State, and Local

Political behavioralists fail to study voting behavior of blacks in
primary elections. They also ignore black participation in general
elections. The student of black political behavior is forced, therefore,
to infer and extrapolate what he can from the vastly uneven literature.
Black voter turnout, existing studies tell us, was low for all elections;
no distinctions are made.

In general elections, the survey data in Table 5.13 reveal that
blacks participate with different degrees of intensity, depending on
the level of the election. Presidential and local elections have the
highest level of black participation, while congressional and state
elections show much lower levels. This changed in 1982 for congressional elections. Among black nonvoters the presidential races capture
the greatest attention, with a tremendous drop of interest in the other
races. Overall, a mean of 55 percent of the black voters declare that
they participated in some kind of general election.

TABLE 5.13. Black Voting in General Elections

Type of General Elections	Percentage of Black Voters	Percentage of Black Nonvoters Had they Voted
Presidential	65.5 (458)	72.4 (221)
Congressional	53.1 (371)	21.6 (66)
House	53.1 (311)	21.6 (66)
Senate	50.1 (350)	17.3 (53)
State	44.5 (311)	18.0 (55)
Gubernatorial	42.8 (299)	16.0 (49)
Lt. Governor	32.6 (228)	8.8 (27)
House	44.5 (311)	18.0 (55)
Senate	34.9 (244)	10.4 (33)
Local	60.6 (423)	10.4 (33)
Mayoralty	60.6 (423)	27.5 (84)
Aldermanic	57.3 (400)	25.5 (78)
County Commissioners	46.1 (372)	20.0 (61)
Mean Four Levels	55.9	34.8
Total Number of Cases	698	305

SOURCE: National Survey Data, 1972-1974.

Using aggregate data from the predominantly black precincts in Atlanta, Table 5.14 shows the turnout of registered black voters in different presidential elections. The fluctuation is more than the SES index can explain for such a short time frame. Other factors, such as the candidates' stands on issues, their popularity, and the kind of support they received from the black community must figure prominently in any meaningful explanation of black voting behavior in general elections.

Finally, the data in Table 5.15, based on surveys conducted by the Bureau of the Census, permit one to see, over eight elections, how blacks voted in five presidential and three congressional contests. Basically in the five presidential elections, the mean black voter turnout was 53.5 percent, while in the congressional elections, it was 38.2 percent.

TABLE 5.14. Levels of Black Presidential Voting Turnout in Atlanta: An Aggregate View

Number of Black Precincts*	Years	Black Turnout (Mean%)
48	1968	61.6
64	1972	52.8
110	1976	58.1
121	1980	57.9

*The precincts in the city for each year with more than 55% black registered voters.

Overall, the mean black voter turnout stood at 48 (47.7) percent. But what the table clearly points out is the vast degree of change in the turnout levels between different elections over time. And the great fluctuations in black voter turnout over eight elections further dramatize the limited ability of the SES index and the racial consciousness model to predict black voting behavior.

The same factors which operated to motivate black voters in presidential contests appeared in an analysis of the five black state legislative districts and the two black state senatorial districts in Atlanta that we have been using as benchmarks and guides in this study. In Figure 5.7 it can be seen that the average number of registered black voters turning out in black state legislative races are significantly higher than the turnout in the primary races. Similarly, the data in Figure 5.8 on turnout for black senatorial candidates show a considerable increase in the turnout of black registered voters.

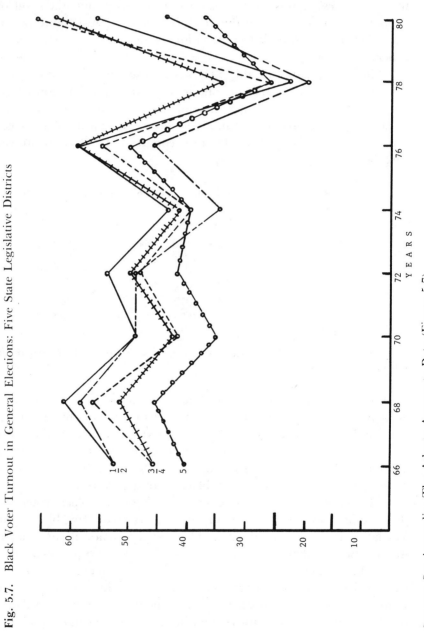

Fig. 5.7. Black Voter Turnout in General Elections: Five State Legislative Districts

SOURCE: See Appendix: The Atlanta Aggregate Data (Figure 5.7)
Numbers 1-5; see The Atlanta Aggregate date—Numbers correspond to the number before

Moreover, upon closer analysis of the aggregate data for Atlanta during the presidential election years, it was found that the Democratic presidential candidates, especially, got more votes (10% more in some instances) in both groups of black legislative districts than did the black House and Senate candidates themselves. In other words, in the state elections, more blacks voted for the presidential candidates than for state-level candidates.

But it should be added that despite the strong support in Atlanta's legislative districts for black Democratic candidates, black Republican candidates who entered the local state races during the general elections received noticeable levels of support. The data in Table 5.16 suggest that if more black Republicans appeared and offered for political office, they would receive some, if not winning support. The level of support seen in the Atlanta districts suggests that black Republicans might possibly win.[63] The questions of black party support will be dealt with fully in the next chapter.

The facts hint at other conclusions, as well. Celebrity status affects black turnout, *at times,* in elections. The turnout for black political celebrities, Julian Bond and Leroy Johnson, in both primary and general elections over several elections, can be seen in Figures 5.9 and 5.10. But even for these celebrities, there is still fluctuation in the black turnout rate in primaries and general elections, even though the turnout for these two well-known black politicians is consistently higher than for their colleagues.

The black voter turnout percentage for State Representative Mildred Glover, who captured and held Bond's old House seat, is lower in both the primary and general elections than it was for Bond. In addition, Bond has been able to get a higher turnout in his Senate district than did the previous black officer holder, who is now a state judge. Celebrity status, however, is tenuous. Johnson, riding a crest of popularity, ran for mayor but lost diastrously. The next year, he also lost his Senate seat. It would seem that good campaign organization is also essential to success.

Finally, the data in appendix B reveal that in these black legislative districts, between the primaries and the general elections, the number of black registered voters rose, sometimes by significant numbers. This rise casts doubt on the usefulness of the SES index and suggests that systemic factors like registration campaigns, the influence of candidates themselves, and organization in the black community are more important. Jesse Jackson's recent efforts are a prime example. In most states where he ran black registration increased significantly.

Fig. 5.8. Black Voter Turnout in General Elections: Two State Senatorial Districts

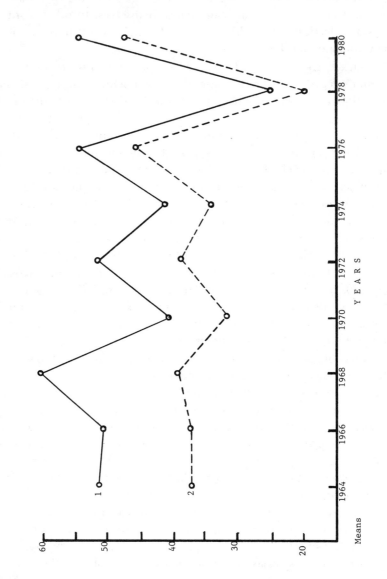

SOURCE: See Appendix: The Atlanta Aggregate Data (Figure 5.8)

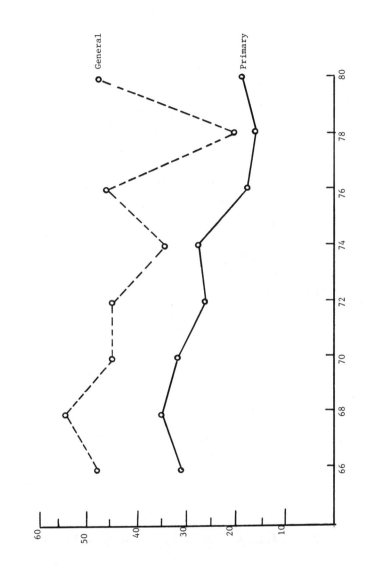

Fig. 5.9. Black Voter Turnout in Primary and General Elections: Julian Bond's State Legislative District

SOURCE: See Appendix: The Atlanta Aggregate Data (Figure 5.9)

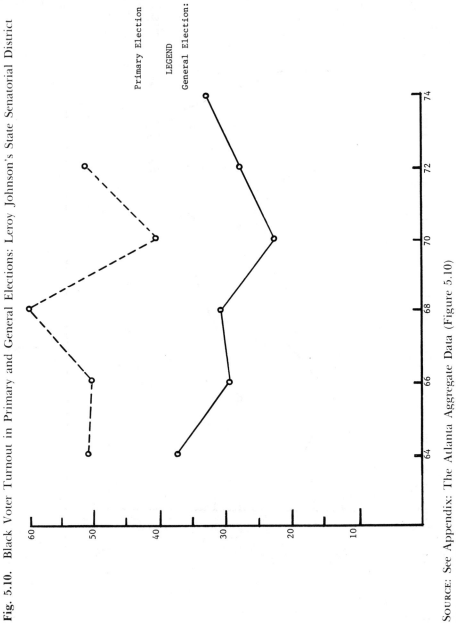

Fig. 5.10. Black Voter Turnout in Primary and General Elections: Leroy Johnson's State Senatorial District

SOURCE: See Appendix: The Atlanta Aggregate Data (Figure 5.10)

TABLE 5.15. The Republican Vote in Black Legislative Races in Atlanta (Percentages)

	House Districts					*Senate Districts*	
Years	*1*	*2*	*3*	*4*	*5*	*1*	*2*
1968	18.9	7.3	NC	NC	NC	19.1	NC
1970	11.4	NC	NC	NC	NC	NC	NC
1972	NC	NC	12.5	NC	NC	NC	NC
1974	NC	NC	NC	16.0*	NC	NC	NC
1976	NC	NC	5	NC	NC	NC	NC
1978	NC	NC	20.7	NC	18.7	NC	NC
1980	3.8	NC	NC	NC	NC	NC	NC

NC = No Candidate

* = Black Independent

Mavericks: Black Independents and Ticket Splitters

There have always been black political leaders who have leaned against the political wind, supported candidates of both political parties simultaneously, or otherwise created new political positions. During the period of supposed Republican hegemony over the black community, black Democrats appeared, ran for office, held office, and maintained support within the black community. During the period of black Democratic hegemony, black Republicans have continued to exist, and viably, in some locales.

In Pittsburg, Robert Lee Vann, editor of the *Pittsburg Courier,* throughout his long career urged blacks to support the unpopular party, and on several occasions he was persuasive enough to break the pattern of black partisan voting. The late Adam Clayton Powell in New York in 1956 "switched" parties in the presidential election by urging his followers to vote for Eisenhower. Although he carried 69.7 percent of Harlem's 16th district on the Democratic banner, his constituents gave President Eisenhower 39 percent of their votes in that district in the same election. In the south, a few black leaders like black newspaper editor John H. McCray in Columbia, South Carolina, and attorney A. T. Walden in Atlanta, Georgia, fought for inclusion in Democratic party ranks. James Meredith has constantly tried to resurrect the Republican party in Mississippi among blacks. He tried earlier in Harlem against Adam Clayton Powell, while a law student at Columbia University.

An even more striking example is the case of Georgia State Representative Hosea Williams. He has sought public office under a variety of banners. He is always an outspoken, uncompromising militant racial advocate, which usually eliminates white support. In the race for vice mayor of Atlanta, Williams in the primary received only 2.4 percent (1,127) of the white vote. And in the run-off he got 3.1 percent (1,771) of the white vote, although the black vote increased nearly 11 percent. Over a five-year period, he has used three different party labels, finally winning under the Democratic label for a seat in the Georgia House. However, he made a strong showing under the other labels as well.

Black nationalist Imamu Amiri Baraka (Leroy Jones) and Black Panther leader Bobby Seale have used black nationalist ideas and symbols to affect political outcomes in mayoral elections. Barkka used his influence to help Mayor Kenneth Gibson win in Newark, New Jersey, and Seale ran himself in Oakland, California.

Black political mavericks have spearheaded political movements with which the majority of the black community sometimes sympathizes. Often, they are trailblazers in a new political territory and pave the way for black political independents.

A 1966 national survey revealed that 5 percent of the registered black voters saw themselves as political independents. An overview of the different polls of the last two decades indicates that the number of black independent voters seems to expand and contract as the two major political parties move to assist or deny black Americans full participation in the society.[64] Despite the fluctuations, the black independent voter remains a meaningful phenomenon.

Moreover, if we use the approach suggested by the late Key in his last work, [65] *The Responsible Electorate,* another portrait of black independent voters emerges. National survey data, as noted in Table 5.17 reveal that in those past five national elections a mean of 13 percent of the black voters were "floating." On the other hand, only about 79 percent of the black voters stood firm with Democrats, while the number standing firm with Republicans is about 21 percent. Shifting from national survey to aggregate data and using the returns from seven black precincts in New Orleans, we can see in Table 5.18 another glimpse of black switching and loyalty in three presidential elections. In seven black precincts in New Orleans in three national elections, a mean of 33 percent of the black voters have been floating. In these precincts, a mean of 67 percent or two-thirds of the black voters stand firm with the Democrats, while one-third or 33 percent stand with the Republicans.

TABLE 5.16 Percentage of Black Switchers and "Standpatters" in Presidential Elections: 1952-1972

Action Category	1952		1956		1960		1964		1968*		1972	
	% D	% R	% D	% R	% D	% R	% D	% R	% D	% R	% D	% R
Black Voting Percentage	79	21	61	39	68	32	94	6	86	12	85	15
Black Switching Percentage			18		7		26		9		3	
Direction of Switch			Rep.		Dem.		Dem.		Rep.		Rep.	

SOURCE: John J. Patrick and Allen D. Glenn, *The Young Voter*, (Washington, D.C., National Council for the Social Studies, 1972), p. 63.

*Estimate

% D = Percent of Democrats

% R = Percent of Republicans

Looking at aggregate data from the black precincts in Atlanta in 1968, we see that the Republican ticket got 2.27 percent of the vote, the Democratic ticket 95.8 percent of the vote, and the American Independent Party ticket 1.9 percent of the vote.[66] By 1972, the Republicans got 10.9 percent of the vote and the Democrats 89.1 percent of the black vote. In 1976, the percentages were 94.9 percent for the Democrats and 5.1 percent for the Republicans. Thus, in Atlanta, switching also took place.

TABLE 5.17 Black Switchers and "Standpatters" in Selected Black New Orleans Precincts: 1952-1960

Action Category	1952		1956		1960	
	% D	% R	% D	% R	% D	% R
Black Voting Percentage	80.7	19.3	43	57	74.4	25.2
Black Switching Percentage			37.7		31.8	
Direction of Switch			Rep.		Dem.	

% D = Percent of Democrats

% R = Percent of Republicans

SOURCE: William C. Howard *et al.*, *The Louisiana Elections of 1960*, (Baton Rouge: Louisiana State University Press, 1963), p. 110. Appendix B, Table 2.

The upshot of this aggregate and survey analysis is that the black independent vote does exist and its fluctuation in various elections cannot be accounted for by an SES index alone. The existence of black political mavericks, independents, switchers, and floaters have made ticket splitting in the black community a reality for a long time. It is not, as the literature suggests, that blacks are an unstable and disruptive force in the electorate.[67]

Those who fail to make a distinction among black voters would easily find only straight-ticket voting in the black community. Many analysts who have relied upon the data of the political behavioralists overemphasized the monolithic nature of black voting. But black voting behavior, like black political behavior is not monolithic. Black party voting has not always been straight-ticket voting. And where it has predominated, studies show that structural forces like ballot forms have contributed significantly to this reality.[68]

Second, because of the limited access of blacks to the various political parties in different regions of the country, black political candidates tend to be concentrated heavily, but not completely, under whatever label is open to them. In these cases, party organization variables are stronger than the psychological variables, and the black voter's choices are systemically limited.

Analysts also fail to see how blacks split their tickets, because they fail to look beyond the presidential level to see how black voters support candidates on the congressional, state, and local levels. Historically, in northern cities like New York and Chicago, blacks often supported one party nationally and another on the state and local levels.[69] In 1966, after having voted strongly against the Republican candidate in the preceding national elections, blacks in Michigan put a Republican, George Romney, into the governorship. Throughout the late sixties and early seventies, black voters supported a wide variety of political candidates regardless of party label.

Black Nonvoting

Political behavioralists have, over the last two decades, devised a variety of terms to explain nonvoting: apathy, alienation, anomie, political cynicism, political futility, political distrust, and low sense of political efficacy. All of them explain nonvoting in sociopsychological terms, making nonvoting a function of individual weaknesses. The individual does not vote because of some "inner" problem.

But in any political system, many more variables than socio-psychological ones operate to inhibit voting behavior. Merriam and Gosnell's pioneering study of nonvoting cited the failure to register as the most important single cause of nonvoting.[70] As this study has shown, the only political failure of many black nonvoters is the failure to vote in a particular election. They might or might not be registered, but they surely hold political opinions, hold political preferences, participate in the spreading and communication of political ideas in the black community, participate in campaigns, and join in pressure-group activities. The label of "nonvoter" hides more than it reveals.

In a contemporary study of the voting behavior of disadvantaged minorities, journalist, Penn Kimball, writes, "The failure of the... political system to engage millions of potential voters is the product of the institutional structure by which people can quality to vote. That structure discriminates most particularly against the poor." She concludes, "Voting in America is enmeshed in a spider's web of prior restraints." Voter registration, she notes, despite its original intent, "operates as an effective system of political control."[71]

In the same vein, another recent work on voting and nonvoting put it this way: "We can nevertheless establish physical difficulties as a major cause of genuine non-voting among registered voters. We found a number of persons who evidently were kept from voting because they had been ill at home or in the hospital, or because they had been away from their city of residence on election day."[72]

The 1963 President's Commission on Registration and Voting Participation similarly found that one-third of the voting age population is not registered because state and local regulations, internal structure, and institutional bias make it burdensome to qualify "if one is timid, unschooled, poor, different or new to the neighborhood, city or region." Jerrold G. Rusk has shown how the poll tax has suppressed voting turnout rates. He writes, "The message of the (data) is straightfoward—both the poll tax and the literacy test laws had independent effects in decreasing voter participation, and when combined, they had a strong cumulative effect, reducing turnout by 47.9 percent from states not having such restrictive legislation."[73]

In 1972, the National Urban League, after conducting a survey including one hundred of its affiliates in thirty-four states and the District of Columbia, concluded that:

> External impediments, and not apathy, are primarily
> responsible for the relatively lower participation of
> Americans, whether black or white....The impediments of
> black participation are widespread...and they take the form
> of clumsy, archaic registration procedures and disqualifying
> factors (such as)...the inaccessibility of registration sites,
> inappropriate registration hours, antiquated residency
> requirements, literacy tests, and the barring of persons with
> felony records from the voting booth. [74]

North and South, the League found that structural and institutional variables had more of an effect on black nonvoting than did apathy or other sociopsychological variables.

Although there is substantial evidence to challenge the behavioralist approach, the question can be raised as to whether sociopsychological variables provide the best explanation for structural and institutional variables. The answer is twofold.

Historically, institutional and structural variables engendered black nonvoting. Any cursory examination of the political history of the black electorate will reveal the numerous legal and illegal barriers blacks had to surmount merely to become voters. Institutional and structural obstacles still bar a large segment of the black electorate from voting. The relationship between the number of black elected officials in the south and the number of requests for changes in election laws in the southern states covered under the Voting Rights Act is clear: as the number of officals rises, the number of requests also rises significantly.[75] Table 5.19 lists the kinds of changes that the southern states requested in rank order. Each change would have increased the difficulty of blacks to register, vote, or build significant political bases of black voters. Dilution and registration are the two most common techniques for reducing black political participation. And despite the continuous complaints to the Justice Department about these new barriers, in most instances, states have put them into practice. Moreover, the situation has continued unabated since the mid-seventies. A United States Civil Rights Commission report issued in 1981 (the data in that report are in Table 5.20) updates the changes requested by states from 1975-1980. In comparing Table 5.20 with 5.19 several things have changed. First, annexation-type changes have taken the number-one position and at-large elections have moved from last to second. Many new techniques, such as a majority vote requirement instead of the old simple pluralities, numbered post, and residency requirements, along with a host of others have surfaced.

And each of these new techniques, particularly annexation and at-large elections, are specifically designed to *dilute* concentrated black voting strength. Seemingly, the move has been from using registration and voting procedures as a means to diminish and halt the black voter in the late sixties and early seventies to the new techniques of dilution of concentrated black voting power which emerged because of patterns of residential segregation. The parallels here between the new techniques instituted since the 1965 Voting Rights Act and those put into effect during Reconstruction are staggering. The future in the region promises more and more restraining mechanisms on black voters. Structural and institutional barriers are indeed far from being eliminated. In the survey, a few black registered voters noted sociopsychological reasons for staying away from the ballot box, stressing instead the political structure and its regulations.[76]

TABLE 5.18. Changes Requested by States Covered by the 1965 Voting Rigths Act: 1965-1973*

Type of Change	Number of Changes Requested	% of Changes
Polling Places	733	24.4
Annexation	705	23.5
Voter Registration & Voting	411	13.7
Government Structure & Operations	376	12.5
Redistricting	363	12.0
Running for Office	171	5.7
Minority Representation	106	3.5
Reregistration	77	2.7
At-large Elections	62	2.0
Total	3,004	100.0

*The data for 1973 cover only January to September 10.

SOURCE: David H. Hunter, *Federal Review of Voting Changes*, (Washignton, D.C.: Joint Center for Political Studies, 1974), p. 74.

Finally, voting as practiced and regulated in America is a middle-class phenomenon, not really for those in the low socioeconomic levels. Penn Kimball writes, "The American system fits the Anglo-Saxon ethic of rugged individualism better than the realities of universal participation.... The posturing of candidates and the promises of parties are simply irrelevant to the daily grind of marginal existence" of most minority groups.[77]

TABLE 5.19. Changes Requested by States Covered by the 1965 Voting Rights Act: 1975-1980.

Type of Change	Number of Changes Requested	% of Changes
Annexations	235	30.5
At-large elections	80	10.4
Majority vote	66	8.6
Numbered posts	60	7.8
Redistricting boundary changes	56	7.3
Polling place changes	55	7.1
Residency requirements	42	5.5
Staggered terms	36	4.7
Single-member districts	26	3.4
Change in number of positions	15	1.9
Multimember districts	13	1.7
Registration and voting procedures	13	1.7
Requirements for candidacy	12	1.6
Election date change	11	1.4
Change in terms of office	8	1.0
Bilingual procedures	8	1.0
New voting precinct	6	0.8
Consolidation and incorporation	6	0.8
Change from appointive to elective/ elective to appointive	3	0.4
Miscellaneous	19	2.5
Total	770	100.1

SOURCE: United States Commision on Civil Rights, *The Voting Rights Act: Unfulfilled Goals*, (Washington, D.C.: Government Printing Office, 1981), p. 69.

E. E. Schattschneider, likewise, sees nonvoting as a result of the extralegal processes, social pressures, and the ways the political system is organized and structured.[78] He sees the electoral system as structured for upper-class participation.

Although, class factors and institutional and structural variables do perpetuate and enhance black nonvoting, there is one additional major factor operative in the nonvoting equation: incentives. Usually, when politicians and organizers are trying to stimulate and increase black voting, they do so on the basis of emotional and racial appeals. But these incentives are fundamentally psychological. Yet in a society that is essentially materialistic, not all of the voters and party workers, black or white, can be effectively motivated by psychological and ideological incentives. Patronage (material rewards) has long been a major motivator in American politics and it is nonetheless true in black politics. And when get-out-the-vote campaigns have combined *psychological* and *material* incentives, particularly where the material incentives reach the masses of people, black nonvoting reaches its lowest possible levels in the black community. And such low levels cannot be reached by the use of one incentive alone.

In short, black nonvoting is a function of both class, structural, institutional, and incentive variables. The decrease of the variables and the use of new material incentives will significantly decrease black non-voting.[79]

Findings from the Second Look

In summary, a reassessment of the literature on black voting behavior reveals that the approach of the political behavioralist to black voting leaves much to be desired. The literature is unsystematic and paints a portrait of blacks in whiteface. The landmark studies supporting the generalizations on black voting have significant methodological shortcomings in numbers and time. Each study includes so few blacks that they are hardly enough, in some instances, to be statistically significant. Moreover, all but two of the major voting studies took place before the 1965 Voting Rights Act, which helped to enlarge black political participation. The picture gathered of the black voter was bound to be a limited one. Adding to methodological problems was the tendency to compare black voters to white voters, i.e., the advantaged to the disadvantaged in society. Blacks with by far the greatest number of handicaps, always fared poorly, giving rise to normative speculations about the need for individual improvement.

A reexamination of black voting behavior using contemporary and historical aggregate and survey data reveals the old theories to be deficient. The new data suggest that systemic and structural variables played a significant role in shaping black voting behavior. Likewise, the new data make note of ebbs, and flows, fluctuations, floatings, turnouts, and switching in black voting behavior for the first time. In short, this second look at black voting seems to reflect responsibility, coherence, and consistency that matches the realities of the black political culture, social milieu, and experience in America.

There is, however, one final thought before concluding. In several localities, where blacks are the numerical majorities, black voters have put whites into office over black candidates. It had happened in the past and it has happened recently and it will happen in the future. There are two reasons for this reality: First there are the situational and contextual variables that make this possible; second, racial consciousness at times dictates that the white candidate be the winner. This aspect of black voting, i.e., voting for a white candidate over a black one, is a feature of black voting behavior in America.

Chapter 6

Black Party Behavior

Black party supporters have always known that structural variables affect their political behavior and often try to tell others. But few paid any attention.

John H. McCray, State Chairman of the South Carolina Progressive Democratic Party (SCPD), told a United States Senate subcommittee hearing on constitutional rights in April, 1959, that blacks in South Carolina had to form a *satellite* political party because they were barred from participation in the regular state Democratic party. "I think, sir," he said, "for 15 years, we have been the Negro Democratic leaders of South Carolina...we operated within the Democratic party...now we are all members of the Democratic party. But in order that we might get together and decide what we should strive for best within that party, we remain in the Progressive Democrats who were organized and functioned from 1944 to 1948 as a seperate and competing party."[1]

Then Senator Olin D. Johnston, a member of the subcommittee conducting the hearing and one of the individuals against whom SCPD had run in 1944, pretended he knew nothing of the party, which suggested its *invisibility*. "I have a statement," note Senator Johnston, from the Chairman of the regular Democratic party in South Carolina, Thomas H. Pope, which notes "that the organization claims to be represented by John H. McCray, as the South Carolina Progressive Democrats, or South Carolina Progressive Democratic

Party, or South Carolina Democratic Organization, whatever he may call it, is not a part of the South Carolina Democratic Party and is not even recognized by the South Carolina Democratic Party in South Carolina."[2] McCray retorted that the National Democratic Party in 1956 "recommended" the SCPD to the state party for inclusion.

Nine years later, John Hulett, chairman of the Lowndes County Freedom Organization, Freedom Party Now, told the U.S. Commission on Civil Rights the same thing at a hearing in Montgomery, Alabama. Mr. Taylor, the commission staff director, questioned Hulett as follows:

> Mr. Taylor: Mr. Hulett, why was it decided to form a third party rather than an independent party, rather than to make an effort to work through the existing party?
> Mr. Hulett: For several reasons. Number one, the existing parties, after Negroes started getting registered to vote, (raised) the qualifying fees to get on the Democratic ballot, they upped the fees by 900 percent, previous to that time if a person wanted to run for sheriff, for example, they only paid $50 and they end up I believe with $500, the school board member was $10 and they moved it up to $100, and since we organized our own political party this year they have lowered the fees back to the normal assessment. That was one of the reasons.
>
> The second place was the large number of people...who couldn't read or write in this country, they wouldn't be able to go to a Democratic primary and vote for a candidate which they wanted to support, because they couldn't read or write. By having your own political party they could go out especially in November and vote a straight ticket by pulling the lever for the political party which you endorse. [3]

Before concluding, Hulett told the hearing that his organization was "an all black political party...It is separate from the Democratic and Republican Party, we organized our independent political party, that's what it actually is."[4]

Because of closed party structures, blacks in one state form a satellite political party, while in another state they form an independent or separate party. In fact, in Alabama in the same year, blacks would also form a satellite party.[5] The state party constitution required all members to uphold white supremacy. In many southern states, the reality was that only whites could join the organization. In the North, separate Democratic and Republican organizations limited black supporters and followers to vote-getting functions and lower-echelon positions. Even today blacks still find organizational structures thwarting them.

Yet, despite the use of closed party structures and various other systemic factors to keep blacks out, the behavioral literature persists in its attempts to explain black party behavior solely from individual factors. Gerald Finch writes, "It is doubtful that socialization is in itself sufficient to stabilize party identification in a group as socially and politically isolated as blacks. They are an electorally vulnerable cast that control neither party, a situation that is likely to retard the growth of lasting party attachments in a system with two internally heterogeneous parties."[6] While using the notion that older blacks were raised by nonpartisan fathers and benefited from little socialization, Finch arrives at the conclusion that blacks are not attached to any political party, making them therefore the most volatile and unstable group in the electorate. Matthews and Prothro used the concept of party image to establish the view that blacks are heavily Democratic, a view that pervades the literature.

Black journalist Chuck Stone, swallowing the behavioralist generalizations about black party behavior, chided blacks for not being politically sophisticated and developed an *oscillating party strategy* for blacks to follow. [7] But Stone's presupposition, and that of many others is, in the words of black comedian Flip Wilson, "jive". It is based on at least two errors. First, it assumes that blacks' access to both parties has been equally free. Second, it assumes that both parties have responded consistently and forthrightly to black needs and aspirations. In addition, it assumes that blacks have been like whites, unfettered in their party participation. Jive presuppositions have led to jive conclusions. At best, blacks' support of parties reflects their experience with the parties. Moreover, black attachment to the Democratic party, despite the percentage point differences, coincides with what most white Democrats were doing; a similar pattern held during Republican Party hegemony.

If masses of blacks identified with a party which did not permit their participation, their behavior would really suggest an abnormal response. Nevertheless, a few blacks have lingered and tried to perform the herculean task of reordering the party priorities toward blacks. And when they have succeeded, the black masses have followed. But seldom, before such massive party priority changes toward the black community, have the black masses switched.

The Literature

Kay Lawson succinctly explains the behavioral approach to party behavior. She write, "it is characterized by an emphasis on the human actors who influence the generation of parties, the acts they perform in the process, and their attitudes and expectations in performing these acts."[8] She continues: "Behavioralists are interested in all three forms of party linked behavior, leadership, activism, and voting."[0] And "if parties *are* what the people associated with them *do*, then information like this can lead to generalizations about the party itself and not just the people in it."[10]

But studies of party activists are scarce because there were so few of them.[11] Instead, the generalizations about black party identification have come from studies of black voters' party support. Aggregate data from black wards and precincts, and the percentage of the votes cast for Democratic candidates and Republican candidates, have been used to establish the existence of black Democratic bias.[12]

Matthews and Prothro, using survey data and the concept of "party image," a sociopsychological variable, arrived at the same conclusion that those with aggregate data did. "The Democratic bias of Negro southerners is so overwhelming that few of them are likely to shift permanently to the Republican camp in the foreseeable future. Not only are they heavily and increasingly Democratic in their party identification, but their images of the parties are extraordinarily favorable to the Democrats and hostile to the GOP."[13]

Previously, observers used socioeconomic and demographic data to argue that the black democratic bias was shaped by class factors. "Those with higher income, education, and occupational status were more likely to vote than those lower with respect to those items, as well as to vote Republican."[14] Democrats, one could surmise, came from the lower SES strata.

Samuel Lubell supported the thesis when he noted in his book, *Revolt of the Moderates*, that "large numbers of persons were rising from working-class to middle-class status, and since the characteristic political behavior of the middle-class person was to vote Republican," the Republicans would shortly become the majority party.[15] Other researchers also delineated the correlation between upward social mobility and Republican party identification.[16]

Eulau, for example, explored interclass perceptions and class- and party-related frames of references. He conluded, that "middle-class people perceived their class as voting Republican, while working class people see their own class as voting Democratic."[17] Those using the SES index perceived that blacks have always "been kept in the lower ranks of socioeconomic status, they are congregated in the least desirable living areas, they have the least formal education and they have the lowest paying jobs."[18] Since these charcteristics were noted to be the same characteristics of those lower-status individuals who supported the Democrats, a major positive correlation seemed obvious. Blacks, because of their SES index, were Democrats. Historians have concluded that blacks are Democrats because of the New Deal.

Currently, those using political socilaization as a theoretical base arrive at the same conclusions as those with aggregate data, survey data, and the SES demographic data. Fred Greenstein describes this approach as follows: "To a considerable extent, party identifications are traditional. Like affiliations in a religious denomination, they are passed on by parents to their children."[19] Leroy Rieselbach adds: " since party identification starts in childhood, it shapes other political perceptions and is extremely hard to change. Thus, the stability of party identification...like most dispositions to which individuals are politically socialized...promotes the continuity and stability of the American political system. It does this by perpetuating the two-party system through the thicket of rapidly changing issues and candidates."[20] He concludes: "More than any other factor, party identification determines how an American will vote."

Hence, Finch's findings, mentioned earlier, that blacks have no history of party identification means that there is nothing to transmit to the next generation; Finch perpetuates the psychological notion fostered by Greenstein, Rieselbach, and others. Wherever one looks, the weight if not the burden of the literature is the same. All of the approaches tell us that blacks are Democratic. Finch's findings suggest that they are momentary Democrats and a threat to the stability of the two-party system.

By 1984, analysts relying on a very small poll conclude that for economic reasons blacks were Democrats. "Different forces" they wrote, "appear to operate at different levels of the black social structure to produce the same results: Overwhelming support for the Democratic party."[21]

All of the literature describing black party behavior as Democratic is based on individual, not systemic variables. In this literature, even the class and SES indices explain party behavior from individual factors. Pompers notes: "Of the various influencing groups, the most important for this voter is his party. Affinity to the Republicans and

Democrats is not unique, but provides a social reference point, much like membership in a union or religious community.... The theme of (these) electoral studies, thus has been 'primarily the role of enduring partisan commitments in shaping attitudes toward politics.'"[22] In short, socioeconomic status and demographic variables made party members dependent party supporters and voters.

All of these four explicans of individual blacks' party behavior have one thing in common: The presupposition that party channels and response were as open and equal for blacks as they were for whites. And if they were, and black Democratic support persisted, then black party behavior would be unusual. But since this is not the case, black leanings toward the Democratic party tell us everything and nothing at the same time. There is nothing to make blacks prone to support the Democratic party except the American party structure and organizations themselves.

The generalizations about black Democratic attachment has been overdrawn. Black adherence to the Democratic party never was monolitic. Other parties receive black support. And Key has shown that inside this democratic trend that significant shifting was taking place.

Finally, Finch's assertion that blacks had nonpartisan fathers and are therefore unstable forces in the party system is not only historically inaccurate, it links stability to purely individual factors.

Before concluding this review of the literature, a word must be said about Eldersveld's study of party activists. But this is risky business. In his 1956 study of the few black party activists in the Detroit area, he found that the black Democratic party leaders were "relatively excluded," while the black Republican party leaders were "almost completely excluded" from the parties, decision-making circles.[23] Then he went on to note that despite the black party activists' great efficiency in getting out the vote and enhancing straight-ticket voting, his presence was dysfunctional for the party organization overall. He wrote: "Negro leaders as subcoalitional representatives may actually stimulate more interest in, and loyalty to, the Negro political movement than the particular party with which they identify. This may be termed the 'Trojan Horse effect.'"[24] A high-level party official, reading these empirical findings repeated throughout the volume, might not see this tendency as a reality of organizational and structural limitations, but as a reason for further limiting black party access or excluding blacks altogether. As noted earlier, this interpretation is risky because the fault here is seen by

Eldersveld as individual rather than systemic. Eldersveld had perceived the existence of closed party structure to blacks before most, but for the wrong reason.

In sum, then, the present portrait of black party behavior as drawn in the behavioral literature is a static one. It paints black party supporters as robots, unthinking and under numerous sociopsychological controls. Moreover, it leads to some peculiar political strategies and approaches to capture or change the black vote. For example, in the 1964 national election, the Republican party strategists and some of its black Republican leaders designed a "King for President" strategy. The plan was developed in the belief that the Republicans would not get any of the black vote that year because of Republican Presidential hopeful Barry Goldwater's stand on civil rights. Therefore, it was decided that if the black bloc vote for the Democrats could be split, a Goldwater victory was possible. Hence, "1,400,000 leaflets designed to influence colored voters in 11 major cities to 'waste' their ballot by writing in the name of Dr. Martin Luther King, Jr. for president" was ordered printed and distributed.[25] "The leaflets, printed on yellow paper in an apparent imitation of a telegram were first distributed in Los Angeles and San Francisco. Reports later came in form Cleveland, Philadelphia, Chicago and Cincinnati, and Atlantic City where they were being handed out in colored precincts."[26] The leaflets bore the caption "Western Unity" and were addressed "To all Negro voters." The text said:

> We can vote for Dr. King for President, a write-in vote for Dr. King shows that we are united. It will prove that Negroes will vote for the greatest Negro in America for President. A write-in vote for Dr. King will tell the world that Negroes will not be led by false prophets. Write in Mr. King for President.

The leaflets were signed by a "Committee for Negroes in Government, Louisville, Ky."[27] In addition to the leaflet, numerous radio advertising spots for the King for President idea were bought and beamed to black audiences. When the scheme was discovered and exposed, black Republican officials denied it was one of their schemes.

Such a strategy not only assumes that black party behavior is static, but also that it will shift in response to black political personalities and promises of civil rights policies. This "King for President" scheme, like the many similar strategies on the state and local level, received little or no support; they all misread black party behavior.

In the 1976 presidential election, Republicans tried a similar scheme. On the day before the November 3 election, someone in the organization sent telegrams to 400 black ministers around the nation, trying to capitalize on an incident in Plains, Georgia, at the Baptist Church to which Governor Carter belonged. The church deacons cancelled services when several blacks, including a black minister who had run for president in 1960 on the Afro-American Party ticket, tried to integrate the church.[28] The telegram suggested that Governor Carter "could not manage the affairs of his own church" and that this incident showed up "some of the inconsistencies in Governor Carter's beliefs on civil rights and religion."[29] But the ploy failed. One recipient of the telegram, the Reverend Alfred M. Waller, pastor of the Shiloh Baptist Church in Cleveland, said, "The prevalance of such a telegram to so many black ministers in the Cleveland area to me seems to be conclusive evidence that this whole episode is designed to embarrass Mr. Carter. I think it is obvious that [those barred from the church] are part of the conspiracy."[30] The father of Dr. Martin Luther King, Jr., said, "President Ford's only hope is to trick black folks into staying home on Tuesday. But that won't work. We're smarter than that now."[31] Numerous other black leaders saw it as a political trick and likewise denounced it. The next day, top Republican leaders denounced the telegram and blamed it on black Republican leaders who acted without White House approval.

But the Republicans didn't give up. When schemes failed to work, the party shifted to images and public relations. In 1977, when "Bill Brock took over" as Chairman of the Republican Party, "his working assumption" based in part on the party's 1976 defeat, was that the "new Republican Majority" would not simply emerge. The party had to be revitalized and out of Chairman Brock's overall strategy "came a plan to deny Democrats the margin of security they routinely derived from an overwhelmingly Democratic black vote." In 1976, the black bloc vote compensated for Democrats' slippage among white voters and helped send Carter to the White House.[32]

Chairman Brock concluded "that Carter's campaign style and Republican indifference" influenced black voters. So in 1977 he recruited "Wright-McNeill and Associates, a black political consulting firm based in Columbus, Georgia to work with his staff and develop an outreach program for black community involvement." Then Brock gave the firm "an office in the RNC's Washington headquarters and...contracts that totaled more than $1 million over the following three years." What were the results of the public-relations firm's efforts? "...Early preelection surveys conducted by RNC political strategist determined that black voters were going to stick with Jimmy Carter or the Democratic nominee no matter what the Republican did in 1980."[33] Therefore, the RNC made an all-out effort to recruit and attract white ethnics and drop any overtures toward blacks. And when Reagan-Bush 1980 Campaign got under-way, the Wright-McNeill firm was told to concentrate on selected congressional and state races, and Arthur Teele was brought in to direct a new appeal to the black electorate. Teele's new public relations strategy failed miserably. The emphasis on an economic strategy to win black votes minus a concern for civil rights main-tained black republican voting at its lowest levels. However in some of the congressional races, special appeals to the black voters did work.

In these congressional races: "Wright-McNeill's job was to provide the Republican contender with information on salient issues in the various black communities, contacts with key black groups and persons of influence and survey research on black voter attitudes and support." In addition, "they promoted media techniques to reach the black electorate and counseled their clients on the selection of message content, timing, vehicles and the use of key words and phrases in speeches and debates."[34] According to Pearl Robinson, "a thorough postmortum of the Democrats' loss of control of the Senate must take into account their party's marginal slippage among black voters in elections targeted by the RNC." However, these appeals work not only because of the public relations efforts but due to the right wing activities of many of the Democratic Senators who sought reelection. Also, closed party structures and legacies of the past have held black voters off. And until the Republican Party on the national level can move beyond a purely economic appeal and embrace civil right and social programs, support for the party by blacks will lag. In 1984, as the Reagan-Bush re-election campaign got underway, word leaked out that again blacks would be written off because all past efforts, i.e., schemes, images and public relations had failed and now Hispanics along with white ethnics would be the new targets for the Party.[35]

Seemingly any technique except a program of mutual political exchange is offered to the black voter. In 1984, the Republican party's "southern" strategy is still in place.

Currently, the Democratic Party, who first offered blacks economic incentives to shift from the Republican party and coupled that later with a strong support of civil rights policies and social programs, basically out of humanitarian and democratic principles, are now in a very competive struggle with the Republicans for the White House. Because of this competitive struggle, which several factions in the party feel the Republican are winning the Democrats are now trying to develop a southern strategy of their own for the party.[36] One has been proposed, and the seemingly tacit acceptance of it by the democratic front runner, led in part to the emergence of the Jackson candidacy, and vigorous black support of his efforts. This kind of in-house or in-party rebellion by blacks didn't occur in the Reconstruction era, when blacks were strongly attached to the Republican party, and the effect was disastrous. Republican party leaders (who felt that they had given blacks all the policy concessions possible: an analogous position is held by the Democrats today) urged black leaders to await a better political climate. Republicans slowly abandoned the cause because a better political time and climate never came. Black Republicans were literally left holding the bag.[37] Slowly, out of this political milieu, with blacks waiting for the Republicans to act the Party developed a southern strategy that excluded blacks. The current black political rebellion in the Democratic party suggests that some black leaders have learned their political lesson and are making possible new directions and party options. Blacks will find new alternatives if both major parties shift to the right and put in place a total southern strategy.[38]

Blacks and the Major Parties: Systemic and Structural Factors

To analyze black party behavior on a sound basis, one needs to see *relatively* unfettered black two-party support over time. Such participation in party politics has not been common in American history, but a view of black party support in the congressional districts of the late Representatives William Dawson and Adam Clayton Powell permits such a view over thirteen elections. In these ghetto congressional districts, blacks had the *relatively* consistent right to vote and choose party label, though they were strongly Democratic districts.

In Figure 6.1, the levels of black support in Dawson's district for the Republican, Democratic, and third parties from 1944 to 1968 are shown. The 1970 data were included because they mark the change in the district from Dawson to Representative Ralph Metcalfe. The mean black Democratic party support is 71 percent while the Republican party support is 28 percent. Approximately one-third of the black voters choose to support the Republican party.

The percentage of the Republican votes ranges from a high of 43.2 percent in 1946 to a low of 9 percent in 1970, when Representative Metcalfe won the district. The Democratic party support ranged from a high of 84.9 percent for Dawson in 1964 and a high for Metcalfe in 1970 of nearly 91 percent, to a low for Dawson of 56 percent in 1946. Third-party support occured in 1948 and ceased after 1950.

Figure 6.2 shows that the mean black support in Powell's district for the Democratic party is 73 percent, over 19 percent for the Republican party, and nearly 7 percent for various third parties. In Powell's district, one-fifth of the black community chose to support the Republican party in an era of Democratic hegemony and even during a period of Republican hegemony in a state that chose Republican Nelson Rockefeller for governor for more then four terms. Support for the Democratic party ranged from a low of 63 percent in 1946 to an all-time high in 1970 of 87 percent for Charles Rangel. During Powell's tenure, Republican party support ranged from a high 37 percent in 1946 to a low of 10 percent in 1964. Moreover, in 1970, the first year that Rangel won, the Republican vote dropped to zero. Third-party support in this district ranges from a low of zero in 1944 and 1946 to highs of 13 percent in 1970 under Rangel and 11 percent under Powell in 1960. Third parties, apparently, flourished in Powell's district but collapsed in Dawson's machine-controlled district after two elections.

Analysis of the aggragate data for both districts reveals that blacks have supported the two parties in varying degres over nearly two decades. Especially in Powell's district, blacks also supported third parties over twelve different elections. Support for the Republican party form one-third and one-fourth of the voters cannot be dismissed or overlooked, especially in periods of Democratic party hegemony.

In the South, aggregate data on black two-party support is scarce, but what little there is suggests some variance with generalizations in the current literature.

Fig. 6.1. Black Party Support: Congressman William Dawson's District: 1944-1970

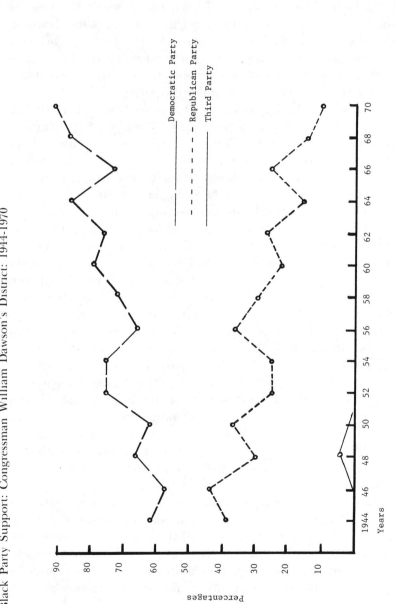

SOURCE: *Official Congressional Directory* (1944-1972) The Election Statistics Sections

Fig. 6.2. Black Party Support: Congressman Adam Clayton Powell's District: 1944-1970

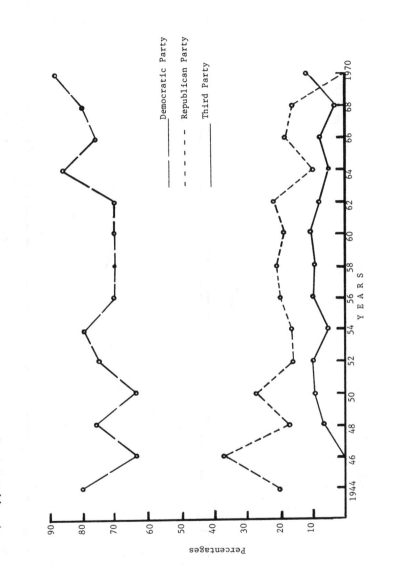

SOURCE: *Official Congressional Directory* (1944-1972) The Election Statistics Sections.

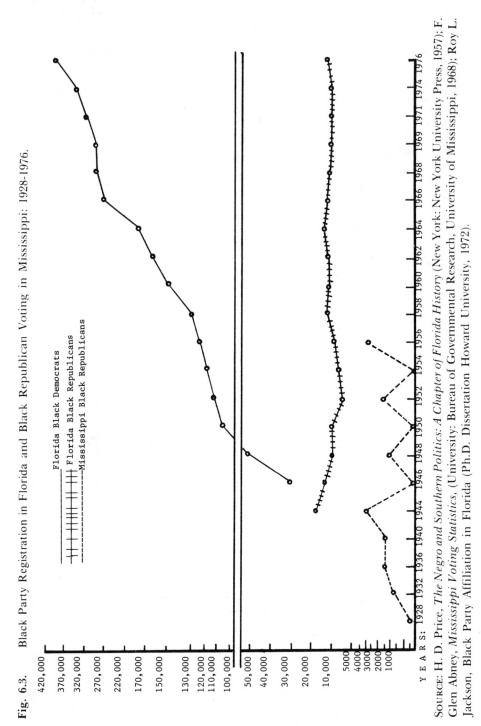

Fig. 6.3.   Black Party Registration in Florida and Black Republican Voting in Mississippi: 1928-1976.

SOURCE: H. D. Price, *The Negro and Southern Politics: A Chapter of Florida History* (New York: New York University Press, 1957); F. Glen Abney, *Mississippi Voting Statistics*, (University: Bureau of Governmental Research, University of Mississippi, 1968); Roy L. Jackson, Black Party Affiliation in Florida (Ph.D. Dissertation Howard University, 1972).

In Florida, black party registration was recorded by race for a time, while in Mississippi the black votes for the Republican party were kept separate for several years (See Figure 6.3). In Mississippi the black vote for the Republican party rose slowly, with some declines, from 1928 to 1956. It was the only party in the state in which blacks could participate. Yet in Florida during the latter half of the same period, black identification with the Republican party dropped and the rose slightly by 1956. But in the same state, during the period of national Republican hegemony, black identification with the Democratic party was rapid and dramatic. In both states, black Republican identificaiton preceded the abolition of the white primary in 1944, when black entrance into the one-party Democratic system in the South was permitted.

Survey data reveal the same kinds of division and two-party flexibility (See Table 6.1). Among black voters, one-third seek attachment outside of the Democratic party. Two-thirds of black nonvoters place themselves outside of the Democratic party.

The NORC data in Table 6.2 show black party preferences as they developed through the seventies and early eighties. Basically, as this Table is contrasted with Table 6.1., it reveals that a shift has taken place, with blacks moving heavily into the Democratic party. The essential reason for this was indicated earlier; the Republican party over this time span has become less and less an attractive alternative on the national level. If it does become attractive then the party shift will recur.

Blacks surveyed indicated that they are attracted to a particular party primarily because of the candidates' stand on issues rather than because of an "image" or the party's historical position of Civil Rights (See Table 6.3). Over two-thirds of both voters and nonvoters are drawn to a particular party because of the candidate's stand on the key issues of the day. Personality and party platform rank low as reasons that blacks forge party attachment.

The implication of both the aggregate and survey data is that black party attachment is flexible, fluctuating in different elections, responsive to closed organizational structures and highly sensitive to issues relevant to the black community. Once the realities of party structure are counted as part of the political equation, the true nature of black party allegiance can be clearly seen. National black party preferences cannot always be equated with local and state preferences. In addition, closed party organizations have given rise to numerous splinter groups among both the Republicans and the Democrats, also creating various black minor parties.

TABLE 6.1. Party Preferences in the Black Community

Party	Percentage (number)	
	Voters	Nonvoters
Democratic Party	61.2 (427)	32.5 (99)
Republican Party	17.5 (122)	14.2 (44)
Black Independents	10.4 (73)	20.7 (63)
Minor Party	1.6 (11)	6.7 (20)
Black Party	1.3 (9)	6.2 (19)
No Preferences	8.0 (56)	19.7 (60)
Totals	100.0 (698)	100.0 (305)

SOURCE: *National Black Survey, 1972-74.*

TABLE 6.2. Self-Identified Political Party Affiliation in the Black Community by Sex: 1972-1982.

Party Identification*	Percentage (number)	
	Black Female	Black Male
Democrat	80 (694)	81 (529)
Independent	9 (79)	9 (56)
Republican	9 (81)	8 (52)
Other Parties	2 (19)	2 (16)
Total		
(Pooled Sample Size - 1526)	100 (873)	100 (653)

*The NORC surveys used an eight-point scale to determine party affiliation. The Democratic and Republican categories used in this table combine all of the various configurations, i.e., strong Democrat, Independent near Democrats, etc., into one category. Only those listed as pure Independents went into the Independent category.

SOURCE: NORC, *General Social Surveys, 1972-1982.*

TABLE 6.3. Factors Affecting Black Party Allegiance

Factors	Black Voters	Black Nonvoters
Positions on Issues	68.1 (475)	62.6 (191)
Candidate as a Person (Personality)	22.1 (154)	14.1 (43)
Party Platform	7.7 (54)	9.2 (28)
Others	2.1 (15)	14.1 (43)
Total	100.0 (698)	100.0 (305)

SOURCE: *National Black Survey, 1972-74.*

Another form of black party behavior arising from closed party structures is the 21st Black Congressional District Caucus, which Congressman Louis Stokes organized in his Ohio district because whites would not permit unfettered black participation in the Democratic party. It is a new and a possible rising form of political attachment in the black community.

Blacks and the Minor Parties

To discern the nature and significance of black participation in various third-party movements, one must examine the political environment that thwarted their involvement in the political mainstream.

One scholar developed a test of significance for the numerous third parties in American history, listing the most significant from 1832 to 1968. Table 6.4 lists the level of black participation in each of these significant third parties.

TABLE 6.4. Black Involvement in Third Parties in Presidential Elections

Year	Party	% of Total Votes	*Level of Black Participation
1832	Anti-Mason	8.0	Extremely Low
1848	Free Soil	10.1	Moderate
1856	American	21.4	Low
1860	Democratic Breckinridge	18.2	None
1860	Constitutional Union	12.6	None
1892	Populist	8.5	High
1912	Theodore Roosevelt Progressive	27.4	Moderate
1912	Socialist	6.0	Low
1924	LaFollette Progressive	16.6	Low
1968	American Independent	13.5	Low

*Hanes Walton, Jr., *The Negro in Third Party Politics* (Philadelphia: Dorrance & Company, 1969).

SOURCE: Daniel Mazmanian, *Third Parties in Presidential Elections* (Washington, D.C.: Brookings Institution, 1974), p. 5.

Black participation occurred in all but the two parties oriented toward slavery in 1860. In every instance, a closed party structure or the political environment stands out as the major determinant in black political participation. In all of the third parties before 1860 only free blacks, not slaves, could participate. Further, only free blacks in certain northern states had suffrage rights. In cases where the political environment did not limit black participation, the political ideology of the party did. Both the nativistic American party and the third parties of 1860 defended slavery as an official party policy. In one parish in Louisiana, blacks were forced to support the party.[39] After the Civil War, black Populists were segregated from white Populists in the southern states before Populism moved to legally disenfranchise black voters. The Progressive Party of 1912 found black voters disenfranchised in the South. But the standard-bearer of the party, Theodore Roosevelt, would not permit southern blacks to join even when they tried valiantly to do so. He upheld southern lily-white Progressivism. The party's 1924 leader, Robert LaFollette, was not much better. At first he refused to recognize blacks, but turned to them in a half-hearted fashion only in the last months before the election.

An analysis of black third-party participation at state and local levels can be even more instructive. Taking the Progressive Party of 1948 as a case in point, we can see that black political attachment and third-party behavior varies by region.

Scholars have established that in the North, especially in predominantly black districts, blacks cast a significant number of their votes for the Progressive Party, led by Henry Wallace (see Table 6.5). But in the South the situation was vastly different (see Table 6.6). The Progressive vote in all black-belt counties having a black majority and permiting blacks to register in 1948 has been totaled and the percentage of votes given the party by these black-belt counties is listed. The picture is clear: despite Wallace's strenuous attempts in the South, few blacks in the black-belt counties voted to support his candidacy. In southern urban areas, his support was much higher.[40] But overall, the southern black Progressive vote of 1948, when compared with the northern black Progressive vote, was indeed small. The crucial factor was the reaction of the white south to the Progressive party and to those blacks who supported it.[41]

Moreover, at this time white southerners resentful of the civil rights proposals of both the Wallace party and the Democratic Party established the Dixiecrat Party. It received some of its strongest support from the black belt area, where whites were not in a majority.

Moving to the senatorial level, we can compare the black turnout in the 1950 race of scholar-activist W.E.B. Du Bois with that for the

TABLE 6.5. Support for the Progressive Party in Selected Northern Cities in 1948

Districts	Votes Cast	% of Total Votes Cast
4 Harlem districts	21,900	15.8
Los Angeles district	4,100	10.1
5 Cincinnati wards	4,300	9.3
Pittsburgh's Hill District	300	2.4
Philadelphia	2,400	NA
Chicago	5,000	NA

SOURCE: Hanes Walton, Jr., *The Negro in Third Party Politics* (Philadelphia: Dorance & Company, 1969), pp. 59-66.

TABLE 6.6. Support for the Progressive Party in Southern Black-Belt Counties in 1948

States	Number of Black-Belt Counties Voting	Total Progressive Votes	Percentage of Total Votes
Arkansas	19	751	2.5
Alabama	62	1,522	4.1
Louisiana	5	3,035	0.2
Florida	2	11,620	0.2
North Carolina	100	3,915	3.5
Texas	21	3,764	0.6
Tennessee	2	1,864	0.1
Virginia	105	2,047	10.0
South Carolina	28	154	18.1
Mississippi	23	225	10.2
Georgia	Unknown*		

*Georgia data were lost. (The total Progressive Vote in Atlanta's three black precincts was 171 votes).

SOURCE: A. Heard and D. Strong, *Southern Primaries and Elections: 1920-1949*, (Alabama: University of Alabama Press, 1950).

Wallace party in 1948. Du Bois ran on the American Labor Party ticket, seeking to capture black support. He polled fewer black votes in every district than a white Progressive two years earlier (see Table 6.7). In all, Du Bois, who placed third in the race, received 11,522 fewer votes than Wallace had in 1948. The crucial difference was the enthusiasm of the black community for the Wallace candidacy and its limited interest in Du Bois's drive and its limited access to the American Labor Party's organizational structure.

TABLE 6.7. Black Third Party Votes for Wallace and Du Bois: 1948 and 1950

Assembly Districts	1948 Wallace Votes	1950 Du Bois Votes
11 (Manhattan)	3,484	2,469
12 (Manhattan)	6,676	3,291
13 (Manhattan)	5,492	2,836
14 (Manhattan)	6,251	5,324
17 (Brooklyn)	5,804	2,265
Totals	27,707	16,185

SOURCE: *Negro Year Book: 1952*

The political environment and party structure play equally important roles in shaping black participation on the state level. All of the states in Table 6.8 are northern except for Virginia, and most of the black candidates were sponsored by left-wing parties. Yet few of these parties let a black head up a state ticket. Nor could blacks expect to win.

TABLE 6.8. Black Third-Party Candidates at State and Local Levels: 1920-1965

Candidate	Party	Position	State	Year	Vote
Mary T. Seymour	Farmer Labor	Sec. of State	Conn.	1920	Lost
Mary T. Seymour	Farmer Labor	Sec. of State	Conn.	1922	6,511
Alexander Wright	Communist	State Legislature	Va.	1936	Lost
Addis Gayle	Communist	State Legislature	Va.	1936	Lost
Josephus Simpson	People party	State Legislature	Va. 1936		Write-in
Frank Sykes	Communist	Lt. Governor	Mich.	1936	Lost
Benjamin Athins	Communist	Lt. Governor	Ohio	1936	Lost
Julian T. Sawyer	Communist	Lt. Governor	N.Y.	1936	Lost
William Clark	Labor Vanguard Demo.	Governor	N.J.	1965	23,402
Ester Nette	Labor Vanguard Demo.	State Legislature	N.J.	1965	Lost

SOURCE: Various Black Newspapers, 1920-1965.

These parties were stigmatized by the media as subversive organizations, so few black voters could truly support these candidates. For instance, when William Clark ran for governor of New Jersey in 1965 against the incumbent Richard Hughes, he found that "when his candidacy was announced he was not only dropped from the relief roles, but was ordered to move out of the housing project where he resided with his five children.[42] Political pressure hit both the party's leaders and supporters. Clark has not run subsequently (see Table 6.8).

Another example of the way systemic forces seek to shape black third-party participation on the local level can be seen in the election of a black Communist candidate to the new York City Council in the forties. Benjamin J. Davis ran on the Communist party ticket against numerous other candidates from Harlem between 1944 and 1949 and was twice elected.[43] Yet, in 1949, when the New York City Council decided that it wanted to rid itself of a Communist member, Davis had to run (from a state senatorial district) against a candidate that had the backing of the Democrats, Republicans, and Liberals. As the Data in Table 6.9 indicate, Davis, despite the fact that "he enjoyed a certain personal popularity in the community and was himself a most able campaigner," lost the election. Black voters avoided this "red" candidate. Davis received less than 30 percent of the entire vote.

TABLE 6.9. Votes Cast in the 21st District New York City Council Race: 1949

Assembly District	Brown	%	Davis	%
7th	29,338	85.7	4,900	14.3
11th	11,768	57.4	8,723	42.6
13th	21,924	72.4	8,339	27.6
Total	60,030	73.2	21,962	26.8

SOURCE: B. Davis, *Communist Councilman from Harlem,* (New York: International Publishers, 1969).

In 1976, several black political activists and elected officials in the National Black Political Assembly decided that neither the Republican nor the Democratic party sufficiently spole to black needs. They organized another black national party, the Independent Freedom Party (IFP), named a standardbearer, and moved to put the party on the ballot of six states to protest the major parties' poor treatment of the black community. Historically, this had occurred numerous times before and each time the newly created party, when put on the ballot of some states received some support from the black community.

In sum, then, the two major forces shaping black third-party behavior are, first, openness of the party organization to blacks, and second, the receptivity to that party, its ideas and programs. Another force is the influence which a particular political machine, as in the districts of Dawson and Powell, might have over the electorate. The stronger the machine's hold, the less likely it is that a black will get a chance to vote for a third party of his choice.

Among blacks there seems to be a tendency to support progressive third-party movements, but this is generally limited to the northern and western states. Most progressive third-party movements in the South, since the failure of the populists, have not attracted blacks or welcomed them on an equal basis. Even the populists had difficulty in accepting blacks on equal terms.

However, it must be added that blacks have also particpated in some of the more conservative and reactionary third parties in both the North and the South, in the latter on a segregated basis. Always, structural barriers inhibited their full participation.

Black Political Parties

All the inhibiting forces mentioned gave birth to the black parties. Leslie McLemore concluded that black third parties developed from racial political discrimination; blacks had no political alternatives except to form their own party.[44] The parties also benefited from the focus of black leadership and determination on specific locales. Alabama, Mississippi, and South Carolina have seen a rash of these new black political vehicles, but Louisiana, Florida, and Virginia did not because these states did not receive the "summer voter drives" and intense organizing efforts of several major black civil rights organizations.

The SES index of the supporters of these parties is worth noting. The demographic characteristics of black party supporters in Alabama and South Carolina reveal that they fall below the poverty line. The median black family income in the five selected Alabama was below the poverty line. "The median black family income in the five selected Alabama counties was $1,987.00, while that in the nine South Carolina counties is $1,581.00. The median schooling for the black population in Alabama was below the seventh grade at 6.4; the median for South Carolina was 5.3"[45] Yet in those five Alabama counties a black political party has captured all offices, and in South Carolina the black party's candidate had turned out 11 percent of the voters.

"Moreover, while the socioeconomic indicators give a picture of a very depressed area, which would not be conductive to high political awareness, this does not hold true for either of the black parties."[46] In addition, the existence of a high illiteracy rate among blacks apparently has not presented a major obstacle for a black party's communication of ideas and programs to the electorate. In this case, the SES indicators cannot explain black party behavior. Blacks in the low SES category support not only black parties and Democrats, but also Republicans and a variety of other third parties.

The potential level of black support for a third party can be seen in one case in Alabama. In 1968, black Democrats in Alabama organized their own party, the National Democratic Party of Alabama (NDPA), offering several black candidates for Congress in four elections prior to 1976. The mean votes cast in four elections was 6,582. The NDPA congressional candidates received a mean of 7.6 percent. This suggests that the voters were dealing with the promises and potential of these particular candidates, and not some abstract national image. In a state where black voters have had so much difficulty in exercising the ballot, this sustained turnout for candidates with small hope for winning, rather than for one of the "lesser of two evils," indicates that problems loom for images of both national and local candidates in the mainstream parties.

Black support for third parties like this one is not a new phenomenon. Historical aggregate data reveal that this type of support, though limited, has been consistent in black political history (see Table 6.10).

Willie Yancey conducted a survey of 136 young black adults in Savannah, an urban area, in 1974, and discovered that among Democrats, Republicans, and Independents, the mean level of support for a black political party was more than 83 percent.[47] No black party has emerged in Savannah, but the state of Georgia did see a Black Statewide Voting League run a black candidate for governor in 1970.[48] This expressed level of support for a black political party suggests that blacks still face problems when they try to enter the regular party organizations.

All the facts suggest that the behavior of black party supporters in the black community is shaped not only by racial discrimination in

TABLE 6.10. Black Voting for Black Political Parties and Black Independent Candidates: 1920-1956

Candidate	State	Party	Office	Year	Votes
J. H. Blount	Arkansas	B=T*	Gov.	1920	15,627
H. Capers	Texas	B=T	Gov.	1920	26,091
Unknown	Florida	B=T	Gov.	1920	2,654
John Mitchell	Virginia	B=T	Gov.	1921	5,036
J. A. Tolbert	South Carolina	B=T	Gov.	1938	283
Kermit Parker	Louisiana	Ind.	Gov.	1952	6,000
Unknown	Florida	B=T	Senator	1920	37,065
J. R. Pollard	Virginia	B=T	Senator	1920	17,576
W. R. O'Neal	Florida	B=T	Senator	1926	6,133
J. A. Tolbert	South Carolina	B=T	Senator	1936	961
Oscelo McKaine	South Carolina	SPDP	Senator	1944	3,214
Electors	Mississippi	B=T	President	1928	524
Electors	Mississippi	B=T	President	1932	1,970
Electors	Mississippi	B=T	President	1936	2,760
Electors	Mississippi	B=T	President	1940	2,814
Electors	Mississippi	B=T	President	1944	3,728
Electors	Mississippi	B=T	President	1948	2,595
Electors	Mississippi	B=T	President	1952	2,966
Electors	Mississippi	B=T	President	1956	4,311

*B=T = Black and Tan Republicans.

SOURCE: F. Glen Abney—*Mississippi Election Statistics, 1900-1967* (Mississippi: Bureau of Government Research, 1968), p. 2; and Hanes Walton, Jr., *Black Republicans*, p. 178.
SPDP = South Carolina Progressive Democratic Party.

the regular political organization but by the various areas of support. Votes for black parties and candidates come from black majoritarian areas, where black inhabitants have low socioeconomic levels. These findings are in direct conflict with the behavioralists' findings.

Black Campaigns

Campaigns are important factors in shaping black party behavior. But Matthews and Prothro suggested the opposite for southern blacks. Northern blacks have been found to be more active and nearly comparable with whites; a recent study rates black campaign activity on a par with, or higher than, whites.

Once again, political structure is crucial. Black political candidates, North and South, have had to run their own campaigns without significant white help. Between 1900 and 1964, most black political candidates ran from predominantly black districts and had to depend upon black volunteers and black support. In the South, the realities were harsher. Here, social conditions and racial beliefs forced blacks to segregate all campaigns.

When blacks supported white candidates, they were segregated from other campaign lieutenants and placed in charge of drumming up black votes. The supporters they garnered also had to work in segregated circles. Northern cities were sometimes little better than southern ones. The urge to elect the "lesser of the two evils" dominated black political editorials, church rallies, and civic associations; it apparently was the motivation behind blacks' acquiescence to the unfair structure.

With the rise of new black politics, the increasing number of black candidates has intensified black participation in campaigning. Most black candidates are still running from black districts and must depend upon black support to survive. The situation is true for both North and South.

However, outside of just campaign participation, most behavioralists have looked only superficially at black campaigning, not bothering to inquire into the role of blacks in the development of campaign platforms and speeches. Yet the reminiscences of black political candidates provide a fairly abundant literature.[49]

The literature reveals that black political candidates shape their platforms and promises in accordance with systemic forces. Black Lieutenant Governor Mervyn Dymally expressed it as follows: "Few blacks," he writes, "represent any economic special interest group such as the oil interest, insurance, or the highway monopoly. The black elected official represents *people*, most poor, minority and discriminated against. His interests are centered on *human* values, not economic interest."[50] Black political activist Fannie Lou Hamer tells us: "As the black politician returns to the scene of politics from years of deprivation he must restore the democratic principles of shared local control and responsiveness to human needs.... It seems to me that the salvation of this nation rests...in the hands of the black striving politician attempting to save his people...."[51]

Black politicians and political activists, and the demographic data from most black electoral districts,[52] indicate that no black political hopeful can ignore the bad housing, low salaries, high unemployment, and staggering human and social needs in their platform promises and campaign speeches and hope to be elected.

Meaningful campaigns and platforms directed to the black community must be attuned to the structural conditions in that community and its environment. Many black politicians have developed techniques for seeing those needs and using them to shape their platforms and campaigns. Bobby L. Hill, former black State Representative and Vice Chairman of Georgia's Black Legislative Caucus was drafted by the local NAACP to run from a predominantly black district. He first scientifically surveyed his district with a questionnaire to determine what his constituents wanted before he drafted his campaign platform and speeches and planned his rallies. Atlanta attorney Marvin Arrington, a black alderman, says he drafted his platform on the basis of experience. "I grew up in the neighborhood, lived there all my life and I knew what the people wanted." A black school board member in Beaufort, South Carolina, Mrs. Freda Mitchell, says, "The black community leaders came to me and asked me to run" and they simply wanted me to "speak out for blacks on the white school board." Most black candidates make an effort to tap "the mind and mood of their black constituents."[53]

Other factors shaping black campaign behavior include political machines, public relations agencies, and the organizational devices of black parties. One such device, often used, is to bring in from the outside well-known black political and civil rights celebrities. This technique is not always successful.

Black Political Money

In the early works on political money, scholars didn't bother to analyze black financial contributions to political parties and candidates.[54] And in the recent explosion of books on money and political campaigns the same trend continues. Black political money, like blacks, is invisible, at least in the academic and popular literature. Yet black political money, despite its small amounts, fills coffers and keep campaigns on the road to victory.

Money for black politics has always been in short supply. Money for basic needs in the black community has been very limited indeed, leaving little for political contributions. Most black political aspirants have to raise money outside their political locality.

When Mayor Andrew Young first ran for the fifth congressional seat in Atlanta, Georgia, he held fund-raising rallies in California, New York, and several other states. In 1976, Howard Lee, the black mayor of Chapel Hill, North Carolina, who was running for lieutenant governor in the primaries and run-off elections, solicited campaign contributions in his wife's hometown, Savannah, Georgia.[55] The lack of economic resources has forced other measures besides these in black political campaigns. Moreover, some blacks worry if raising money outside the black community will not burden black officials with additional constituencies they will have to serve. When outside sources are not tapped, campaigns must do without massive publicity, huge printings of posters, and comprehensive media coverage. Yet many black candidates win with poverty campaign budgets. Again, the socioeconomic explicans are clearly deficient.

In Table 6.11, the money that blacks for Congress spent in the general election campaign can be seen over five elections, from 1974 to 1982. The black incumbent Democrats' total expenditures have moved in this time period from less than a half-million dollars to more than 2.6 million, with the mean rising from $38,000 to nearly $150,000 dollars.

TABLE 6.11. The Campaign Expenditures by Blacks for the House of Representatives: 1974-1982

	1974	1976	1978	1980	1982
Incumbents[1]					
Total	$422,421	$655,739	$1,454,115	$2,152,674	$2,626,380
Expenditures	(N=11)*	(N=14)	(N=16)	(N=17)	(N=18)
Mean per					
Incumbent	38,481	46,838	90,882	126,627	145,910
Challengers					
Total	$188,560	$159,325	$ 134,861	$ 119,457	$ 238,470
Expenditures	(N=10)	(N=13)	(N=11)	(N=15)	(N=17)
Mean per					
Challenger	18,856	12,255	12,260	7,963	14,027

[1]The term incumbent here refers to not only those in office but also those who won vacated as well as newly created seats.

*N = number of individuals and this varies either because of missing data, no opposition or failure to report.

SOURCE: *The Almanac of American Politics: 1978, 1980, 1982, 1984.*

However the story for the Republican challengers is much different. Starting in the Watergate era, their expenditures dropped significantly each year until the Republican revival in 1982 with Ronald

Reagan. And this is likewise true of mean amount spent by each candidate.

The holistic picture presented by the table masks some different individual realities. For instance, in 1974, Congressman Charles Diggs only spent $400 to win his seat, while his opponent lost with $194 as his expenditures. This is the lowest recorded amount ever spent by a black congressperson when opposed to win reelection. On the other hand, the largest amount recorded in the data sources spent by a black congressperson was $617,007—spent by Congressman Dymally in 1980, the first year he ran for his seat.

In terms of Republican challengers, in 1982, of the eighteen black congresspersons who faced opposition, eleven challengers spent no money at all. And in this entire five-year period, Republican challengers have only outspent their Democratic opponents on three occasions. It occurred twice in 1974, when Congresspersons Collins and Nix were outspent (both won) and in 1978 when Congressman Diggs was outspent and he won. Thus, to date, no black Congressperson has lost or been unseated because of money.

The second reality about black political money, at least in Congressional elections, is revealed in Figures 6.4 and 6.5. In the first graph, mean black expenditures are compared with mean white expenditures. On the whole, black Democratic incumbents have much less money to spend than do white candidates. And in the second graph, the data confirm that Republican challengers have a great deal less money to spend than their Black Democrat counterparts. Part of the reason lies in the poverty-stricken nature of the black community. The poor economic conditions in the black community limit the ability of black candidates to raise money there.

The situation gets even worse when one moves to the national level. Of Jesse Jackson's presidential fund raising efforts, a reporter notes: "Personally conducting his fund-raising, an unorthodox technique for a presidential candidate has become practically a daily feature of Jackson's campaign schedule." She continues:

> Where other candidates hold cocktail parties and small,
> high-priced dinners to raise money—with surrogates actually
> putting the touch on people—Jackson performs the ritual
> himself—in black Baptist Churches, gospel conventions,
> school auditoriums—starting with a handful of $1,000
> checks and ending with a foil-covered bucket, wastebasket,
> hat or church collection plates full of dollars and coins.

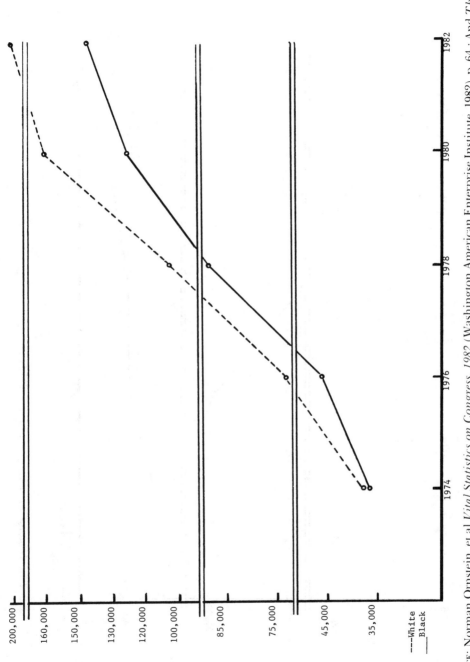

Fig. 6.4 A Comparison of the Expenditures Made by Black and White Democrates in Their Congressional Races, 1974-1982

Source: Norman Ornstein, et al *Vital Statistics on Congress, 1982* (Washington American Enterprise Institute, 1982), p. 64.; And *The Almanac of American Politics, 1974-82.*

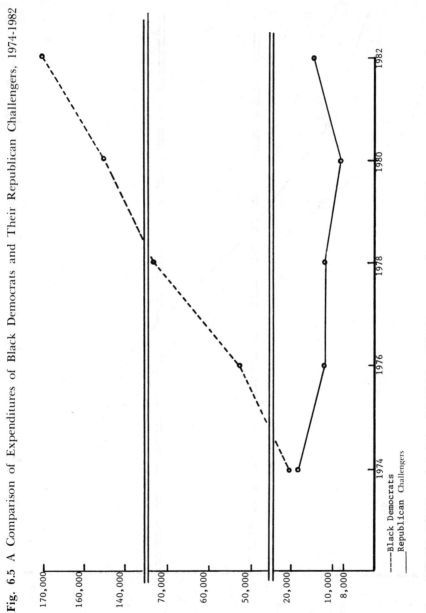

Fig. 6.5 A Comparison of Expenditures of Black Democrats and Their Republican Challengers, 1974-1982

------Black Democrats

———Republican Challengers

SOURCE: *The Almanac of American Politics: 1974-82*

At the halfway point, the campaign had raised "about $2 million, about one-third from collections taken after speeches or rallies...another third comes from fund-raisers...(and) a smaller amount is raised by direct-mail solicitaiton." Thus, Jackson: "operates in hand-to-mouth fashion, spending what he gets as soon as it is received."[56] And because of this his campaign didn't buy any TV or newsprint political ads, yet the word got out.

Attorney Martin who watched the local Jackson campaign in Chatham County, GA concurs on the money situation. "Most of the money raised locally was sent to the national headquarters to help with Jackson's transportation expenses in getting from one state to the next. "Black People," Martin notes, "didn't raise a lot of money and how could they with such techniques as house parties, oyster roast and dinners where they charged three dollars to get in."[57] Martin is right, black political money is always, whether in national, congressional, state or local races, in short supply and this is due to the limited economic resources in the community.

Black Convention Behavior

The literature on black convention behavior is nearly nonexistent.[58] As in other facets of black political life, black activists have struggled with structural and legal obstacles in their attempt to participate in national, state, and local conventions.

In their review of recent Democratic party developments, Lucius Barker and Jesse J. McCorry clearly show how such obstacles persist: "Formulas for selection of delegates to national conventions are determined by the national party committees, which act under the authority of their previous conventions. Accordingly, the Democratic National Committee, acting on the recommendations of the Mc-Govern-Fraser Commission, announced two major reforms for selection of delegates to the 1972 convention."[59] One of these reforms, which required black representation in each state delegation to be in "reasonable relationship to their presence" in the population of each state, permitted black representation at the National Democratic Convention in 1972 to reach its highest *ever* (Figure 6.6). "However, after the 1972 elections, party regulars charged that it was this very quota system...that led to the disastrous defeat of the McGovern led Democratic ticket. They could recall vividly and with rancor how 'upstart insurgents' such as Alderman William Singer of Chicago and the Rev. Jesse Jackson had successfully ousted the 'veteran-loyal-party-regular,' Mayor Richard Daley," even from the floor of the convention.[60] Barker and McCorry show that the Democratic Party "in its first mid-term conference to consider recommendations for a new party charter...shied away from the quota provisions of the 1972 convention. Rather, the 1974 Kansas City Mini-Convention, as it was known, called for the adoption and implementation of 'affirmative action programs' in delegate selection and party organization at all levels.'"[61] This new procedure caused the number of black convention delegates to drop by about 15 percent in 1976.[62] At the Republican Convention that same year, black convention delegated dropped from the 4.2-percent level of 1972 to 3 percent. The number of black delegates, to the Republican convention however, increased (see Figure 6.6). Moreover, the black delegates to the 1976 Republican convention split not only over whom to support, President Ford or Governor Reagan, but also over whether the party could be forced to put into the party's platform better recognition of the needs of the black community.

Black Democrats, meanwhile, formed the Caucus of Black Democrats, held a convention in Charlotte, North Carolina on April 30-May 1, adopted several key issues vital to the black community, and then invited several Democratic presidential contenders to state if they could support their demands. Four candidates, Governor Jerry Brown, Governor Jimmy Carter, Senator Frank Church, and Representative Morris Udall, indicated they would. The issuance of these positions also guided the twenty blacks who sat on the full platform committee and the three who worked on the drafting subcommittee. They saw to it that black needs would be reflected in the Democratic platform in 1976[63] Yet these efforts, while quite laudable and a sharp break with the past, made little impact in terms of public policy for the black community. Therefore in 1980, the Caucus of Black Democrats held a similar convention in Richmond, Virginia. Again several presidential contenders were invited, as well as the Democratic president Jimmy Carter. President Carter and several other candidates refused to come. However, beyond citing their dissatisfaction, the Caucus did little other than promise some vague punitive action, Thus, the 1980 effort ended much like the 1976 effort, having little policy impact. But it did set the stage and the need for more dramatic efforts in 1984 and beyond. Hence, new black political convention strategies and innovations had to be born.

In both parties, systemic forces had to be overcome for full black political participation. Surely these barriers have shaped black political behavior. C. Vernon Gray, in his comprehensive analysis of black convention politics, has shown that rules and racial discrimination barred northern blacks from Republican conventions until 1916

Figure 6.6

Number of Black Delegates to Democratic and Republican National Conventions:1868–1980

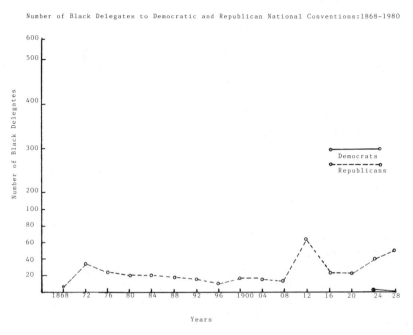

Figure 6.6   Part II

Number of Black Delegates to Democratic and Republican National Conventions:1868–1980

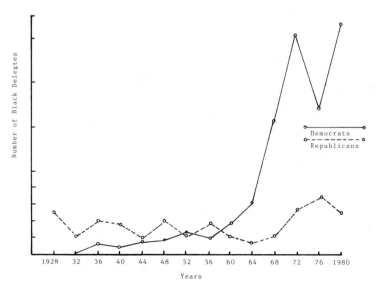

Source: Hanes Walton, Jr. & C. Vernon Gray, "Black Politics at National Republican and Democratic Conventions:1868–1972," <u>Phylon</u> (September,1975),pp.269–78. Data for 1976 and 1980 supplied by authors.

and northern and southern blacks from Democratic conventions until 1936.[64] It should be noted that blacks attended many conventions even when they were not delegates, to see if they could affect the party platform and prioities. Usually they were dismissed.

Jesse Jackson's bid for the 1984 democratic party's nomination created the potential and possibility for a new black political convention strategy: called the balance-of-power strategy, i.e., when two Democratic contenders arrive at the convention with nearly an equal number of delegates, the black candidate can use his delegates to make one candidate the nominee. And that strategy was not completely effective, thus, Jackson's candidacy makes possible a second strategy, the newly mobolized and energized third-party effort.[65] The third strategy is that beyond 1984, if the Democrats do not adopt policies that affect the community, then the long-time alignment of blacks with the party may slowly start unraveling with significant consequences for the years ahead.[66]

Therefore, added to the old strategies of trying (1) to get delegates, (2) increasing the number of delegates, and (3) influencing the presidential contenders, are the three new ones borne of the Jackson candidacy. But these are not all. In addition to the convention strategies, Jackson attacked the rules of the democratic primaries —the 20 percent threshold rule which requires that a candidate get 20 percent of the vote in each congressional district to get one delegate. Even the Chairman of the Democratic Party, Charles T. Manatt, agreed at the midpoint of the primary season that the rule discriminates. "Manatt agreed yesterday that the system has deprived Jackson of delegates and said he will urge state party leaders to include additional people (as delegates) representing the Jackson campagin ...because of the way the system has worked."[67] However, prior to the beginning of the primary season, Manatt refused to consider the request that the rules be changed because they were discriminatory.[68] At midpoint Jackson had "won 17.8 percent of the popular vote in primaries and caucuses (but) has won only 7 percent of the delegates ...."[69] However, two black political scientists have argued that this concern with the rules is not worth the trouble. "Jackson's challenge of the Democratic Party delegate selection rules is a cause of concern because, the merits of the challenge notwithstanding, it runs the risk of deflecting media and public attention away from the substantive issues that constitute the central focus of the campaign.[70] And for them, this central focus is the continuation of the liberal agenda and progressive heritage of the party. But whether Jackson can achieve that or not, new forces were underway to limit his impact in every particular facet of the process.[71]

In sum, blacks have developed numerous strategies and tactics to impact national convention politics and a new group of techniques were borne during the 1984 democratic presidiential primaries. But with each new tactic and achievement comes new structures, rules and policies to delimit or circumscribe the political power of blacks.

The Second Look

The latest comprehensive survey study of American voting behavior was issued in 1976; it was based on data from 1952 to 1972 and revealed that "blacks are perhaps the most pro-Democratic (large) minority in the country."[72] Blacks were also the most liberal group on all issues. In addition, the study showed that all other groups in society were dropping their party partisanship and shifting to personal "issue" positions as guides to political action and behavior.

All of our data suggest that the behavioralist notions about black party behavior are not quite accurate. To be sure, there is a marked Democratic tendency among blacks, but this tendency is fueled by factors behavioralists ignore: black candidates, black needs, and the black social environment, to say nothing of a wide variety of parallel black political Democratic structures and organizations as well as the closed structure and the inertia of the Republican Party.

Barker and McCorry conclude: "Unlike other citizens who had recourse to lower levels of the political system, that is, the parties at the local or state levels, black exclusion from participation at these intermediate levels forced them to turn to "the national one."[73] But few surveys look beyond or use aggregate data, and so do not take into account black floaters, switchers, and independents plus the black supporters of third parties, the Republican party, and new black parties. This kind of support averages at least one-third in some locations, sometimes even winning.

Secondly, the specific nature of political organizations in some localities shapes local behavioral patterns.[74] Closed structures, semi-closed structures, machine-operated and manipulated structures, and national-party issue positions help determine black involvement.

Some of these force black political participation in third and black parties.

Individual variables and factors are just not enough to explain black party behavior at all levels and in different party organizations, at conventions, or in raising money for political campaigns.

Chapter 7

Black Legislative Behavior

In the next few chapters an analysis is made of those blacks who are elected or appointed officials, and of the forces that the behavioralists point to as shaping legislative, judicial, and administrative behavior. Again the question is whether scholars have relied too heavily on sociopsychological explanations and too little on systemic and structural forces.

The focus in this chapter is on black legislative behavior on the congressional, state, and local levels. Although the recent upsurges in black legislators have been studied, little systematic and comprehensive research has been done specifically on black legislators and their political activities. To be sure, the black legislative caucuses, especially the Congressional Black Caucus, have come under limited journalistic and scholarly examination, but little work of any real substance had focused exclusively on black legislative behavior in terms of the influence of systemic variables.[1]

The Literature

Political behavioralists working on legislative institutions and processes have developed many diverse approaches. Meller, summarizing the literature up the 1961, wrote, "Studies are getting too scattered and lack corroboration over time; and conflicting findings have not served as stimuli for further clarifying research."[2] After 1961, Eulau and Hinckley discerned a similar diversity but also "an increasing tendency toward a more concise and coherent conceptual framework."[3] However, none saw a general theory about legislative behavior flowing from all this work.

Wahlke noted that the inquiries up through 1961 tended to fall into two categories: the "studies of the character and recruitment of representatives;" and studies of "motivation and behavior of individual representative bodies."[4] Eulau and Hinckley found Wahlke's categories to be too narrow in light of new research. Wahlke's typology was focused on individual legislative behavior, they argued, and failed to include "institutional processes, substructures and policy outcomes."[5] Eulau and Hinckley developed a new typology to improve Wahlke's. Their conceptual schema stressed the fact that "research on legislatures split fairly early along the lines of two models," the "inside" model and the "outside" model.[6]

> The 'inside model,' concerns legislative behavior and actions as revealed in the growth of formal and informal substructures, groups, authority relations, influence patterns and so on, within the legislature. The 'outside model' concerns the legislature and the legislator's activities as products of forces or influences beyond the institutional boundaries of the legislature...the electoral constituencies, district parties, pressure groups, executive agencies, and those socio-economic and predispositional attributes that legislators input form the 'outside.'[7]

They noted, however, that studies done in both categories tended to explain legislative behavior in terms of inside or outside forces. In fact, the legislator is pictured "as the ploy of an assortment of forces either in his constituency and personality makeup or inside the legislative halls and processes." But in neither model, outside or inside, noted Eulau and Hinkley, was there any direct proof to substantiate this "ploy" theory of legislative behavior. Linkage between inside and outside forces, they stressed, was in almost all instances a matter of implication rather than valid evidence, no matter how ingenious the methodology or design.[8] In most instances, those using the inside model rarely coordinated their efforts with those employing the outside-model approach. Hence, two literatures tended to coexist without any significant bridging efforts between them.

They lauded as innovative and theoretically advanced the work by Wahlke, et al., entitled *The Legislative System: Explorations in Legislative Behavior,* which attempted to analyze legislative behavior in terms of a legislative system, i.e., a system model which would encompass both inside and outside forces as well as public policy outputs. But they hastened to note that the Wahlke study was in conclusive on what it found.[9] In short, the ploy theory of legislative behavior tended to predominate.

In fact, a recent study on legislative behavior using the Wahlke system concluded that what a legislator "seeks to accomplish when he reaches Washington will be influenced by his previous experiences; the values acquired from his family, school, or church, and the lesson learned in various forms of employment. . . ."[10] Legislative behavior, in short, is an outgrowth of the lawmaker's functional beliefs and values acquired during the early years of his personality maturation. Individual legislative actions and voting arise and flow from social-background characteristics and attributes. Here is a classic restatement of the behavioralist notion that all political behavior, whether in the electoral process, the political entities, or the decision-making institutions, is a function of sociopsychological variables. What does this ploy theory of legislative behavior tell us about black legislators?

Not much behavioral research has been devoted exclusively to black legislators. Much of what exists deals with or flows from the historical, descriptive, and institutional perspective.[11] The leading behavioral piece that stresses the ploy theory is the well-known article by James Q. Wilson, "Two Negro Politicians: An Interpretation."[12] In this essay Wilson demonstrates the impact of Powell's and Dawson's personal styles on their respective electoral organizations. He endeavors to show how their own organizations determined their legislative behavior. In short, both Dawson and Powell were ploys of their respective political or electoral machines. To some supporters of Powell, this conclusion came as a surprise, for many saw him as being his own man, not a tool of his legislative districts.[13]

Besides Wilson's study, little was written about black legislators until the recent upsurge in their numbers. Most of the contemporary research on black legislators tended to be journalistic, aimed at describing obstacles and problems.[14] Many focus on black female legislators. However, a few tried to be comprehensive and systematic in a chronological way. *America's Black Congressmen* is one example. It begins with the first black congressional legislator and proceeds one by one in a biographical manner to the latest one elected.[15] In the fall of 1971, Alvin D. Sokolow published an article on the patterns of bill sponsorship by the black legislators in California, breaking the biographical pattern.[16] Maurice Woodard attempted to evaluate formally the legislative record of the late Representative Adam Clayton Powell.[17] Jewel Prestage made a statistical analytical study of black women state legislators.[18] And black legislators in Illinois, headed up by State Senator Richard H. Newhouse, set up a black legislative clearinghouse which would not only hold conferences and public hearings and record bill sponsorship patterns of black legislators in the state of Illinois but also would make their findings available and grant assistance to other black elected officials.[19] Yet even with innovative approaches to black legislative activities, few follow-up studies and little synthesizing of the trends have been done, and much remains to be done.

However, Freddie Colston's work stands out not only as a major pioneering effort, but as the most comprehensive and systematic study yet done.[20] Colston analyzed the black legislators in the Ohio House of Representatives.[21] Although he used all of the methods favored in behavioralism such as interviewing, questionnaires, direct observation, and content analysis, Colston did not conclude that the black legislators were ploys of their constituencies. His approach focused on the black legislators as an informal group in the house and noted the role that race played in affecting their behavior.[22] Although he looked at their background characteristics, he developed an index to measure their influence as an informal group in the state house.[23] He concluded that an "examination of the five indices in this study confirms the black legislators' influence in the House,"[24] a finding true both individually and for the whole group. Colston's study is well structured and is most likely to become the model for other state studies of black legislative behavior.

However, although these works are quite informative on the factors affecting black legislative behavior and the role of race in influencing black legislative activity, little has been done on the role of structure, most notably, reapportionment.

Reapportionment

The role of reapportionment in the rise of black legislators is crucial. Colston found that four factors typified black legislators in the Ohio

House of Representatives: racial identity, predominantly black constituency, urban residence, and party loyalty.[25] A key variable here is the urban residence. In the South, it is typically both urban and rural.

The focus upon behavior alone diverts attention away from the impact the political sturcutre had in making the election of black legislators possible: the roots of black legislative representation centers on the creation of political districts with black majorities. Black legislators, with a few exceptions, have always emerged from predominantly black electoral districts.

In Georgia, the election of black state legislators is a direct result of the destruction of the old Georgia country unit system, a change which gave more representation to the urban areas. [26] The majority of the black legislators in the state are from urban areas. In South Carolina, the recent black victory in a reapportionment suit netted more than twenty possible seats; in Mississippi, Alabama, Florida, Tennessee, and Arkansas, the situation is similar. Likewise, in northern states, the creation of black political districts gives rise to black legislators. In short, a change in the political structure meant a change in black legislative representation. Now, inside the state houses, the structure of race relations is significant indeed. Colston writes: "The state legislature is a microcosm of the larger society where race relations are indeed problematic."[27]

The Social Backgrounds of Black Legislators

To provide insight into the varied backgrounds of black legislators, an analysis will be made of those in Congress; those in Georgia, Illinois, Missouri and Ohio; those black alderpersons in Athens, Atlanta, Savannah and Thunderbolt, Georgia (Alderpersons are the major policymakers on the local level); and a black county councilperson (commissioner) in Columbia, Maryland. this will provide a four-level portrait of black legislators, which should suggest possible general patterns and trends in the social background of black lawmakers.

Table 7.1 reveals the major demographic characteristics of black congresspersons over a full decade. By looking at 1972 and 1982, the beginning and ending years of the decade, one can see the changes and continuities during this time frame. Basically, there has been a substantial increase in the total number of representatives, a rise from 15 to 21, or an average increase of one congressperson every election year and this increase in the total number has resulted in an increase in their percentage in the House, from 3.6 percent to nearly five percent in 1983. In 1972, there were ten states and the District of Columbia with black congresspersons and California sent the largest number—three. By 1983, there were still ten states (Georgia had dropped out and Tennessee had joined and the District of Columbia, but the largest number came from both California and New York, which had four representatives each. The only other states to increase their numbers were Illinois and Missouri, by one each.

In 1972, there were sixteen representatives, but in 1983, only eight of those sixteen remained. Four had retired, two died, one was defeated and one resigned. Between 1972 and 1982 some nine new members had joined the original eight and four more were newly elected in the fall of 1982.

In terms of the black population in each district, the most striking feature of Table 7.1 is that in 1972 only 23 percent of the black representatives came from nonblack districts. By 1983, that had risen to 43 percent. Put differently, over three-fourths of the black representatives in 1972 came from predominately black districts, while in 1983 just over 57 percent came from these districts. This indicates that during the recent congressional reapportionment, fewer overwhelming black districts were drawn and that some black congressional candidates have mastered the technique of effectively appealing to the white and black electorates jointly. The mean black population in 1972 was 60 percent, and in 1982, 58 percent.

This decade also shows a sharp rise in the number of black men elected to Congress and a small decline in the number of black women elected and running for Congress. Along with these gender changes came a change in the age category. Essentially, the group with some eight returning representatives grew older. In 1972 the majority of black representatives fell into the 35-44 age group. Ten years later they fell into the 45-54 category. The mean age in 1972 was 47, in 1982, 51. The oldest representative in 1972 was Robert Nix (D.—Pa.) at 67 and the youngest was Barbara Jordan (D.-Tex.) at 36. By 1982, the oldest representative was Augustus Hawkins (D.-Calif.) at 75 and the youngest was Alan West (D.-Kan.) at 30.

In the decade, the largest number of representatives had either college or graduate and professional-school training, and new members had the same background. The religious background also remained unchanged, the majority being of a protestant orientation. This reality did not hold for the professions. In ten years, the number

TABLE 7.1. The Demographic Characteristics of Black Congressmen: 1972 and 1982

Demographic Character-istics	*1972*		*1982*	
	Number	*%*	*Number*	*%*
Total Number	16	3.6	21	4.8
Region				
Northeast	5	31.3	7	33.3
Midwest	6	37.5	8	38.1
South	2	12.5	2	9.5
Far West	3	18.8	4	19.1
District % Black				
21 - 50%	3	18.8	9	42.9
51 - 60%	5	31.3	2	9.5
61 - 70%	4	25.0	3	14.3
71 - 80%	3	18.8	5	23.8
81 - 90%	1	6.3	1	4.8
91 - 100%			1	4.8
Sex				
Male	13	81.2	19	90.5
Female	3	18.8	2	9.5
Age				
25-34	0		1	4.8
35-44	8	50	4	19.1
45-54	5	31.3	9	42.9
55-64	1	6.3	5	23.8
65-94	2	12.5	2	9.5
Educa-tion				
High School	1	6.3		
College	2	12.5	6	28.3
Graduates & Professional	12	75.0	13	66.7
Others	1	6.3	1	4.8
Religion				
Catholic	3	18.8	3	14.3
Protestant	13	81.3	18	85.7
Occupation				
Attorney	6	37.5	6	28.3
Businessman	1	6.3	2	9.5
Minister	2	12.5	2	9.5
Educator	4	25.0	4	19.1
Other	3	18.8	7	33.3

SOURCE: *The Alamanac of American Politics: 1974-82.*

of attorneys declined below their one-third position and a wide variety of other occupations that ranged from accountants, newspaper publishers, judges, social workers, pharmacists and morticians came to dominate. Surprisingly, the number of ministers in the group remained the same despite the powerful role that the black church plays in black politics. Moreover, in terms of political experience, fourteen (or two-thirds) have either served on the city council or in the state legislatures or on the bench or as appointed officials. One, Dymally, had been Lt. Governor of California for at least one term. Only seven (or one-third) had had no political experience at all and nearly the majority (ten) had served in the state legislatures, either the upper or lower houses.

Recaptulating, black congressional representatives over the decade 1972-1982 gradually shifted from being male lawyers who were young, college-educated protestants to being from a variety of occupations who are male, middle aged, college and professionally trained protestants.[28] Thus the major change in the decade came in terms of absolute numbers, geographical locations, age and occupations of the representatives, and the percentage of the black populations in the districts. The number of blacks in black congressional districts declined significantly.

Shifting from the national level to the state level, Table 7.2 reveals the demographic characteristics of black state legislators in Georgia, 1972; Illinois, 1971; Ohio, 1971; and Missouri, 1969. In the beginning years it can be seen that the southern state dominates with the largest number but the midwestern states, particularly Illinois, are very close behind. Moreover, Illinois clearly has more blacks in the upper House than Georgia. And in all four states the legislators are from the urban centers. While this is clearly acceptable and proper for the midwestern states, the southern state has a very large rural black population that is not represented by black legislators. Definitely black representation in the southern state is not balanced between the black urban and rural sectors of the state.

In terms of sex, males dominate, in terms of age, the southern state legislators are much younger than the rest. Here the entrance into the political system differed significantly for the regions, occurring in the South only in the late sixties and early seventies. However, the educational levels tended to be the same nearly across the board. The data on religion was not collected systematically in each study so no solid picture emerges. But in terms of occupations, attorneys, businessmen, ministers, and educators tended to dominate.

These were the traditional occupational areas open to blacks and they tended to stand out in the intial years of analysis and study.

Since the data in Table 7.2 were adapted primarily from dissertations[29] (the lone exception being Georgia), and because these dissertations focused on only one legislative term, data are not yet available for longitudinal analysis. But when the 1982-3 data is juxtaposed against the early data, some changes and continuities can be seen. Table 7.3 quickly reveals that Georgia had the largest growth of black state legislators in the decade. There was a 50 percent increase in the number in the state senate and 30 percent increase in the state

TABLE 7.2. The Demographic Characteristics of Black State Legislators in Georgia, Illinois, Ohio and Missouri

Demographic Characteristics	Georgia House	Georgia Senate	Illinois House	Illinois Senate	Ohio House	Ohio Senate	Missouri House	Missouri Senate
Total Number	14	2	14	5	10	2	13	0
Sex								
Male	14	2	13	5	12		12	
Female	2		1		0		1	
Age								
25-34	6						3	
35-44	1	1	5		4		2	
45-54	4	1	6		3		7	
55-64			3		3		1	
65-70	3		5					
Education								
Grade School	1							
High School	4		7		2		3	
College or more	9	2	12				7	
Unknown							3	
Religion								
Catholic	1							
Protestant	12	2						
Unknown	1		19		12		13	
Occupation								
Attorney	5	2					1	
Businessman	1		10		4		5	
Minister	1		1		1			
Educator	1				3		1	
Politician	1						1	
Consultant	1							
Other	4				2		5	
Unknown			8			2		

TABLE 7.3. Selected Black State Legislators: Changes and Continuities in Social Background

State and Social Background	Years: 1969-1972	Year: 1982	Changes
Georgia	*1972*		
Total Number	16	25	+9
Senate	2	4	+2
House	14	21	+7
Sex			
Male	14	20	+6
Female	2	5	+3
Illinois	*1972*		
Total Number	19	21	+2
Senate	5	6	+1
House	14	15	+1
Sex			
Male	18	15	-3
Female	1	6	+5
Ohio	*1971*		
Total Number	12	12	0
Senate	2	2	0
House	10	10	
Sex			
Male	12	11	
Female		1	+1
Missouri	*1969*		
Total Number	13	18	+5
Senate		2	+2
House	13	16	+3
Sex			
Male	12	14	+2
Female	1	4	+3

house. Missouri became the next state with the largest increase. It had a clear 100 percent increase in the state senate and a little more than a 20 percent increase in the state house. And both states saw a dramatic increase in the number of black female legislators. The number went from a total of three in 1969 and 1972 to nine in 1982.

But if two states saw dramatic increases, then two states showed only marginal increases or none at all over the same decade. Illinois added only two more members to its black delegation, while Ohio had no growth at all in terms of total numbers. However, even if the growth rate slowed, there was both change and continuity within the total numbers. And in both states the number of women increased.

Illinois added five different female legislators, while Ohio increased its number of females by one. There were other changes.

As the data in Table 7.4 indicate, Ohio, which saw no growth, had eight of its early members remain in office. Both of the state senators were reelected and six of the original ten state house members. Georgia, the state with the greatest increase over the decade, had in the summer of 1982, seven of its original members for a 44 percent retention rate. Although both of the state senators were gone, one state legislator, Julian Bond in a political deal, moved from the state house to the state senate during Carter gubernatorial term. The other six members were continually reelected to the state house.

TABLE 7.4. Rank Ordering of States by State Legislators with Longevity 1969-82

States	Total Members 1969-72	Number Remaining 1982	% Remaining
Ohio	12	8	67
Georgia	16	7	44
Missouri	13	5	38
Illinois	19	5	26

SOURCE: Joint Center for Political Studies; *National Roster of Black Elected Officials* (Washington, D.C., Joint Center for Political Studies, 1982). This list was made by comparing the names in each doctoral dissertation and the Georgia membership roster with the current list given in the National Roster.

In Missouri, only five, or 38 percent, retained their seats over the decade. Like Georgia, both state senators lost their seats, and one state representative, J.S. Banks was able to move from the House to the State Senate. The other four members were continually reelected to the state house. Illinois, however, presents a totally different picture. Only five, or one in four, were able to keep their seats over the decade. The turnover rate in Illinois was the largest of all the states surveyed. Three of the five state senators and only two of the fourteen house members were continually reelected. Many new freshmen legislators continued to join the black delegation in Illinois. One state legislator, however, Harold Washington, was elected to Congress and in 1983 was elected to the Mayor of Chicago to become the first black mayor in the city's 150-year history.

To recapitulate; on the state level, one is apt to find more variation among black legislators. But *even* with this wide variation and some of it due to systemic factors like the *date* that blacks could enter the political arena, each state shows that college-educated individuals dominate; protestantism dominates in the religious categories; and white collar professional and businessmen dominate the occupational areas. Over the decade, there were both inter-and intra-delegation changes. The inter-delegation changes suggest that some states are possibly reaching a maximum point, while other states like Georgia might still be years away from reaching their black legislative potential in terms of absolute numbers. The intra-delegation changes reveal that there was both a rapid turnover rate and generally speaking a retention rate of less than 50 percent. This means that the high turnover rate decreases the chances of blacks receiving chairmanships and gaining institutional power in American state legislatures. Only one state showed significant stability in retaining and continuing in office black representatives. And, finally, upward mobility either did not exist (as in one state) or was limited to only one person in each of three states; two moved to the state senate and one went to Congress and later to a mayorship. Another, Ben Brown of Georgia, got an appointment at the Democratic National Committee because of his electoral work for Jimmy Carter but lost the position with Carter's defeat in 1980.

In analyzing the black alderpersons in four Georgia cities, Table 7.5 demostrates that a clear majority of them are young, colleged-educated protestants who are businessmen, attorneys, and professionals. Although the table does not show it, the group in the early seventies was predominately male. By 1983, the profiles were nearly the same. The group was predominately college-educated males who were attorneys and businessmen. The real differences, as shown in Table 7.6, is in actual number. In Atlanta the group has risen from 9 to 12 and now holds the chairmanship of the council and the majority of seats. In Savannah, despite the fact that the number has increased by one, the council has been enlarged by an annexation scheme so that the percentage of blacks stays below the original high of one-third. In Thunderbolt and Athens, the numbers remained the same but in the former city, the one black alderman is now Vice Mayor due to his longevity on the council.

In terms of continuity; three in Atlanta remain of the nine; none of the two in Savannah; two of the three in Athens; and in Thunderbolt, the single alderman has continued. Thus, one city has had a complete turnover, one has had a two-thirds turnover rate, and one a one-third rate and one a zero rate. Basically, it has been in the two very large urban areas that the greatest turnover rate has occurred.

On the whole, the social backgrounds of black alderpersons on the local level has remained basically the same and quite similar despite the large turnover rates in the large urban centers. Other studies, with few exceptions, suggest similar social backgrounds elsewhere.[30] Mack Jones in a pioneering study in 1969, performed a systematic and comprehensive analysis of local black office holders

TABLE 7.5. The Social Background Profile of Selected Black Alderpersons: 1969

Profiles	Atlanta[a]		Savannah[b]		Athens[c]		Thunderbolt[d]	
Age
25-34	(6)	67%	(1)	50%	(2)	67%		
35-44	(1)	11						
45-54					(1)	33%	(1)	100%
55-64	(1)	11	(1)	50				
65-69								
70	(1)	11						
Education
Grade School								
High School	(2)	22			(1)	33		
College or more	(4)	44	(2)	100	(2)	67	(1)	100
Unknown	(3)	33						
Religion
Catholic								
Protestant								
Baptist					(2)	67		
Methodist			(1)	50	(1)	33		
Episcopal								
Congregational								
Other			(1)	50				
Occupation
Attorney	(1)	11						
Businessman	(4)	44	(2)	100	(1)	33		
Minister								
Educator							(1)	33
Politician	(1)	11						
Consultant	(2)	22			(1)	33	(1)	100
Other	(1)	11			(1)	33	(1)	100
	(N = 9)		(N = 2)		(N = 3)		(N = 1)	

[a]Of all 18 aldermen in Atlanta, 9 were black—50%.

[b]Of all 6 aldermen in Savannah, 2 were black—33%.

[c]Of all 10 aldermen in Athens, 3 were black—30%.

[d]Of all 6 aldermen in Thunderbolt, 1 was black—16.6%.

and discovered that the majority were males; over 72.7 percent had college training or higher; 56 were 49 years of age and younger; and educators, doctors, lawyers, and successful businessmen predomin-

TABLE 7.6. The Social Background Profile of Selected Black Alderpersons: 1983

Profiles	Atlanta[a]	Savannah[b]	Athens[c]	Thunderbolt[d]
Age				
25-34	2			
35-44	6	2	2	
45-54	3	1	1	
55-64	1			1
65-69				
70				
Sex				
Male	10	3	3	1
Female	2			
Education				
Grade School				
High School	2	1	1	
College or more	10	2	2	1
Unknown				
Religion				
Catholic				
Protestant				
Baptist				2
Methodist				
Episcopal				
Congregational				
Other				
Occupation				
Attorney	3	1		
Businessman	1	1	1	
Ministers				
Educators	1	1	1	
Politician				
Consultant	3			
Other	4		1	1
	(N = 12)	(N = 3)	(N = 3)	(N = 1)

[a]Blacks are 66% of the aldermen in Atlanta.

[b]Blacks are 33% of the aldermen in Savannah.

[c]Blacks are 30% of the aldermen in Athens.

[d]Blacks are 17% of the aldermen in Thunderbolt.

ated.[31] Though his data concerned black city councilmen, Jones found it to hold true for county commissioners, school board members, and law enforcement and judicial officers. Thus, earlier findings and current findings are quite similar, and this has continued to be the fact over the last decade.

Therefore, the basic fact that emerges from this survey of social-background characteristics of black legislators on three different levels is that they are surprisingly similar. Some variation must account for the differences and wide behavioral responses amongst black legislators. For instance, if you correlate black bill sponsorship patters with social background features, then all you will find will be individual factors explaining legislative behavior. While these social background characteristics do help illuminate and distinguish these black legislators from one another, these individual characteristics cannot fully explicate bill passage ratios, and the creation of more new black districts through legislative bodies. Thus, if only socieconomic-status factors are all that are put into the behavioral equation, then the parameters are foreclosed and, as is the case in so much of the behavioral literature, only individualistic factors such as roles and role perceptions will evolve as the explanations for black legislative behavior. Other factors, particularly external and systemic ones must be taken into account.

The Electoral Milieu of Black Legislators

One of the major external factors that must be considered in the study of black legislative behavior is the socioeconomic composition and electoral makeup of the constituency, because despite his or her personal characteristics, the services rendered to his constituency are crucial and will eventually result in his or her being retained or removed. In Table 7.7 the data show that the mean vote received in the 1972 base-line year was 77 percent compared with the 1982 fall elections where the mean vote had risen to nearly 81 percent. Overall the percentage of blacks in the congressional districts had also risen, while for some individual districts the number had dropped.

The second group of black congresspersons in their initial election year captured 85 percent of the vote but by the fall of 1982 got only 83 percent of the vote. Surprisingly the number of blacks in the districts of this group was quite similar to the number in the first group. This suggests that the large black composition of the original group was reshaped by population losses and reapportionment during the last congressional reapportionment drive.

The last four recently elected black representatives were able to capture 73 percent of the vote while the mean black population in their districts stood at 37 percent.[32] In fact, the key factor that sets this last group of black representatives off from the first two groups is that only about one-third of their districts are black, whereas nearly two-thirds of the former groups' districts are black. Yet despite this drop

TABLE 7.7. The Population and Electoral Milieu of Black U.S. Congressmen: 1972 and 1982

Congresspersons	First Year Vote Percentage	Black Population	Last Year Vote Percentage	Black Population	Mean Percentage
Original Group	1972		1982		
W. Clay	63%	54	66%	65	65%
J. Conyers	90	70	97	87	94
R. Dellums	56	26	56	24	56
W. Fauntroy	62	71	74	70	68
A. Hawkins	83	54	80	50	82
P. Mitchell	80	74	88	79	84
C. Rangel	98	59	98	54	98
L. Stokes	87	66	86	79	87
Total Mean	77.4	59.3	80.6	63.5	
Later Group	1st Winning Year				
C. Collins	93		87	50	90
G. Crockett	92		89	79	91
J. Dixon	100		81	50	91
M. Dymally	64		72	36	68
H. Ford	50		73	63	62
W. Gray	82		77	75	80
M. Leland	97		85	43	91
G. Savage	88		87	77	88
H. Washington	95		97	91	96
Total Mean	84.5		83.1	62.7	
Recently Elected	Fall 1982				
K. Hall			57	24	
M. Owens			91	54	
E. Towns			83	45	
A. Wheat			59	23	
Total Mean			72.5	36.5	

SOURCE: "Returns for Governor, Senate and House," *Congressional Quarterly Weekly Report* (November 6, 1982) pp. 2818-2824.

in black population, the last elected group are getting nearly three-fourths of the vote. This put them only slightly behind the first two groups which are getting nearly eighty percent of the vote. And currently, the few opponents which black congresspersons face in the general elections find it difficult to gather more than 30 percent of the vote.

On the state level, the picture is quite similar. In Ohio, the mean vote captured was over 89 percent and the majority of black districts ranged from 60 to 90 percent black. Two districts were about half and half and a black senator represented a predominately white district. In Georgia, in the 1972 state election most of the black legislative districts were predominately black, averaging 75 percent and higher. As for the mean vote, the fourteen representatives captured roughly 4,431 votes—and eleven of the districts received 100 percent of the vote cast. Of the remaining three, one got 88 percent, two received 80 and 70 percent. The mean percentage was 96 of the vote. In terms of the two black senators they both got 100 percent of the vote and had a mean vote of 16,508 votes. By the 1982 fall elections, the mean vote was 4,381 and nineteen of the twenty-one legislators got 100 percent of the vote and one got 67 and the other 87 percent. In the senate, two of the four got 100 percent of the vote and the other two received 72 and 84 percent, respectively. The mean vote for the four senators was 12,635 votes. This was a sharp decline from the vote in 1972.

The electoral and population milieu on the state level is similar to the one on the congressional level in terms of being predominately black. On the state level it is even more pronounced and the small data base suggests that as the districts increase in size, the white population tends to rise. However, there is a major difference between the state and congressional levels. Republican and independent opposition, especially in Georgia—a one-party state—is nearly non-existent in the black legislative districts and where it does exist, the electoral power of such candidates is lower than 30 percent of the voting electorate.

The picture changes when one moves to the local level, as seen in Table 7.8. In Atlanta, most of the aldermanic wards are heavily black. Only two wards, One and Eleven have more than 50 percent white registration. Second, only two of the nine blacks are Republicans, but even these two are quite an exception for a predominately southern democratic city that has few Republican elected officials, white or black. In both instances the black Republican candidates significantly outpolled their Democratic contenders. The black Democratic candidate in the Ninth Ward barely held off his Republican opposition. The black Democrats on the average attained a major portion of the votes cast and with one or two exceptions they had a 50-percent voter turnout. However, those blacks who ran at-large—a Democrat, a young articulate black attorney named Marvin Arrington, and one Republican, a middle-aged black realtor—got only a nominal percentage of the vote beyond those registered in their districts. By 1983, this entire reality had changed dramatically. Four alderpersons and the President of the City Council, Marvin Arrington ran at-large and won. The electoral structure of the city had changed and the black population had significantly increased.

In Savannah both black aldermen had to run at-large; they received nearly as many votes as the liberal incumbent mayor. Both men are Democrats and received nearly unanimous support of the black community and its key organization, the local NAACP. By 1983, the city fathers, fearful of a black takeover had annexed a white area to the city and reorganized the political districts. Now there are six districts and two at-large seats. Three of the six districts are overwhelmingly black, and whites won the at-large seats. No blacks ran at-large in this new electoral arrangement.

However, in a much smaller community, where no major black community organization exists, the black alderman had to run as a coalition candidate, the only black man on the ticket. And of the total 740 votes cast out of 800 eleigible voters in the small city, he received only 37 percent of the 92 percent voter turnout. In fact, it appears that his votes were close to the total number of eligible black voters in the city. the other black candidate on the other coalition ticket ran almost as well, which indicates that neither man could have received much white support. This was the situation in 1974. Alderman Merritt was reelected in 1976 with 321 votes, of which nearly 175 were black. In 1982, he got 345 votes.

In Athens, Georgia, two of the black aldermen, Turner and Mack, come from a ward that is evenly split between blacks and whites, but where black registration is higher than the white registration. Since Athens has five wards, with two representatives from each ward, the third black alderman represents a predominantly white district. All of the aldermen are Democrats.

In sum, the electoral makeup of black legislative districts is mixed, with heavy black populations in the national Congressional districts and in the state legislative districts in Georgia. But the makeup of local districts is generally determined by the type of

Table 7.8. The Electoral Milieu of Selected Black Aldermen

District	Alderman	Party	Registration White	Registration Black[1]	Votes	% of Votes	Votes for opposition	% of votes for opposition	% of voter turnout
Atlanta's black population is 54% of the total city population[1]									
1	John H. Calhoun	Rep.	3,933	5,792	2,381	75.5	771	24.5	32.0
3	James Howard	Dem	337	16,452	4,742	57.4	3,521	42.6	49.3
4	James Bond	Dem.	1,276	13,100	4,816	62.6	2,876	37.4	53.5
5	Morris Finley	Dem.	60		1,959	58.2	1,405	41.8	46.9
9	Authur Langford	Dem.	308	14,440	3,464	50.1	3,450	49.9	56.6
10	Ira Jackson	Dem.	381	18,839	6,500	59.7	4,387	40.3	32.2
11	Carl Ware	Dem.	6,035	12,135	3,597	61.5	2,256	38.5	
14	Marvin Arrington	Dem.	1,613	29,525	34,883	100.0	none	none	at-large
17	Q. V. Williamson	Rep.	689	33,279	43,704	61.8	26,932	32.2	at-large
Savannah's black population is 44.5% of the total city population[2]									
At-large	Boles Ford	Dem.	N.A.	N.A.	15,194		8,130		
At-large	Roy Jackson	Dem.	N.A.	N.A.	14,618		8,527		
Thunderbolt's black population is 40% of the total city population[3]									
At-large	John Merritt	Dem.	480	320	280	37.8*	247	33.3	92.5
Athen's black population is 30% of the total city population									
	Ed Turner	Dem.	N.A.						
	Charles Mack	Dem.	N.A.						
	John Taylor	Dem.	N.A.						

[1]Atlanta...1973 election data taken from *Atlanta Constitution* & Director of Aldermanic Staff.

[2]Savannah...1974 election data taken from *Savannah Morning News* and P.U.S.H. Organizer.

[3]Thunderbolt...1974 election data supplied by Alderman.

*740 people voted.

electoral structure present, whether wards, or at-large, or both. In ward areas, the districts tend to be heavily black, and in at-large situations, they tend to be mainly white. In combination systems, the ward is black, but the at-large positions are mainly white again. This generally means small support for black legislators from white voters. Despite the black population in any legislative district on any level, it must be clear that these districts are the creation of political bodies that blacks rarely control and that these districts can be changed, manipulated and rearranged to affect black legislative behavior. For instance, when Savannah didn't have any black districts, the city fathers made a deal with the black community and responsible elements in the white community to *give* blacks the two at-large seats. The word went out quietly to have whites vote for these *chosen* black candidates. When the arrangement changed so did the way that blacks sought political office. Therefore, in any final analysis, factors like reapportionment and annexation and consolidation must be included along with personal social factors in determining black legislative behavior.

Caucuses

Inside Congress, "various types of informal groups exist. The most nebulous of these are friendship or social groups."[33] However, "more important are the avowedly ideological or policy oriented informal groups," such as the liberal Democratic Study Group (DSG). "Southern Democrats have their own Caucus and the liberal and moderate Republicans have their Wednesday Club which has its own staff and serves as a source of information for its members." These groups, expressing common social concerns, class interests, ideological outlooks, or geographical loyalties, have been least-studied facets of the legislative institutions. Yet they have fostered an internal structure that, although informally, shapes and instructs new and old legislators in their behavior.[34] Given the existence of such informal structures, it was only a matter of time before blacks in these bodies would develop similar organizations based on *race*. Because of the diffculties imposed upon blacks in the larger society and in these legislative decision-making bodies, black caucuses arise almost naturally to increase the political clout of black lawmakers and their constituencies.

In Congress, blacks at first formed the Democratic Select Committee under Adam Clayton Powell. But as their number grew, the

Congressional Black Caucus (CBC) was officially formed in 1971 to the accompaniment of much press coverage. The informal group set up a staff and office in downtown Washington. Internally, the CBC set up several committees and selected a chairman to run the caucus and institute its programs. In 1974, the caucus chose Congressman Charles B. Rangel (D.-NY) as its chairman and Congresswoman Yvonne B. Burke (D.-Calif.) as vice-chairwoman. By 1983, Congressman Julian Dixon would be chairperson.

The caucus began a series of hearings throughout the country to determine the legislative needs of blacks. However, this approach was soon abandoned for a political and policy-making role, i.e., getting legislation important to blacks passed. This is its current procedure and approach.

In addition, the caucus has met with the past four presidents, soliciating their support for actions that would benefit black Americans. To support its programs and pay staff and operating expenses, the organization has sponsored money-raising galas. However, the development of a staff, a program, and techniques to implement the program has given rise to some disagreement among members. Members hold a variety of ideological views, which at times, threaten the unity of the caucus. Nevertheless, it has survived.

Black Congressmen are relative newcomers and their organization is still too young to allow a full assessment of its accomplishments. It can be said, however, that such caucus programs as its conferences on education, black elected officials, and health care proved to be quite useful sources of information.[35]

The political leadership of the caucus during the national elections of 1972, 1976, and 1980 was quite notable, especially in fighting representational battles and setting priorities among the issues. But its attempts to pressure Republican presidents have not been entirely successful. Their experience with Democratic Presidents, however, might prove different, although it did not under Carter.

In May of 1975, the "racial" makeup of the caucus was challenged when a white California Democrat applied for membership. Representative Fortney Stark (D-Calif.) indicated that his district had some 30 percent Spanish-speaking or black citizens and suffered from urban poverty as well.[36] The caucus, after a month of deliberation, turned down Stark's application, noting that "representing black constituents alone is not a valid determinant for caucus membership." Chairman Charles Rangel (D.-NY) stated: "Just as the Democratic and Republican Caucuses have unique interests to protect and would not include non-party members in their respective groups we too, have the same needs and concerns." In one analysis and evaluation of the Caucus, Marguerite Ross Barnett had noted that the caucus has since its formation transformed itself three times and undergone three stages. First, the collective stage where the caucus tried to act as a single unified national leader. It failed and this led to the second stage, the ethnic phase, where the caucus members acted as individual legislators which undermined unity. This stage failed and the third stage has emerged which is a sysnthesis of the first two. Barnett writes: "In a broad sense, the false consciousness contradictions, false starts and oscillations associated with CBC history are part of the general black political dilemma in the United States."[37] She concludes by saying: "The Congressional Black Caucus, in order to be effective within the electoral context, would have to understand and directly attack the structural conditions of black subordination. Otherwise, structural constraints will continually undermine...advances won through electoral politic...."[38]

Like their counterparts on the national level, blacks in various state legislatures have formed informal groups on the basis of race. In Ohio, reports Colston, "The black legislators, due to a long history of racial discrimination existing in the society at-large feel impelled to assemble as an informal group to protect and oversee 'black interests.'"

During the 107th General Assembly in 1967, black legislators "began to meet informally to discuss legislation pending before the house as it affected the interests of their constituents and other common problems." Meetings of the group are led by a chairman selected by the body and are held weekly or monthly, as need indicates. However, the black legislators as an informal group do not sponsor legislation; they do so individually and then request colleagues' support.

Unlike the Congressional Black Caucus, the Ohio Caucus is not incorporated and does not have an office or staff; an executive secretary sends out notices of meetings. The group has attempted to find jobs in state government for blacks and met with the president of Ohio State University about the firing of the school's Black Studies director. The organization is made up entirely of black Democrats. The one black Republican in the House did not associate himself with the group because he represented an almost all-white district.

Similarly, black legislators in Georgia organized at first along very informal lines, forming a loose confederation with no rules, binding agreements, or elected chairmen. Popular and charismatic State Representative Bobby Hill recalls:

> We always met, talked about common issues.... About three years ago we decided that by being totally unstructured, we were not in many, many instances communicating with each other sufficiently to have the kind of impact that we sought to be having; for example given a piece of legislation coming up on the floor affecting black people, affecting poor people, affecting our districts generally, coming up abruptly, we were then put in a position where we had to guess where the other blacks were going with it or in many instances somebody might have a better appreciation of the net effect of this piece of legislation. Thus, we would go our separate ways on the vote, because some of us didn't appreciate what was coming off, so we organized the Caucus, at first, primarily to get that kind of discussion out and debated pro and con. We got a convener and then we designated one or two people to review the legislative calender periodically or at least enough to keep us apprised and to take those things off the calender and synthesize and digest them and communicate it to the rest of the group and let the other members decide strategy.... This occurred every morning as an amended calender, which was designed to keep the black members well informed of what was coming up.[39]

This tactic, Hill felt, helped to get blacks together because in the Georgia State Assembly, "many votes went off by ten votes, win or lose. Being fourteen, we got the bloc vote."

Even though the Black Georgia Caucus was calling itself a caucus, saying it to the press and even meeting with the governor, it remained unorganized until 1975 because of a reluctance to elect a chairman. Hill explained: "Everybody thought that if somebody else got elected chairman, they would become spokesman for the group and egos just didn't allow us to organize and we avoided it a long time—because a fear existed that a spokesman would make a statement probably attributed only to himself but held out to be a statement for the entire group." The wrong leader could harm the equality of the members and the integrity of the individuals. "The first convener, Rep. Ben Brown," Hill noted, "didn't abuse his position and always noted that any statement he made was only attributed to himself."

Even when it was organized only informally, the Georgia Black Legislative Caucus was active, holding "Soul Food Dinners" to improve relationships with white counterparts, distributing issues of *Ebony Magazine* to white legislators, 60 percent of whom had never heard of it and 90 percent of whom had never read it,[40] and pushing members of the group for leadership positions in the House. The group also met with the governor to express their views on important legislation affecting blacks.

In Georgia, the road to an organized Black Caucus was a long, evolutionary one plagued by members' fears of colleagues' ego-tripping. To be elected to public office, Hill noted, a person had to be "handsome, charismatic, rich, intelligent, etc.," and "no one black legislator wanted to recant and let the group have a major spokesman, that might supersede his position." Eventually the fear subsided.

The group organized formally during the 1975 session at the prodding of a newly elected representative, black political scientist Robert "Bob" Holmes,[41] but didn't become legally incorporated until 1983. The Black caucus of the Georgia General Assembly established several task forces, which according to former Caucus Chairman Ben Brown would "address problems which the Caucus has deemed as priority concerns of Black Georgians."[42] Six task forces were set up, with caucus officers serving as ex-officio members of each.

Each committee develops its own tactics and strategies for achieving a more equitable share of state services and opportunities for Black Georgians. Ben Brown and Bobby Hill initially served as chairman and vice-chairman, respectively, and the twenty-two-member caucus includes both state representatives and state senators. In 1977, Hill became chairman when Brown was appointed by President Carter to become Deputy Chairman of the Democratic National Committee. In 1983, Representative Holmes indicated that it looked as if the caucus would finally achieve something after all.

In 1974, the Caucus members supported the efforts of two blacks, one a businessman from Valdosta, Freddie Rayford, and the other, an insurance executive from Louisville, George Boatwright, who were running in districts having near majorities of blacks and who were given a good chance to win. The caucus gave these two candidates financial support as well as campaign endorsement and electioneering support. However, in rural Georgia, this was not enough; white candidates defeated both of the candidates in the primaries.

The two black aldermen of Savannah's six-man board obviously would not be organized. However, they do "get together" in an "informal" way before voting on issues. Alderman Roy Jackson puts it this way:

> Personally, I would not describe it as being a Caucus as such, but it is an informal union.... We do have a communication; if there is an issue that is particularly sensitive to the black community, then we don't need to caucus on it, yet we have always been of the same opinion. This is due, in part, to our communication with the community through the political advisory council. On other issues which pertain to the community in general, if I am pushing for a certain view on it, I contact Alderman Boles Ford and see where he stands on it and if it is an important issue I will try to make sure that we are of the same opinion. Personally, I try not in many cases to oppose him if he feels strong about the issue, yet we vote differently a lot....[43]

Alderman Jackson is the younger of the two and serving his first term. Alderman Ford is serving his second term. Both are successful businessmen in the city.

The structure of the city government in Savannah, which has a council-manager form of government rather than the strongly centralized mayoral form of Atlanta, Athens, and Thunderbolt, makes the use of other techniques, devices, and strategies necessary for these black alderman.

Black aldermen do not have to rely upon a caucus or even an informal union for political cues or to succeed in their legislative efforts on behalf of the black community. Alderman Jackson says, "The tragic thing I found is that blacks don't pressure enough...the issue has to be real pertinent...very hot, very meaningful to them to get them up into arms to pressure the City Council...for the Council is very responsive to pressure."[44] He continues,

> We could get a lot more out of the City Council, if we pressure more...but we won't do it. Even the NAACP won't come out on every issue...it could get a lot more done if it would mount the needed pressure and keep it there...but for the organization to move it must be a particular kind of issue...such as civil rights, but not in the area of economic rights except in job discrimination. The branch may also feel that it has its input and representation through the black councilmen on the board,

and I agree with that contention, but still being in the minority that we are in, we cannot get anything passed alone.... We can vote the way the community wants us to vote, but that still doesn't turn the tide, that doesn't swing the vote for you, you need to swing some other folks which are white folks and if there was more pressure brought to bear then it could be done and it would make our position that much stronger and job a lot easier.[45]

Alderman Jackson felt that this criticism also applied to the fledgling PUSH organization in the community. "PUSH is relatively new in this community and we have gotten no kind of pressure from PUSH on any issue." Moreover, he felt that PUSH and the NAACP "never come together on any issue and work for the good of the community." The alderman also felt that the Black Ministerial Alliance could mount enough pressure to affect policy matters in the city if it would try, but it had not done so. Nor did it join issues with other groups. In other words, the factionalism among the major black groups in the community only further weakens them.

In Savannah and similar communities, the power of the small number of black aldermen is further limited by the lack of organized pressure from blacks; the city manager acts only when the council responds to this sustained pressure. In a council-manager form, a caucus would be fruitful only if it were a majority voting block, or were supported strongly by black community action. Here is an instance where political structure determines much of the effectiveness of a black informal organization.

By 1983, the newly elected Alderman Otis Johnson, who holds a Ph.D in Social Work and chairs the Social and Behavioral Sciences Department at Savannah State College agreed with Jackson's earlier assessments about the absence of local black pressure groups.[46] "Six months into his first term, he has seen no single black group that monitors the action of the city council and this all new group of black aldermen in regard to long term policy concerns for the black community." What he has seen is "special interest black groups, like a particular black church that wants to build a parking lot, a neighborhood group that wants a new park, and a neighborhood association that opposes a new liquor license application for a store in their neighborhood,—all of these groups are concerned with a single issue and all come out for this one shot affair."

As for a black caucus, this newly elected group began meeting regularly one hour before the regular council sessions to develop their positions on agenda items. Recently, however, one alderman has indicated that he cannot make these meetings and in at least one open session voted against the other two. Whether this is a harbinger of things to come, only time will tell. In summary, then, a limited caucus has been formed, and while one-shot black pressure groups have increased in this community, no single continuing group has yet to emerge.

In Thunderbolt the lone black alderman, John Merritt, finds that he must get his political cues from black individuals in the small community of approximately three thousand persons.[47] The city has no large black organizations to dramatize the black situation, hence there are no factions or group pressures. In cities like this, the black alderman must find his way by responding to individual demands with political astuteness. He is on his own to develop political clout. For instance, in June 1981 the mayor of Thunderbolt resigned. The customary procedure was to designate the new mayor *pro tem* by giving it to the second highest vote getter in the last city election. but using the secret ballot, the city council this time selected another, for Merritt was the second highest vote getter. Angered by the situation and having little or no organized help in the community, Merritt went to the local news media and leveled charges of racism at the city fathers.[48] He argues that "the altered balloting process" was used only because of him. "The remote possibility of my one day becoming mayor is what scared them." After the situation was exposed in the local press, the city council relented and gave Merritt, the sole black on the council, the position.

In this same city, is Savannah State College with an enrollment of nearly 2,300 black students. However, the student government has not ventured to promote the registration of the black student body— partly because of what happened to a sister black state institution, Fort Valley State College, located in the middle of the state in Fort Valley, Georgia.

The student government at Fort Valley State, after the passage of the amendment giving 18 year olds the right to vote, moved to gain political control of the town and found themselves confronted with a political suit from the white political leadership. The suit claimed that the black college was a diploma mill and needed to be desegregated. The suit halted, temporarily, the black takeover of the town and nearly closed the black college.[49] As a result of the action in Fort Valley, the Savannah State College students have not attempted either to take over or participate in Thunderbolt's city politics.

However, the Savannah State situation is somewhat different from that of her sister institution, because in Savannah there is a predominantly white state college. In Thunderbolt, no caucus or significant black political pressures exist.

There is no informal organization of the black aldermen in Atlanta. The basic reason for this is the existence of two major factions, dubbed by one alderman as the "old guard" (those blacks who have been on the board for two or more terms) and the "young turks" (those blacks who are presently serving their first term).[50] However, one of the aldermen failed to fit into either group and he followed a separate path. It was suggested that his advanced age and his inexperience forced him to go his own way, attorney Marvin Arrington, of the old guard, has tried to bring the two groups together on critical issues, but he has not always been successful, and on noncritical issues the groups tend to go their own ways. Alderman Arrington explains, "Black elected officials are individuals, and from time to time, will disagree over a particular issue. Normally, where we feel that an issue is important to the black community, we will come together in voting on that particular issue...but we are not *always* able to come together and support each other." He adds, "normally, we [the black aldermen] do not sponsor ordinances and resolutions as a group, but we sponsor said legislation in our individual capacities and try to get broad represention on said legislation. I personally have sponsored legislation in the past, and have always attempted to get two or three white city councilmen to cosign the bill to assure the passage of said legislation."[51]

The black mayor, Maynard Jackson, occasionally called the group together to urge their support of critical policies he was about to put to the full coucil for passage. His pleas were not always enough. Arrington points out that there were issues "which the mayor and black councilmen, were heatedly divided on."

One such issue, writes Arrington, was the Neighborhood Planning Units (NPU).

> Certain black members on the council and the mayor
> have not been able to structure the planning units. The
> black council members have contended that under the
> mayor's proposal, there is too much citizen participation,
> and it does not allow councilmatic input. The mayor on
> the other hand has contended that the way the black
> members have proposed structuring of the NPU's would be
> too complicated and would put citizens against citizens."

Eventually, the mayor vetoed the plan proposed by the council,and strongly supported by several black councilmen.[52]

On another issue, the fight between the mayor and some of his black councilmen ended in an odd fashion. The mayor sought to fill a vacancy on the Marta Board with a black female, Dr. Johnnie Clark, Ph.D., of the Business Department of Atlanta University. The majority of the black council members wanted Dr. Joseph Lowry, minister of the Central United Methodist Church, instead. Arrington recalls,

> The debate was heated and the mayor advised the group that he was going to submit Dr. Clark's name to the full council, and that if black members wanted to vote against Dr. Clark, they would have an opportunity to do so on the day the nomination was put forth. Several black council members advised the mayor that he was putting them in a very precarious position, and that they would vote against Dr. Clark if he submitted her name as a nominee before the council. At the next council meeting the mayor, in fact, submitted Dr. Clark's name, and she was approved unanimously. The majority of the black council members who were opposed to Dr. Clark, I feel, were still opposed to her nomination on the day of the meeting, but wanted to avoid an all out fight with the mayor on the council floor.[53]

By 1983, when Arrington had become President of the City Council and the oldest member on the board, no formal black caucus existed and he had to occasionally meet with the black mayor Andrew Young, who travels frequently outside of the city, to get reacquainted. The local press described the situation thusly: "Young comes home from his Middle East trip on Tuesday. On Thursday evening, he stopped by Arrington's house. The council president made coffee. Mrs. Arrington roasted peanuts. Then the mayor and the council president sat down to watch the NCAA basketball playoffs and talk politics."[54]

Arrington told the press: "We just reacquainted ourselves with each other. We just talked. He didn't have a security guard with him. We just talked on a one-to-one basis about politics, of the city.

"That summit conference was followed by a news conference where Arrington and Young announced a new harmony between the executive and legislative branches of city government."[55]

These examples clearly show how black elected officials will fight each other using various tactics to establish their hegemony. The also demonstrate that race might be a fairly effective tool to unify blacks in the electoral arena but it is not always meaningful or even useful in the decision-making area. Black legislators have had a great deal of difficulty in continually organizing around race alone.[56]

In Athens, Georgia, there are three blacks on a ten-member city council. And although Alderman Ed Turner has been on the board longer than the two others, this proved an obstacle to their quickly forming an informal black caucus. The Athens caucus has no officers as such, no regular meetings, and no agenda or list of priorities. However, when crucial issues regarding the black community do arise, the three black members go into action to decide their strategy. According to Alerman Turner, "The emergence of key crucial issues is not the only reason for the informal black caucus' existence. The other reason is that white councilmen meet secretly and privately at clubs and develop goals, approaches and strategies and put them through the council with little or no debate or discussion. Every time a white council proposes a motion, it is quickly seconded and unanimously supported by the other white members."

Sometimes the black councilmen's only recourse is to adopt methods of publicly exposing the white councilmen's actions. "Usually this means going to the local press but because it is hostile and no black newspaper exists in the city, black mass meetings must be held at local churches throughout the city." Normally these meetings are sponsored by the NAACP, which is headed up by Councilman Turner.

The main problem facing the small black group in Athens, however, is that one of the three represents a nearly all-white district and normally votes against the black Caucus stand. His support for the group is in spirit and presence only. The group thus fraternizes socially but votes separately because of difference in their constituencies.

However this changed in 1982 when a black was elected to the Clarke County Commission. His election forced communication between the Athens city Coucilmen and their counterpart on the County Commission because problems facing blacks in the city and county had to be resolved as much as possible in a common and unified manner. Thus, a black caucus had to be formed primarily as a communication device between the two groups of elected officials. Thus, finally one exists and it was born out of necessity.

The Los Angeles black caucus is even more unusual. In a recent interview that city's first black councilman, Gilbert Lindsay, responded to a question about how closely he worked with the other black councilmen "in hammering out a unified stand on the issues" by saying: "I'm not a black councilman. And I don't consider the other three minority blacks, black councilmen. We act like everybody else. We're just councilmen."[57]

He continues: "We don't operate on the council as blacks. I don't have any more dealings with the black councilmen than I do with the others. Shoot, I've torn up the black councilmen the same as I would anybody else when they stepped on my toes."[58] He went on to state that the reasons for his acting alone and using his "wits" and political acumen was due to his long tenure on the council as the single black member. "Prior to my election," he avers, "there had never been a single Negro on the council. Once I was elected, they treated me as though I wasn't there! I didn't get the same respect. I didn't worry about those things."

How then did he influence the council, being a single and disrespected member? The answer is simple. It took patience, forebearance, and potitical sophistication. "I knew that some day, however long it took," he argues, "that they would need me. So I waited on the perimeter of the council and waited for that day to occur. And so, when some councilman needed to save his political life, and he didn't have the votes, he would approach me with hat in hand. I would never go to him. I always made him come to me. . . . In actuality, I bailed plenty of them out when they were desperate."[59] Thus, Lindsay, through patience, endurance, and a correct reading of the political wind used his one vote to improve conditions in the black community.

How could one man on a fifteen-member council through political maneuvering and strategy make a difference? He explains: "Oftentimes, there's only a quorum present, which means ten members. In those cases, it requires all ten votes to pass something. My one vote could make all the difference in the world. I could tie up the council for at least a week under the law. When I saw that my vote was needed, I would look up at the vote board and know that I ran the city."[60]

By the time other blacks had been elected to the council, Lindsay had learned to rely on his individual political skills and maneuvering as a loner rather than to operate as a member of a team united around the issue of racial concerns. A black caucus organization, in his view would be unnecessary.

The influence of informal black legislative groups on the behavior of black legislators is varied. In some areas, they do not even exist. Where they do exist, their influence is minimal because they have internal problems and/or external difficulties. And in yet other areas, they promise to become quite influential because they are rapidly developing a sound structure, agendas, strategies, leadership, and policies for coalitions and alliances. Where such groups succeed, sociopsychological variable cannot and will not be the sole determinants of black legislative behavior.

Committee Assignments

In Congress, the standing committees in the House and Senate have been assigned by scholars to certain categories based on their importance in each house and the kind of issue they deal with. Generally, Senate Committees are divided into major and minor ones, while those in the house are divided into exclusive, semi-exclusive, and non-exclusive categories.[61] Using these categories, we can assess the kind of committee assignments that black legislators and Representatives have received from their white counterparts.

In 1974, black Representatives were, in the main, not placed on committees in the exclusive category; the largest number was assigned to committees in the semi-exclusive category. Although membership in the semi-exclusive category permits membership on two or three committees, nine (or more than half of the other black Congressmen in 1974) had only one committee assignment. Moreover, only two, Rep. Rangel (D.-NY) and Rep. Mitchell (D.—Md.), had positions on select committees. The former served on the Select Crime Committee and the latter served on the Small Business Select Committee.

Of the black Representatives in 1974, only two, Diggs (D.-Mich.) and Rep. Nix (D.-Pa.), held subcommittee chairmanships. Diggs was chairman of the Foreign Affairs Subcommittee on Africa, while Nix was head of the Foreign Affairs Subcommittee on Asian and Pacific Affairs. However, only Diggs has used his subcommittee chairmanship to help African countries. "Rep. Nix," write Barone, Matthews, and Ujifusa, "has contributed little to the debate on Vietnam which is both Asian and Pacific."[62] By 1977, Rep. Nix became chairman of the House's Post Office and Civil Service Committee over stiff opposition within the House. In 1978 then, only four blacks have held House chairmanships. By 1978, Nix had lost re-election and Diggs resigned his chairmanship when he was convicted of federal charges of payroll padding and accepting kickbacks from his employees.

Starting with 1979, all of this would change. Black chairmanships would rise from zero to an all-time high. Robert C. Smith writes, "In part as a result of...reforms (and the rapid turnover in membership in recent Congresses) blacks in the House have done very well in the competition for subcommittee chairs."[63]

Table 7.9 reveals that "in spite of their low seniority, more than half of the black delegation in the House have achieved leadership in the subcommittee structure." But all of the subcommittees that blacks chair are in the semi-exclusive and non-exclusive categories. Not one member of the black delegation chairs an exclusive committee's subcommittee.

TABLE 7.9. Black Members of the House—Subcommittee Chairs, 96th Congress

Committee	Subcommittee	Chair
Education and Labor	Employment Opportunities	Hawkins
Banking, Finance and	Domestic	
Urban Affairs	Monetarycy	Mitchell
	Human and Community	
Budget	Resources	Stokes
Government Operation	Manpower and Housing	Collins
Administration	Printing	Hawkins
Judiciary	Crime	Conyers
Post Office and	Postal Personnel and	
Civil Service	Modernization	Clay
Ways and Means	Health	Rangel
District of Columbia	Fiscal Affairs and Health	Dellums
	Government Affairs and	
	Budget	Fauntroy

SOURCE: List of Standing and Select Committees of House of Representatives together with Joint Committees of the Congress (Washington, D.C.: Government Printing Office, 1979).

Analysis reveals that in regard to the full standing committees in the House, "blacks rank in the middle or near the bottom in committee seniority," and "of the twenty-two standing committees in the House, there is black representaion on all save five: Agriculture, Science and Technology, Public Works, Standards of Conduct, and Veteran Affairs" (See Table 7.10).[64] Moreover, of the twenty-two committees, only one is chaired by a black. Congressman Ronald Dellums (D.-Cal.) chairs the District of Columbia committee—which is, as far as the House committee ranking is concerned, not an important committee, but which is as far as the black residents of the District and its black government are concerned, an extremely important one.

Thus, with an average of 9.2 years of seniority, blacks hold one committee chairmanship and ten subcommittee chairmanships (Congressman Hawkins chairs two subcommittees—Employment Opportunity and Printing. But in the final analysis, while the number of subcommittee chairmanships have increased, the number of full chairmanships have declined by one. And the one committee which blacks continue to chair, the District of Columbia committee, at least in recent years, can be considered important at least to blacks in that area; blacks in other areas do not benefit as much. By 1983, blacks had obtained four committee chairmanships. Dellums headed the District of Columbia Committee, Hawkins the House Administration Committee, Mitchell the Small Business Committee and Stokes the Standards of Official Conduct Committee. In a decade things had changed structurally somewhat.

In concluding, it must be noted that the performance, productivity, and numbers of black congressmen are circumscribed by structural and systemic forces and not simply individual ones. Even such a systemic force as reapportionment can determine the numbers of blacks who go to Congress and thereby the extent of black national representation.

In Georgia, the two black senators found themselves on a total of six committees; each man served on three committees and each had a vice-chairmanship in his first term in 1975. Senator Horace Tate, in addition to serving as vice-chairman of the Senate Committee on Retirement, was also a member of the Education Committee and the Committee on Offender Rehabiliation. Senator Julian Bond was vice-chairman of the committee on Economy, Reorganization and Efficiency in Government and was a member of the Consumer Affairs and the Human Resources committees.

However, in the Georgia House the situation was different. Of a total of twenty-seven committees, blacks served on twenty-two, or about 82 percent. This is indeed significant, in light of the fact that blacks made up only about 11 percent of the total house. In Table 7.11, for 1975, it is noted that blacks served as chairmen of only two standing committees, the Human Relations and Aging Committee and the Special Judiciary Committee. On the former committee blacks had a numerical majority. Its chairman was seventy-four years of age. Moreover, one of the three vice-chairmanships held by House

TABLE 7.10. Black Democratic Members of the House: Committee Assignments and Rank-Standing Committees of the House, 96th Congress*

Committee	Democratic Members	Black Members and Rank
Exclusive		
Appropriations	36	Stokes - 5
		Dixon - 35
		Stewart - 36
Ways and Means	25	Rangel - 7
		Ford - 14
Rules	11	Chisholm - 6
Semi-Exclusive		
Agriculture	27	None
Armed Services	29	Dellums - 16
Banking, Finance and Urban Affairs	28	Mitchell - 19
Education and Labor	24	Hawkins - 4
		Clay - 8
Budget	17	Stokes - 4
		Gray - 17
Foreign Affairs	22	Diggs - 4
		Gray - 18
Judiciary	20	Conyers - 5
Interstate and Foreign Commerce	27	Leland - 26
Public Works	31	None
Science and Technology	27	None
Non-Exclusive		
Administration	16	Hawkins - 4
District of Columbia	9	Diggs - 2
		Dellums - 1
		Leland - 7
		Gray - 9
Interior and Insular Affairs	26	None
Post Office and Civil Service	16	Clay - 5
		Leland - 10
Government Operations	25	Conyers - 8
		Collins - 9
		Mitchell - 7
Standard of Conduct	6	None
Veterans Affairs	21	None
Merchant Marine and Fisheries	25	None

*To facilitate presentation, Congressman Evans, the Republican Delegate, was excluded from the table. He is a member of the Armed Services, Interior and Merchant Marine and Fisheries Committees where he ranks 16 of 16, 15 of 15 and 15 of 15, respectively.

SOURCE: List of Standing and Select Committees of the House of Representatives of the United States together with Joint Committees of the Congress (Washington, D.C.: Government Printing Office, 1979).

blacks was also in this committee. Overall, the tendency seemed to be one of assigning black lawmakers to the Human Relations, Health and Ecology, State Planning and State Institutions committees. The Ways and Means and the Finance committees had few or no black lawmakers at all.

In 1976 the picture still had not changed much. The number of committees and subcommittees on which blacks served had gone down. Chairmanships had also shifted, and the Human Relations Committee remained the one committee with a black majority. In the Georgia Senate, blacks were on six of the nineteen committees, and were vice-chairmen of two. However, they headed up no subcommittees nor served as vice-chairman of any. In 1983, Julian Bond chaired the State Senate Committee on Consumer Affairs and the other three blacks served as vice-chairman of the Higher Education, Retirement, and Offender Rehabilitation committees. In the state house, two blacks had chairperson positions. One served as chairman of the Special Judiciary Committee and a black woman served as chairperson of the Human Relations and Aging Committee. Three had vice-chairperson positions and only one held a secretary's position. In a decade, institutional power for blacks in the Georgia Legislature had declined significantly in terms of the the numbers and types of position held, although in 1983 the number of blacks in each body

TABLE 7.11. Black Committee Assignments in the Georgia House: 1975 and 1976

Assignments & Offices	1975	%	1976	%
Committees	27	100	28	100
Subcommittees	54	100	54	100
Committees with Blacks	22	81.4	20	71.4
Subcomittees with Blacks	28	51.8	24	44.4
Committees with Black Chairmen	2	7.4	2	7.1
Committees with Black Vice-Chairmen	3	11.1	2	7.1
Committees with Black Secretary	4	14.8	3	10.7
Subcommittees with Black Chairmen	7	12.9	6	11.1
Subcommittees with Black Vice-Chairmen	4	7.4	6	11.1
Subcommittee with Black Secretary	6	11.1	7	12.9
Committees with Black Majority	1	3.7	1	3.5
Subcommittees with Black Majority	0	0	0	0

SOURCE: *Committees of the House of Representatives*, (Georiga: Secretary of State, 1975 and 1976).

was much higher. Turnover had eliminated long tenure. And switching blacks from one committee to another had prevented some blacks from chairing very important committees.

The picture in Ohio and Missouri is quite similar to Georgia in the early years. Perry writes of Missouri, "Of the forty committees appointed by the speaker, the thirteen black members occupied seats on twenty-one" and had a lower average of assignment per member, than non blacks in the House."[65] He concludes, "In essence the black representatives held no positions of leadership on any of the major committees of the House," and "the five functioning committees with black vice-chairmen were given a total of 135 bills or slightly more than ten percent of all bill referrals."[66] Of Ohio, Colston says, "The largest percentage representation of blacks on any committee is on Health, Education and Welfare," and "black legislators are under-represented on the Finance Appropriations, Reference, and Rules Committees."[67]

The patterns of assigning black lawmakers on the state level follow the patterns on the congressional level. Blacks are placed on minor or moderately important committees and not on the more important ones. The same holds true for committee chairmanships and vice-chairmanships.

In Thunderbolt, Alderman John Merritt chairs the Health and Sanitation Committee, which is charged with garbage collection and city beautification, and he co-chairs the Street and Water Committees. (See Table 7.12) This small city has seven committees with the following budgetary allocations for 1975: In the original budget, Alderman Merritt's committee was given no allocation because the garbage collection operation was "expected to be self-supporting and operation expenses would be covered by income from the residents." Each resident had to pay for his own service. Alderman Merritt's function was to see to it that such service existed and that customers received it. Later the city budget was amended to give him some money for administrative expenses. The other two committees, on which he served, however, got 29.7 percent of the budget.

Alderman Merritt's situation brings into focus a situation un-covered by Jones. He writes, "When Joseph Pete, one of the South's first black councilmen, was elected in Crowley, Louisiana, in 1954, for example, he was given an inconsequential committee assignment. However, after he painstakingly researched city records and presented evidence that white councilmen who had represented his ward in the past had always been given major committee assignments, the mayor relented and gave him better assignments. Since that time, Mr. Pete has chaired all of the council's major committees."

TABLE 7.12. Committee and Budget Allocations: Thunderbolt, 1975

City Committees	% of Total Budget
Administrative and General	32.04
Police	32.16
Water	15.11
Street	14.62
Youth Activities	2.66
Fire Department	2.48
Library	.89
Health & Sanitation	.00

SOURCE: Alderman John Merritt.

Black aldermen like Adlerman Merritt must strive for committee assignments and committee chairmanships that control major budgets and have significant economic control. And they must do so without the help of other blacks in a caucus and black pressure organizations that lobby the legislative body. As is indicated both on the national and state levels, the existing political structure is designed to keep blacks out of these positions. Yet, the "point of power," as C. Vernon Gray has so eloquently phrased it, must be the chief focus.[68]

The situation in Athens highlights this even more. In that city, there are four committees, with black representation as shown in Table 7.13:

TABLE 7.13. Black Committee Assignments in Athens, GA: 1975-1984

Committee	Total Members	No. of Blacks
Finance	5	1
Public Works	5	2
Streets, Parks, and Recreation	5	2
Public Safety	5	2

The all-important finance committee has only one black member. According to Alderman Turner, the lone black can never get a motion passed or put on the agenda because none of the white members will second it. In fact, on the finance committee all the black-advanced proposals died because of the last of a second for the original motion. This tactic continued until the late seventies when a female was elected to the council and place on the finance committee and a new black member was elected to replace Charles Mack. Now the lone black member on the Finance Committee does get support for his motions from the white female, according to Councilman Ed Turner (interview, August 20, 1984). However, the key reality here is that nine years later, there is still only one black on the finance committee. Obviously the political structure attempts to control black political behavior.

In Savannah, the situation, though different, is essentially the same. The difference is that the city has a council-manager form of government. Hence, there are no committees. And because open council meetings preclude the city manager's directly controlling the proceedings, the manager, notes Alderman Jackson, holds "pre-council sessions" with all the aldermen so the open city council meeting will flow with ease and in a predetermined fashion. These sessions, argues Alderman Jackson, are both positive and negative. They are positive in the sense that "they give you a chance to make an assessment of the vote before it comes to council to actually find out how it's going to come out, plus it gives you a chance to open up and air any kind of difference you might have before you get to city council..."

However, he feels, they are negative in that the "mayor uses the pre-council sessions to kill those issues that he does not want to come out before council in an open session..."

In these sessions, if "objectionable" matters are raised, "they are beaten to the ground and never acted on by regular council. Therefore, the city manager never gets directives to act on these matters." Jackson says. He has therefore adopted a strategy of "waiting until the open council meeting before airing an important issue and if it is the kind of issue that they cannot back away from then you can get support for it at the open council meeting and favorable reaction, especially if the black community is present."

In the council-manager form of government there is the constant employment of adminstrative fiat. "The mayor at times functions as a full-time mayor...and as a result decisions are made adminstratively...and that is a handicap, because it takes the alderman out of the decision-making process.... I have experienced this recently, for nothing at times come to council other than routine matters." Overall, pre-council sessions and adminstrative fiats are structural forces that operated in this city to shape black legislative behavior.

In regard to the pre-council sessions noted by Jackson, Alderman Johnson indicated in 1984, that they still exist but have now been renamed: the City Manager briefing sessions. "All racial matters are dealt with and hammered out in these sessions so that they will not evolve into and become media issues or potential explosive community matters." Thus, the device to contain and manage conflict, i.e., racial issues and matters, continues in place.

In Atlanta, in 1973, there were nine standing committees, and blacks held the chairmanship of five, and of the other four committees, blacks are vice-chairmen of three. By 1983, there were ten committees and blacks held the chairmanship of five of them: particularly the powerful Finance committee.

However, despite being chairmen of the kind of committees that in Gray's terms are "points of power" because of their budgets, focus, and the individuals they employ, blacks in 1973 did not head the city's Finance, Public Safety, Executive, and Human Resources committees. Three of these committees are powerful in themselves. The Finance Committee recommends on matters "pertaining to budgets; taxing ordinances; public revenue; tax officials and collectors; department of finance; and license and pension funds." The Public Safety Committee oversees the Police Department, Fire Department, and city prison, while the Executive Committee provides legislative oversight of the mayor; city purchasing; and intergovernmental relations with the county, state and federal authorities. The Human Resources Committee recommends on city parks and recreation, the public library, model neighborhood programs, and education and welfare programs.

Legislative bodies can change, as governments modify their number of committees or change the appointments to them. Whenever this happens, committees that control large budgets, focus on human concerns, and employ many individuals should become a matter of concern for black legislators, for they have more power and influence than other committees.

Clearly, black legislative committee assignments are used to manipulate black political behavior. On the national and state levels, blacks are appointed to minor and moderate committees limiting their legislative clout. Granting blacks chairmanships to committees of limited power complements the first strategy and grows out of it. The practice is seen on the local level, too. The budget is also a tool. Blacks are assigned to head committees with little or no budgets, furthermore, keeping blacks off the finance committee obviously has an impact on their performance. Finally, forms of goverment affect black legislative influence, as we have seen in the case of the council-manager form.

The discussion of legislative behavior of black County Commissioners has been avoided until now because of the desire to focus on that behavior as it deals with specific legislation (i.e., anti-black terrorist groups' legislation). In looking at the behavior of black congresspersons, alderpersons, and state legislators, it was clearly shown that the structure of the legislative bodies had impact which modified and proscribed their behavior. Now the question is how would these legislative structures affect the behavior of a black legislator when he is not trying to promote progressive legislation and assist minority groups, but when he is trying to stop and/or regulate the behavior of anti-black white terrorist groups?

C. Vernon Gray is a Professor of Political Science at Morgan State University in Baltimore, Maryland and a member of the Howard County Council, in Columbia, Maryland, where he lives. Blacks are about 12 percent of the population. The county council is composed of five member—one black and four whites. Gray was elected in an at-large system as part of a slate of candidates, in 1982, for a four-year term. In this county, the council was a "committee of the whole and also sits as the Liquor, Zoning and Health Boards." According to Doctor Gray, "there is not a lot of give and take or a lot of disagreements on the council at it meetings." This, he says, came as something of a surprise to him.

In terms of procedure, the Council usually holds a legislative session on the first Monday of each month to (1) introduce bills and (2) to pass bills that are ready and completed from earlier sessions. On the third Monday, a second legislative session or hearing is held to discuss bills introduced on the first Monday and let the public react to these new legislative proposals. This is usually considered a work session and amendments can be introduced to bills if there are any. "It is at this session that each County Council member can talk with other members to get them to support their legislation and out of common courtesy let each other know if an amendment is in the offing. But most important no formal voting or motions are made at these sessions."

Prior to his winning a seat on the Council, there had been Ku Klux Klan activity in the county, where county property was defaced with Klan insignias. After getting on the council, black firefighters called to say that Klan literature was being distributed at the public-supported fire station. Gray met with the firemen and adopted a plan called "politics of exposure."[69] This included (1) contacting the local newspaper for a story; (2) informing County and State Human Rights Commission for an investigation, (3) meeting with all the black firefighters in the County (4) getting a hearing before the County Council and (5) introducing legislation and (6) sending letters to all County agencies asking that this activity be prohibited on public lands and buildings.

At the hearing, some 30 people came at County Councilman Gray's request to testify and back his Anti-Klan resolution bill. His "colleagues were both surprised and overwhelmned." Prior to the hearing on the bill, they gave him the "silent treatment on the issue." On all other matters, colleagues would initiate discussion and get a conversation going. But on this Klan issue, they said nothing—"no one would broach the subject, not even the liberal member of the council. And on the first Monday when the resolution was offered, an amendment was put forth to delete an important line from the resolution" Gray was caught off guard because it had been a matter of common courtesy to let each member know when an amendment was in the offing. He had not been afforded this courtesy. The Amendment was passed to delete the line from the resolution. Even the liberal members voted for the amendment. After the resolution had been watered down, it was still passed by only a 3-to-2 vote.

According to Gray, however, Klan activity continued and he moved to introduce a bill making it a misdemeanor for the Klan to deface county property. On this occasion, his proposed measure was subjected to a harsh review and a quickly prepared resolution was drafted (again without his knowledge and the policy of common courtsey was abandoned) to make his bill unnecessary and useless. To fight off this approach, Gray went to see the Executive Secretary of the council who schedules all bills and resolutions in terms of the order that they come on the floor to see to it that his bill came up before the hastily drafted resolution. It did, and again the bill passed by a 3-to-2 margin.[70]

The point with this Klan legislation is that the same legislative structures that hamper black legislative behavior in its efforts to get progressive legislation can prove quite difficult when violent and terrorist groups need to be checked in the society. In closing, it can be noted that county legislative structure also shapes black political behavior.[71] In short, whether on the national, state, or local level, other variables are operating to shape black political actions and responses than purely personal motives and drives.

Black Female Legislators: A Research Note

In anlayzing the characteristics of black legislators, we have included both sexes without distinguishing between black male and female legislators on the national and state levels. No black women were present in the local governments discussed.

Presently, all serve on local school boards, and thirty-eight serve as state legislators, with four in Congress. The Congresswomen represent urban areas, Rep. Yvonne Burke (D.-Calif.) comes from the West; Rep. Cardiss Collins (D.-Ill.) from the Midwest; Rep. Shirley Chisholm (D.-N.Y.) from the East; and Rep. Barbara Jordan (D.-Tex.) from the South. In addition, all of the black legislators in Kentucky are women. All in all, black women are 17 percent (684) of all black officials in the nation in 1974. In 1982, there were 1,081 black elected women, of which two were in Congress, 64 in the state legislature and the rest in county and local level positions except for two regional officials.

In her pioneering study of black women state legislators,[72] Jewel Prestage found them to be similar to black male legislators in education, occupational status, and age. Nearly half were married or widowed and most had children.[72] Prestage's findings note similarities in personal characteristics, but did not look into committee assignments, bill sponsorship patterns, and the like, leaving these open for further study.[73] However, what she did find out about black female political behavior in general ran counter to findings on militant black women. Inez Smith Reid found that militant, "together" black women were not traditional political animals. She writes, "We discovered in our survey that the majority of women (104) identified with no political party...nor did the women tend to participate in other aspects of traditional politics such as working in political clubs or engaging in formal debates and discussions about candidates and issues."[75] She continues, "Many of the women in our survey, for example, indicated that they simply did not vote." She suggested that "together" black women reject black politicians and the Civil Rights Movement as being useful to them. The apparent contraditions between Prestage's and Reid's findings must be resolved in the future not only for accurate information regarding black female legislators, but black female political behavior in general.

Black Local Legislators and the Political Structure: A Research Finding

We need to analyze not only the ways that the *internal* political makeup of legislative bodies shape black legislative behavior, but also the ways that it is affected by the *external* political structure. Clinton Jones has examined the ways that both structural and demographic forces act on black political representation on city councils.[76]

Jones looked at the impact of electoral systems, i.e., organization into at-large and regional districts, on blacks elected to city councils as well as "the relationship of demographic and socio-economic variables to the elections of blacks to councils.[77] In both instances, Jones used the "black representation ratio" as his dependent variable. This ratio is established by "dividing the black percentage of a city's population into the black percentage of the city's council seats. The black representation ratio will equal 1.00 when the black percentage of council seats is equal to the black percentage of a city's population. It will be more or less than 1.00 depending on whether the black percentage of council seats is more or less than the black percentage of the city's population."[78]

Jones found that the data from 136 cities supported the hypothesis "that at-large systems restrict black membership on city councils. The mean representation ratio for at-large cities is 0.43 compared with 0.61 for district cities, a difference of 0.18."[79] And "when region is controlled for," Jones found that "black membership on city councils with districts remain higher than in cities with at-large systems, with the South and Northeast showing the greatest differences...."[80]

Jones, using the Pearson's correlation coefficient (Table 7.14), found that the fewer seats that there are within at-large systems, the smaller the number of blacks that would be elected:

> Without controlling for region, the correlation of the
> number of seats in at-large systems with black
> representation ratios is $R = 0.93$ and significant at the .001
> level; however, when region is controlled the predominating

influence of the South on the strength of the relationship becomes clear.... As a matter of fact, when region is controlled, the correlations between number of seats and black representation ratios are negative in the Northeast and insignificant in the West. The data on the South and North Central do clearly support the propostion that few seats in at-large systems tend to restrict black membership on the city councils.[81]

TABLE 7.14. Pearson's Correlation Coefficients Between Number of Council Seats and Black Representation Ratio

Regions	Correlations	Significance Level
North Central (N = 20)	.6816	.001
North East (N = 16)	−.0791	N.S.
South (N = 53)	.9610	.001
West (N = 17)	.2972	N.S.
All Regions (N = 106)	.9343	.001

SOURCE: Professor Jones' Paper—Table II.

In looking at the influence of socioeconomic variables, Jones found them to be significant in different regions. "In general," he writes, "greater black resources in terms of education, income and size are associated with greater black electoral success but the impact of these variations is somewhat situational, with different factors being significant in various regions."[82] For instance, only in the Northeast did a higher level of education correlate significantly with a higher black representation ratio. Only in the South and West was a higher income significantly correlated with black representation ratios.

Jones' research clearly demonstrates that the political structure, especially at-large systems with few seats, greatly hampers blacks in getting equitable representation in city councils. In addition, his study found that it was generally, not always, Southern cities with large black populations that employ at-large methods of electing city councils. Black political hopefuls in these kinds of political structures would obviously have to modify their political behavior to get elected and maintain their elective offices.

Coupling Professor Jones' findings with earlier data, we conclude that both external forces such as the political structures like at-large systems and internal political structural forces like budget committee assignments and adminstrative decrees can and do shape the behavior of black elected officials as readily as do socioeconomic background and personal perceptions. Recently, some scholars have argued quite forcefully "that it is the disparity in politically relevant socioeconomic resources possessed by blacks and whites which better explain blacks severe underrepresentation on city council within the south," if not elsewhere, instead of structural arrangements like at-large election devices.[83] And these scholars concluded that improvement will not come until improvements are made in black socioeconomic conditions rather than a switch to district-type elections. This is the classic argument: as soon as blacks improve themselves, not the imperfections in the political system, they will improve.

Another group of scholars, using a different statistical method, retested this observation and found that: "Clearly, structural alterations can be expected to have a more profound immediate impact on underrepresentation in the South than would change in relative socioeconomic conditions."[89] Therefore manipulation of structural arrangements will bring more progress than increasing socioeconomic conditions, which is a long term matter.

However, the key point here is not what one statistical model found vs. another (for a good case can be made for both statistical models) as much as it is the *conceptualization* of all of the forces shaping black legislative and political behavior. It is not an either/or or even a combination of the two but a host of forces as well as the continual manipulation of the community by external and internal forces that must be added to the equation for a full understanding of all of the forces shaping and determining black legislative and political behavior. In fact, it is the contention of this work that behavioralists have overemphasized one variable at the expense of other important ones—usually for policy implications. However, black politics and political activity have proceeded along an array of fronts and have worked on many factors at the same time.

Patterns of Bill Sponsorship

Since there is a strong interplay between external and internal structural political forces that is not readily apparent when political behavioralists look only at individual and personal characteristics, the continuing practice of looking at how a particular legislator voted on a certain bill only clouds the issue and excludes the role of the political structure on political behavior. We cannot expect to explain black legislative voting behavior by rooting the explanation in the solon's voting record. This much too narrow approach must be broadened to include variables besides his personal perceptions and background.

To get a multidimensional picture of black legislative voting behavior, a bill sponsorship pattern index would be quite useful. Such an index, initially used by Alvin D. Sokolow, would include the three dimensions he used and could also include the one most commonly employed by political behavioralists, voting patterns.[85]

The index includes: (1) the number of bills introduced, (2) passage ratios, the number of bills passed in relationship to those sponsored, (3) the areas of bills, and (4) how the legislator voted during the entire session on all bills.

Using this type of approach, one can see the roles both of the structure and individual factors. For instance, the number of bills introduced would suggest the predominant concerns of the electorate and legislator. Moreover, the passage ratios tell us how the black representative was supported by white legislators and by fellow party members. Likewise, they say something of black power and influence in the legislative body. If he or she continually has a low passage ratio, it might be that the political structure is arrayed against him.

The areas of legislation reveal both district or constituency needs and the beliefs of the legislator about what is in the public's best interest. One can also watch for shifts in black legislator's concerns.

Last, a legislator's voting record can reveal: (1) his individual preferences for bills he sponsored or assisted and (2) how he reacts to bills that he did not sponsor or help develop. For instance, if black legislators have low bill-passage ratios, it would mean in most cases they have been voting on white-sponsored and backed legislation which might be detrimental to their constituencies.

Taken together, the four broad areas of legislative performance will give a much clearer and multifaceted picture of a black legislator's behavior than his voting record alone would. Except for Sokolow's work on black legislators in California this approach has not been fully employed. However, experimental probes with the index have produced new insights.

If one looks at the bill sponsorship patterns of black legislators in Congress starting with the year that they organized the Black Caucus, one can clearly see the role of structure in shaping black legislative behavior. Though organized informally in 1969, the black Congressmen formally announced late in 1970 the formation of a "shadow cabinet" to oversee federal enforcement of Civil Rights Laws.[86]

Starting in 1970, the black Congressmen introduced a total of 32 bills; the number the next year reached a high of 76, falling to 39 in 1972, and then going to a new high of 77 in 1973 and then to about 50 in mid-1974. In the 4½-year period, only one bill passed the House, but it never got out of the Senate. Even in the midst of the recession of 1975 and 1976, Rep. Hawkins' bill on full employment (HR-7248) failed to become a law. Later it did.

Moreover, it is not possible to compute the success ratio of black Congressmen except in the year 1971, when one bill passed, for a success ration of 1.30. The mean number of bills introduced by each black Congressman came to 5.6, with a mean passage rate of 0.076 percent each. In the other years the mean passage rate and the success ratio was zero.

In short, despite numerous attempts, each black Congressmen had only one piece of legislation pass the House. Can this low record be attributed solely to their inner personal motives and drives? The data suggest otherwise.

The bills fell into the following broad subject areas: House rules and Congressional representation for Washington, D.C., education, economics, housing, foreign affairs, welfare, and civil rights. By 1972, to these seven areas were added poverty and welfare reforms and busing. In 1973, Congressman Ron Dellums (D.-Calif.) added the area of defense. Overall, the legislative sponsorship patterns reveal that black Congressmen seem to be concerned with traditional civil-rights issues, but also with "class" legislation of importance to low-income persons and the educationally disadvantaged. On the other hand, the hearings conducted by the Caucus around the country dealt primarily with the problems inherent in combating racial discrimination and the role the government could play in alleviating them. Moreover, comparison of the categories of legislation introduced by the black Congressmen with the sixty recommendations given by them to President Nixon, reveals little connection. Few pieces of their legislation related to their demands to the executive branch.

Most black Congressmen, in their ultimate political act, had to vote on legislation sponsored by white Congressmen, in many instances, legislation that had little to do with the subjects of their own bills. Hence, their voting patterns seem at times random; both supportive of and in opposition to their party's legislation.[87] Thus, analysis of their party voting record might not always show a high party unity score, but not because of lack of party loyalty.[88]

On the state level, a pattern that emerges seems similar. Black legislators tend to introduce a large number of bills, have a low passage-success ratio, and sponsor legislation in people-oriented categories. However, in some states blacks are in both houses and can get bills passed in both. On the state level there is also a greater concern with constituencies and more co-sponsored legislation.

Analyzing black legislators in California, Sokolow found that "the black assemblymen sponsored more bills, on the average, than any of the group of white assemblymen."[89] Yet, he discovered that "much more striking are the differences in the average number of bills passed per group and in the percentage of toal bills this represented. On both measures the black assemblyman came last, falling far behind the white groups, particularly in bill-passage ratios. Less than a quarter of the bills sponsored by the five black assemblymen were passed by the legislature as compared with half the bills introduced by Republicans" and one-third by liberal white Democrats.[90]

Using the black members of the California legislature of 1967-1971 as the basis for his analysis, Sokolow found that the lone black senator had a much higher bill passage ratio than the black assemblymen. In the Senate, Senator Dymally, now lieutenant governor (1974-1978), "ranked 18th for both bill introductions and success ratio." His "success ratio was 48.7 percent in 1969 and this was more than twice as high as the 23.3 percent average of the five black assemblymen."[91]

Table 7.15 shows the subject areas of bills introduced by the black assemblymen as a percentage of the total bills sponsored in 1969.

TABLE 7.15. Black Legislative Concerns: California

Subject Area of Bills Introduced	% of All Bills Introduced
Natural Resources	4.6
Business Regulation	21.3
Welfare-Health	22.4
Education	20.7
Transportation	2.9
Criminal Law	17.8
Public Employment—Retirement	0.6
Elections—Political Parties	3.4
Others	5.1
Total	100.0

SOURCE: Sokolow, *Black Politician*, op. cit., p. 25.

Clearly, black legislators sponsor bills that seek to help low-income persons, the educationally disadvantaged, and the defendant in criminal cases. Sokolow concluded that black legislators in California have shifted from a concern with traditional civil rights to class legislation for the lower strata in society. And he also found that black legislation tends to be geared to the concerns of individuals in their districts rather than to the concerns of local governments and governmental agencies, which is the case with the white assemblymen.[92]

In Georgia, Willie Woods, Director of the Southern Public Policy Center at Clark College in Atlanta, found in 1973 that 37.8 percent of bills co-sponsored by blacks passed both houses, 19.2 percent of bills sponsored by blacks passed both houses and 50.2 percent of all bills introduced by blacks passed the House. The black bills tended to fall into the following categories: crime, education, consumer protection, and health and welfare. Woods' findings nearly parallel those for California. In both cases, there are low passage rates in both houses, a large number of bills introduced, and a prevalence of people-oriented legislation. In Ohio, Missouri, and Illinois, the findings are nearly the same.[93]

However, black state legislators generally find themselves having to vote little or not at all on black-sponsored legislation and more on white-backed legislation, which may be more concerned with governmental agencies and local government than with people and governmental services for the disadvantaged.

The task of mapping out the bill sponsorship patterns on the local level is difficult because of the lack of agencies that keep records on aldermanic sponsorship of city ordinances and resolutions. Moreover, the constant shifting in local governments makes it difficult to gain full insight into the legislative behavior of local black elected officials. Given the wide variety of city structures and the disarray of black caucuses on this level, it is hard even to generalize. However, one recent case study of local black elected officials in 16 New Jersey cities was made. The author of that study, Leonard Cole, analyzed the voting patterns of blacks in those cities and concluded that while "there were tendencies toward bloc voting," the "overriding feature remains the frequency of unanimity in all councils" of black voting with whites,[94] which was especially true in the bedroom or suburban communities. Passage rates were mixed, as were the subjects of the various resolutions and ordinances that were introduced. However, when solely black proposals were introduced, they usually failed.[95]

Cole's findings suggest difference in the suburbs but similarities in the central cities.

A Look to the Future

Black legislative behavior is still growing and has yet to reach maturity. Reliance upon any one index will consequently not give a true, multidimensional picture. Neither does black legislative behavior match the picture painted in the behavioral literature. The backgrounds and personal characteristics of black legislators at all levels are diverse. Several categories now seem to predominate, but by no means are all black legislators young, educated, Protestants. Generalizations about their constituencies are equally difficult to make. While a significant number come from urban and black districts, others represent white districts and rural areas. In fact, the number representing rural blacks has slowly begun to grow, suggesting the potential for many more.

The black caucuses in the various legislative bodies range from the nearly nonexistent ones to highly organized and functional ones. These organizations hold only a spiritual power over their members, uniting them in their common desire to help with the problems of their racially identifiable districts.

Since the legislative bodies to which black legislators are elected are microcosms of the larger society, black legislators find themselves affected by the same forces that structure black political behavior generally, a fact which can be seen in black committee assignments and black bill-passage ratios.

Another important factor in black legislative behavior is the lack of concerted, unified lobbying. Few black lobby groups exist, and black pressure seldom arises except in times of crisis when the legislators, who are always in the minority, need backing for their efforts. However, the potential may be realized in the future.

Chapter **8**

Black Judicial Behavior

Behavioralist studies of black judicial activity has been like its analysis of other areas of political science. Black judges have been thoroughly analyzed, their behavior is said to be determined by socioeconomic factors, by their social backgrounds and their role perceptions, by political socialization agents, by the nature of justice itself and societal reactions to their judicial pronouncements. Socio-psychological theory of stimulus-response and conversion, with the individual as the central unit of analysis, dominates this area of political science also.

The Literature

The literature tends to follow particular patterns. First, a significant number of the writings dwell on the social backgrounds and attitudinal characteristics of judges. They relate such factors as party affiliations, law schools, and jurisprudence to performance on the bench and decisions on specific cases.[1]

Besides the variables of age, education, sex, income, and the like, some of the literature probed the cultural environment of judges to determine the influence of popular customs, current notions of justice, and legal norms such as constitutions, statutes, judicial precedents, and administrative regulations. Normative stimuli came to be considered by some political behavioralists to be just as important as social background and role perception.

Some students of judicial behavior sought to discern the pressures arising from judges' interactions with legislators on both state and national levels and to evaluate presidential pressures in the instance of high-court opinions.[2] The influence of other agencies upon the judge's decisions were known and the behavioralists sought to explain it in clear-cut terms. Next, the judges' behavior was analyzed in terms of the impact of public responses to their decisions. Public reactions to court adjudication in church and religious cases, criminal cases, political matters such as reapportionment and civil rights sometimes became sustained, vociferous, and threatening, and there was much interest in assessing the possible impact of such outbursts upon future judicial action.

Finally, the focus on judicial biography started to take shape. This approach, like the current psychological approach to political leadership, emphasized "the judge's personality, background, and belief system to his conduct on the bench and impact on the law and politics of his time."[3] It urged biographers to discontinue "indulging in personality cults, for choosing subjects and evidence according to subjective and non-verifiable assumptions of interest, importance, and personal empathy"[4] and to produce data that could be empirically tested.

Despite all the attention given to judicial behavior, the data on the behavior of black judges are scarce. In fact, there is so little information that one might conclude that black judges do not exist. Such an assumption would be most wrong. "President Franklin D. Roosevelt," writes Helen Edmonds, "started the practice of appointing black federal judges in 1937 and each President since has continued it."[5] On the state level, black state judges appeared first in New York, Pennsylvania, Ohio, Illinois, and then California. Other western and midwestern states followed. Only in the South did black judges not arrive until the late sixties.[6]

Although the political behavioralists might have passed over black judges, they did not go entirely unnoticed. Black journals and periodicals are filled with descriptive analyses, short biographical sketches, and revelatory articles. Recently, articles revealing black judges' departures from the standard canons of jurisprudence and dealing with black defendants in more humane terms have appeared.[7]

The biographical approach to black judicial decision-making is exemplified in Randall Black's book on Supreme Court Justice

Thurgood Marshall.[8] This work does not employ the new psycho-historical approach so prevalent in current leadership studies. It is more traditional in its description of Marshall's life and social background. In many ways, Marshall's life and liberal attitude on civil-rights cases would seem a perfect fit to the behavioralist approach because they would correlate so well with those background factors that are supposedly related to liberal judicial decisions. But the limitations of such an enterprise are quite grave. There are several other black federal judges with similar backgrounds whose judicial attitudes are very different from Justice Marshall's. Judge George Crockett, Sr., in Michigan is but one example.[9]

Smith, in a recent paper, has tried to discern the "relationship between certain social background characteristics (such as birthplace, present residence, age, and family socio-economic status) and their role perceptions of themselves as black judges."[10] He went on to indicate that in addition to the background factors "their low academic rank and the influence of law school on their thinking and subsequent carreers" would be studied.[11] Smith's sample included 185 judges out of the 288 who were sent a questionaire. He found that the "most striking pattern about the background is the number of judges who were born in the South. Over half of the respondents were from that region."[12] About 70 percent were from 45 to 64 years of age, yet some were in their twenties, while others were over seventy years old. Most of the judges came from working-class families and black colleges provided the chief undergraduate training. Moreover, Howard University's Law School was the main training ground for the judges,[13] and most of the respondents noted that they ranked in the top third of their classes.

Finally, Smith's study found that a correlation existed between the black judges' law school, academic rank, and law school influences, on the one hand, and their actions, on the other.[14] "Those judges," he writes, "who graduated in the top third of their classes and those who considered law school very important on their thinking and subsequent careers were most likely to think that black judges should not provide special protection for black interest."[15] Those judges who did not think this way, Smith felt, did not take a professional view of the black judges' role.

Black political scientist Gilbert Ware, using a nonbehavioral approach in the first major study of blacks in the judicial system and black legalists (i.e., judges and attorneys) in politics, arrived at a completely different view of black judicial behavior.[16] In this work, which will cast a towering shadow over future explorations into black judicial politics, Ware let black jurists speak for themselves and the "process" system in which they find themselves. Their utterances, as he recorded them, reveal numerous behavior-shaping forces. He writes, "black judges can go only so far in flailing racism and classism. They must restrain themselves for fear of running afoul of judicial disability commissions, newspapers, and police officers' associations. They must avoid alienating colleagues who they need to persuade to a different way of thinking and acting. They cannot start lawsuits, defend litigants, or engage openly in the rough-and-tumble politics that, directly or indirectly, determine whether justice will be done or done in."[17] Black jurists caught up in such a political system of conflicting demands, Ware finds, must shape some of their judicial behavior according to these systemic and structural forces.

The literature on black judicial behavior is very spare indeed, and what little does exist sees the influence of indiviudal personality variables along with systemic and structural ones, with the former dominating. Any thorough analysis of black judicial behavior must consider both the political structure and the definition of justice in the political system to achieve a multidimensional view.

Black Judges and the Political Process

To probe black judicial behavior, some pertinent questions must be raised, not only about the individual, but about the political system and its structure as well. For instance, why was it not until 1852 that the first black judge, the Honorable Robert Morris, was appointed to Boston's Magistrates Court and why is it that currently the total number of black judges is less than 330.[18] More important is the question of whether this is the fault of the black individuals seeking judgeships or the fault of the system.

Part of the answer lies in knowing how, when, and where black judges have arisen in the American political system, information that must be taken into account if one is to discern the interplay of other variables beyond individual and personal characteristics.

Helen Edmonds, in her careful analysis, has clearly shown that in the past, systemic and regional variables limited both the number and the types of black judges.

Table 8.1 shows that in 1970 only sixteen black federal judges were still serving, out of a one-time high of nineteen. In the state courts, only one hundred and twenty-five blacks have donned the dark robe. When Edmonds reflects upon the types of positions held, she notes that most blacks who serve in the state courts are "near the bottom of the state system of courts, i.e. as city and municipal judges."[19] Moreover, she found that, except for the federal judges, "the largest number of black judges were to be found in the large industrial cities of the northeast, north-central, and western regions, the same cities that had the voting power to elect black Congressmen and members of state legislatures. The presence of black judges in the courts located in these cities is the result, direct or indirect, of that black voting power."[20] Appointed black judges were and still are fewer than elected black judges. And in the South, the elected judges account for almost all black judgeships, major or minor. In the 14 years since Edmonds' study, the story has changed very little.

TABLE 8.1. Black Judges: 1937-1970

Location	Number
Federal District Courts	9
Other Federal Courts	7
State Courts	
Northeastern Courts	
New York	23
Pennsylvania	9
Maryland	5
Connecticut	
North-central Courts	
Illinois	9
Michigan	11
Ohio	14
Missouri	4
Indiana	2
Iowa	2
Colorado	7
Western Courts	
California	14
Washington	4
Nevada	1
Southern Courts	
North Carolina	1
South Carolina	1
Tennessee	1
District of Columbia	3

SOURCE: Edmonds, *Negroes in Government*, op. cit., pp. 152-161.

Figure 8.1, where the total number of black judges throughout the country is plotted and compared with the total number of black judges in the South, where more than one-half of the black population still resides, reveals that the number of black judges is very low. In Mississippi, no black judges have yet won office or been appointed to the bench. The low number of southern black judges obviously is explained by systemic and structural factors. For example, there were few black law schools in this region, reducing the number of black lawyers.[21] Second, the small number of blacks who passed state bar examinations in the region further reduces the number of potential black judges. Third, those blacks who surmounted these hurdles could not expect to be appointed by segregationist legislators and governors in the regions, and furthermore, the black electorate itself was burdened with systemic forces that made election of blacks to the bench a difficult if not impossible task. Thus, few blacks in the region took seats on the bench.

Beyond the actual numbers are the percentages. In 1970-71, blacks were not much more than 1 percent of the total number of all judges on the state and local level, and about 6 percent of all judges on the federal level. Of that tiny percentage on the state and local level, "two were on state supreme courts, and seven were on intermediate state appellate courts,"[22] which correlates with the earlier findings of Edmonds that black judges hold only the low-echelon positions.

In addition to their few numbers and low positions, black judges are not evenly distributed around the country. Ware writes, "More than half the black judges in America are in six cities, namely New York City, Philadelphia, Washington, Chicago, Detroit, and Los Angeles.[23]

In sum, the political process has played a major role in determining the actual number if not also some of the judicial behavior of black judges. The social milieu has, to some extent, determined the cities where black lawyers and thereby black judges might find a livelihood. Crucial in the entire political process is the fact that most states elect most of their judges.[24] By barring blacks from the voting booths, the bar rosters and associations, law schools, and full participation in the political arena, states have determined to a great extent the parameters of the black judiciary. Just how much this has shaped judicial actions and response must still be explored.

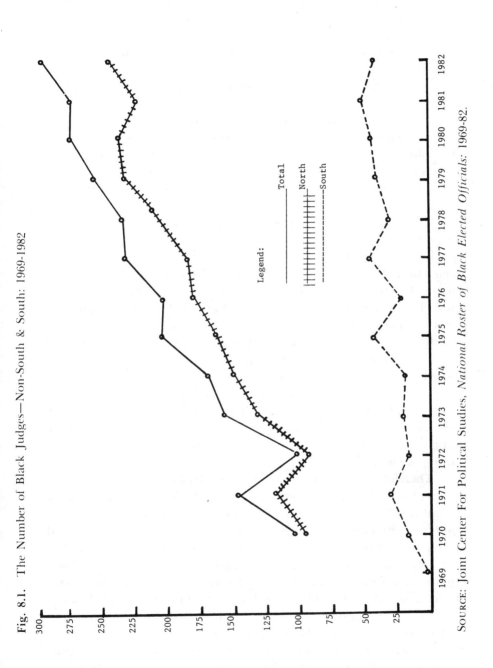

Fig. 8.1. The Number of Black Judges—Non-South & South: 1969-1982

SOURCE: Joint Center For Political Studies, *National Roster of Black Elected Officials:* 1969-82.

Judicial Behavior in Context: The National and Subnational Levels

Black judicial behavior, like other forms of black political behavior, is not a simple response to individual motivations. Black judicial behavior is determined by the numerous complex systemic and structural variables present in the political process. As these variables continue to change, so shall that part of black judicial behavior that is responsive to them. In addition, black judicial behavior must be seen at the different levels on which it interacts with other variables in the political process. Black judicial activity must be seen in context if it is not to seem out of step with contemporary judicial policy, procedure, and management. That context includes the plight of the black community.

Congress, within the framework of the Constitution, has over the years set forth how federal judges and Supreme Court justices would obtain office; the President plays an important role in the appointments of both. If a President is not persuaded or cannot be persuaded by the Judicial Council of the National Bar Association that blacks should hold federal judgeships, then black judges on the national level do not appear.[25]

It took one-hundred and seventy-eight years of national existence before the first black Supreme Court justice was appointed. Nominated by President Lyndon B. Johnson on April 17, it was not until August 30, 1967, that Thurgood Marshall was confirmed by the United State Senate. He was nominated by President Johnson not only because of his race, but also because of his long and continuous support of civil rights and civil liberties, in which the President had a strong interest.

Therefore, to compare Justice Marshall's civil rights voting record with his socioeconomic background, the procedure of most political behavioralists, is to engage in something of a self-fulfilling prophecy. Likewise, there is little use in looking at Marshall's record in relation to his SES index, as many of the cases on which he has voted had little or nothing to do with blacks, minorities, or civil rights. His liberalism in one area of constitutional law would have little to do with his voting record in other, unrelated areas. Finally, the traditional approach would tell us little about his relationship to other justices, as individuals, or as a group.

Justice Marshall's voting record and judicial behavior should be approached as a unique case, for it has no historical antecedants. An examination of Justice Marshall's voting patterns in all civil rights and criminal cases from 1967 through the summer of 1976 follows: he concurred a total of 231 times, dissented 107 times, and abstained 21 times. He concurred with the majority of the court two-thirds of the time and dissented or abstained one-third; his dissenting votes rose slowly and steadily in the early and mid-seventies. In summarizing the 1978-79 term, Bruce Fein writes; "In the realm of Criminal Justice, Rehinquist, Burger, and Blackmun solidly supported the government whereas Brennan, Marshall, and Stevens were steadfast in opposition."[26] Usually they held for the accused or inmate.

"In the area of Civil Rights Jurisprudence," Fein, using a selected sample of twenty cases, notes, "Rehnquist voted only once with civil rights advocates, who managed only two votes from Burger. In contrast, Marshall championed civil rights in all twenty cases and was joined by Brennan and White eighteen and thirteen times, respectively."[27]

Below the national level there is not much hard information, but a recent journalistic study based on numerous interviews provides some insights into black judicial behavior and legal activity in Washington, D.C. from earliest times to the present.[28] This portrait of the black judiciary in Washington, D.C., also included the black lawyers who worked for the Justice Department.

The series shows how the systemic variables have made it extremely difficult for a black person to move through a law school to become, first, a lawyer and eventually attain the staus of judge.

The study told of Louis Mehlinger, who became a clerk on June 4, 1921, and passed the District of Columbia bar in 1922; he was the sole practicing black attorney in the Justice Department during the presidency of Warren G. Harding.[29] However, it was a black Republican political appointee to the Justice Department, attorney Perry Howard, who was to be responsible for moving Mehlinger from a position as law clerk to assistant attorney and set the stage for his final move to senior attorney in the department.

Mehlinger's long struggle against the city's judiciary structure led him to create and run a black night law school from 1935-1950; the Robert H. Terrell Law School graduated 600 black lawyers, including some of the current black jurists. He also helped organize the black bar association in the city in 1925.

The same qualities of the system that led the only "colored" man at justice to this activity also led the black firm of Houston and Houston to develop and implement a systematic legal strategy for dismantling racial segregation.[30] Charles H. Houston was a lawyer, schoolteacher, and later the head of the NAACP legal defense fund from 1934 to 1938. Among those Houston taught was none other than Justice Thurgood Marshall.

Like Mehlinger and Houston, A. Mercer Daniels, librarian of the Howard Law School, struggled against the closed legal structure. Before 1941, black law school graduates were banned from the law library in the federal courthouse, and before 1947, blacks were barred from bar review courses. Daniels, to help blacks break through this systemic barrier, tutored students in his home.

The study found new, current barriers which continue to hamper black activity in the legal circles of the district.[31]

Focusing on the history of the rise from legal circles to the bench, the study found similar stories. President Taft appointed the first black lawyer of recent times to the district courts in 1909, who continued in the post until his death in 1926. After Robert Terrell came James Cobb, who held on until a black Democrat was appointed by President Franklin Roosevelt in 1934. After Roosevelt, the study found that the federal bench in the district remained entirely white until the mid-1960's when President Lyndon B. Johnson selected Spottswood Robinson III, William Bryant, Joseph Waddy, and Aubrey Robinson, Jr. for the U.S. District Court.[32] President Nixon added one black to the federal bench and five to the local bench, but Attorney General Saxby recommended to President Gerald Ford that a vacancy on the District's Court of Appeals be filled by a white surburan resident.

However, the local courts in the District got a black majority when home rule was granted to them through the efforts of Black Congressman Charles Diggs (D.-Mich.) and D.C. Judicial Selection Commission was granted the powers to name judges. The power to appoint federal judges in the district, however, still resides with the President. By 1984, that power had been modified somewhat because the Commission was granted the power to recommend D.C. Judges for appointment by the President.

The social milieu in the District has profoundly affected the black judges. First there is the matter of treatment from colleagues on the bench. "The white municipal court judges," write Whitaker and Meyer, "excluded Judge Scott from parties they held" and as he became a "senior judge, he literally got a broom closet for his chambers and presided most" over "drunk court." Next there was the matter of treatment from defendants in the court. As a judge, Scott would ask the defendant if has anything to say. The (white) defendants would say, "yes, no nigger judge is going to put me in jail." Scott would then "recess for 45 minutes for himself to cool off and then sentence them."[33]

In regard to the present, Whitaker writes: "Judge Bryant has never favored long prison sentences and each case that could result in incarceration causes him personal agony. (And) because of his highly sensitive and sometimes time-consuming approach to making decisions, Bryant has gained the distinction of having the slowest work record of any judge in court."[34] Other black judges have been subjected to other types of systemic influences,[35] suggesting a wide variety of behavioral actions and responses shaped not only by the structure but by the types of cases which the judges hear. Professor Ware's recent analysis of black jurists in several cities yielded results similar to the patterns revealed in the series on the District of Columbia.

Black judges find themselves involved in a system of justice that dispenses both justice and injustice; they must deal with the sundry forces in the system that demand certain kinds of justice in certain situations Hence the judges' backgrounds, law schools, and personalities are not the only forces seeking to influence their behavior. There are forces inside the judicial system, that affect behavior just as powerfully as external forces. Elected black judges are as profoundly affected as appointed ones. Another major problem for the black judiciary is the dispensing of justice to those in a racial minority.

Some Concluding Thoughts

The study of the attitudes of black judges by using their voting records is limited, and it can be counterproductive. When the results of such studies are presented as knowledge the insights at best are only half truths.

The study of black judges' personal backgrounds and educations is no better, for the results are bound to be unidimensional and sketchy. When combined, the two approaches are only individualistic perspectives that note some of the forces and motivations for action in individual cases.

Content analysis of judicial decisions is not solution either. Even undergraduates learn that some of the "landmark" Constitutional decisions, like *Marbury* vs. *Madison,* are political rather than Judicial decisions. Analysis of individual records and decisions will not necessarily reveal the weight and influence of these outside political forces.

The systemic forces are ever present and influential. Black judges live, breathe, and issue judicial decrees amidst these forces. To ignore them or assign them to noninfluencial roles, or to construct a paradigm of black judicial activity without including them invites distortions, functionally useless generalizations, and strained pictures of reality.[36] Black judicial behavior is an interplay of internal and external factors which must be studied by methods and techniques that account for both sets of forces. As more black judges occupy seats at the bench, a better multidimensional picture of black judicial activity will slowly surface.

Chapter 9

Black Political Leadership Behavior

Political leadership has long been studied by both scholars and layman. The social psychologists, the historians, the journalists, the psychologists, the sociologists, and the political scientists have all probed the characteristics, the backgrounds, and the fall of those who have headed political units and organizations throughout the world. Ethnic and minority group leadership is no exception to the rule.

The Literature on Leadership

When the behavioral revolution hit political science, the probing of political leadership became deeply inbued with psychological and psychoanalytic theory. The question raised most often was that of Harold Lasswell in one of his pioneering studies: "What are the relationships between a man's personality and his political behavior?"[1] Slowly, political scientists, following the path blazed by Sigmund Freud and others of the psychoanalytical school, developed a theory of political leadership motivation. This theory, which dominated the literature from Lasswell's original work to the late sixties, can be called the *displacement* or *tension-reduction theory*.

Of the political personality, Lasswell writes: "Our key hypothesis about the power seeker is that he pursues power as a means of compensation against deprivation. Power is expected to overcome low estimates of the self, by changing either the traits of the self or the environment in which it functions."Hence, according to Lasswellian model, "the perfect power type is wholly absorbed with advancing the value position of the 'scared me' (not 'us'). Therefore he scarifices anyone and everyone...for his power."[2]

Individuals and leaders, noted psychologist Gordon Allport in explaining the theory, are motivated by "a state of tenseness that leads us to seek equilibrium, rest, adjustment, satisfaction or homeostasis."[3] In short, change, new events, and social dislocation produce tension and frustrations which, in turn, lead individuals, in Lasswell's view, to displace these "private affects upon public objects."[4] Leaders work out these frustrations through the attainment and manipulation of political power. Because of this drive, "the primary goal is to relieve through aggression, in the form of agitation, this profound psychological tension or frustration" and "the literal attainment of particular objectives is only a secondary consideration."

In a study of the mayor of Chicago, Anton J. Cermak, Alex Gottfried found a relationship between the mayor's gastrointestional disturbances and his political leadership.[5] "Cermak's surface attitudes throughout his life," writes Gottfried, "were those most typical of the 'gastric type' patient..."[6] He continues, "Cermak demonstrated the characteristics of the 'anal' person in a whole congeries of related traits: his hostility, suspiciousness, lack of warmth, reluctance to delegate responsibility...and finally, in the central characteristic of his personality, the demand for power."[7] Gottfried concludes: "The dynamic background of Cermak's illness as formulated by Alexander and other writers allow us to place this politician rather squarely in the category of power-seeking personalities suggested by Lasswell and a number of psychologists." In this study, the public good which Cermak sought was only a secondary consideration, because his primary goals were the relieving of his frustration and tension arising from his stomach disorders.

The Cermak example is only one of the many studies developed on the basis of the behavior model structured and informed by the work of Freud and Lasswell. Political scientist Harold Zink made a similar psychological analysis of a Klan leader;[9] Adorno and his associates, using the Lasswellian schema, "uncovered" the "authoritian personality."

Following the school of thought that explained political leadership as a result of "intrapsychic" tension, was political scientist Robert E. Lane. His "grammar of political motives" saw political activity as serving some six general human needs.[10] Yet his attempt to extend and enlarge Lasswell's model suffered from the same lack of specificity that Lasswell's model had. Hence, his study made few meaningful advances.

But political scientists and psychologists were not the only academicians to be attracted to the "intrapsychic" tension theory. Historians also produced their share of works using this model. "Many historians, " writes Gerald Sorin, "have characterized their work on abolitionist leaders with similar themes referring to the reformers' motivation as a function of 'maladjustments,' 'desire for martyrdom,' 'the easing of guilt,' 'psychic forces clamoring for expression,' and as an 'outgrowth of desperate inner needs.'"[11] Historians like David Donald, Stanley Elkins, Fran Brodie, and a host of others employed the "intrapsychic" tension theory to explain radical leadership in history.[12]

Sociologists, too, followed the political scientists and historians. Seymour Martin Lipset described the American radical right leadership as being motivated by status dislocation and its ensuing frustrations.[13] In fact, right-wing leaders and their ideologies have come to be explained in most of the behavioral literature as evolving from personality disorders. "Conservatism," noted Herbert McClosky, "appears to be far more characteristic of social isolates, of people... who suffer personal disgruntlement and frustration...poorly integrated psychologically, anxious, often perceiving themselves as inadequate, and subject to excessive feelings of guilt; they seem inclined to project onto others the traits they most dislike or fear themselves."[14] Lispet had continued this tradition in his most recent work, which developed out of the Wallace-for-President movement in 1968.[15] Along with Lipset's contemporary analysis, is some of the work of Robert Coles, who found segregationists to be disturbed,[16] and the writings of Alexander George, Sigmund Freud, and William Bullitt on President Woodrow Wilson.[17]

However, these explorations and explanations of leadership ran into some stiff criticism, which led to the second behavioral theory of leadership. Critics of Lasswell's ideas argued that his model sees all public leaders as neurotic and the personality disorders of the leader, then the merits of his claims can be easily dismissed or forgotten.

"The methodological mistake of psychoanalytic explanations, notes Heberle, consists "in the direct, unmodified application of categories of personality psychology to the analysis and characterization of highly complex and flexible social groups."[19] And in so doing, it becomes extremely difficult "to determine the exact frequency of certain motives among a multitude of individuals...."

Erich Fromm has gone on to suggest that the entire "society as a whole may be lacking in sanity," and that the rebel or radical leader might not be neurotic or sick but "genuinely attempting to correct the irrationality of a given social order."[20] Finally, there were those critics who asked: why is it that the extremist, the conservatives, and the radicals are sick or neurotic, but never the moderates and the liberals? Behavioralism, cry these critics, leaves the liberals and moderates as always psychologically sound.[21]

A second model or theory was soon born. This second behavioral theory of leadership, simply put, stressed the notion that the "leadership" personality was shaped during the individual's adolescent years. This theory still employed psychoanalysis but shifted away from personal tensions and frustrations to survey the leader's childhood and maturity and personal crisis of identity. Although Lasswell had suggested this approach along with the frustration-tension paradigm, the major progress came with the work of Erik Erikson. His *Young Man Luther* and *Gandhi's Truth* blazed a new path.[22] The last book won for him the Pulitzer Prize and increased his already immense reputation.

Of Erikson, Wolfenstein writes that he "provides life developmental concepts which nicely complement Lasswell's more psychodynamic approach."[23] Erikson constructs several stages in a person's psychosexual maturity and outlines the influences that these stages might have on a person's development of his own identity. For him, "the process of character formation begins at birth, if not before, and is largely completed by the end of adolscence. Man thus matures emotionally over a long period of time."[24] "It is human,"Erikson argues, "to have a long childhood, it is civilized to have an even longer childhood. Long childhood makes a technical and mental virtuoso out of man, but it also leaves a lifetime residue of emotional immaturity in him."[25] In a word, the child is constantly haunting man in Erikson's scheme of things. The important stages , according to his theory, are the oral phase, the genital or oedipal phase, and the latency period.

Armed with Erikson's insights, the political behavioralist started to seek out the influence of a person's childhood on his motivations and public actions. Fred I. Greenstein, following this lead, attempted to clear away the "underbrush" in political science literature: "It follows that social and personality characteristics are in no way mutually exclusive. They do not complete as candidates for explanations of social behavior, but rather are complementary. Social 'characteristics' can in some way be more important than personality characteristics."[26] Nevertheless, Greenstein leaves the reader in limbo. What is the connection? And what are the guidelines that one should follow when he discovers that a particular researcher pointedly emphasizes personality factors over systemic and structural variables?

E. Victor Wofenstein went even further. He attempted to relate early childhood and adolescent experience to particular types of leadership and followers. In his first book, he sought to find those traits inherent in revolutionary personalities. However, he concluded after studying Lenin, Gandhi, and Trotsky that he could not be definite. "Political men and political processes, like revolution, are complicated things; and it is not presumed that ideas developed in this study provide definite solutions to any of the problems we raised...For there is more to understanding men than can currently be gleaned from psychological knowledge; and there are other useful perspectives on revolution than the psychological."[27]

However, he continued to look for those characteristics that produces political philosophers, political leaders or statesmen, and those that produced political adherents or followers. In the first category, he examines the early life of Friedrich Nietzsche; he examined Winston Churchill for the second category; and he explored Malcolm X's early life for the third category. He concluded that "by using psychoanalytic theory (he) was able to find connections among the various life experiences of each man which were not discernible on the manifest level. In each case (he) found that political activity served as a vehicle for managing the guilt that accompanied the father-son relationship. For Churchill an identification with his father formed the psychological basis for his capacity to lead. *Malcolm X's adherency to Elijah Muhammed and the Nation of Islam grew out of his need to be a loyal son to his father.* Nietzsche's philosophical activity allowed him to express his highly ambivalent feelings for the father he manifestly loved."[28]

But Wolfenstein wondered out loud about the approach. "Psychoanalytic theory involves," he wrote, "joining two not entirely compatible qualities." To do a good job, a person must identify with his protagonist but must simultaneously be detached from him. Second, Wolfenstein indicated that "one must be sensitive to the broad social and historical context within which the person lived... (for) ignoring such factors results in a psychological reductionism which obscures as much as it clarifies...[29] And last, he admitted that "psychoanalytic theory...directs (one's) attention toward the individual."[30] But despite his caution, Wolfenstein's findings must be taken with great care because Malcolm X moved from follower to leader and Wolfenstein's psychoanalysis does not explain the change.[31]

Though much criticism of this approach is developing, for the time being it holds sway over the literature and methodolgy. Wolfenstein's assessment is typical: "Despite the ambiguities and difficulties involved, despite the residue of what cannot be explained, it is worthwhile to continue studying human nature in politics."[32] Recent research has suggested that personality characteristics are but one source of explanation and that a multivariate and multidimensional approach is better.[33]

In sum, two theories dominate the behavioral approach to political leadership. One explains leadership from intrapsychic tensions and the other from factors and forces operating in the person's early childhood and adolescence. The latter is more clearly in vogue and is widely used despite its weaknesses and limitations.

These two versions of the behavioral study of political leadership are not the only techniques that have been employed to study political leaders. In addition, there is the elitist approach, which studies reputations and strategic positions to designate political and community leaders. Since much has been written about this approach and it has been little employed in the studies of black political leadership, we can move to the third typological method.

The typological method uses schema of leadership types based on personality factors and techniques; this method currently dominates the literature on black leaders, delineating, describing the nature, scope, functions, and significance of black leadership. Other methods have been advanced as being appropriate but few of them have captured much attention and usage. Lester Seligaman, for instance, noted that leadership can be studied as a function of social status, as a form of organizational function, and from the standpoint of political biography.[34] However, the behavioral techniques presently hold sway despite their limitations.

The Literature on Black Leadership

Since "political activity in the black community has often been dependent upon a single strong leader," argues K. C. Morrison, "there seems to be a disproportionate number of studies on ...(black) leadership" especially in the South.[35] Morrison is right. By the mid-sixties, works on black leadership filled the library shelves. The nature and significance of the actions of Southern black leaders were constantly analyzed. White academicians and journalists constantly interviewed black leaders to determine their concerns, goals, and strategies.[36] But the 1960's, wrote Morrison, "brought such disparate leadership and mass participation that (it) is (now) difficult to see how these old studies could be useful in the same way." Thus the end of the leadership studies seems to be near and appropriately so! The present electoral black leadership is in many ways vastly different from the old charismatic leadership of the pre-sit-in days.

Out of the literature of this period one work neatly summarizes the early studies, synthesizing their findings with new data and new interviews: Everett C. Ladd's *Negro Political Leadership in the South*.[37] Ladd's work did not break out of the earlier studies. In fact, in its attempt to decrease the confusion about typologies, it ends up by only offering a new typology. "The typology used here contains three categories," writes Ladd, "which have been labeled conservatives, moderates and militants. We are saying that militant leaders in each race relations situation are, in their rhetoric, goals, and means, less acceptable to the dominant group of whites than are moderates, who in turn are less acceptable than conservatives. Southern whites certainly use these descriptive categories to indicate the extent to which they will accept the styles of leadership."[38] Thus, Ladd defined black leadership behavior in terms of its relationship to the white community.

Although very few studies employed behavioral approaches in studying black leaders, there were exceptions. E. Victor Wolfenstein did a piece on Malcolm X, and black political scientist Cedric Robinson tried to apply the Weberian concept of charisma to Malcolm X; both had some difficulties.[39] Wolfenstein's use of psychoanalysis on Malcom X almost stands alone. But great flaws in his work indict this methodological approach as being of extremely limited value. Malcolm X, as Wolfenstein categorizes him, becomes a political adherent, a follower, not a leader. Applying psychoanalytic theory to Malcolm X's psychosexual maturation, Wolfenstein discovered that "Malcolm had accepted Elijah Muhammed with a truly filial love, he had trusted him as one ideally trusts one's father; and it was the prophet who had given him, if not life itself, at least rebirth, a new name and something approaching psychic harmony."[40] Wolfenstein summarizes: "Only by submitting to the prophet, by wielding to him the prerogative for all judgments and decisions, was Malcolm able to accept his feelings of guilt. Only by accepting the role of Elijah Muhammed's son and allowing himself to be absorbed into the family of Islam was he able to cast off his sense of impotence, of powerlessness...Elijah Muhammed gave him, in short, the gift of belief, of a holy cause to serve."[41]

But early in 1964, after his pilgimage to Mecca, Malcom broke with Elijah and set up the organization of Afro-American Unity. He became a leader and a major influence on the black radicals of the period. Yet Wolfenstein characterizes him as a follower—who later became a leader; something is wrong. His childhood cannot be said to have prepared him to be a follower when he himself later became a leader, unless there is something the Wolfenstein psychoanalytical approach missed.

But Wolfenstein was not finished with Malcolm X. In 1981, he would produce another book that would attempt to answer some of the unanswered questions in the first volume.[42] And in this new book, Wolfenstein would combine Freudian psychoanalysis with Marxist class analysis to explain Malcolm's journey from an individual with a false consciousness to a follower of Elijah to finally a radical leader and his tremendous role in the black revolution. In the book, psychoanalysis explains the inner realities of Malcolm, while Marxism explains the outer or external realities of Malcolm's environment. This new Marxist framework permits the author to move beyond the limitations of his earlier study because it provides an explanation of the social and historical conditions of blacks in America, and the former technique shows how Malcolm mentally adjusted to these external class problems and obstacles. Although this new approach directs one's attention to both the individual and his surrounding environment, ultimately Wolfenstein suggest that Malcolm's leadership mantle can be best explained by his own internal subjective responses to his surrounding external conditions. In Wolfenstein's view, the right combination of economic, historical and personal factors leads to radical black political leadership. Thus despite this new addendum model of Marxism, the final insights remain inside the psycho-historical construct. Individualistic factors still hold the key to explanation. But the question remains: What are the ingredients and the right combination of the ingredients?

The Typological Approach

The typological approach to black political leadership likewise has serious deficiencies. The proponents of this methodology assign black leaders to specific categories on the basis of the *speed* with which they wanted integration to occur and on the basis of the kinds of goals they sought (status, welfare, improved race relations, etc.). But goals and strategies are crude tools with which to analyze black leadership.

In crisis situations, the typologies become blurred. Millitants and moderates become hard to distinquish. Rapidly changing events force black leaders to change their strategies. And, most important, the goal of integration itself comes under strong attack. The typologies developed during the forties, fifties, and early sixties were useless during the turbulence of the "black-power era." Men and strategies changed so rapidly they were impossible to type. Lerone Bennett commented, "It is hard in a revolutionary age to identify the real revolutionaries...it is very difficult to tell whether a given revolutionary prophet was born prematurely or posthumously..."[43] Moreover, the aftermath of the revolution made possible the emergence of a large array of black electoral leaders and organizations that now competed with the nonelectoral organizations in the black community for a leadership role. In this period, goals and strategies also changed with the rise of new black caucuses, parties, political assemblies, and the leaders who headed these organizatons. The old typologies simply could not deal with movements and leaders that fell outside the integrationist perspective.

The second major problem with the typological approach is that most of the types were developed during the segregationist era, when pressure-type black leadership predominated, those who operated in a "closed" enviroment. The validity of a typology predating a major electoral era must be questioned. *Typologies are static concepts trying to grasp dynamic and changing realities.* They are inherently weak tools. In revolutionary times, times of great upheavals, great stress and tension, they cannot keep pace.[44]

By 1984 a black political scientist made a serious effort to enhance and improve the typological methodology as it related to the study of black political leadership. In the most comprehensive and systematic analysis of black leadership yet, Robert Smith provides the most thorough critique currently available of the black leadership literature. Based on the deficiencies and limitations which he found, he developed a new modified typological technique. He writes: "The leadership typology was disaggregated into its three constituent elements—beliefs, methods, and rhetoric—and then applied fruitfully to the available data on Black leaders, thereby permitting the distinguishing of leadership militancy on the basis of each element." And in this manner, "means need not be subordinate to ends." A new typological methodology which is sensitive and redefined so that it can grasp the realities of black political leadership is a major improvement over the old technique.[45]

An Ideological Approach: The Cruse Model

It was in the midst of these changes that Harold Cruse developed an ideological approach to the study of black leadership. His approach broke with tradition; in being a pioneer of sorts, Harold Cruse became both a much-lauded and much-criticized figure. Blacks and whites alike attacked and praised him. Yet few saw him as a theorist of black leadership behavior. But he was. In fact, he developed a model for black leaders to follow in order to achieve black liberation in America.

Cruse's analysis of black leadership falls into two phases. In phase one, as noted in Figure 9.1 Cruse sees all black leadership as embracing either integrationist or nationalist idelogies, in one degree or another. But because of the nature of the struggle in America and the existence of "cultural imperialism," black leaders are forced to move to the final ideological state of Marxian-socialism. The embracing of this last ideology, Marxism-socialism, *insures* complete failure of the black liberation movements, as well as the failure or "crisis" of black leadership.

As Cruse sees it, the sundry shades of integrationist ideology and the varied and myriad facets of nationalist ideology are simply not strong enough tools to organize the black masses for a final liberation movement. Once black leaders see this, then they are prone, in Cruse's analysis, to take the fatal step toward communist ideology, which will prove even more ineffective as an ideological tool with which to move the black masses. Not only is its utility within the black community limited, but the white left itself, according to Cruse, is shot through with misunderstandings of the black presence and movements in the

United States. Thus, the white left in America is in a hopeless state and cannot lead anyone, not even itself.[46]

In his first work, Cruse used Harlem as the model community and his own experiences to bolster his view of black leaders' ideological failings. His attack upon the white left is clear and perceptive.[47] But after making his analysis of what is wrong with black leaders' ideological orientations, Cruse then prescribes the type of ideology that black leaders should embrace and that would liberate the black masses. That ideology is *culturalism,* presumably black culturalism. This is the second phase of Cruse's analysis or model. "It is not yet understood that without a cultural philosophy (or methodology) suitable for radical politics within the interracial context of American realities, it is impossible to organize the Negro masses around the political or economic reforms of black power."[48] He continues:

> In the same way that the nation of Islam used religion to bind Negroes together into a social and economic movement (without politics), the secular black radical movement must use the cultural ingredient in black reality to bind Negroes into a mass movement with economics and politics. This has to be done through a cultural program that makes demands for cultural equality in American society. Without cultural equality there can be no economic and political equality.[49]

Since "the white Anglo-Saxon protestant group set the cultural standards for all other groups" in America, no black movement can ever fully establish its cultural identity. Therefore, "for the Negro" argues Cruse, *"social revolution is impossible without a cultural revolution."* Hence, black liberation for the black masses would be possible if black leaders developed an ideology based on black culturalism. However, exactly what black culturalism is, Cruse only partially defines in his writing. His thesis leads one to believe that it would include a new set of values, a new sense fo justice, and a new philosophy of life, as well as a reordering of human priorities. The Cruse model is indeed provocative. In addition, it is one of the clearest statements to the black community since King's non-violence and other theories of black power.

Cruse's critics claim that his analysis is just one way of looking at the facts and then ordering the world. As for his proposal of

Fig. 9.1. Harold Cruse's Analysis of Black leadership

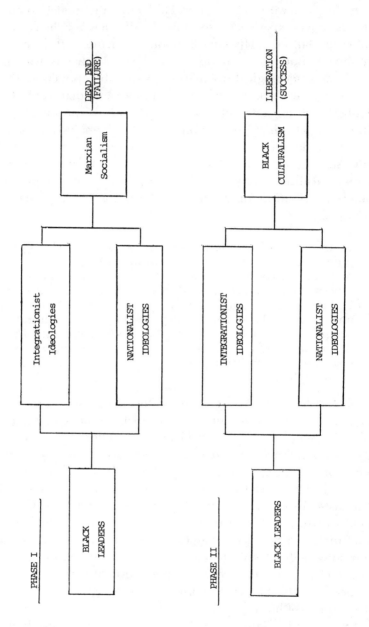

culturalism as an ideology, they note that it must be identified, transmitted, and inculcated. Finally, they ask, how does a minority transmit fundamental values which set into motion a new reordering of values first to itself and then to the majority?

Cruse has continued his incisive analysis of black leaders' idelogical shifts using his original model. Most recently he has strongly attacked Imamu Amiri Baraka (Leroy Jones) for his shift to Marxian socialism.[50] Few others are seeking to analyze black leadership behavior from an ideological perspective. Despite some problems in the Cruse model, the approach brought to light a major dilemma in black leadership that other methodological approaches passed over.

The Dilemma of Black Leadership

Black leaders, like any other heads of political and social units and organizations, have invoked ideologies to mobilize their followers. Many different ideological outlooks have been employed throughout black history, with varying degrees of success. The use of nonviolent ideology by Martin Luther King, Jr., is both well known and an excellent example.[51]

However, black leaders must move a race of people, whereas other leaders are concerned with socially defined groups: workers, unions, political parties, nations, and *ad hoc* movements. When racialism (nationalism) is combined with a particular ideology, contradictions arise both for the integrationist and the black-nationalist leaders.

For instance, when integrationists seek to mobilize the black masses to work toward an integrated society by employing "race" as a mobilizing technique, they must play up the achievements and pride of race and other positive aspects of the black past and call for black unity and pride. These same leaders must then play down or limit this feature as the the black masses approach the goal of integraton. The positive features of integration must then take precedence over the positive features of the black past. This was the issue to which many black power advocates spoke in the mid-sixties.

On the other hand, the black nationalists' use of race as a mobilizing device also meets contradictions when their followers look around them in society. Black nationalists who talk of the glorious black past, the great black empires and nation-states and the existence of great black contributions throughout the world, soon must leave their halls and walk into a society where they are the minority, in minority positions of power and influence. The realities conflict violently with the exhortations. In short, nearly all black leaders must deal with contradictions that eventually cause problems and raise questions of credibility both from within and without their movements. Herein lies the dilemma, for the contradictions cannot readily be solved.

To escape this dilemma, some black leaders and intellectuals have moved to class-based or religious-based ideologies, i.e., to something larger than race. Cruse pointed out the dilemmas facing these pioneers. Yet his cultural approach, while interesting, also eventually succumbs to the same dilemma: credibility.

Functional Black Leadership in a Southern City: A Community Study

Black leadership has arisen to serve needs within the black community. To be sure, some black leaders have sought to serve their own selfish interests, and others have sought to serve white interests Ultimately, however, black leaders have had to respond to the myriad concerns and hopes in the black community. Any analysis of how black leaders behave must attune itself to those needs and aspirations.

Moreover, most studies of black leadership have focused on the dilemma facing black leaders and not the needs being addressed in the black community. Hence, they dwelled on the man, his shortcomings, and his colorful and at times contradictory behavior. In addition, they told of the vast number of black leaders, their factionalism and their efforts to eliminate each other. Finally, their failings were eventually blamed on them and their methods. However, inside any black community there are a variety of black leaders: educational, religious, social, fraternal, professional, and artistic—all seeking to address their own narrow concerns as well as those of the larger black community. Clearly these community leaders will clash, unify, change allies, change strategies and tactics, and rise and fall as resources, money, and skills permit.

The social and political structure also plays a major role in shaping black leaders. Too many of the earlier studies ignored the context out of which black leaders arose and the situation that they addressed, which were powerful systemic forces affecting them and their actions. To exclude these forces from analysis is to eliminate a crucial variable in their motives. Second, to overlook what effect the structural and contextual variables had upon their pronouncements and programs, is to see the black leaders as inevitably performing for others and not for the black community.

E. Franklin Frazier long ago said; "The position of a Negro leader on the race problem is being determined more by the outlook and ideology of the group which he represents than by the fact that he is radical and conservative."[52] In short, Frazier argued that in time, as social, economic, and political fortunes changed in the black community, they developed a diversity of interests within the community. The result was the emergence of *functional leaders.*[53] When viewed and understood in this fashion, the "chaotic condition of Negro though," and the "conflicting viewpoints" and "incessant backbiting and factionalism" among black leaders becomes something else entirely—forces arising naturally from a diversity of needs and aspirations within a particular community.

Those who condemned this reality and "sought a black spokesman" eventually developed in their writing what might be labeled the "Booker T. Washington leadership syndrome." Although we shall discuss the tendency later, it is necessary at this point to discuss the functions that various black leaders serve in the black community.

Using a single community approach, we will look at the functions that black leaders perform in their various organizations within the black community. In each of these organizations, philosophies and tactics as well as the constant pressure of sytemic and structural forces continue to work in formative ways. The leaders interviewed in this survey are: (1) a traditional black civil-rights organizational leader, (2) a black religious leader, (3) a black grassroots leader, and (4) a black *ad hoc* leader. The list is not intended to be exhaustive, but it will permit a close examination of some of the key current functional leaders within the black community, their functions, and the interfacing of systemic variables on their course of action.

Leadership in Traditional Civil-Rights Organizations:

W.W. Law has been president of the Savannah, Georgia Chapter of the NAACP since May 1950. He has stood for election and reelection twenty-six times in the last twenty-six years and won each time.[54] The perspective from which he views things and the type of black leadership philosophy he has developed—meshing his own goals and aspirations with those of black people whom he has tried to serve and with the program and the ideals of the national organiza-tion—have bred an outlook that is neither static nor formal. Law describes the framework that confines and molds black leadership. "If anybody is working on the problem, that hasn't changed in 50 years, not just the sixties, it hasn't changed in a hundred years."

"Basically the Negro is here to stay and he must develop the mechanism for getting what it takes to exist and to survive in this country...Thus, the struggle is one of continuously confronting their consciousness" as well as a process of "wrestling from the man who got it all, some of it for black folks who have nothing...."

"The real struggle and fight," he continues, "for Negro advance-ment lies in the day-to-day confrontation of every decision; where monies are to be appropriated, where the appointments are to be made.... These are the places and not just at election time." At this point Law paused, frowned, and noted: "This is where the white man has sold us out, because he comes to us at election time, but we must *go to him whenever things are coming up to affect our lives*—he will not seek us out when he is getting ready to appropriate monies for causes, for the various community projects and it is at that point that we have to confront him—seek him out."

Law is also clear about the mechanism to be used in this struggle. "From the standpoint of history," he argues, "the one mechanism and organization that has done more to protect the hide of black people and done more to make him a real competitor with white folks, is the NAACP.... And rather than to spend a great deal of time trying to fashion a new tool, *I will and black people should* take this tool, sharpen it up a little bit and continue on hammering on the problem."

If Law's commitment to the organization is clear and basic, he is equally clear about the germane force which he feels ties the organization to the masses. This tie is, simply, *trust.* He states,

> The real leveler for me and the other leaders; for all
> black leaders is to be responsible to the plain folk...for
> black folks do trust us, they have trusted their religious
> leaders, they have trusted their political leaders, the early
> efforts for our black businesses was a matter of trust, and
> it is something that we oughta deal with and handle with
> a great deal of care, for too often they don't know and

they are willing to go along with the guys who they think
do know...and that puts a heavy responsibility on the
black leaders....

Understood in this manner, black leaders then become, in Law's
view, "primarily a vehicle for getting something for black people who
have nothing and *must get* something." "It should not be," he
insisted,

> too much *I* or too much *me*. Black officeholders, and
> black leaders, must be individuals who serve at the
> pleasure of the black community and whenever that
> community says, either officially or unofficially, that we
> feel that somebody else can better serve us at this point
> than you, then the leader oughta be gracious enough to
> step aside...black leaders must not be wedded to the office
> but let the best interest of the people determine who will
> be in office. In other words, I do not think we (black
> folk) can afford to create the same kind of professional
> politicians that are constantly running for office which
> predominates in the white community. We need to spend
> more time in fitting the man to the needs he is to serve.

In short, Law feels that black leaders need both *training* and a
social consciousness to be effective. Black leadership in his view,
however, faces numerous systemic constraints and obstacles. Law put
it bluntly: "Black political leaders should not go into office too
hungry—nor should they speak somewhat at variance to the others,
for if so, whites immediately begin to center in on him to enhance
this divergent opinion to emphasize to the other black leaders that
'y'all aren't together, when y'all git together, y'all come back to us.'"
He repeatedly encountered this tactic over the years simply
because "the white man is looking for someone who agrees with him,
in part or in whole and that if he can get this, he need not change any
of his thinking, he was right all the time, in what he was doing, in
what he was thinking and in what he was preparing to do." But this
tactic is not the only one, Law argues. If dissension-creating tactics do
not work, other tactics are: (1) "to begin to give awards of various
kinds;" (2) "promote or give the wives a good job;" (3) "look out for
the children when they finish school," (4) "and use their economic
advantage...it is the one thing that perhaps they use more than any
other because they have these things; they have money and positions
that they can use at will."

If black leaders are to evade these manipulating tactics, Law feels "that the black elected official and leader "oughta at least have some basis in the black community for his economic survival and be that whatever it is, he ought to be willing to live on that, so when he goes into a political situation he doesn't have to expect to profit off of black folks." Otherwise, a splitting of black leadership occurs, and the black community is sold out.

His view of black leadership, Law told the interviewer, arose from his background and maturation in the black community in Savannah. Law painted a vivid picture of these background influences, which started in the Depression era.

> My father died because he lost his job and developed a
> leaking heart, and after that I can recall standing in bread
> lines when my mother would go for flour in order to feed
> us and blacks were in charge of those lines to give staples
> to black families and as a small boy I stood there with my
> little wagon and saw my mother stand half a day and
> black leaders (a teacher, social worker and relatives of a
> prominent Negro leader) would issue out this food to their
> friends through the back door. And oftentimes when we
> got half-way up the line they would say to those waiting,
> there is not more today...you come back tomorrow; I saw
> this being done by Negroes on other Negroes...we went to
> a dairy for the milk and whites were in charge here. We
> got the milk *generally* on a regular basis...as a boy, I
> saw white lawyers bragging that they had so many 'nigger
> votes' in their pockets. And I saw black political leaders
> being given pay-offs for their leadership for whites.... One
> thing I clearly remember was a swimming pool which the
> city built for Negroes—it was nothing more than a mud
> hole—but the Negro who was given charge of the pool
> was a black political leader and he was allowed to pocket
> the nickels and dimes and fifteen cents that we paid to
> swim and that was his pay-off.... At other times black
> church leaders who supported white politicians were given
> neon signs for their churches as pay-offs...." "*All of these
> things I saw and vowed to change once I became a black
> political leader.*"

Reacting to this pattern of white manipulation and black personal aggrandizement, Law elevated over them the interest and needs of the black community. As head and leader of the local

NAACP, he has established a regular mass meeting where all of the local black elected and appointed officials supported and put into office by the NAACP must give an account to the black masses for their actions and policies.

Nearly all black political aspirants for public office in the city who hope to be successful must go to the organization and submit themselves and their program to the political advisory council for scrutiny and analysis. Few black political candidates in the city have won without the support of the political advisory council.

The organization itself goes out and "corrals the black electorate and forms the necessary coalition for its chosen black candidates—so they can be free to serve the community" without any harmful entanglements "or political alliances."

Law takes great pains to emphasize that "the local NAACP is a reluctant leader in political action. "Political animals," he argues, "cannot always protect minority people and it is too easy for the majority to wipe out gains made by blacks in the political arena." Thus, "the organization should not spend all of its time and efforts wheeling and dealing politically, for if it does, it is bound to lose the trust and faith of the black community" when these efforts are stymied by the white community or personal greed. "The organization should continue its efforts in pressing for black folks "with class action suits and in other cases of personal and individual discrimination." For Law the concern of the local organization is now twofold, political action and action against racial discrimination. Efforts in one area do not cancel out the other area, nor should blacks put too much emphasis upon political "animals," for in his view they are prone at times to be destructive.

Law suggests that black people should "hang on to their roots and their past and carry these things with them so that a successful linking on for the future can be made." Thus, for him, although he is head of the NAACP, integration is not so much a matter of race mixing as it is "equal participation in the things which America has to offer."

The lesson from Law is specific and instructive. Black political leadership in traditional civil rights organizations must merge a sense of community, personal aspiration, and organizational ideas. Then these organizations must serve the community both in the area of political action and to correct discriminatory practices and policies. Black leadership of this type of organization faces strong external forces that seek to shape it and minimize its representation of the black community's needs. And these forces can have telling and powerful adverse effects on minority organizations.

Law's kind of leadership can cause problems within the black community and outside it. Such a philosophical posture on behalf of the black lower class tends to clash with middle-class aspiration at times; new and emerging political elites in the city have their own designs for the organization.

Leadership in Religious Organizations:

A common feature in most urban centers in the black church and the black preacher who sooner or later dabbles in the politics of the area.[55] In fact, black ministers have long known of their power over certain individuals within the black community and the central role of the church in the community. From time to time they have employed their influence and the church for both good and bad purposes. Occasional black ministers have formed black ministerial alliances, which have come to function in a variety of ways within the black community.

The Reverend Matthew S. Brown is both a mover and leader in the Black Ministerial Alliance in Savannah, Georgia. He has significant power both inside the organization and in the community as well. Key individuals, blacks and whites, come to him for political advice, along with many parishioners in his large congregation at the St. John Baptist Church.[56] His philosophy of leadership is significant.

In his assessment of the functions of black religious organizations and black ministers in political leadership roles, the Reverend Brown is frank and incisive. The compulsion to lead, he avers, comes from two forces. "Black preachers have always wanted to be *the* leaders of their people because when we read in biblical history about biblical leaders and how they led their people into salvation...we want the same kind of image." This individual compulsion, Brown notes, is enhanced by a community one.

> People come to the black religious leader because they still feel that the minister, the preacher-prophet has some spiritual and mystical connection with God and with God there is still power. Although some people feel that God's power has been diminished, not all of them feel this way

and many assume that God will hear the preacher-prophet a little bit better and a little bit quicker than themselves."

Brown quickly adds, "People also come because they respect your opinion and because they may feel that you have your finger on the pulse of many of the problems in the community and you will be instrumental in alleviating some of their difficulties." In short, people and politicians want the influence of the church behind them and their programs.

Thus, black religious leaders, as Brown sees them, serve two functions, one on an individual plane and one on a community plane. As Reverend Brown points out, these two functions are not always served. "Because of economics," he argues, "the individual's compulsion didn't always benefit the community. There was a time," he muses, "when black people thought that many black preachers were in politics for personal aggrandizement and subsequently didn't fully trust them." He hastened to add that

> The black preacher was the most under-paid professional man in the black community and the black preacher had the same financial responsibility of other professional people; in fact, his responsibility might have been a little bit more, and that might be a reason why some black preachers saw an opportunity to get an extra dollar.
>
> But that time is now gone, we are moving out of that era and black preachers are somewhat better paid, we are now moving up to the norm. Now the church is nicer to us, thereby we can now be our own man; we can now put on our own suit of clothes and can say to God when we wake up in the morning: Lord use me like you want to use me and not like the mayor of the city wants to use me!

On the matter of serving community needs, Brown is perceptive about realities. Part of the reason why the black church leadership cannot always deliver to those coming to it for help, he notes, is the "brainwashing" efforts of the political system and other barriers constructed by the system.

> There are some things we cannot pull off by ourselves. And the white man will only work with black leaders when it is something that will benefit the white community. When you are out there fighting a totally

black cause, you will have problems with white leadership.
I've run into that problem time and again and I think
every black leader has run into that kind of problem. The
white man doesn't want to become tainted with something
wholly black.

Coupled with this the Reverend Brown insists, is the fact of
brainwashing. "There are things that white folk want black folks to
believe. We've heard so long that politics is dirty business. Well the
white man has brainwashed us with that idea, because everything we
do deals with politics, regardless of how you work it out; even inside
the church, politics is important."

"Another myth is the notion that black folks cannot get together.
I refuse to believe that black people cannot come together. We came
together in the sixties and when the cause was strong...I see black
people getting together every Sunday morning and during the week at
church meetings, fraternity meetings, sorority meetings." He goes on
to say that this perception "stems back to the slave ships when white
folks mixed the various African tribes so that blacks could not get
toegether and it is something in black folks' background that they had
to overcome. And it currently works at times to stymie organizing."

In addition to these barriers, Brown points to the fact that there
are those in the religious community who are confused about the
statement, "On this rock, I will build my church and the very gates of
Hell shall not prevail against it."

"Many people," he suggests, "have become confused over the
statement and eschew political action by the church and relgious
people." But in trying to set the record straight, Pastor Brown, as he
calls himself, argues that "if the church does not prevail against the
gates, then the gates will prevail against the church and the church
will not survive." "My philosophy," he emphasized to the writer, "is
that you cannot divorce the church from the community. The church
has a definite part to play and if it is going to survive, the church has
to get its hands dirty if it is going to move into the mainstream of
things." This reluctance to see and accept this role for the church
hampers the leadership of religious leaders.

Yet, Brown ends on a positive note: "Black leadership," he
declares, "may not be achieving all that we would like to achieve in
all areas, but we are certainly not failing."

Thus, black religious leadership serves specific functions and has
roles to play within the black community, just as do traditional and

new black civil rights organizations. The problems faced by black religious leaders are not ones that arise merely from personality traits and socioeconomic background. The Reverend Brown's remarks indicate major systemic barriers facing black religious leaders. These are limited white cooperation, biblical misinterpretation, economic insecurity, unfounded myths and brainwashing, and the lack of self-sufficiency within the black community.

Leadership in Ad Hoc Political Organizations:

Observers of the black community are quick to point to the wide variety of black organizations and their incessant bickering as a reason for their failure. The existence of numerous organizations and the continual establishment of new ones within the black community are hard to deny. The sheer numbers of these organizations, however, should not be blamed for their ineffectiveness and failures. To do so is merely to see the problem as an organizaitonal one and to refuse to see the obstacles facing the organizations.

Ad hoc political organizations tend to emerge and disappear at all levels in the black community. Some succeed, some fail and other make only a small impact. They all serve a function for the black community or for certain segments of that community. This analysis of Political Summit-74, one such *ad hoc* black political organization, attempts to portray the functions such organizations fulfill in one black community.

Thomas H. Byers has always been a black political activist.[57] In 1948, he was canvassing the southern black community for the Progressive Party of Henry Wallace. In the sixties, he was a freedom fighter and a supporter of the Great Society. By the late sixties, he had acquired a doctorate in political science and history and moved to the deanship of one of the outstanding black state colleges in the country.

Therefore, in 1974 when the Savannah mayoral election campaigns were beginning, he joined with other progressive blacks in the city and began talking about the possibility of a black mayor. When existing black organizations in the city did not take the lead, Byers and several of his peers established Political Summit-74 (PS-74).

PS-74, Byers declared,

> started as an effort to get greater unity in the black community. We saw as we looked at the community and

also based upon some studies made on the black leadership
in this community that there was great fragmentation[58]
And we felt that the time was approaching when blacks
could successfully run a candidate. Moreover, if blacks
wanted a chance for success, then all of the different
organizations that are involved in politics in the city ought
to get together to give the community in general a chance
to express themselves to determine: (1) if it was time to
offer such a candidate for mayor and (2) or whether blacks
ought to strengthen the postion we had on the city council
and express themselves about who these candidates should
be.

Byers goes on, "That is why we called it Political Summit,
because it would be a summit meeting of the leaders of all the black
organizations in the community." He paused and then noted, "We
were successful in getting all of the major black organizations as well
as sororities and fraternities and other groups that had not previously
been involved in politics, i.e., partisan politics, at least, to come in
with us and help sponsor a convention."

How did they accomplish this feat? The organizations agreed,
Byers argued, "on the basis that we (PS-74) would hold a covention at
which time we would discuss issues that were pertinent to the black
community and the possibility of running a candidate for mayor
and/or alderman. All parties agreed to the convention."

"But before we could get the convention off the ground," Byers
said in a surprised tone, "one of the traditional black civil rights
organizations in the city backed out on the grounds that if we opened
the process up as widely as we wanted to, it would leave the door
open for a candiate who might have mass appeal but who would not
have the necessary 'qualifications.'"

At this point, Byers intimated that he thought the real reason was
because old established political alliances were threatened by the
possibility that new connections or coalitions would be formed. But
being an old political pro, Byers revealed the "the organizer of PS-74
were committed; we had gone around speaking to groups; we had
secured a building for the convention and we had gone to the news
media.... We felt that we had made too much of a commitment to
back down, so we went ahead, knowing that the withdrawal of this
traditional civil rights organization meant that the convention would
not be well supported, attended or backed."

As PS-74 proceeded, they "found that there were many people whose support of the forthcoming convention were contigent upon its partial sponsorship by the old-line organization, which had withdrawn. And there were many comments from people in the community that what we were starting was simply another group rather than serving as an umbrella for all the groups in the community and this would result in splitting up the black vote."

Therefore, in deference to this criticism, Byers emphasizes, "PS-74 decided to take a low profile in the campaign and refused to identify or align with any of the particular candidates, black or white, that by now had thrown their hats into the political ring." This action, he says, kept the primary purpose of the organization untarnished; it would be an umbrella group.

Although the convention was delayed until well into the campaign so that PS-74 might overcome its problems, a convention did take place. Byers describes the convention. "We had workshops devoted to some of the specific issues which plagued the black community such as employment opportunities, voter registration, educational opportunities, etc. Each one of these workshops considered some position that they felt would be beneficial to the black community and then made reports to the total convention that resulted in some resolutions about positions which the black community would support."

Byers went on to say that the "convention itself decided that the role PS-74 would play would be to address itself to the various candidates' stands on issues and make sure that the black community knew how such candidate stood on the issues before it. Secondly, PS-74 would try to get the candidates to take favorable positions on issues pertinent to the black community."

After the convention, having chosen to play an educational rather than king-making role in the election, PS-74 tried in the last days of the campaign to act as a political broker.

Byers describes this role as follows: "We played a key role in getting the black mayoralty candidate to negotiate his position with the leading white candidate and withdraw from the race for a compromise position as alderman on the other slate.... We got the negotiations started but because of several miscues the meetings were never completed." The political brokerage role of PS-74 thus failed. "PS-74 faded," Byers concluded, "but it might revive again in 1978 if not earlier." By 1978, PS-74 was reorganized and restructured as the

Black Summit, an organization concerned with black issues in the community. Since its emergence, the group has held conferences on Selective Buying Campaigns, Black on Black Crime, and Busing. Currently, it does not endorse any political candidate, only creating the black position on issues.

The impetus for this *ad hoc* black political organization came from concerned and astute observers of the local black political scene. Sensing the needs of the black masses and the ripeness of the times, this handful of observers tried to move the black community and many of its organizations in a new political direction and to a new level of political awareness. Difficulties in achieving their goal stemmed not from poor personality traits and poor child rearing practices, but from old alliances, coalitions, and entanglements inherent in the black community. The loss of benefits from these entrenched connections spawned numerous obstacles and caused PS-74 to shift functions and purposes as political events progressed and changed. But the changes were not enough to overcome the obstacles. In the end, therefore, PS-74, had only limited success and had to reorganize.

In the future, PS-74, or a new *ad hoc* organization inspired by their meager efforts, may go on to raise the black community to a new political level. The PS-74 revolt has shown a new way, as have so many similar organizations in black communities throughout the country.

Leadership in Grassroots Organizations:

White policemen are still shooting, supposely in self-defense, black assailants in the ghetto.[59] Such an incident in Savannah recently led not to a major riot but to the creation of an urban black grassroots organization.[60] Jimmy Bennett, a young ghetto warrior who is street wise, took this opportunity to organize the urban black masses into a force to shape their own destiny and achieve self-determination.[61]

This shooting angered the black community, and the regular black civil-rights organizations proved generally ineffective in getting quick justice and meaningful relief. Filing law suits and registering complaints and resolutions did not satisfy the hot anger which insisted that something be done "now." Nor did these responses stop local governments from whitewashing the shooting. In an atmosphere of grief and sadness, many new black organizations were born. Jimmy Bennett and his grassroots movement are typical.

"This grass roots movement," Bennett said, "has two major purposes. First, it seeks to be a catalyst for change—social, economic, and political change—within Savannah." And second, "We hope we can work specifically in the inner city of Savannah and can reorder the priorities of the city government to make it address itself more to blacks in particular and the overall community."

He continued, "We feel that the growth of the overall community is predicated on the growth of the black community. And that if the black community is up to par then the whole community will be up to par; the lesser the crime, the more jobs, the lesser the people will be on the street, robbing, etc."

In a quiet and reasoned tone, Bennett went on to say: "We also feel that we ought to have the recourse to march, to boycott, yet we should be trying to raise the consciousness level of the people, putting information out where they can get to it, make it freely accessible to all the black citizens as well as white citizens."

"Ultimately," noted Bennett, "we see ourselves as tree shakers. We will take any problem, make the problem known to the overall community and move in a type of productive and forceful manner to bring about change."

Bennett then turned his attention to the matter of allies and tactics. "We don't want to negate, neither is it our position to supplant the old line black leadership but rather to complement their actions with a direct action type of program. One of the main purposes of the grassroots movement is the coalition with all other organizations in the community and we feel that the old line leadership will be attracted and attuned to our positive agenda."

Although Bennett indicated time and again that his organization is open and welcomes allies if they want to support the movement's agenda, he is less sanguine about real allies. "Our biggest problem," he insisted, "is within the black community because the leaders of the black community have let caution put them into a position of cowardice. And those young blacks who have espoused positions of self-determination will have the greatest struggle with these leaders."

"These leaders," Bennett felt, "have predicated their and the black community's progress on white progress and simply believe that something will eventually happen to improve conditions within the black community. Their limited participation in white-owned things, such as country clubs, private restaurants, and other exclusive social, political, and economic entities, caused them to become more responsive to the white man and his needs than to the black community. And hence most often before the white man can respond to defend his position, these blacks are defending it."

In his eyes the old-line black leadership has other failings. "The old-line black leadership," he argued, "constantly talks about the need for keeping a line of communication open with whites, but never talks about how productive it is. A line of communication ain't nothing if it ain't producing nothing. I wouldn't mind seeing the line of communication broken down for six months and total chaos and at the end of that time then talk about something meaningful and constructive." Bennett went on to repeat himself to dramatize his point. "As a struggling organization of young people who are independent in their thinking and who feel that black people ought to assist themselves and ought to administer things rather than being administered to all the time, we are going to find the biggest struggle within the black community also from the strongest ideology and overriding one which rules in our community, that of integration— usually just for integration's sake. They [the old-line black leaders] don't realize that integration without a sound plan for self-determination built in is absent of any real change." Moreover, "the integrationists' policy of being close to the power, then we as black people are safe, has also to be opposed because we must move to gain control over those things that affect our lives. We are talking about lending self-sufficiency to blacks as a community, whereas the old-line leaders talk about contributing to the welfare of someone else's community."

Then Bennett said that the integrationist faith that something will happen is nonsense:

> Young blacks, cannot sit and wait until something
> happens, they will have to pressure the city and the county
> administration, and the state and Congress to make things
> happen. We hope that the old-line leadership will realize
> that our position is not totally a powerless position but a
> powerful position in terms of the fact that we are the
> undergirders of the inner city economy. In the inner city,
> the white economic well-being is related to us and our
> participation and...using this as a fulcrum we can make
> them focus in on our problems and be in a situation to
> demand some returns when they say they cannot coalesce
> with us because ours is a totally black cause.

"We no longer have to ask for things; black people have been asking for too long. We are in a position to demand things. Somewhere along the line whites have to come to the black community if not to support their stores and enterprises, then to deal with us and here is where we can make our demands. And we would be demanding things which are rightfully ours.

Bennett reverted momentarily to say that if "programs are creatively developed and presented to the black masses, they will support and sponsor them economically themselves." This money can be generated, he felt, not from wealthy blacks but from the "average working man." He concluded, "Blacks should be able to take up their own positions and foster their own concerns through their own resources and skills."

To overcome the old-line black leaders and their politics of cooperation and support of progressive white programs, Bennett suggested all that grassroots movement needs to do "is to do something positive." "Blacks," he argued, "don't have any reinforcements and this is our plan." In addition, the movement will attract "numerous old blacks with progressive ideas, especially those who have been beaten down by the established black leaders long ago."

As for whites and their reaction to the movement, he smiled, paused, and began to "rap" again. "Whites," he charged, "don't know what we are really about. They think that the current black struggle is a gigantic power play to see who will get the right to go down to city hall and make the deal with them. But when they finally realize what we are about, they will be in trouble. Presently, they are constantly telling the old-line leaders to get control of their community."

Bennett's insights revealed that many of the current methods employed by black middle-class leaders and organizations are dysfunctional for the black masses. He noted that the ideological notions of middle-class black leaders are flawed because they leave out black innovation and black self-determination. Finally, he felt that coalescing with whites on matters that are in the black community's eventual interest is much too slow and of limited use to the black masses. He felt that concerned blacks should seize any dissatisfaction and discontent in the community to organize the masses and reshape urban priorities. His comments bring to mind the situation that Charles V. Hamilton found in Harlem. There, numerous fledging black organizations used the funds generated from President Johnson's Great Society poverty programs to set up organizations and challenge entrenched or old-line leaders. Upon getting such funds, these new black organizations, jealous of their new-found life, refused to cooperate with each other. "Within a four and one-half square mile area in Harlem...I counted 212 different organizations serving the community. Yet programs within blocks of each other will not get together."[62]

In short, not only will black grievances serve as a tool for organizations, economics can act as a catalyst as well. These are just two of many factors that can give impetus to the organization of blacks and the use of black leadership.

Arising from this single community analysis of the southern city, there are some startling similarities, revealed in terms of functions. Each individual sees a problem and due to his particular form of socialization and acculturation in the community, these individuals have shaped a social and political philosophy as to how the problem or problems ought to be handled. This philosophy also serves as a guide to evaluate and come to grips with the role that other black community organizations shall play. Finally, this philosophy determines, if not defines, the man, his leadership and his organizational thrust. Thus, the focus of a functional approach moves the emphasis away from the individual-centered deprivation to community-centered deprivation and how best those deprivations can be eradicated.

This approach also reveals the dissimilarities between leaders. Each leader saw the black community from a slightly different perspective and vantage point and this led each individual to develop a solution to the problem which was unique to his own abilities and talents. In fact, the solution and organization chosen was always one in which individually possesed skills and traits could evolve. In other words, these individual wanted to be leaders and given the avenues available, they tended to gravitate toward the organization where they could emerge and make the most and greatest contribution. Here, one sees individual needs being served as well as those for the community as a whole.

Finally there is the matter and nature of the black problem. The social and political system has divided up the problem into: a housing problem, a welfare problem, an education problem, a health problem, a political problem, a voting problem, etc. Thus, because of this fragmentation of the problem, it has made possible many types of functional solutions and thereby functional leaders. And this fragmentation is clearly seen in this southern community and how leadership evolves to address the problem in various ways.

Black Leadership in Other Organizations

The preceeding was an analysis of some of the types of functional leaders within a black community; there are others. Black leaders of social organizations and political organizations exist within the confines of the black community, and they serve a myriad of purposes for the community and the people they represent. The interplay of national and state leaders should not be overlooked, for these forms of leadership are very important to the black community, as are the increasingly numerous black elected officials and black radicals such as Eldridge Cleaver and Stokely Carmichael (Kwame Toure) who seek to regain leadership status.

Local black leaders were chosen because of the methodological problems posed by the elitism that surrounds national leaders. Analysis of leadership at the national and state levels makes it appear as if black leaders are all-powerful and that they gained support through rhetoric, slogans, charisma, or oratory. The truth of the matter is that all black national leaders have worked through the ever-present local leaders. King used SCLC and other organizations to put him in touch with the masses. Likewise, Marcus Garvey, Elijah Muhammed, Jesse Jackson, Roy Wilkins, W.E.B. Du Bois, and Frederick Douglass all worked through local groups. We need to know much more about the ways black leaders through the years have used this linking and supporting process to further their causes.

The primary purpose of these case studies was to cast light upon another way to understand black leadership behavior; in this instance, to see it in terms of functional roles, rather than as an outcome of inner stresses and one's adolescent years.

The four case studies reveal that black leaders not only serve themselves, their personal philosophies, their organizational concerns, the black community, and the needs of black people, they also interact and collide, and cooperate with and counteract the white community. Second, these studies reveal that leaders within the black community will face challenges and reassessments and criticism, and that in the process of reevaluation they may face demise, dismissal, or negation, as well as growth and enlargement. Finally, these studies reveal that black leaders are aware of shifts in the relative status of the black community and what these mean for them and their policies. They use what they learn in the struggle for power and transmit it to those next in line. A dynamic picture of black leadership behavior emerges from this functional analysis.

The Black Appointed and Annointed Leaders: Administrative Behavior

Not all black leaders emerge or arise inside of the black community. Some black leaders serve in the black community for organizations and indivudals and groups that are external to the community, while others work in organizations and institutions that direct programs, policies and activities which are designed for the black community and at times to that community's third-world allies. And the administrative and leadership behavior of these individuals are truly determined by systemic and structural forces which give rise to their leadership "mantle."

The first of these leaders are the black appointed leaders. James E. Mock writes: "Of particular interest has been the output resulting from black voting and how such outputs relates to interest of the black community... . Perhaps the most obvious policy output for blacks involves changes in personnel at the highest levels of govern-menn."[63]

In fact, the oldest and perhaps the best-known and most-used techniques to pay off blacks for their voting and party fidelity has been political recognition. "This pay-off technique involves appointing blacks to a few executive postions," such as, on the presidential and gubernatorial levels, cabinet and sub-cabinet posts; and on the county and local levels, individuals to the mayor's, city manager and city hall offices and commission chairman, commissioner manager and county offices. "The use of this high visibility tool garners much support and euphoria. The black educator Mary McLeod Bethune said: "My people will not be satisfied until they see some black faces in high places."[64] Unfortunately this techniques is wearing thin and is proving to be not enough for the black community. But it does in the short run create another group of black leaders.

"In the emergent literature on black political participation and power in the United States, there is a lack of attention to black appointed officials as a subgroup in the burgeoning black political class."⁶⁵ And clearly one of the major reasons for this was the tragically few black appointed officals down through the years.

This all changed when President Franklin D. Roosevelt appointed so many at one time that they got to be called the "Black Cabinet." Generally speaking, historians identify this group, their sub-cabinet positions, and the role and function that they played, as essentially advisory. Robert Brisbane, a black political scientist, says:" [the term]. . .applies usually to whatever group of Negro leaders happened to be exercising some influence with the party in power in Washington, D.C." or holding a federal appointment.⁶⁶ By the Johnson administration, Journalist Chuck Stone wrote of the "Black Cabinet," "The fact is that these showcase appointments have not substantially changed adminstrative and policy-making patterns of government."⁶⁷ Yet despite their influence, it is certain that their numbers have been increasing.

For instance, President Carter and Reagan have each appointed as many women and blacks as did the previous six presidents combined.⁶⁸ And because of this rise in the numbers of appointed black leaders and a rise in the number of black political scientists, studies of this type of leadership have begun to appear. But basically these early studies have centered upon the types of individuals selected by these administrations.

Of these individuals, Smith writes: "They are of course better educated, disproportionately male, and more likely to be products of the advantaged stratum of the black community in terms of family background. But in terms of religion and region of birth there is fundamental congruence between this element of the black elite and the masses."⁶⁹

James Mock, who has analyzed these appointees from 1961 through 1980 indicated that "the data show that the Black political executives are a highly educated group whose families principal wage earners were more educated and had higher occupational standing than the masses of black people. We conclude that Black political appointees are an elite group with advantaged backgrounds." Mock also found that "the number of Black political executives increased over time; more Blacks were appointed in Democratic than Republican administrations, and appointees in Democratic administrations held more powerful positions."⁷⁰

This increased black presence, however, has not meant influence and power. Two scholars write: ". . .despite the fact that higher percentages of female and black cabinet officers hold advanced college degrees and have prior experience in national government, no woman or black has been appointed to what Cronin terms an inner-cabinet post."[71] Based on the roles that cabinet officers perform, Cronin has made a distinction between "inner and outer cabinet departments."

"The secretaries from the inner cabinet departments, State, Treasury, Defense, Justice serve as counselors to the president, while the others the outer-cabinet secretaries assume advocacy roles on behalf of their partiuclar agencies."[72] They concluded: "Female and black cabinet secretaries have been restricted to supervising client-oriented, outer-cabinet departments rather than serving in position as counselors to the president."[73]

On this point, Smith has found that in order to increase their influence and power, these "appointees indicated that they have tended to form informal caucuses or cliques in their efforts to pursue black interest; that they have tended to pursure their goals through strategies of quiet negotiations, and that their effectiveness has been limited to minor matters of patronage rather than the shaping of board administration policies on questions of race."[74]

Smith's research also uncovered the "Council of Black Appointees," "It was started late in the fall of 1969 as the first year of the Nixon adminstration was drawing to a close."[75] Samuel Jackson, a black official in both the Johnson and Nixon Adminstrations was the principal organizer. However, this council died with the arrival of the Carter administration.

During this adminstration, only *ad hoc* and informal groups of blacks came together as a clique to discuss problems and inform each other about their different agencies. Several individuals in the Carter Administration argued that there was no need for such a group due to the power and prestige of the black appointees and to the absence of perceived hostility in the early years of that administration.[76]

In the Reagan Administration, black appointees decided that they would not get together and to stay away from working on racial issues. In point of fact they decided to specialize in non racial matters. Smith writes: "Blacks in the Reagan administration came into office determined not to follow the traditional pattern of black appointees focusing on "black issues'. . . . In other words there was to be no collective action by blacks in the administration on behalf of black interests."[77] But by 1982, the Reagan administration was under such critical attack from the black community that Melvin Bradley, the senior black in the White House Staff was given responsibility for the "black community." In addition, the black Republican appointees formed in 1982 an informal network to assist each other as the criticism continued to mount. Out of this informal network, they sent suggestions to the White House for consideration.

But despite these formal and informal communication networks, and the increase in their numbers, structural forces have limited significantly the powers and influence of these appointed black leaders. Lenneal Henderson writes: "(black) adminstrative advocacy (i.e., appointees that speak out for the black community) may spark controversy and disapproval from bureaucracy decision-makers who may argue that advocacy...may be harmful to the agency interest."[78] And when such is perceived to be the case, the administrative behavior of black appointed leaders is circumscribed by the individual or organization to whom the bureaucracy is ultimately responsible.

Now what of the second category of black leaders, the annointed ones? Usually these individuals are referred to as "responsible," "moderate," and "acceptable" leaders. Inside the black community, they may be called "uncle Toms," and "Oreo cookies." Black political scientist, Matthew Holden, Jr., developed the concept "clientage" leaders to describe this group. It is by far one of the most useful concepts to emerge in black politics and he defines it as follows; "The rule of thumb which the practitioners of clientage seemed to follow," he writes, "might be stated as *Find a basis for coexistence by choosing objectives which the more influential outsiders (in this case whites) will support, and by their support offer protection against those outsiders who are your irreconcilable enemies.*"[79] The prime example of clientage leader in Holden perspective is none other than Booker T. Washington.[80]

Washington, his allies, and his disciples, notes Holden "operated on a political logic that *Blacks must be willing to withdraw from open political competition with whites,* because white antagonism was so great that it could not be reduced so long as the possibility of direct electoral confrontation or influences existed." He continues: "Clientage, particularly in the manner practiced by Washington, should be regarded...as the most fundamentally political conception one could image. That is, *it worked,* it could not but have penetrating effects on the structure of social competence and power."[81]

But the reality and fact is: "That the strategy did not work (and) was apparent before Washington's death. Not only did unsympathetic critics see it, but so did faithful allies."

Washington was the quintessential clientage politican, and the strategy continued in the South long after his death. The northern environment inhibited it to some extent and no other black leader of Washington's ability embraced it with such dedication and fervor, although some did try. Thus, the appointed leader went slowly into decline until a new racial crisis emerged. Then the white political establishment sought such leaders once again. The classic example for the sixties occured when J. Edgar Hoover, Head of the FBI, decided that Martin Luther King, Jr. was no longer a "responsible" black leader whom whites could control, and he decided with others in the organization to discredit him, his organization, and program and to advance another responsible black leader like Samuel Pierce, the only black cabinet officer now in the Reagan Adminstration.[82]

Recently this tendency for appointing emerged again during the 1984 Democratic presidential campaign when several of its comment-ators and opinion leaders of the new media tried nearly throughout the campaign to discredit Jesse Jackson to black folks and make him appear as a radical and violent leader supposely not in the tradition of his "mentor" Martin Luther King, Jr. Both electronic and print media were filled with allusions to other "responsible" and more acceptable potential black presidential canidadates. But this new appointing effect didn't work because the more the media tried to appoint a leader the stronger the black community supported Jackson in the primaries.

Giving the black community its leadership had, by the eighties, run into very stiff opposition. But the tendency didn't stop, at least, in the political area. Political parties appointed black leaders by having them become spokepersons and appologists for policy programs and proposals directed toward the black community. The latest crop of appointed leaders operating under the guise of spokeperson are the new black conservatives.

Basically, they advance economics and the free-market system as the *solution* to black problems. Big government and social programs are castigated as twin evils that are destroying the black community, black initiatives and individualism. Their clients have elevated them to very powerful positions of prestige and influence in the white and black world, like Washington's white clients had done. The sponsor-ship of these ideas by black conservatives who have taken stands against minimum wage, affirmative action, busing, social programs and civil rights, has meant that they have appeared in nearly all of the leading opinion journals, magazines and newspapers. And blacks who advocate liberal ideas and concepts borne of the New Deal now find themselves debating not the white governmental leaders, but these other blacks. And behind all of the glib defenses and rationalizations for laissez-faire economics, there are some of the same reasons that Washington and his allies had advanced—that blacks must withdraw from open competition with whites. Listen as Thomas Sowell speaks: "We certainly do not need to let emotionally combustible materials accumulate from ill-conceived social experiments." He continues: "The mass internment of Japanese-Americans just a generation ago is a sobering reminder of the tragic idiocy that stress can bring on. We are not made of different clay from the Germans, who were historically more enlightened and humane toward Jews than any other Europeans—until the generation of Hilter and the Holocaust." Then he concludes: "The situation in America today is, of course, not like that of the Pearl Harbor period, nor of the Weimar Republic. History does not literally repeat, but it can warn us of what people are capable of when the stage has been set for tragedy."[83] This argument clearly indicates that the massive power of the majority and their control of the political system led in part to his personal conservative posture and to his urging other blacks to accept such a posture for their own survival in the future. Although this small insight tells us about the "why" of this particular person's conservation position, many critics of these individuals usually dwell on the "how" which can be easily stated or seen as being because the current conservative administration wants him to be a leader.[84]

The extremely limited literature on black conservatives does not disclose whether these leaders come to this persuasion because of (1) socialization and training; (2) because it is a road to power in the black community; (3) or because the white power structure nurtured and fertilized the leadership ground to germinate these leaders; (4) or because they are genuinely committed and serious about the philosophical and political posture; or (5) some combination of the above.[85]

But this tactic of having black leaders speak for the program and policies of political parties is not new to black politics. For instance, Val Washington made and did similar things in 1955; "Negroes have fought hard to obtain first-class citizenship. The development and success of this progressive movement...could not be properly documented without showing the important part the Republican Party has contributed to this aggressive drive." He continues: "In order to be successful in (their) struggle Negroes had to have friends. This is where the Republican Party comes in and from Abraham Lincoln to Dwight D. Eisenhower...Republicans have been their friends."[86] Prior to Washington, there were individuals like Frederick Douglass.

Thus, in both parties and institutions either liberal or conservative appointed black leaders have come forth to rationalize and promote the polices and practices of these positions.

And what of the lastest spokemen and appologists? Pearl T. Robinson writes: "Many black Republicans would like to continue the Brooke approach (i.e., economic and social problem legislation in the broadest possible terms). But Reagan's decision to make inflation fighting the number one economic priority of his administration has brought budget cuts that imperil black enterpreneurs as well as the poor and disadvantaged," and numerous social programs. Intense lobbying efforts by black economic groups "have not succeeded in altering the administration's course of action. In effect, black Republicans find themselves the unwitting victims of power asymmetry within the GOP. Under such conditions, they have little ability to block or control policy outcomes."[87] In short, the economic approach that the current black conservative spokesmen promote for the GOP hasn't been embraced by that organization, and the question remains: shouldn't they first try to convert their clients and white allies?

In the final analysis, the appointed and annointed black leaders are under more constraints and systemic forces that shape their leadership behavior than some other type of black leaders.

Moreover, avoiding the "why" gives an incomplete picture of black leadership behavior, and it edges toward an ideology of black leadership that suggests that the only road to power and the only avenue that might succeed in problem-solving in the black community is a reliance on whites. There *are* those who are trying other avenues. The new approaches call into question both the old syndrome and the theories of intrapsychic motivation. Lurking somewhere in the background are systemic and structural forces that shape minority leadership.

Chapter 10

Black International
Political Behavior

Although nation-states are the major actors on the international plane, studies of the impact of indivudals and groups on international relations have been done. But black Americans are not among those studied. Few words by political behavioralists on international politics have ever included, in any fashion, black groups and individuals as forces and actors. In an age of the emerging third world, such scholarly omissions are staggering.

The Literature

Two questions are important. First, have blacks as individuals and groups sought to influence international politics and foreign policy? Second, have there existed trends and tendencies in the behavioral approach to the study of international politics as there did in the other areas of political science?

Taking the last question first, the answer is a mixed one. No one particular tendency stands out, but the behavioral revolution *has* affected the study of international relations and politics.

Primarily, the behavioralism revolution in international politics has consisted of the application of various behaviorally oriented techniques to the study of nation-states and national decision makers. One of the first works on the subject examined in detail the relevance of the sociopsychological approach to international relations and concluded that there were some problems with the approach.[1] Kelman, who introduced the topic and defined the parameters, also tried to summarize the efforts of the other scholars involved in the projects. "We have defined our focus," wrote Kelman, "as the social interaction of individuals within an international relations context. Yet the designation 'processes of interaction in international relations' suggests another possible focus, namely the interaction between nation-states."[2] In the end, however, Kelman found the behavioral approach to be much more relevant to "the international behavior of individuals" than to the "study of international politics and foreign policy...."[3] "It is much easier to establish the relevance of social-psychological approaches," Kelman proffered, "insofar as they are concerned with studying the international behavior of individuals, that is the ways in which individuals relate themselves to their own nation and other nations, to the international system as a whole, to foreign policy issues, and to the broader questions of war and peace; and to the actual interactions between individuals of different nationalities, than interactions of nation-sates."[4] He added, "When we turn to social psychological research that deliberately addresses itself to issues of international politics and foreign policy, the question of relevance takes on a different character...(and) no matter how interesting and worthwhile these studies may be in their own right, however, insofar as they are presented as contributions to the understanding of international politics and foreign policy, it is entirely fair to apply more stringent criteria of relevance to them."[5] Then he brings the matter full circle: "It becomes important to ask whether they tell us anything about the factors that enter into foreign policy decisions."[6] At this point Kelman begins to have some second thoughts about being too self-critical and undermining his own methodolgy. In the very next paragraph he writes: "It is usually not very fruitful to pose the question in such absolute terms, that is to debate whether these studies have any political relevance *at all*.... The real question concerns the *kind* of relevance that such studies have for international politics and foreign policy and the *limits* of this relevance."[7] In the rest of his summary and conclusion, Kelman tried to establish ways in which the social-psychological method could contribute to the study of nation-states. He noted that this methodological approach would be open to a major criticism. "Extrapolation," he writes, "from individual to state behavior is open to the charge of personifying the nation-state."[8] This "temptation to personify the nation-state and the glossing over of historical and political factors that constitute the conditions within which state actions are carried out, represent real dangers to which we must always remain alert."[9] In short, Kelman tried to suggest great possibilities for his social-psychological method and then deny or severly restrict those possibilities. In so doing, he pointed up a key dilemma in the behavioral approach to international politics and relations: Can the individual's internationalism be better studied than the nation-state? However, few political behavioralists were ready to stop there, and consequently a variety of studies have emerged.

Models and simulation experiments of international politics were common.[10] Game theoriests came forth with a variety of "gaming" techniques. A variety of studies applied mathematical analysis to conflict behavior and political violence.[11] Modified versions of decision making and group-behavior theory found new applications in terms of bargaining and negotiating models,[12] and psychological theories of frustration and aggression were expanded to the international political realm and pressed into service. Human-nature theories and psychopathological ideas also became explicans.

Later, in an ironic twist, socioeconomic indexes were correlated to a variety of state actions and national variables to determine "causal" effects; the results were not quite satisfying or convincing. Hence, some scholars applied cybernetics and communications theories, while others updated the systems theory and theories of integration and societal development. Harold Lasswell proposed the study of "elites" in each nation-state as the behavior of nation-states, but after a time this led back to the dilemma posed by Kelman. Then, some scholars called for the use of computers to analyze the behavior of nation-states.[13]

The development and use of numerous behavioral techniques to explicate the behavior of nation-states rather than that of individuals and to move beyond the dilemma which Kelman noted led to confusion, distortion, and fanciful manipulation in the field. In some instances the enterprise became counter-productive.

To bring order to the chaotic state of the subject, several symposiums were held to discuss the trends and tendencies in the field. The effort at summation was not altogether successful in pointing out new areas to explore.[14] On the other hand, the search was not entirely futile and unimaginative. Some scholars who took part in and edited the results of several conferences began to develop a middle-ground idea. It was, in a word, the concept of "linkage," i.e., the convergence of national and international systems.[15] Rosenau described it: "We wish to identify and analyze those recurrent sequences of behavior that originate on one side of the boundary between the two types of systems and that become linked to phenomena on the other side in the process of unfolding."[16] *Linkage,* in short, could be defined "as any recurrent sequence of behavior that originates in one system and is reacted to in another."[17]

Since the development of this notion, theory building, using linkage as the basic unit of analysis, has continued and promises much for the future. Presently, the linkage framework has been applied to foreign policy studies for insight, but not always to the degree that the proponents of the concept would like.[18] And in many ways this new middle ground brings one nearly full circle, back to the study of individual attitudes about internationalism further, i.e., to determine the "connection" between intranational entities, their ideas and actions, and the nation-state's interaction in the international realm. This led, therefore, to the first question raised about blacks and the international system.

The answer to that question, then, is complex. Yes, blacks have tried as intranational entities to influence America's international relations and foreign policy. But, the behavioralists in international polititics have not studies this process systematically. They have sought to find, on a very limited basis, black attitudes toward international relations and foreign affairs. And the major effort, to date, has been that of only one scholar, and he looked primarily at the attitudes of southern blacks. Occasionally, where the data permitted, he compared southern blacks with nothern ones.

In the early sixties, Alfred Hero undertook, as a part of the work for the World Peace Foundation, a systematic analysis of the international attitudes of southern Negroes based on the data collected by the National Opinion Research Center (NORC), the Survey Research Center (SRC), and the American Institute of Public Opinion (AIPO); data were collected between 1945 through 1959. Although there were some major methodological problems with these surveys, such as the small number of blacks included in the sample and the fact that many blacks were interviewed by whites, Hero made his projections with this limitation in mind.[19] The picture he constructed, however, is highly questionable.

Hero began by noting that "Southern Negroes as a group have been consistently less informed about virtually all international questions than both southern whites and northern Negroes."[20] This arose from the fact that with the exception of a few middle-class blacks, "readership of international news and, especially, editorials in local daily papers has been much less prevalent statistically among southern Negroes than among southern whites."[21] Hero arrived at this conclusion, while simultaneously he had the knowledge that "habitual readers of the Negro press among the interviewees noted that the independent movements in Africa and developments subsequent to termination of colonial control had in recent years received increasing attention in many Negro popular periodicals."[22]

Hero's summary of his "Exposure to Mass Media" section is contradictory. "Unfortunately," he wrote, "no systematic examination of the international content of the Negro press has come to our attention." But in the next paragraph he notes, "Most editorials on Africa and other world issues seem superficial and generally poor, and even the news presented was frequently overly dramatic and sensational.. .."[23] Exactly how and where he got the information to draw that conclusion, one is hard-pressed to find.

However, having noted that blacks had little interest and knowledge about world affairs and poor mass media exposure to world events, Hero went on to describe the role that black groups play in organizing blacks around world issues. "Only the most self-assured, urban Negro cosmopolitans of college backgrounds have participated in desegregated discussions of foreign relations in groups composed mainly of whites." Hero continues:

> A few service, luncheon, or dinner groups among professional class Negroes have in recent years devoted some relatively responsible attention to international affairs, particulary to Africa south of the Sahara and other issues related to the Negro and race relations. Among these have been the Hungry Club in Atlanta and the Frontiers Club in a number of cities.[24]

Coupled with these, Hero found that Professor, now President, Samuel Cook inaugurated Town Hall meetings at the Atlanta University Center, and the Crossroads Africa Program, all of which were centered in Atlanta, Georgia. According to his findings, the media was helped little by black organizations and informal groups in enlarging black knowledge about world affairs. The reason for this "sad" and "deplorable" state of affairs, noted Hero, was socioeconomical. "Demographic and social factors alone go far to explain the phenomena just described."[25]

Having then assessed the knowledge of blacks and their attitudes toward world affairs, Hero turned to describe black attitudes toward foreign policy. However, before Hero started his analysis, he prefaced his remarks with some *questionable* psychological insights. Hero opened with this statement:

> Given the concentration of isolationist sentiments among the less informed and little interested, the *subconscious* learning of most Negroes who have ventured no opinions probably have not tended to support activist foreign policies, particularly those demanding individual sacrifice, such as military service and foreign economic assistance. Moreover, the intensity of most international opinions offered by Negroes has been low; it is questionable that the answers many have offered have been seriously enough held to create a preference strong enough to determine important aspects of their behavior, like their votes at the polls.[26]

Moving from these assumptions and broad generalizations, Hero noted blacks' attitudes on specific foreign policy issues. Blacks, he found, tend to be isolationists and advocate "reductions of United States military and other commitments abroad."[27] Moreover, they opposed, he found, alliances like NATO, SEATO, OAS, and the UN police action of Korean War. Likewise, few blacks supported the Truman Doctrine, the Marshall Plan, and economic aid to America's anticommunist allies.[28] On the other hand, Hero's data have led him to write that "Negroes have appeared more 'liberal' than whites in the south primarily on those international issues wherein Negroes tend to identify to some extent with equalitarian foreign policies of our federal government or with Negroes in foreign countries...."[29]

Hero concluded that it is only a few blacks of the middle class who are truly knowledgeable about world affairs and therefore comparable to whites. But "even by 1967 only one southern Negro adult out of four was registered to vote" and " the proportions who actually voted in congressional primaries or elections were considerably less than figures suggest." Hence, blacks in Hero's estimation would have little influence on foreign affairs. This small knowledge and political impact, Hero concluded, resulted from "demographic factors alone."[30]

In sum, Hero, using questionable and limited data, developed a jagged portrait of black international political behavior, surrounded with vague generalizations, presuppositions, and contradictory and repetitious statements. Many students reading Hero for the first time have come to accept his erroneous conclusions, as we shall see shortly.

Before subjecting Hero's ideas to a systematic analysis, we should reflect upon a basic trend in the scholarly literature which followed on the heels of Hero's attitudinal analysis. This trend structures a conceptual framework to explore the role of race in foreign policy and international relations.[31] This approach, which some of its proponents hail as pioneering, seeks to identify "the significance of color in transnational relationships."[32] Those presently using the approach are developing models, stratification systems, typologies, definitions, and systematic patterns about race in shaping international political behavior.

Proponents are right in claiming that little has been done in the area and that it is a virgin area for research. Rosenau agrees: "If one looks at virtually any textbook published in the field of international relations one will find virtually no discussion of racial factors."[33] But they are wrong in assuming that they are pioneering in the area. Presently, they have made little advance beyond the efforts of some black political scientists in the fifties.[34] Among contemporary writers about black participants in international affairs, several are of Hero's disposition, saying that blacks know little and have little influence. Moreover, a few of these writers have brought to full-blown proportions a muted theme in Hero's work.[35] This theme, which emerges from their reading of history, is that blacks have shown little concern for black Africa and Africans, their ancestral homeland. These writers have concluded that if blacks have shown limited interest in Africa, then it logically follows that they have had no or only passing concern for other international entities. In addition, this focus on "what blacks did on the African question" has led to shortsighted comparison between blacks and Africa and Jews and Israel. The conclusion is always the same. Blacks have not been as concerned with Africa as Jews have been with Israel. The comparision is of little value and in any case is incorrect. A close look at the literature discussing American blacks in relation to Africa reveals obvious flaws.[36]

Victor Ferkiss merges the African approach and Hero's theses. His work, therefore, shares the same ambiguities and contradictions. "The American Negro," he writes, "has been torn between assimilation in America and identification with Africa in a manner exhibiting striking if not complete parallels with the problems of American Jews vis-a-vis America and Israel."[37] Having drawn his parallels, Ferkiss then reviews blacks' interest and concern with Africa from 1788 to the mid-sixties, and en-route, he draws numerous conclusions. "The new American Negro pride in things African," he noted about halfway through the book, "has even led to some tendency to rewrite history and to over-emphasize the extent to which a few lonely voices in the Negro community spoke up for Africa in decades past."[38] In fact, Ferkiss thought he saw a "general American Negro disinterest in Africa throughout the period from the Civil War to World War I...."[39] As for matters between the two wars, Ferkiss said, "In general—American Negroes were only marginally more concerned with Africa than were white Americans prior to World War II, and white Americans were very little concerned....Africa had almost dropped out of American sight."[40] "World War II did little" in his view to "alter the picture." In fact, in his estimation it was President Kennedy who revived both black and white interest, but this, too, quickly faded. Ferkiss concluded: "In the final analysis, despite what happens in Africa, the American Negro is most concerned with what happens at home. Negro criticism of the Johnson administration's African policy is muted because of its confidence that he may...lead the United States across the river into the promised land of racial equality."[41] and "as long as the Negro march toward equality in this country continues unchecked, any adminstration will have great freedom of action in Africa."[42]

Black philosopher and essayist Alain Locke would have agreed. "Except from the point of view of religious missionarism," wrote Locke in 1924, "it has been until recently almost impossible to cultivate generally in the mind of the American Negro an abiding and serious interest in Africa...other than one that has therefore been sporadic, sentimental and unpractical."[43] Then, in a curious twist, he claims that "the great concerns of this great continent have engaged the Caucasian and primarily the European mind."[44]

Black Africanists Adelaide Hill and Martin Kilson partly agree and partly disagree with these positions. The agreement is that they see little black concern for Africa before the 1880s but they disagree about the level of concern which appears thereafter. They say, "The period of a conscious search among Negro Americans for, and understanding of, and identity with their African heritage began during the mid 1880's when there appeared the beginnings of a Negro American intelligentsia."[45] Starting with that period, Hill and Kilson attempt to "fill in the variegated picture of the long history of the relationship of Negro Americans to Africa and to assess its dimension as illustrated in the words and deeds, thoughts and actions, of the Negro intelligent-sia."[46] But the truth of the matter is, and Hill and Kilson note it in their introduction, that black interest goes back much further than the 1880s, as indeed does the black intellegentsia. Hill and Kilson make Ferkiss's view of black concerns with Africa appear faulty.

Overall, then, the literature on black international political behavior is limited and replete with errors. It has made few attempts to probe beyond old attitudinal data and model building. The attitudinal data are both time-bound and the data bases limited. Consequently, the literature tells us nothing much of the past, the present, or the future of black international politics.

Black Internationalism: A Historical Review

In reality, the black presence began to affect the international arena with the beginning of the slave trade and it has not ceased since. As a matter of fact, one of the earliest consequences of this trade was the British Navy's effort to halt it.[48] In the Revolutionary War, blacks fought on both sides, with the Americans and with the British. In addition, blacks were imported from Haiti to fight in the battle of Savannah in 1779. Many of the blacks who fought with the British later took up residence in Canada and Nova Scotia. After the war, Congress and the United States Navy made a feeble attempt at suppressing the slave trade. Shortly after the War of 1812, a free black, Paul Cuffe, returned several black immigrants to Africa. Later this action was to be continued by the American Colonization Society backed by a grant of money from Congress, culminating in the founding of Liberia. In each instance, black individuals and groups supported and attacked the colonization movement.

By 1833, blacks like the Reverend Nathaniel Paul carried the black plight to England to seek friends and financial support. Blacks from America went as delegates to the World Anti-Slavery Conference held in London in 1840. Here, they tried to attract not only worldwide attention to the black predicament but also to internationalize America's domestic problem. This effort was followed in 1845 with black journalist Frederick Douglass's crossing the Atlantic to seek allies for the black cause in Ireland and England.

There were other international activities by blacks in the pre-Civil War era. Black slaves who escaped the mainland and fled to the Bahamas caused extraordinary problems between the United States

and Great Britian.[49] During the Mexican War of 1848, blacks entered
the fracas, opposing the war and trying to influence the government's
foreign policy on the matter.[50]

In addition, there were blacks' continuing efforts to emigrate.
Robert Campbell traveled to Africa and explored the Niger Valley for
a black colonization organization which was white financed, while
Dr. Martain Delany went at the same time for a black nationalist emi-
grationist organization.[51] After the war, Henry McNeil Turner and
Chief Albert Sam would continue these projects.

Prior to the Civil War, a delegation of blacks led by a leading
black anti-slavery figure, George T. Downing, met the exiled Hungar-
ian leader Louis Kossuth. This leader of the unseccessful rebellion in
his country in 1848 was on a nationwide tour to raise funds "for the
renewal of the revolutionary struggle against the Hapsburgs." He
heard a black delegation read a statement to him saying, "Yes! illus-
trious patriot, may Hungary be free! May the world rejoice in her
speedy disenthrallment. May the joy be twofold in that Hungary shall
be redeemed and not Hungary alone, but with her the world, and
mankind."[52] When Kossuth refused to take a stand on American slavery, Frederick Douglass published an open letter to him in the February 26, 1852, issue of the *Liberator,* reminding him that on the matter
of slavery and the oppression it wrought, "there is not neutral ground
here for any man."[53]

During the Civil War, the Southerners sought European allies
and the Confederacy sought diplomatic recognition. Shortly after the
war, a trickle of black diplomats representing the United States was
sent to the black republics; later, black diplomats would go to various
European and Asian outposts.

When America's Age of Imperialism arrived, both black supporters and black opponents to imperialism were active. Both sides tried
vigorously to influence the course of events, the conquest of the colo-
nies, and the campaign of subjugation waged to get them. Willard B.
Gatewood notes: "Because Negroes recognized the degree to which
racism pervaded American society and thought, they could never
become wholly reconciled to the arguments of either the imperialists
or anti-imperialists." He continues, "At one extreme (in the black
community) were the enthusiastic pro-war advocates whole bellicose
rhetoric placed them in the vanguard of most strident jingoists.....
Opposing such views were the highly vocal, anti-imperialist elements
within the Negro community who were also concerned about the
impact of the quest for empire upon black American."[54] Black organi-

zations, like the National Colored Protective League, and key individuals, like Lewis A. Douglass, son of the famed Frederick Douglass, condemned America's expansionist policies in the darker nations of Cuba and the Philippines.

Black military men served in World War I. In France, this black participation caused the French government to issue memos regarding black-white contact so as not to offend white Americans.

After the war, W.E.B. Du Bois developed the first Pan African Congress, which became a prime focus behind the League of Nation's mandate system.[55] Several other Pan African Congresses were held and several black individuals and organizations petitioned the League or took up negotiating with it for the darker races of the world. Such individuals included Monroe Trotter and Marcus Garvey.

Moreover, even a cursory examination of the debate regarding the defeat of the League of Nations treaty in the Congressional records immediately calls into question the standard answer offered in the textbooks, that its defeat was the result of conflict between Senator Henry Cabot Lodge and President Woodrow Wilson. While this may have been one key concern, the record shows clearly that "racial matters" were also a major concern for the U.S. senators. Some senators recoiled at the prospect of having white men sit down with and accept as equal, black delegates to the proposed world body. It is important that this debate be brought to light.

Emerging fascism found strong opposition in the black press, as did the invasion of Ethiopia by Mussolini. In fact, as mentioned in Chapter Two, the *Pittsburg Courier* increased its black circulation by sending a correspondent to Africa to cover the war and giving it first-page headlines.

When the U.N. became a reality, blacks petitioned the world body on numerious occasions for assistance. In the same period, a black, Ralph Bunche, became an employee of the world body and helped to resolve the Arab and Israeli conflict of 1948. Walter White in this era led the NAACP on a campaign to generate support in the black community for the Zionist movement. The Cold War period saw Richard Wright go to the 1957 Bandung Conference, which dealt with the problems of the colored races of the world.[56] During this period and later, black newspapers and organizations continued to try to influence the masses as well as the national foreign policymakers.

The comparison of Israel and Africa is weak for other reasons as well. First, Israel never had the negative image that Africa has born for centuries as the dark continent. Second, African religion and ethics have never had the impact in America that the Judeo-Christian ethic has had. Third, Jews could become much more easily assimilated in America than could blacks. And finally, the economic and political power of Jews within America has not waxed and waned as blacks' power has. The parallels are grossly inadequate and fail to note the structural burden on blacks.

Black interest and activity on international affairs have existed throughout black political history, but they were not always influenctial, consistent, systematic, and powerful. Moreover, much of the activity stemmed from key black individuals and small organizations which have sought to arouse and awaken the black masses.

Black International Attitudes

Much-needed studies of black opinion on international affairs do not now exist; nor do the needed studies of past black responses to international matters or the impact of black efforts on the shaping of foreign relations. From the fragmentary data we do have, we can see that black international behavior has maintained some constant themes in the midst of many changes.

Black Americans seem to watch international political events with a brooding constancy, ever watchful and ready to spring into action when international matters are judged to be of strategic importance to the black community or of benefit to other darker races. Attention to the ways international relations might affect the black community seems to have been one of the significant features of black international behavior. This constancy, in particular, can be seen in American blacks' interest in Africa.

In September 1970, Leroi Jones and other black writers and intellectuals revitalized the Pan-African Movement and tried to fashion a grassroots movement amongst the folk.[57] The seventies saw the Congressional Black Caucus attempt to improve U.S.-African relations and to prod the Secretary of State, Henry Kissinger, into developing a coherent and meaningful African policy.[58] Moreover, the Caucus visited Africa and talked with several leaders to discern needs and establish brother-to-brother ties.[59] In 1977 former-Congressman AndrewYoung became U.N. Ambassador and an outspoken critic of human relations in Southern Africa and of flaws in American foreign policies past and present. His attacks on racism and vigorous support of Third World nations led to enourmous criticism of him and cries for his removal. Later Young was removed from his UN position for not applying administration policy and then lying about it. Secret intellegence reports to the president showed that Young had been meeting with members of the Palestine Liberation Organization.[60] However, many black leaders condemned the administration for not applying the policy even-handedly and dismissing Young. Nothing came out of the protest.

Prior to Young's arrival at the UN many black men and women served as delegates to the world body and several of them protested American policy at the world organization but the structure of the State Department and its foreign policy-making machinery made little adjustment in America's foreign-policy posture. Prior to the arrival of black delegates, many black groups, notably Mary McLeod Bethune and the National Council of Negro Women organization— which she headed, constantly sought to move the American policy at the world body in a more humane direction. Success, if it did arrive, came in bits and pieces.

Beside black representatives at the United Nations, there have also been black diplomats sent to a limited number of countries, primarily third-world nations and several of these diplomats have tried to refashion and reshape American policy toward these nations. Usually, however, the requirements of American policy have prevented these efforts from being completely successful.

Finally, the sixties, seventies, and eighties have seen a procession of black groups and organizations, dubbed "non-state actors" operating on the international plane to assist black liberation movements in third-world nations and to try and block and prevent American involvement and assistance to racists and "outlaw" states. These groups have likewise protested "imperialistic" American actions. Among some of these actions, particular ones stand out: (1) Malcolm X's address at the Organization of African Unity and his effort to get African Diplomatic support for UN debate on racial oppression in the United States, (2) the African Liberation Support Committee and the African Liberation Day marches, (3) Stokely Carmichael's All African People Revolutionary Party that emerged out of his temporary exile in Africa and (4) the emergence and growing influence of Trans-Africa.   Perhaps the most unique and permanent of these non-state black political action groups in TransAfrica. This organization is the "Black American Lobby for Africa and the Caribbean." Beginning in 1982 the Organization started to send out "Issue Briefs" and a newsletter which alerted their membership and individuals in the Congress and the foreign policy-making community to matters of concern for blacks. Besides these briefs, the organization publishes *Trans-Africa Journal* which is directed not only to its membership but to the intellectual and academic community and it is devoted to a scholarly discussion of African and Caribbean foreign policy matters from a black perspective. There are also special issues of the Journal issued when major policy crises and concerns arise.[62] To further facilitate matters, the organization brought all black ambassadors together for a meeting to discuess common problems and difficulties in their behavior and assistance action to third-world nations.[63] The organization is currently sponsoring a "Cultural Boycott Campaign" Artist and Athletes Against Apartheid. It is being headed by Harry Belafonte and Arthur Ashe.[64] In addition to these endeavors, the organization lobbies Congress for both aid and assistance programs for third-world nations and seeks to block legislation that will be harmful to these countries.[65]

Overall, black political history suggests anything but a lack of concern either in international affairs or Africa. Hill and Kilson were correct when they wrote, "The sentiment of American Negroes toward Africa (and international affairs)...should not be considered out of the context of Americans in general, nor out of the context of the Negroes' politically and economically weak positions in America in particular."[66] Understood this way black interest in shaping international affairs can be seen to have been strong, though actual black influence in shaping U.S. foreign relations was very limited. This is why the comparison of blacks and Africa with Jews and Israel is so dubious.

But what about matters only peripheral to or superficially linked to the concerns of the black community? On this score, fragmentary evidence, both traditional and behavioral, suggests flux, changes, and division.

Present evidence suggests that mass black involvement in international affairs and foreign policy matters in not constant. Marcus Garvey, Chief Albert Sams, the Ethiopian War, and the world wars have generated mass black interest and participation, but even in these cases not on a continuous level for long periods of time. On the other hand, black leaders and people in the black news media have sometimes shown a persistent interest in stimulating and directing black international activity. Du Bois' Pan Africanism and Pan African Congresses are excellent examples. Black artists like Leroi Jones, black intellectuals, and small black African organizations may have shown sustained interest, but however persistent, this is not involvement. Nonetheless, interest like this should not be written off as noninvolvement, as some writers have dubbed it.

Blacks' attitudes about international events are affected by their environment and perceived community needs. In 1974, for instance-, what black voters and non-voters felt about foreign aid was established (see the survey data reported in Tables 10.1 and 10.2) But five, ten, or even three years from now, will these same attitudes prevail, or will they have changed because of changes in subjective or objective conditions? To be frank, change could occur in several directions.

Table 10.1 shows that black voters and nonvoters alike want to see foreign aid flow to black African nations; their second preference is for countries with democratic regimes. Both categories of black participants desire a decrease in foreign aid (Table 10.2). This attitude might reflect the economic dislocation that blacks have experienced during an inflationary spiral and rising unemployment. While more black voters than novoters wanted to see an increase of aid, more nonvoters than voters wished to see the level of foreign aid spending kept at the present level.

TABLE 10.1 Opinions of Blacks Regarding the Direction of Foreign Aid

Category	Voters	Nonvoters
African nations	72.9 (401)	62.4 (133)
Communist nations	11.5 (63)	5.2 (11)
Democratic nations	14.4 (79)	30.5 (65)
Others	1.3 (7)	1.9 (4)
No opinion	– 0	– 0
Total	100.0 (550)	100.0 (213)

SOURCE: National Black Survey, 1972-74.

TABLE 10.2. Opinions of Blacks Regarding Level of Foreign Aid Expenditures

Category	Voters	Nonvoters
Increase	11.1 (54)	8.8 (25)
Decrease	73.9 (359)	62.1 (177)
Keep Same	7.8 (38)	19.6 (56)
No opinion	7.2 (35)	9.5 (27)
Total	100.0 (486)	100.0 (285)

SOURCE: National Black Survey, 1972-74.

Looking at how black foreign policy attitudes shifted and changed during the decade of 1973-82, Tables 10.3 and 10.4 use the actual numbers of blacks that answered the question in each year instead of the percentages. Because the numbers were so small, as the reader can see, the percentages using these small numbers would have had a masking effect and created a false impression and conveyed a greater sense and degree of accuracy. At best all the numbers can convey is a hint.

In Table 10.3, the general pattern established by the actual numbers is that American spending on defense, military and armaments have been "about right" except for 1973 and 1980 when blacks in this survey felt that spending was too much the first year and too little the last year.

TABLE 10.3. Black Attitudes on Spending for the Military, Armaments, and Defense: 1973-82

Years	Too Little	About Right	Too Much	Total Number
1973	30*	54	76	160
1974	32	66	53	151
1975	28	69	49	146
1976	25	59	30	114
1977	24	70	53	147
1978	28	77	32	137
1980	69	44	14	127
1982	22	63	67	152

*These are the actual numbers of blacks who answered the question instead of the percentages.

SOURCE: *NORC General Social Surveys, 1972-1982.*

In Table 10.4, the pattern established by the actual numbers clearly suggests that, for every year under analysis, the Government has been spending too much money on foreign aid as far as blacks in this group of surveys were concerned. Although the earlier survey, conducted especially for this book, probed to see the direction of aid, the NORC surveys didn't. And because of the small numbers in the NORC surveys, all that can be said is that blacks feel that too much is being spent by America on foreign aid and that up until 1982, military spending was about correct.

These few insights into black international attitudes cannot be taken as a full exploration of black attitudes on foreign matters, but they do provide points of departure. They do suggest that blacks are concerned with how these affairs can affect the black community.

TABLE 10.4. Black Attitudes on Foreign Aid Expenditures: 1973-1982

Years	Too Little	About Right	Too Much	Total Number
1973	16*	32	120	168
1974	15	20	128	164
1975	18	31	102	151
1976	5	20	96	121
1977	15	45	95	155
1978	19	36	88	143
1980	18	25	92	135
1982	20	25	102	147

*These are the actual numbers of blacks who answered the question instead of the percentage.

SOURCE: *NORC General Social Survey, 1972-1982.*

Knowing this, one does not have to make the mistake of one black political scientist, who said that "in areas such as foreign affairs blacks continue to be almost entirely uninvolved, even when their interests are clearly at stake."[67] Historical records, contemporary activities, and a sampling of black attitudes all belie such a conclusion.

Systemic and Structural Factors

The study of an individual's internationalism does not explain the behavior of nation-states. More importantly, it reveals little or nothing about the impact of systemic and structural variables upon the international political activities of blacks.

Any cursory content analysis of the numerous emigrationist schemes in America, from Martin Delany's to Marcus Garvey's, reveals that social, economic, and political discrimination in America was the driving force and motif. In short, a key to black involvement with the international arena is institutional racism. Moreover, black ideologies such as Pan Africanism and schemes like the Pan African Congresses, the mandate systems, and plans for African and Afro-American unity developed from a "concern for the plight of the darker races in the world." The massive efforts of blacks in the sixties and seventies to shape America's African policy grows out of South Africa's apartheid system and Rhodesia's minority rule. Finally, black radicalism finds impetus in the wish to internationalize the race problem, to interest other nations in the black man's plight, and to seek allies and friends from beyond the horizon. Such efforts are not all

recent ones; they include the pre-Civil War efforts of Frederick Douglass, the recent efforts of black leaders in the sixties and seventies like
Stokely Carmichael and Eldridge Cleaver, or those of the forties and
fifties, like Paul Robeson and William Patterson. The plight of the
minority groups in America has been both a triggering and sustain-
ing force. All of which brings us to one final point.

Internationally oriented black leaders who have sought allies for
blacks from countries that are ideologically opposed to capitalism and
belong racially to the darker people have likewise met with exploiting
systemic factors. Alex Poinsett, the first writer to analyze these leaders
as a group, and one of the few to discuss their systemic problems,
notes that treatments of them tend to capitalize upon their problems,
which are used as a political football in world power politics, much
to the dismay of Cleaver and the group he represents. He writes,
"Cleaver's theorizing has convinced him that revolutionary societies
outside the U.S. would aid the burgeoning revolutionary movement
within the country. His travels from Montreal to Cuba, Albania,
North Korea, China, Vietnam, The Soviet Union, and the People's
Republic of the Congo taught him otherwise, however. By 1972, his
flagging belief in international proletarian solidarity was shattered by
chairman Mao Tse-tung's welcome of President Richard M. Nixon to
China, world leader of revolutionary struggle. One by one the pillars
of Cleaver's world view crumbled to dust."[68]

Usually such radicalism means the repression of the leader at
home, as Poinsett aptly shows, and the eventual abandonment of his
cause internationally. Ultimately, in most cases, the international
leader is left without allies. The recent flight, exile, and return of
Eldridge Cleaver is a prime example.[69] He was preceded by others like
Robert F. Williams and John Clytus.[70] International black leaders
have yet to solve their problems of "linkage" with the international
allies. They quickly find themselves seeking to return and rebuild an
internal domestic base.[71] Cleaver, however, found a new base when he
returned. He moved to the right, and became a born-again Christian.
In 1984, "nine years after returning from exile in Cuba, North Korea,
Algeria and...other Communist and third world countries, he is profoundly disillusioned with his once beloved Marxist-Leninist ideology. He is now a pro-Reagan, anti-Communist crusader." Besides
running as an independent for Congress, "he...considers himself to
be a Christian and a conservative."[72] And in launching his campaign
for Congress against Congressman Ronald Dellums (D.-Calif.) he
announced, "...I look upon the United States of America as being

revolutionary. The Declaration of Independence to me is the most revolutionary document in the world. So I consider myself to be a constitutionalist."[73] The role that systemic and structural forces play in these flights and returns is crucial and obvious. The successes and failures of black internationalists are determined, in part, by the actions and reactions of the nation-state that spawned him.

Future Research Needs and Opportunities

To study black international attitudes solely to determine and analyze black international political activity is to end up with not only a limited picture of reality but one that is time-bound and static. Hero's analysis, for example, fails to take into account the fact that blacks and international affairs both would change over time. Moreover, his analysis makes it seem as if the lack of individual knowledge and low socioeconomic status determine black international behavior. Not only does the SES index for blacks not allow for change (international events are far more fluid than the SES index for blacks has been) but this emphasis on individual variable blocked from view such systemic forces as the rise of black elected officials; the Congressional Black Caucus; the heading of the African Subcommittee, for a while, by black Congressman Diggs; the rise of several mass movements headed by activists and concerned individuals, and guerilla wars in southern Africa. Probing for individual variables blocked out any searching for the reasons and motivations among structural and systemic variables in the sociopolitical system.

Given the great increase in black international activity in the late sixties and seventies, hard data should be emerging for further analysis and testing of the linkage theory regarding the impact of intranational minorities on foreign policy.

Chapter 11

Black Political Participation: A New Portrayal

It is downright difficult to discern a coherent vision of black political participation in political behavioralism. The reasons are basic. First, what data there are, are dispersed throughout innumerable books and articles. Second, political behavioralism is divided into subfields, each supposedly requiring specialists. Finally, it has failed to cover all phases of black political behavior, leaving broad gaps between heavily trodden areas.

Moreover, the problem goes beyond simple addition. The literature on black voting cannot be added to the literature on the black socialization process and that to black party partisanship and so on to achieve a full view. Incompatible techniques and strategies have been used in the search of individual political motivation. In the area of black party behavior, for example, four or five research strategies have been employed.

However, if it is clearly understood that the chief focus and the prime unit of analysis of the behavioral methodology is the individual, then some semblance of order and structure can emerge.

The Old Portrait in the Literature

The behavioral portrait of black political behavior either omits the culture or treats it as dysfunctional. It posits a culture that incorporates none of the supposedly pertinent values and belief systems that promote stability (regime norms). The behavioral portrait of the black political socialization process reveals serious discontinuities that are the consequence of the decline or dysfunction of the three principal socializing agents, School, Family, Media. Thus, the transmission of political ideas and values from one black generation to another cannot take place, further incurring the likelihood of political instability of the group. Moreover, the protrait shows that even if the agents of socialization did their job, the lack of a political culture would leave nothing to transmit.

The behavioral portrait of black political opinions and attitudes depicts them as ideas that are not properly formed and shaped, that are not distributed effectively, and that manifest themselves only in hostile and antisystemic beliefs.

The behavioral portraits of the black voter bring to light alienated, apathetic, unregistered, uninformed, miseducated, fearful, and easily manipulated, if not irrational, ballot markers. Further, black Democratic party partisanship is pictured as evolving out of "images" rather than family affiliation. Therefore, the attachment is portrayed as unstable, volatile, subject to swift change and possible disruption to the two-party process. Currently many political behavioralists see the electoral arena as mirroring the racial polarization which exists in society, with whites choosing one electoral side and blacks supporting another. Black political behavior at conventions, it is noted, is apt to be devoid of compromise, bargaining, and negotiation and instead reflects emotionalism, racism, and no-win strategies.

Behavioralism portrays black legislators and judges as pawns and dupes of their own personal social experience, disproportionately interested in civil rights. Group interest, we are told, exceeds community or social interest. Behavioralism portrays all black leaders, on the whole, as overly concerned with speedy change in civil rights as a result of childhood maturation practices. Most black leaders, if they are not moderates, are radical neurotics or conservative Uncle Toms. Finally, in regard to foreign affairs, blacks are ill informed and uncaring, even when they should be vitally concerned.

Such a portrayal of black political behavior, especially when it is juxtaposed with a white control group, generates a dismal, pitiful, and disturbing vision of political reality. In many ways, it can be likened to the "denegrating" portrait the early behavioralists developed of the American voter.[1] This portrait, which Pomper labeled

"The Dependent Voter," pictured the American electorate "as un-responsive and unknowing" and possibly "potentially dangerous" to democracy. "In particular," he writes, "the voting studies provide data on two related subjects: The political capacity of individual voters and the causal influences on balloting. Dependent voters are deficient on both grounds. Few give serious consideration to public matters. Even the majority who do vote are not greatly concerned over the outcome. Beyond voting, most refrain from further participation in organized political life...."[2] Thus, some political behavioralists, Pomper writes, "without malicious intent, but still with real con-sequences" have portrayed voters "as limited in their capacity to understand political events and issues, and as subject to devious manipulation. The danger of such statemetns is not only that they may be false, or true only in some circumstances, but that they may be believed."[3]

The behavioral portrait of black political participants is striking. In all the correlations, tables and graphs and statistics, the indicators point to the ground—if not below. Black political participants, they imply, do few of the things expected of, and performed by, average citizens.

In sum, the behavioralist view of the black political participant is that he is a creature motivated by individual forces, clearly explaina-ble by low socioeconomic traits which, in turn, insure low levels and abnormal forms of political behavior. Such a portrait, created with the demographic data, is self-evidencing, self-fulfilling, self-justifying and self-correcting. It is a theoretical construction, out of touch with reality, easily citicized—either as a whole, or by part.

The Validity of the Behavioral Approach to Political Science

To question the validity or veracity of the behavioral portrait of black political participation, boders on the sacriligious. Here, only the most basic concerns can be aired.

Writing in 1959, V.O. Key and Frank Munger urged the political scientist to look beyond the narrower social determination found in the early voting studies.[4]

> In research, the answers one gets depend in part on the kinds of question he asks. If one inquires about social characteristics and political preference, he finds out about social characteristics and political preference. If one puts

other sorts of questions into the research mill, he might well bring out other and more complex characteristics of the process of electoral decision.т

In short, Key and Munger noted that "social characteristics determined political preferences" only if this was all the reasearcher was looking for.

Of the political behavioralist's narrow perspective, Robert Black has written that "with the current stress placed on socioeconomic variables, the fact that the political system itself is significant in determining the political activity of its members is many times ignored."[6] And the reason for this, Black finds, is "because social and economic indicators are easily quantifiable and readily available, (thus) political variables have been relegated to a dependent capacity."[7] In his study, Black concludes that "a refocusing of attention from" the socioeconomic variables "to the political characteristics themselves was necessary to provide a more balanced perspective" of political reality.[8]

Some other scholars have looked at the interplay of individual and systemic variables and concluded that the "differences in rates of registration and these in turn reflect to a considerable degree local differences in the rules governing...and...handling...the registering of voters."[9] A later study had similar findings,[10] but a recent attempt falls back on individual variables, offering a poor explanation as to why the South showed up as an exception to individual factors.[11]

Although Key and Black and the others' comments were primarily concerned with voting behavior, their insights are pertinent to the other areas of political science where the political behavioralists have made inroads.[12] But Key and Munger and Black and a few others are lonely voices raising some penetrating comments.[13] Others have instead chosen to develop theories and ideologies based on the findings of the political behavioralists.

Political Behavioralism and the Political Ethos

The tendency to build ideology and construct theory on the basis of only a partial vision of political reality is exemplified in the work of Banfield and Wilson. It was developed under the rubric of a value premise, dubbed "public regardingness."[14] Both men, not seeing their work in the ideological tradition and shifting attention away from the basic causes of the problem, bifurcated the political world into "we" and "they" camps. Using black and white aggregate voting data on municipal bond issues taken from several northern cities such as Chicago and New York, they showed, without any sleight of hand manipulation of the data, that blacks tended to vote selfishly and *against* "public" projects that would have been beneficial to the city as a whole, while whites tended to vote for citywide public projects. They concluded that blacks were not public minded and went on to suggest that "public regardingness" as a major and significant value premise was held only by the "we" camp (meaning whites).

However, had they expanded their data base and looked at some southern cities, their conclusion might have been reversed. During the bond referendum in Atlanta, Georgia, in 1963, the voting was as noted in Table 11.1. In eight selected predominantly black precincts, the voting was much higher and more in favor of the bonds than in eight comparable predominantly white precincts. Only for the school bond did whites show any support for the general public bonds. But this was no fluke. In 1961 the very same type of pattern can be seen; blacks then too were strongly supportive of public matters, whereas whites voted strongly in opposition to citywide measures.[15] In this

TABLE 11.1. Breakdown by Race and Issue: The Bond Issue Referendum of 1963

Bond Categories	Race	Votes	For %	Against Votes	%
School Bond	Black	6,160	90.2	672	9.8
	White	2,755	56.5	2,347	44.5
Sewer Bonds	Black	5,950	87.3	867	12.7
	White	2,533	48.3	2,606	51.7
Library Bonds	Black	5,506	88.4	724	11.6
	White	2,037	40.3	3,022	59.7
Auditorium Bond	Black	5,728	87.7	806	12.3
	White	2,140	41.5	3,019	58.5
Traffic Bond	Black	5,832	89.3	699	10.7
	White	2,451	47.1	2,751	52.0
Urban Renewal Bond	Black	5,744	88.8	726	11.2
	White	1,890	40.5	3,181	59.5
Park Bond	Black	5768	89.4	780	10.6
	White	1,890	37.3	3,181	62.7

SOURCE: General Consolidation Sheet: *City of Atlanta Bond Election,* (May 15, 1963), Office of the City Clerk, Atlanta, Georgia.

instance, blacks seem to have a so-called public regardingness value premise and whites do not.

Several studies on other cities have not found the Wilson and Banfield bifurcation of the political world to hold, nor did they find it to be consistent with political reality.[16] In the Atlanta case, more information is needed if interpretation is to be valid. In southern political history, blacks are known to have been permitted to vote so that public bond issues could be passed in times when white voters were staunchly opposed. Such factors cannot be ignored. Hasty generalizations point back to the comments of Key and Black. Naturally, by excluding part of political reality, one can always find what one looks for!

Political Behavioralism and Ideology

Joining the criticism of others are the arguments of William Ryan about the ideology of political behavioralism. "Blaming the victim" writes Ryan, "is an ideological process, which is to say that it is a set of ideas and concepts deriving from systematically motivated, but *unintended* distortions of reality."[17] "The new ideology," Ryan continues, "attributes defect and inadequacy to the malignant nature of poverty, injustice, slum life, and racial difficulties. The stigma that marks the victim and accounts for his victimization is an acquired stigma, a stigma of social rather than genetic origin. But the stigma, the defect, the fatal difference though derived in the past from the environmental forces—is still located within the victim, inside his skin."[18]

Ryan describes the process, noting that "the problems of slum housing are traced to the characteristics of tenants who are labeled as 'Southern rural migrants' not yet 'acculturated' to life in the big city. The 'multiproblem' poor, it is claimed, suffer the psychological effects of improverishment, the 'culture of poverty' and the deviant value system of the lower classes; consequently, though unwittingly, they cause their own troubles."[19]

The proponents and adherents to this ideology, Ryan argues, include "sympathetic social scientists with social consciences in good working order, and liberal politicians with a genuine commitment to reform. They are very careful to dissociate themselves from vulgar calvinism or crude racism; they indignantly condemn any notions of innate wickedness or genetic defect."[20]

However, victim blamers arrived at their conservative ideological posture, agrues Ryan, because of the benefits they derive from the status quo.

> They cannot bring themselves to attack the system that has been so good to them, but they want so badly to be helpful to the victims of racism and economic injustice." To solve this dilemma, they develop a compromise which explains what is wrong with the victim "in terms of social experience *in the past,* experiences that left wounds, defects, paralysis, and disability." Then they develop solutions by analyzing the victim carefully, scientifically, mathematically, and objectively to determine the causes, which usually lie in a lack of job skills, education, poor values, bad habits, apathy, and "deviant low class cultural patterns."[21]

In so doing, those who blame the victims for their own shortcoming leave much undone.

Ryan's insights, while partically helpful in pinpointing some of the problems inherent in the political behavioralist orientations, rest themselves on an intrapsychic mechanism: a guilt complex or conscience. What Ryan failed to see, and what fails to develop from his point of view, is the way in which this complex has assisted and developed systemic, institutional, and organizational arrangements in the political arena to protect and perpetuate injustice. Systemic vairables become forces that ensure the victims' plight.

A recent example of this ideological description of blacks and black politics came during the 1984 presidential primaries. Theodore H. White put it this way: "What black leadership shares with most of the other movements...is a common purpose—to transform the traditional credo of American politics, 'equality,' into the credo of 'group equality'...what blacks want most is public acceptance of equality, not only on the basis of individucal merit but of group results and group shares—in short 'quotas' or 'goals' and 'timetables'.[22]

He continued this flawed ideological description of black politics: "...the black movement has introduced a new thought: that America is not a nation of equality of individual opportunities, but a coalition of races, each required to be equal in group results or entitlements."[23] This demand of black politics, he argues, is destructive, for it will lead to the "Lebanonization: of the American political system."

How does he arrive at this conclusion? There is no substantial body of public opinion data that shows blacks to be demanding this. In the political rhetoric of black leaders, civil rights, and political leaders, there is no call for this. In the campaign demands of Jesse Jackson there is no demand for entitlements and group equality, or quotas, or timetables. And if one looks at how quotas and timetables evolved in Congress, they were not advanced by blacks. So just how does White arrive at this conclusions? What makes White interpret black concerns in this way? The answer is obvious. He feels that there is nothing truly wrong with the American system, that certin uncompromising groups in the system don't understand the way it works, and that they ought to behave politically. It is simply an ideological perspective borne of the behavioral persuasion. The problem isn't the system, it is the people.

The Key Determinants of Black Political Behavior:
A Concluding Note

The misconceptions about black political participation cannot be corrected simply by reanalyzing the survey data or renewing emphasis on the question of black invisibility. To begin with, most survey data either omitted blacks or included only a very few of them. For instance the current three volumes that contain the same findings of Gallup polls from October 1935 through December 1971 will not even reveal questions on race relations until the early sixties. One of the earliest polls on black voting behavior appeared October 24, 1962, dealing with congressional elections of that year.[24] The second problem arises from the survey question themselves. Most addressed concerns in race relations, civil rights, and the integration of education, instead of crucial political matters. A third problem is awesome: the problem of regionalism. In the South, political participation was linked to the system. In the North, it took place, at least in some areas, on a segregated basis. Hence, it was only in national surveys where it was noted that these major incongruencies created at best, a fragmented or fractured picture in the final data. To get around this problem, many studies simply included more blacks from the South and generalized that participation was low throughout. Finally, given the wide variety of surveys, done by different groups for different reasons, even similar results were interpreted differently.

To attempt to reconstruct another view of black political activity from this morass of material would be nearly impossible because the prime thrust of the surveys was to find individual rather than systemic and structural motivations and influences. Merely emphasizing the inclusion of more blacks into the surveys will not resolve the major problem, because the surveys were looking for individual influences.[25] Thus, the major findings of this study grow out of the search for other forces shaping black political activity. These findings are not at all like those of studies seeking only individual influences.

The black political universe finds itself enmeshed in a complex web of systemic and structural influences. The black community has almost always been confronted with outside forces designed to shape its attitudes, its economics, and its politics. The black community also has found itself confronted with diverse internal forces seeking to influence its politics from, among others, a black nationalist perspective, an integrationist perspective, a Marxist-Socialist perspective, a religious perspective. These external and internal forces inevitably clash, producing change and compromise. But, most of all, they exert influence. Out of these myriad forces come black political responses. These responses vary with time and changing impacts.

As the preceding chapters have indicated, national black political behavior is not always the same at the state, local, and congressional levels. The forces and influences at one level, in one region, and of one kind, differ both in kind and degree from those at other levels at other times. Patterns emerge and thrive; they also disappear, collapse, reverse themselves, and begin anew. Therefore, to assume that black political participation is *solely* determined by SES indices or any other individual characteristics is to ignore political reality.[26]

Black political behavior is best understood as the result of indivudal, community, systemic, and structural factors, which over the years have all acted together in a complex, changing fashion. At one time, all of these forces and factors seemingly converged to produce a cry and demand for civil rights policies. The demand for political and social justice pushed the demand for economic justice, most of the time, to the background. The task of trying to return it to the black political agenda fell to small ideologically radical groups and individuals operating on the fringes of the sociopolitical system. But the modern civil rights movements—beginning with the 1963 march on Washington, the March for Jobs and Freedom, and King's Poor Peoples March, once again put economic progress back on the agenda with civil and political rights. By the mid-eighties, black political behavior, electoral leadership and other behavior were beginning to converge. Blacks were demanding civil, social, and economic policies that never materialized because King's effort had been cut short with his assassination. In addition, the Reagan Administration, with all of its dramatic economic cutbacks, had dramatized to the black community, possibly anew, to see the need for economic justice to eridicate the ghetto, improve slum housing, alleviate massive unemployment, police brutality, drug addiction, etc. Reagan, by making the economic issue dominate, permitted the economic concerns in the black community once again to join in with civil right demands. Thus, the legacies of racism in the political, economic, and social sectors will in the years ahead become the *key* determinants of black political behavior.

The Methodology, Survey and Questionnaire

This book is based on a data base that is both national and local in scope. The techniques of data analysis explored for both systemic and individual influences on political behavior and action, making the work both unique and pioneering. Data collection and data analysis procedures are described here in detail.

The primary data collection techniques were: (1) a national black population survey; (2) a collection of aggregate voting data; (3) a variety of extended open-ended interviews; and (4) some case studies, of both the traditional and behavioral genre.

The data analysis procedures employed were: (1) standard statistical techniques and inferences, and (2) historical analysis and representation of existing materials and data.

Together, the collection and analysis techniques and procedures sought not only to determine the existence and impact of systemic forces, but also the interrelationship of both individual and systemic (internal and external) variable.

The National Black Survey

The development and the administration of the national survey, though separate acts in themselves, are clearly interwoven. It was necessary to devise, construct, administer, and estimate the cost of surveys; a special concern was finding a way to carry out a national survey with limited resources.

First, problems had to be defined. Then procedures to overcome or minimize the problems had to be devised. As a first step to resolve these problems, various local surveys were conducted. Next came a statewide survey,[1] and then the presampling in mid-1972 for the survey. Revisions were completed in the summer of that year and on the basis of accumulated experience, techniques for the national survey were developed. Finally, of course, the matter of the demographics of the black electorate had to be addressed.

The Demography of the Black Electorate

Shortly after Professor C. Vernon Gray took over as research-director of the Joint Center of Political Studies, he asked the author to develop a full study of the black electorate based on the Bureau of Census demographic data for 1960 and 1970. Using the 1970 Census data and insight developed from the study, we developed a demographic profile of the black electorate for the national black survey. Using the Census-derived demographics and the black voting age population (BVAP) to define the parameters for the black electorate, we established key sampling units for (1) counties with black majorities; (2) counties with near balances of blacks and white, and (3) counties with blacks in the minority. Along with the sheer numbers of blacks in the population as a guide, we also used, of course, the socioeconomic variations and breakdowns.

After constructing the questionnaire and locating the key sampling units, we began the interviewing. This took place in several stages from 1972-74.

A word should be said at this point about the division of the respondents into black voters and nonblack voters, as opposed to the standard techniques of having nearly equal black and white groups. (A similar approach was used in *The Voter Decides*). First, the latter technique does not permit in-depth intragroup analysis because of the heavy intergroup comparisons. Second, to construct a more valid picture of black political participation, benchmarks should be established from either within the group, or at least with other similarily located minority groups, and not with the dominant majority.[2] Few in the majority have experienced the full range of systemic constraints that the black minority has. Third, nonvoting blacks, as we have seen, may participate politically in many ways, excepting only voting. Therefore, they influence and help shape some of the activities of those who do vote. Moreover, their individual perceptions are sometimes different from those who do vote. Finally, because many individuals move back and forth between the two groups, it is essential to collect information from both.

A sample of 1,200 persons was planned, but due to dwindling resources, only 1,100 questionnaires were adminstered. The response rates were as follows:

		%
Completed questionnaires	1003	91.2
Unusable questionnaires	97	8.8
Total	1100	100.0

		%
Total Interviews	1003	100.0
Black Voters	698	69.6
Black Nonvoters	305	30.4

The over-sampling toward the black voter category was deliberate so that this particular group could be seen in a larger portrait.

The Aggregate Data

The aggregate data for Atlanta from 1968 to 1976 was purchased on computer printouts from the Fulton County Office of Voter Registration. The data for 1962 to 1968 was supplied from the same office on Xerox hand-prepared pages for the black area. The office also provided maps and other helpful material.

The data on Atlanta's black aldermen, Savannah's Black aldermen, and the first election after reapportionment for the black legislators from Atlanta came from black and white newspapers. Data on black legislators in other parts of Georgia came from the Georgia State Archives and the *Georgia Official and Statistical Register.*

The data for Louisiana came from Perry Howard's book, as indicated; for New Orleans, from William Harvard's book; and from Florida, from Hugh D. Price's book. For the Congressional Districts, *The Official Congressional Directory* for each two-year period was employed. Sources for other aggregate data used in this volume are specified in footnotes.

The Atlanta Aggregate Data

Normally, studies on political behavior rely either on survey research data or on aggregate data. Survey data are used more often because most scholars want to avoid the so-called ecological fallacy. However, in developing the research design for this work, we decided to use both survey and aggregate data not only so that vivid comparisons and contrasts could be made but also for greater range, depth, and heightened dimensional insights. The use of aggregate data permits researchers to overcome the "snapshot" fallacy of the survey approach.

The Atlanta aggregate data were chosen for two reasons: first, they permit a significant degree of accuracy in regard to what blacks do in terms of voter turnout, and second, they permit a longitudinal look; which gives perspective and a chance for a time-series analysis.

When the Supreme Court destroyed the Georgia county unit system in the early sixties and set into motion the reapportionment of the Georgia State legislature, numerous black districts were created. I selected for analysis five House districts (out of the more than twenty-two) and the two black senatorial districts on the basis of the continuity of the various candidates in office. Moreover, Fulton Company had available both registration and voter figures for the various elections, thereby permitting a full analysis of turnout rate over time. Third, these five black house districts and two black senate districts are predominately black in their voting-age composition as well as the number of registered voters. The range in these districts runs from a low just over 80 percent blacks to a high of nearly 96 percent. Thus, one can contrast survey data about black turnout with aggregate data on how blacks as a group actually turn out, providing insight into possible differences between what people say they do and what they actually do. Moreover, since the same candidates in these districts stood for reelection several times, the fluctuation in turnout rates must take into account other factors such as campaigns, the times, and events. Finally, of the individuals analyzed here, two had national exposure: Senators Johnson and Bond. Overall, the findings from the aggregate data are clear and illuminating.

Researchers should note that aggregate data obtained from the Office of Voter Registration on registration differ from the data from the Board of Elections in Fulton County. For every year from 1968 to 1976, I used the figures from the Board of Elections. For the years 1964, 1965, and 1966, I used data from the Office of Voter Registration and estimated the percentages from that information. For example, on the Senate data sheet, primary and general percentages for 1964 and 1966 were calculated from the Board data. This is true for the year 1966 for the House data.

Senator Johnson's district was first created in 1962 and a second black senate district was created in 1964. Therefore, I have used 1964 as the starting date. In the House, special elections were first held in 1965 and again on a regular basis in 1966. For those wishing to see election data from the other black legislative districts in Georgia, which now number twenty-two, the *Georgia Official and Statistical Register (1966-1980)*, lists the primary and general election votes but not registration data. Additional data can be obtained from the Georgia Department of Archives and History microfilm section.

In regard to the following tables, the reader should note that, in some instances, the total number voting in the primary and the primary vote as well as the total number voting in the general election and the general election vote for the candidate listed do not always coincide. This simply means that the candidate had one or more opponents. But in every instance, the primary and general election percentages were calculated from the total number of persons voting, i.e., turning out in the election. The number of votes the candidate received was only of secondary importance in the research design. Of prime importance was the determination of the number of blacks in the aggregate turnout over time in primary and general elections for different political races.[3]

Interviews with Black Decision Makers

The interviews of the black legislative decision makers and the black organizational leaders were open-ended. They attempted to put "other kinds of research questions" into the research mill. Each person was chosen so as to add perspective and depth; the choices were not random. The cities were chosen for similar reasons. For instance, in Atlanta, blacks were one-half of the aldermatic board and the city itself is a major urban center with a still-vital downtown. Savannah, on the other hand, while an urban area, is watching the downtown decline. Unlike Atlanta, it did elect its aldermen on a citywide basis. Moreover, blacks on this board were only two, far less than 50 percent. Athens, a much smaller city but with three black aldermen, reflects another type of political milieu. And Thunderbolt, a very small city with only one black alderman, is the site of a major black institution, Savannah State College.

As for the choice of decision makers, black attorney Marvin Arrington was chosen because he was one of the first younger black alderman to win citywide and he had watched as the number of blacks on the board increased to the point of parity. In Savannah, Alderman Roy Jackson was chosen not only for his longevity and insights, but because he represents a new wave in city politics for the future. Ed Turner in Athens has been involved in that city's politics and as leader of the NAACP for many years, being the first among the few black alderman there. In Thunderbolt, the first black alderman, Leroy Brown is deceased; John Merritt, not only a much younger man but new to the community, works at the major black institution in the small coastal city.

On the state level, attorney Bobby Hill was then not only a six-term state legislator, he was vice-chairman and later chairman of the black state legislative caucus. Moreover, he was a significant force in the election of one of the state governors and in Governor Carter's presidential campaign.

W.W. Law, as president of a local branch of the NAACP in the South for more than twenty-six years, has seen the events of three very different decades from the vantage point of leader of a black organization. His perspectives were indeed important additions to our data.

The Reverend Matthew S. Brown has been a strong religious force in two urban black communities and therefore had a cross-community view. Moreover, he sees the church as playing a social as well as a religious role for its parishioners.

Thomas Byers had a long history of involvement with new and progressive organizations, while Jimmy Bennett is a street man, perpetually organizing the community for various benefits and self-help efforts. Finally, every individual was re-interviewed after an extended period for a longitudinal perspective.

A Final Note to the Reader

There are three things which the author feels he should bring to the reader's attention. These matters not only pertain to the discussion in the text, they will facilitate reading of the text by bringing into clearer focus the author's orientation and some of his predispositions.

In some chapters, the reader might wonder: why did the author not create more indices and provide deeper analysis of some issues? The answers are twofold. Most works on political behavior are books on voting behavior or the processes of political socialization, and their authors can thus deal with all connections and interrelationships. This volume, however, is a broad survey of a wide range of political activities. Chapters 2-4, on black culture, black socialization, and black opinions, deal with key theoretical issues; chapters 5-7, on black voting and party behavior, deal with matters of individual and organizational participation; chapters 8-10 concern themselves with black decision-making behavior; while chapter 11 moves to matters in the international arena. Chapter 1 offers a definition, while chapter 11, seeking some type of summary, covers both the past and future. Overall, the approach in this volume differs from the reductionistic approach so prevalent in the literature, and attempts to provide a comprehensive view instead of probing fully any one area.

As for indices, the issue is primarily, but not completely, a matter of methodology. Indices are developed to deal with inherent deficiencies, which Hennesy noted. Such research, he says, is "a tissue of assumptions and inferences." In other words, since the researcher cannot be sure of what the interviewee tells him, it becomes necessary for the researcher to map out the interviewee's attitudes and opinions in order to predict his behavior in the future. To do this, every questionnaire must include a number of co-relative questions, which buttress and extend each other, to provide the survey researcher with a broad view of the individual's political personality. During final analysis, these questions are grouped together, a scale is formed, and the index is born. It is a clever procedure but it has problems.

First, not all the questions composing the index are answered in postive or supportive fashion. Second, most indices, like behavioralism itself, assume that all the motivations for political actions are individualistic. Few indices include systemic realities. As a result, the wide array of existing indices need further study.

Finally, the reader might want to ask why I used the term "*ad-hoc* black political leaders" instead of a term such as "local black political convention organizers and leaders." The selection was purely one of individual preference and was like several others, which were not chosen as hard and fast terms, but to indicate tentative categories and break new ground.

In the final analysis, my aim is to stimulate further research in this vast and little-explored realm.

The Survey Questionnaire

Only the basic questions used for analysis in the following questionnaire have been included. Other items were dropped in the interest of saving space. Before the questionnaire was developed, the author obtained various questionnaires developed by blacks for use in the black community. Also, most of the questionnaires used in works devoted to the analysis and study of black attitudes and opinions were obtained. Finally, the various manuals on questionnaire construction and procedures issued by the Institute of Social Research of the Survey Research Center of the University of Michigan were consulted. Each set of questionnaires was carefully analyzed, along with some of the usual index scales in survey research. Several versions were developed before the final form was achieved.

Opinion Continuum

1. Have you heard of the following political terms? Liberals, Moderates, Conservatives.
_____ Yes
_____ No (move to next section)
_____ Other
_____ No Opinion

2. How often have you heard the terms used?
_____ Regularly
_____ Sometimes
_____ Once in a while
_____ Not at all
_____ Other

3. Do you consider yourself to be familiar (knowledgeable) with the terms?
_____ Yes
_____ No
_____ Uncertain
_____ No Opinion

4. In general political matters, which term would you use to describe yourself most of the time?
_____ Liberal
_____ Moderate
_____ Conservative
_____ Other
_____ No Opinion

5. On racial matters relating to the black community, which term would you use to describe yourself most of the time?

_____ Liberal
_____ Moderate
_____ Conservative
_____ Other
_____ No Opinion

Political Involvement

1. Do you talk about political happenings and events to family, friends, or neighbors?

_____ Yes
_____ No
_____ Other
_____ No Opinion

1. Did you vote in 1968?

_____ Yes
_____ No
_____ Other
_____ No Opinion

2. Did you vote in 1972?

_____ Yes
_____ No
_____ Other
_____ No Opinion

Political Concern

1. Do you feel that people should take part in politics (talking, giving money, campaigning, running for office, etc.)?

_____ Yes
_____ No (if no, conclude the interview)
_____ Other
_____ No Opinion

2. Do you know anyone in your community that is involved in politics?

_____ Yes
_____ No
_____ Other
_____ No Opinion

3. Do you feel that black participation in politics is useful (worthwhile)?

_____ Yes
_____ No
_____ Other
_____ No Opinion

4. Are you personally interested in politics?

_____ Yes

_____ No

_____ Other

_____ No Opinion

5. In terms of your interest in politics, would you say you are:

_____ Very interested

_____ Fairly interested

_____ Not interested

_____ Other

_____ No Opinion

6. If interested would you give money or time or other resources to political candidates or organizations?

_____ Yes

_____ No

_____ Other

_____ No Opinion

7. Have you ever contributed any form of support to political candidates and organizations?

_____ Yes

_____ No (Move to next question)

_____ Other

_____ No Opinion

8. Can you always participate politically when you want to take part?

_____ Yes

_____ No

_____ Other

_____ No Opinion

9. Do you care to name some personal and nonpersonal reasons why? (Personal—explain as individual ones) (Nonpersonal—explain as external)

Personal	Nonpersonal
1.	1.
2.	2.
3.	3.
4.	4.
5.	5.

Political Evaluation

1. Do you think people have feelings about how the government operates and affects them?

_____ Yes

_____ No

_____ Other

_____ No Opinion

2. Do you know people who have strong and/or negative feelings about government actions and policies?

_____ Yes

_____ No

_____ Other

_____ No Opinion

3.Do you have definite feelings about governmental policies and programs?

_____ Yes

_____ No

_____ Other

_____ No Opinion

4. Of the following terms, which one would you use to describe your feelings about government?

_____ Favorable

_____ Unfavorable

_____ Other

_____ No Opinion

5. Of the following presidents, which do you consider to have been most important for blacks?

_____ Lincoln

_____ Roosevelt

_____ Truman

_____ Kennedy

_____ Johnson

_____ Nixon

6. Of the following presidential programs, which do you consider to have been most important for blacks?

_____ New Deal

_____ Fair Deal

_____ New Frontier

_____ Great Society

_____ Other

7. Of the following Surpreme Court decisions, which do you consider to have been most important for blacks?

_____ Brown Decision 1954

_____ 1964 Civil Rights Decision

_____ 1965 Voting Rights Act

_____ Other _____

8. Of the following terms, which one would you use to describe your feelings about the Supreme Court?

_____ Favorable

_____ Unfavorable

_____ Other

_____ No Opinion

9. Of the following terms, which one would you use to describe your feelings about the founding fathers?

_____ Favorable

_____ Unfavorable

_____ Other

_____ No Opinion

10. Of the following terms, which one would you use to describe your feelings about the Senate filibuster?

_____ Favorable

_____ Unfavorable

_____ Other _____

_____ No Opinion

11. Of the following terms, which one would you use to describe your feelings about the current welfare policy?

_____ Favorable

_____ Unfavorable

_____ Other _____

_____ No Opinion

12. Of the following terms, which one would you use to describe your feelings about the current educational policy?

_____ Favorable

_____ Unfavorable

_____ Other _____

_____ No Opinion

13. In your opinion, which of the following public issues is the most important one facing blacks?

_____ Poverty

_____ Civil Rights

_____ Education

_____ Welfare

_____ Other _____

_____ No Opinion

14. In your opinion, should welfare payments be:

_____ Increased?

_____ Decreased?

_____ Remain the same?

_____ Other _____

_____ No Opinion

Political Learning and Communication

1. Do you think that there are groups, organizations, agencies, that help to shape people's opinion?

_____ Yes

_____ No

_____ Other _____
_____ No Opinion

2. Do you know of any individuals who have had their opinions changed because of various groups and/or organizations?
_____ Yes
_____ No
_____ Other _____
_____ No Opinion

3. Have you ever changed any of your political ideas and opinions because of groups, family, friends, or organizations?
_____ Yes
_____ No
_____ Other _____
_____ No Opinion

4. In your opinion, which of the following organizations have had the greatest amount of influence on your opinions?
_____ The black church
_____ The black minister
_____ Black schools
_____ Your friends
_____ Radio & TV

5. How much attention do you pay to political matters in the media?
_____ A great deal
_____ Some
_____ None at all
_____ Other _____
_____ No Opinion

6. Of the following national and local newspapers, which do you read the most?

National	*Local*
_____ PITTSBURGH COURIER	_____ CHICAGO DEFENDER
_____ AFRO-AMERICAN	_____ ATLANTA DAILY WORLD
_____ NEW YORK TIMES	_____ NEW YORK AMSTERDAM NEWS
_____ WASHINGTON POST	_____ OTHER

7. As a source of political information, which of the following types of newspapers do you consider most important?
_____ Black
_____ White
_____ Both
_____ Other _____
_____ No Opinion

8. Which national magazines do you read most often?

_____ EBONY   _____ ESSENCE
_____ JET   _____ NEWSWEEK
_____ ENCORE AMERICAN   _____ TIME
_____ SEPIA   _____ U.S. NEWS & WORLD
                                              REPORT

Voting Behavior

1. Are you familiar with the following types of elections?

A. Primaries   B. Run-Offs   C. General
_____ Yes   _____ Yes   _____ Yes
_____ No   _____ No   _____ No
_____ No Opinion_____ No Opinion   _____ No Opinion

2. Have you ever discussed with family or friends the following elections?

A. Primaries   B. Run-Offs   C. General
_____ Yes   _____ Yes   _____ Yes
_____ No   _____ No   _____ No
_____ No Opinion_____ No Opinion   _____ No Opinion

3. Have any of your family or friends ever voted in any of the following types of elections?

A. Primaries   B. Run-Offs   C. General
_____ Yes   _____ Yes   _____ Yes
_____ No   _____ No   _____ No
_____ No Opinion_____ No Opinion   _____ No Opinion

4. Which of the following types of primaries do you vote in regularly? (If nonvoter, would like to vote in)

A. Congressional Primaries B. State Primaries C. Local Primaries
_____ House   _____ Gubernatorial   _____ Mayoralty
_____ Senate   _____ Lt. Governor   _____ Aldermanic
                      _____ House   _____ County Commis-
                      _____ Senate   sioner

5. If the following primaries included black candidates, which ones would you vote in regularly? (If nonvoter - would like to vote in). Check as many as voted.

A. Congressional Primaries B. State Primaries C. Local Primaries
_____ House   _____ Gubernatorial   _____ Mayoralty
_____ Senate   _____ Lt. Governor   _____ Aldermanic
                      _____ House   _____ County Commis-
                      _____ Senate   sioner

General Elections

1. Would you call yourself a regular voter in general elections? (If nonvoter, would like to be).

_____ Yes
_____ No
_____ Other
_____ No Opinion

2. Which of the following types of general elections do you participate in regularly? (If nonvoter, would like to participate in regularly). Check as many as voted.

A. Presidential B. Congressional C. State D. Local

__ Yes	__ House	__ Guber- natorial	__ Mayoralty
__ No	__ Senate	__ Lt. Go- vernor	__ Alder- manic
__ No Opin- ion		__ House __ Senate	__ House Commis- sioner	__ County

Nonvoting

1. Are you always able to vote as regularly as you like?
_____ Yes
_____ No
_____ Other _____
_____ No Opinion

2. Would you mind stating some of the reasons why you cannot vote regularly?
1. _____
2. _____
3. _____
4. _____
5. _____

3. Are you planning to try and vote more often despite these problems?
_____ Yes
_____ No
_____ Other
_____ No Opinion

4. Are you planning to register to vote soon?
_____ Yes
_____ No (If no, move to next question)
_____ Other
_____ No Opinion

5. Would you mind naming some of the reasons why you are not registered to vote? (personal or otherwise).
1. _____
2. _____
3. _____
4. _____
5. _____

Party Behavior

1. What are your preferences in terms of political party affiliations? (If nonvoter, would like to be affiliated with)

_____ Republican

_____ Democrat

_____ Independent

_____ Minor

_____ Black

_____ No Preference

_____ Other _____

2. Which one of the following factors is most important in determining this preference for you? (If nonvoter, would be if you voted)

_____ Issues

_____ Candidate's personality

_____ Party Platform

_____ Others _____

_____ No Opinion

3. For what party did you vote for in 1968? (If nonvoter, would have voted for).

_____ Republican

_____ Democrat

_____ Minor

_____ Other

_____ No Opinion

4. What party did you vote for in 1972? 1974?

1972

_____ Republican

_____ Democrat

_____ Minor

_____ Other

_____ No Opinion

1974

_____ Republican

_____ Democrat

_____ Minor

_____ Other

_____ No Opinion

International Attitudes

1. How often do you keep up with international affairs?

_____ Regularly

_____ Sometimes

_____ Not at all

_____ Other

_____ No Opinion

2. Do you feel that the recent presidential trips to Russia and China were beneficial to blacks?

_____ Yes

_____ No

_____ Other

_____ No Opinion

3. In terms of foreign aid, which of the following categories of nations should the United States give aid to?

_____ African

_____ Communist

_____ Democratic

_____ Other

_____ No Opinion

4. In your opinion, should we increase or decrease or maintain at present, the level of American foreign aid?

_____ Increase

_____ Decrease

_____ Keep same

_____ Other

_____ No Opinion

Appendix B.

Black Legislative Districts

TABLE B 1. Black Voting and Turnout in Selected Black State Legislative Districts in Atlanta, Georiga: 1965-1980

Black State No. Representatives	House District	Primary Registered Voters	Primary Total No. Voting	Primary Votes	Primary %'s Turnout	General Election Votes	General Election %'s Turnout	General Elections Total No. Voting	General Elections Registered Voters
LEGISLATIVE RACES: 1965									
1. W. H. Alexander	133	N.A.	N.A.	1,165	N.A.	2,468	N.A.	N.A.	N.A.
2. J. C. Daugherty	134	N.A.	N.A.	1,814	N.A.	2,822	N.A.	N.A.	N.A.
3. Ben Brown	135	N.A.	N.A.	1,025	N.A.	2,608	N.A.	N.A.	N.A.
4. Julian Bond	136	N.A.	N.A.	1,244	N.A.	2,320	N.A.	N.A.	N.A.
5. Grace Hamilton	137	N.A.	N.A.	852	N.A.	1,475	N.A.	N.A.	N.A.
LEGISLATIVE RACES: 1966*									
1. W. H. Alexander	133	11,407	N.A.	2,503	26.0	3,402	47.8	N.A.	N.A.
2. J. C. Daugherty	134	14,027	N.A.	1,987	22.5	3,688	42.2	N.A.	N.A.
3. Ben Brown	135	12,494	N.A.	2,728	24.6	3,855	42.1	N.A.	N.A.
4. Julian Bond	136	7,334	N.A.	1,376	30.9	2,192	47.8	N.A.	N.A.
5. Grace Hamilton	137	7,557	N.A.	1,350	19.4	1,804	35.5	N.A.	N.A.
LEGISLATIVE RACES: 1968									
1. W. H. Alexander	108	18,340	5,008	5,008	27.3	8,862	57.1	10,922	19,118
2. J. C. Daugherty	109	12,513	2,630	2,630	21.0	6,308	52.5	6,803	12,947
3. Ben Brown	110	12,586	2,991	2,991	23.8	5,928	46.7	5,928	12,696
4. Julian Bond	111	7,230	2,501	2,501	34.6	3,887	53.5	3,887	7,267
5. Grace Hamilton	112	7,965	1,373	1,373	17.2	3,402	41.7	3,402	8,153

#	Name	District								
LEGISLATIVE RACES: 1970										
1.	W. H. Alexander	108	22,387	5,746	5,746	25.7	9,092	44.7	10,267	22,976
2.	J. C. Daugherty	109	13,511	2,849	2,849	21.1	5,126	37.4	5,126	13,717
3.	Ben Brown	110	12,431	2,889	2,889	23.2	4,815	38.3	4,815	12,586
4.	Julian Bond	111	7,430	2,397	2,397	32.3	3,325	44.5	3,325	7,467
5.	Grace Hamilton	112	8,115	1,291	1,291	15.9	2,540	31.1	2,540	8,159
LEGISLATIVE RACES: 1972										
1.	W. H. Alexander	38	13,639	4,140	3,811	30.4	7,352	50.0	7,352	14,695
2.	J. C. Daugherty	33	12,505	3,042	2,322	24.3	5,764	43.9	5,764	13,137
3.	Ben Brown	34	13,176	3,982	3,042	30.2	5,664	46.1	6,471	14,024
4.	Julian Bond	32	11,305	2,928	2,928	25.9	5,826	45.4	5,826	12,840
5.	Grace Hamilton	31	10,209	2,120	1,810	20.8	3,912	37.1	3,912	10,535
LEGISLATIVE RACES: 1974										
1.	W. H. Alexander	38	14,598	3,008	3,008	20.6	5,820	39.4	5,820	14,789
2.	J. C. Daugherty	33	11,713	2,789	1,639	23.8	4,129	35.1	4,129	11,769
3.	Ben Brown	34	12,705	2,721	2,721	21.4	4,771	37.3	4,771	12,790
4.	Mildred Glover	32	11,692	1,870	1,870	16.0	3,138	30.2	3,734	12,347
5.	Grace Hamilton	31	9,279	2,214	1,394	23.9	2,995	32.1	2,995	9,326
6.	Robert Holmes	39	16,224	4,725	1,658	29.1	5,706	34.7	5,706	16,442
LEGISLATIVE RACES: 1976										
1.	Henerita Canty	38	14,918	2,296	2,296	15.4	8,496	54.6	8,496	15,556
2.	J. C. Daugherty	33	10,957	2,179	1,537	19.9	5,683	50.9	5,683	11,158
3.	Ben Brown	34	12,432	2,690	2,476	21.7	6,726	54.6	7,081	12,963
4.	Mildred Glover	32	11,525	1,207	1,207	10.5	5,115	42.1	5,115	12,154
5.	Grace Hamilton	31	8,658	1,763	941	20.4	4,085	46.3	4,085	8,818
6.	Robert Holmes	39	16,730	3,200	2,510	19.1	9,024	50.3	9,024	17,940

TABLE B 1. Black Voting and Turnout in Selected Black State Legislative Districts in Atlanta, Georiga: 1965-1980

		Primary				General Election Votes	General Election %'s Turnout	General Elections	
Black State No. Representatives	House District	Registered Voters	Total No. Voting	Primary Votes	Primary %'s Turnout			Total No. Voting	Registered Voters
LEGISLATIVE RACES: 1978									
1. Henerita Canty	38	14,768	4,481	3,418	30.3	3,883	26.5	3,883	14,644
2. J. C. Daugherty	33	10,204	1,275	1,275	12.5	2,281	22.2	2,281	10,271
3. Lottie Watkins	34	12,248	3,669	2,130	17.4	2,910	31.2	3,668	11,774
4. Mildred Glover	32	11,528	1,060	1,060	9.2	1,788	15.4	1,788	11,605
5. Grace Hamilton	31	8,309		950	11.4	1,483	21.8	1,824	8,356
LEGISLATIVE RACES: 1980									
1. Lorenzo Benn	38	15,795	2,593	2,593	16.4	7,747	50.8	8,052	15,845
2. J. C. Daugherty	33	10,155	1,353	1,353	13.3	3,529	34.7	3,529	10,168
3. Tyrone Brooks	34	13,316	3,844	1,152	28.9	5,788	43.4	5,788	13,331
4. Mildred Glover	32	12,512	1,103	1,103	8.8	3,952	31.5	3,952	12,546
5. Grace Hamilton	31	8,287	995	995	12.0	2,447	29.5	2,447	8,297

*Percentages estimated from Board data.

N.A., not available.

SOURCE: *Georgia Official and Statistical Register* and materials supplied by the Fulton County Office of Voter Registration: 1965-82.

TABLE B 2. Black Voting and Turnout in Selected Black State Senatorial Districts in Atlanta, Georiga: 1965-1980

Black State No. Senators	Senate District	Registered Voters	Total No. Voting	Primary Votes	Primary %'s Turnout	General Election Votes	General Election %'s Turnout	Total No. Voting	Registered Voters
								(General Elections)	*(General Elections)*
SENATE RACES: 1964									
1. Leroy Johnson	38	33,493	—	12,536	37.4	21,035	51.9*	26,956	44,761
2. Horace Ward	39	26,637	—	4,326	16.2	10,289	36.5*	10,369	26,630
SENATE RACES: 1966									
1. Leroy Johnson	38	—	—	—	28.6*	—	51.0*	—	—
2. Horace Ward	39	—	—	—	19.0*	—	36.5*	—	—
SENATE RACES: 1968									
1. Leroy Johnson	38	43,439	13,614	13,614	31.0	21,794	60.2	26,956	44,761
2. Horace Ward	39	26,162	5,217	5,217	19.9	10,369	39.0	10,369	26,630
SENATE RACES: 1970									
1. Leroy Johnson	38	44,484	10,350	10,350	23.3	18,748	41.3	18,748	45,369
2. Horace Ward	39	23,610	3,801	3,801	16.1	7,828	32.4	7,828	24,143
SENATE RACES: 1972									
1. Leroy Johnson	38	35,896	9,718	9,718	27.1	19,740	51.5	19,740	38,362
2. Horace Ward	39	32,445	6,949	5,764	21.0	13,275	38.1	13,275	34,852
SENATE RACES: 1974									
1. Leroy Johnson	38	36,457	12,029	5,759	33.0	Lost in primaries		—	—
1. Horace Tate	38	36,457	12,029	6,272	33.0	15,275	41.6	15,275	36,748
2. Julian Bond	39	30,680	8,407	6,676	27.4	10,556	33.6	10,556	31,377

TABLE B 2. Black Voting and Turnout in Selected Black State Senatorial Districts in Atlanta, Georiga: 1965-1980

Black State No. Senators	Senate District	Registered Voters	Total No. Voting	Primary Votes	Primary %'s Turnout	General Election Votes	General Elections		
							General Election %'s Turnout	Total No. Voting	Total No. Registered Voters
			SENATE RACES: 1976						
1. Horace Tate	38	35,957	8,535	7,602	23.7	19,975	53.8	19,975	37,159
2. Julian Bond	39	28,947	4,947	4,947	17.1	13,811	45.9	13,811	30,068
			SENATE RACES: 1978						
1. Horace Tate	38	34,764	10,257	8,360.	29.5	8,903	25.4	8,903	—
2. Julian Bond	39	27,825	4,358	4,358	15.7	5,552	19.8	5,552	—
			SENATE RACES: 1980						
1. Horace Tate	38	36,022	7,499	7,499	20.8	16,336	45.3	16,336	36,101
2. Julian Bond	39	29,058	4,355	4,355	14.9	11,573	39.7	11,573	29,116

*Percentages estimated from Board data.

NOTE: The registered voter data supplied for the year 1980 in both the legislative and Senate districts was date 10/20/80 for the primary and 11/15/80 for the general election. The primary was held on 8/5/80 and the general election on 11/4/80.

SOURCE: *Georgia Official and Statistical Register* and materials supplied by the Fulton County Office of Voter Registration: 1964-82.

Notes

Notes to the Preface

1. Other personal journeys with the behavioral approach are described in Heinz Eulau, "The Behavioral Movement in Political Science: A Personal Document," *Social Research*, Vol. 32 (Spring 1965), pp. 1-29; and Robert A. Dahl, "The Behavioral Approach in Political Science: Epitaph for a Monument to a Successful Protest," *American Political Science Review*, vol. 61 (December, 1961), pp. 763-772.

2. Two of Brisbane's major works that note some of the limiting forces under which black politics operate are *The Black Vanguard*, (Valley Forge: Judson Press, 1970), and *Black Activism*, (Valley Forge: Judson Press, 1974).

3. See his *Negro Politicians*, (Chicago: University of Chicago Press, 1932).

4. See U.S. Commission on Civil Rights, *Hearing Voting*, Vol. I (Washington, D.C.: U. S. Government Printing Office, 1965), pp. 207-215, for Testimony of Professor Prothro.

5. Samuel Cook, "Introduction. The American Liberal Democratic Tradition, The Black Revolution, and Martin Luther King, Jr.," in Hanes Walton, Jr., *The Political Philosophy of Martin Luther King, Jr.*, (Westport: Greenwood, 1971), p. xxvi.

6. W. E. B. Dubois, *Dusk of Dawn*, (New York: Harcourt, Brace, & World, 1940), p. 130.

7. Richard Wright, "Introduction" in St. Clair Drake and Horace R. Cayton, *Black Metropolis*, Revised Edition, Volume I (New York: Harcourt, Brace & World, 1970), p.xxviii.

8. Ralph Ellison, *Invisible Man*, (New York: Signet Books, 1953).

Notes to Chapter One

1. See his "Tradition and Innovation: On the Tension Between Ancient and Modern Ways in the Study of Politics," in his (ed.),*Behavioralism in Political Science*, (New York: Atherton Press, 1969), p. 17; *Micro - Macro Political Analysis: Accents on Inquiry, (Chicago: Aldine Publishing Co mpany, 1969), p. 152; Political Behavior, (Gencoe: Free Press, 1956), p.3; The Behavioral Persuasion in Politics*, (New York: Random House, 1963), pp. 13-14; *Political Behavior in America: New Directions*, (New York: Random House, 1966), p. 5.

2. S. Sidney Ulmer (ed.), *Introductory Readings in Political Behavior*, (Chicago: Rand McNally, 1961), pp.3, 2.

3. Lester W. Milbrath, *Political Participation*, (Chicago: Rand McNally, 1969), p. 3.

4. David Apter and Charles Andrain (ed.), *Contemporary Analytical Theory*, (Englewood Cliff, N.J.: Prentice-Hall, 1972), p. 14.

5. William Welsh, *Studying Politics*, (New York: Praeger, 1973), p. 63

6. Lawrence Mayer, *Comparative Political Inquiry: A Methological Survey*, (Homerwood,Illinois: Dorsey Press, 1972), p. 191.

7. G. David Garson, *Handbook of Political Science Method*, (Boston: Holbrook Press, 1971), p. 24.

8. Nelson Polsby et al.(ed.), *Politics & Social Life: An Introduction to Political Behavior*, (Boston: Houghton Mifflin, 1963), p. 172

9. Theodore L. Becker (ed.), *Political Trials*, (Indianapolis: Bobbs-Merrill, 1972, and Leon Friedman (ed.), *Southern Justice*, (New York: Meridian Books, 1967).

10. Lois B. Moreland, *White Racism and the Law*, (Ohio: Charles Merrill, 1970), and Louis Knowles and Kenneth Prewitt (ed.), *Institutional Racism in America*, (Englewood Cliff: Prentice Hall, 1970).

11. See Arnold J. Herdenheimer (ed.), *Political Corruption*, (New York: Holt, Rinehart and Winston, 1970), and John Gardiner and David Olson, *Theft of the City Reading on Corruption in Urban America, (Bloomington: Indiana University Press, 1974)*.

12. *Murray B. Levin, Political Hysteria in America: The Democratic Capacity for Repression*, (New York: Basic Books, 1971).

13. Heinz Eulau, *Micro Macro Political Analysis, p. 2.*

14. *Ibid., p. 3.*

15. *Stephen L. Wasby, Political Science: The Discipline and Its Dimensions*, (New York: Charles Scribner & Sons, 1970), pp. 44.

16. Milbrath, *Political Participation*, p. 5.

17. Garson, Handbook, p. 25.

18. Arthur J. Brodbeck, "The Problem of Irrationality and Neuroticism Underlying Political Choice," in Eugene Burdbeck & Arthur Bodbeck (ed.), *American Voting Behavior, (Glencoe: Free Press, 1959), pp. 121-135*

19. *Eugene Burdick, "Political Theory and the Voting Studies," Ibid., pp. 138-139, 140.*

20. *V. O. Key, Jr., The Responsible Electorate*, (Cambridge: Harvard University Press, 1966), p. 7.

21. See Philip E. Converse, review of *The Responsible Electorate* in the *Political Science Quarterly*, (December, 1966), Vol. 81, pp. 628-633.

22. Thomas Dye and L. Harmon Zeigler, *The Irony of Democracy*, Second Editon, (California: Duxbury Press, 1972), p. 363.

23. For this argument see B. F. Skinner, *Walden Two*, (New York: MacMillan, 1978), and Melvin M. Schuster, "Skinnner and the Morality of Melioration," in Peyton Richer (ed.), *Utopia/Dystopia*, (Massachusetts: Schenkman, 1975), p. 108

24. Henry Etzkowitz and Gerald M. Scholflander, *Ghetto Crisis: Riots or Reconciliation*, (Boston: Little, Brown and Company, 1969,), pp. 120-127

25. Richard Dawson, "Political Socialization," in James Robinson (ed.), *Political Science Annual*, (New York: Bobbs-Merrill, 1966), p. 3.

26. Eulau, *Micro-Macro Political Analysis p. 7.*

27. *Ibid.*

28. *Don R. Bowen, Political Behavior of the American Public*, (Ohio: Charles Merrill, 1968), p. 7.

29. See also William Raspberry, "Victimism," *Washington Post*,(July 7, 1976), pp. A-15. In addition, see William Ryan, *Blaming the Victim, (New York: Vintage Books, 1971)*.

30 .Edgar Litt, *Ethnic Politics in America*, (Illinios: Scott, Foresman and Company, 1970), p. i.

31. Leslie Burl McLemore, "Toward a Theory of Black Politics: The Black and Ethnic Models Revisited," *Journal of Black Studies*, Vol. 3 (March, 1972), p. 323.

32. Quoted in Ibid., p. 324.

33. McLemore quoted in Ibid., p. 323

34. Quoted in Ibid., p. 325.

35. Charles S. Bullock and Harrel R. Rodgers, Jr. (ed.), *Black Political Attitudes: Implications for Political Support*, (Chicago: Markham Publishing Company, 1972), p. 6.

36. Milton D. Morris, *The Politics of Black America*, (New York: Harper and Row, 1975), p. 282.

37. Ibid., p. 200

38. Donald Matthews and James Prothro, *Negroes and the New Southern Politics*, (New York: Harcourt, Brace and World, 1966), p. 324.

39. Margaret Law Callcott, *The Negro in Maryland Politics: 1870-1912,,*(Baltimore: The John Hopkins Press, 1969), p. ix

40. Ibid.

41. Ibid., pp. ix-x

42. Frederick M. Wirt, *Politics of Southern Equality: Law and Change in a Mississippi County*, (Chicago: Aldine Publishing Company, 1970), p. 298.

43. Johnnie Daniel, "Negro Political Behavior and Community Political and Socio-Economic Structural Factors," *Social Forces*, Vol. 48 (March, 1969), p. 277; the same article appeared in the *Journal of Social and Behavioral Sciences*, Vol.14 (Fall, 1968), pp. 41-46, however without the footnotes.

44. Ibid.

45. Ibid., p.278.

46. Bowen, *Political Behavior of the American Public*, p. 125.

47. Ibid.

48. These early studies merit a study in themselves: At Chicago, see Joe Elmer Henderson, "A Study of the Basic Factors Involved in the Change in the Party Alignment of Negroes in Chicago, 1932-1938," (unpublished thesis: The University of Chicago, 1939); At Columbia, see John Morsell, "The Political Behavior of Negroes in New York City," (Ph.D. thesis, University of Pennsylvania, 1945); at Atlanta, see Cleo Roberts, "Some Correlates of Registration and Voting among Negroes in the 1953 Municipal Election of Atlanta," (Master's thesis, Atlanta University, 1954); at Emory, see William C. Hamann, "A Study of Voting Participation, 1945-1954, in an All-Negro Precinct in Atlanta, Georgia," (M.A. thesis Emory University, Atlanta, 1955) and Hugh C. Owens, "The Rise of Negro Voting in Georgia, 1944-1950, (M.A. thesis, Emory University, Atlanta, 1951).

49. The articles and book in this area are numerous: Mack H. Jones, "Black Officeholders in Local Governments of the South: An Overview," *Politics 1971*, pp. 49-72: Joe Feagin, "Black Elected Officials in the South: An Exploratory Analysis," in Jack Van Der Slik (ed.) *Black Conflict with America*, (Ohio: Charles Merrill, 1970), pp. 107-122: Joe Feagin and Harlan Hahn, "The Sound Reconstruction : Black Political Strength in the South," *Social Science Quarterly*, Vol. 1 (June, 1970), pp. 44-45; Douglas St. Angelo and E. Lester Levin, "Black Candidates: Can They Be Aided by a New Populism," *Journal of Black Studies, Bol. 38 (December, 1971), pp. 167-182; John Kramer, "The Election of Blacks to City Councils: A 1970 Status Report and a Prolegomena," Journal of Black Studies*, Vol. 39 (June, 1971), pp. 443-476; Charles S. Bullock, III, "Southern Elected Black Officials," a paper read at the 1973 Annual Meeting of the Southern Political Science Association, (November 1-3, 1973); Clinton Jones, "Structural and Demographic Correlation of Black Membership on City Councils," a paper read at the Fifth Annual Meeting of the National Conference of black Political Scientists, Atlanta, Georgia, (May 2, 1974); and Mervyn M. Dymally (ed.), *The Black Politician: His Struggle for Power*, (Belmont: Duxbury Press, 1971); John Conyers and Walter Wallace, *Black Elected Officials*, (New York: Russell Sage, 1976); Leonard Cole, *Blacks in Power*, (Princeton: Princeton University Press, 1976); William Nelson, Jr. and Philip J. Meranto, *Electing Black Mayors*, (Columbus: Ohio State University Press, 1977); and Albert Karnig & Susan Welch, *Black Representation and Urban Policy*,(Chicago: University of Chicago Press, 1980).

50 Gabriel Almond, "Comparative Political System," *Journal of Politics*, Vol. 18 (August, 1956), p. 396.

51 See Gabriel Almond & Sidney Verba (ed.), *The Civic Culture Revisited (Boston: Little, Brown, 1980).*

52 *Herbert Hyman, "Surveys in the Study of Political Psychology* (San Francisco: Jossey-Bass, 1973), 322.

53. John Robinson & Phillip Shaver, *Measures of Social Psychological Attitudes* (Michigan: Survey Research Center, 1970); his *Measures of Occupational Attitudes and Occupational Characteristis (Michigan: Survey Research Center, 1969). See Howard Schuman & Stanley Presser, Question and*

Answers in Attitude Surveys: Experiments on Question Form, Wording, and Context (New York: Academic Press, 1981).

54 For further details see appendix A.

55 See Angus Campbell, "Recent Developments in Survey Studies of Political Behavior," in Ranney,*Essay on the Behavioral Study of Politics* (Urbana: University of Illinois Press, 1962).

56 Ibid., p 34.

57 On this matter, see William Welsh, *Studying Politics,* (New York: Praeger Publishers, 1973), pp. 171-173.

58 Kenneth R. Hoover, *The Elements of Social Scientific Thinking,* Third Edition, (New York: St. Martins Press, 1984), p. 150.

Notes to Chapter Two

1. Almond and Verba, *The Civic Culture Revisited,* p. 26

2. Ibid., pp. 27-28

3. Lucian W. Pye, "Political Culture," *International Encyclopedia of the Social Sciences* (New York: Free Press, 1961), p. 218.

4. Lucian W. Pye, "Culture and Political Science: Problems in the Evaluation of the Concept of Political Culture," in Louis Schneider and Charles Bonjean (ed.), *The Idea of Culture in the Social Sciences* (New York: Cambridge University Press, 1973), p. 67.

5. Almond and Verba, *The Civic Culture Revisited,* p. 15.

6. Hanes Walton, Jr., "Black Political Cultural Institutions: L. H. Stanton, C. L. Holte, *Continental Features* and *National Scene*" in his *Black Politics & Black Political Behavior: A Linkage Analysis* (forthcoming).

7. Almond and Verba, *The Civic Culture Revisited,* p. 23.

8. Alan I. Abramowitz, "The United States: Political Culture under Stress," in *Ibid.,* pp. 180-181.

9. Dwaine Marvick, "The Political Socialization of the American Negro ," *Annals of the American Academy of Political and Social Science,* Vol. 361 (September, 1965), pp. 112-27.

10. Donald R. Matthews and James W. Prothro, *Negroes and the New Southern Politics* (New York: Harcourt, Brace and World, 1966), p. 276, footnote 3.

11. Ibid., p. 219.

12. Ibid., p. 277.

13. Harry Holloway, *The Politics of the Southern Negro* (New York: Random House, 1969), pp. 82, 102, 314, 321.

14. Nathan Glazer and Daniel Moynihan, *Beyond the Melting Pot* (Massachusetts: M.I.T. & Harvard University Press, 1964), p. 53.

15. Ibid., p. 33.

16. John Szwed, "Introduction," in Arthur H. Fauset, *Black Gods of the Metropolis* (Pennsylvania: University of Pennsylvania Press, 1971), p. vi.

17. Ralph Ellison, "A Very Stern Discipline," *Harper's* (March, 1967), p. 84.

18. John Hope Franklin (ed.), *Three Negro Classics* (New York: Avon Books, 1969), p. 81. See also Ronald Walters, "The New Black Political Culture," *Black World*, Vol. 22 (October, 1972), pp. 4-17.

19. The debate is clearly stated in E. Franklin Frazier, *The Negro in the United States*, revised edition, (New York: MacMillan, 1975), pp. 4-21.

20. See Melville T. Herskovits, *The Myth of the Negro Past*, (New York: Harper & Brothers, 1941).

21. Franklin Frazier, *The Negro Family in the United States*, (Chicago: University of Chicago Press, 1968), p. 16.

22. *Ibid.*, Alex Haley's *Roots* shows the weaknesses here.

23. See Charles Keil, *Urban Blues*, (Chicago: University of Chicago Press, 1966).

24. See Ulf Hannerz, *Soulside*, (New York: Columbia University Press, 1969).

25. Roger Abrahams, *Positively Black*, (Englewood Cliffs: Prentice Hall, 1970), and his *Deep Down in the Jungle: Negro Narrative Folklore from the Streets of Philadelphia*, (Chicago: Aldine, 1970). For a recent and similar thesis see Lawrence Levine, *Black Culture and Black Consciousness*, (New York: Oxford University Press, 1977).

26. Eugene Genovese, *Roll, Jordan, Roll*, (New York: Pantheon Books, 1974).

27. Peter Wood, *Black Majority: Negroes in Colonial South Carolina from 1670 through the Stono Rebellion*, (New York: Knopf, 1974).

28. Gerald W. Mullin, *Fight and Rebellion Slave Resistance in Eighteenth Century Virginia*, (New York: Oxford University Press, 1974).

29. St. Clair Drake and Horace Cayton, *Black Metropolis*, revised edition, Vol. 2, (New York: Harcourt, Brace and World, 1970), p. 396.

30. Ibid.

31. St. Clair Drake, "The Social and Economic Status of the Negro in the United States," in K. B. Clark and T. Parsons (ed.), *The Negro American*, (Boston: Houghton, Mifflin Company, 1966), p. 7.

32. Ibid.

33. W. Lloyd Warner, "A Methodological Note: The Conflict in American Ideolgoies, in Drake and Cayton," *Black Metropolis*, pp. 769-770.

34. Margaret Walker Alexander, "Culture: A Nation of Nations," *The Urban League News* (May, 1976), p. 19.

35. Ibid.

36. Daniel Thompson, *Sociology of the Black Experience* (Connecticut: Greenwood Press, 1974), p. ix.

37. Ibid.

38. W. E. B. Du Bois, *The Negro*, revised edition (New York: Oxford University Press, 1970), p. 115.

39. Ralph Bunche, *The Political Status of the Negro in the Age of FDR*, edited by Dewey W. Grantham, (Chicago: University of Chicago Press, 1973), p. 87.

40. Drake and Cayton, *Black Metropolis*, p. 383.

41. See Hanes Walton, Jr., *Black Political Parties*, (New York: Free Press, 1972).

42. Bunche, *Political Status of the Negro* op. cit., p. 87.

43. Hanes Walton, Jr., "Black Political Thought: The Problems of Characterization," *Journal of Black Studies*, Vol. 1 (December, 1970), pp. 213-218: and his "The Political Theory of the Black Muslims," *Faculty Research Bulletin*, Vol. 27 (December, 1973) pp. 148-59.

44. The work on the Black Muslim (now Bilalian) is very extensive indeed. See the unusual treatment by Edgar Litt, *Ethnic Politics*, (Illinois: Scott, Foresman and Company, 1970). For an excellent treatment, see Oliver Jones, Jr., "The Black Muslim Movement and the American Constitutional System," *Journal of Black Studies*, Vol. 13 (June, 1983), pp. 417-437.

45. A current work on Black Nationalism only devotes four pages to this major phenomenon. Alphonso Pinkney, *Red, Black and Green: Black Nationalism in the United States*, (New York: Cambridge University Press, 1976), pp. 93-97. See Jane Bayes *Minority Politics and Ideologies in the United States*, (California: Chandler & Sharp, 1982).

46. Reo M. Christenson, et al., *Ideologies and Modern Politics*, (New York: Dodd, Mead and Company, 1971), p. 18.

47. Philip Foner (ed.), *The Black Panther Speaks*, (Pennsylvania: J. B. Lippincott, 1970).

48. Stokely Carmichael (ed), *Stokely Speaks*, (New York: Random House, 1971); see also Donald J. McCormack, "Stokely Carmichael and Pan-Africanism: Back to Black Power," *Journal of Politics*, Vol. 26 (May, 1973), pp. 386-409.

49. See Numan Bartley, *From Thurmond to Wallace: Political Tendencies in Georgia*, (Baltimore: John Hopkins Press, 1970).

50. For more on this question of Foreign Policy see Chapter 10.

51. John Kincaid (ed.), *Political Culture, Public Policy and the American States*, (Philadelphia: Institute for the Study of Human Issues, 1982), p. 6.

52. Statement by L. H. Stanton, editor and publisher, interview with the author, New York City, September 2, 1977.

53. See "National Scene Family News Supplement," *The Charlotte Post*, (November 27, 1971), pp. 1-8; Carlayne Hunter, "7000 Books on Blacks Fill A Home," *New York Times*, (March 18, 1972), p. 1 and "Clarence Holte's Search Into the Black Past," *Ebony Magazine*, (April, 1976), p. 96; *Hanes Walton, Jr.*, "The Literary Works of a Black Bibliophile: Clarence L. Holte," *The Western Journal of Black Studies*, Vol. 1 (December, 1977), pp. 286-287.

54. Leila Sussman, "Mass Political Letter Writing in America: The Growth of an Institution," *Public Opinion Quarterly*, Vol. 23 (1959), pp. 203-213. And her *Dear FDR: A Study of Political Letter-Writing* (Totowa, New Jersey: Bedminster Press, 1963).

55. For a pioneering look at another black political culture-bearing institution, see Leslie McLemore, "Black Political Socialization and Political Change; The Black Panther Party Platform as a Model of Radical Political Socialization," *Negro Educational Review* Vol. 26 (October, 1975), pp. 155-166.

56. Editors, "Jackson Jumps In," *The New Republic* (November 28,

1983), p. 9.
57. Ibid.
58. Ibid.
59. Ibid. Somehow the Editors seem to have forgotten that Bradley lost in California.
60. Ibid.
61. Ibid.
62. Ibid., p. 10.
63. Ibid.
64. Ibid.
65. The magazine continued to attack Jackson: see Editors, "Jackson and the Jews," *The New Republic* (March 19, 1984), pp. 9-10.
66. See Julian Bond, "What's Next?" *The Negro History Bulletin.* (July-August-September, 1983), Vol. 46, pp. 78.

Notes to Chapter Three

1. Herbert Hyman, *Political Socialization* (New York: Free Press, 1959).
2. Jewel L. Prestage, "Black Politics and the Kerner Report: Concerns and Directions," in Lenneal Henderson (ed.), *Black Political Life in the United States* (San Francisco: Chandler, 1972), p. 187.
3. Ibid.
4. McLemore, "Toward a Theory of Black Politics: The Black and Ethnic Models Revisited" *Journal of Black Studies,* Vol. 3, (March, 1972) pp. 155-166.
5. See Kai T. Erikson (ed.), *In Search of Common Ground, Conversations with Erik H. Erikson and Huey P. Newton,* (New York: Laurel Books, 1974), p. 126.
6. Pat Watters and Reese Cleghorn, *Climbing Jacob's Ladder,* (New York: Harcourt, Brace and World, 1967), p. 77.
7. Ibid.
8. Kenneth P. Langton, *Political Socialization,* (New York: Oxford University Press, 1969), p. 4.
9. Milton Morris and Carolyn Cabe, "The Political Socialization of Black Youth: A Survey of Research Findings," *Public Affairs Bulletin,* (Southern Illinois University at Carbondale), (May-June, 1972), p. 6.
10. Ibid., pp. 5-6.
11. See Bullock and Rodgers, *Black Political Attitudes,* pp. 9-163.
12. Ibid., p. 7.
13. Paul R. Abramson, *The Political Socialization of Black Americans: A Critical Evaluation of Research on Efficacy and Trust,* (New York: Free Press, 1977), p. 113 & 109.
14. Ibid., pp. 108-109.
15. Ibid., pp. 90, 99.
16. Ibid., p. 90.
17. Ibid., p. 20. For a different point of view see, Herbert Jacobs, "Problems of Scale Equivalency in Measuring Attitudes in American Subcultures," *Social Science Quarterly,* Vol. 62 (June, 1971), pp. 61-75.

18. See Sanders Anderson, "The Political Socialization of Black Children: An Analysis of the Attitudes of Children in Three Pan African Schools and a Longitudinal Study of the Attitudes of Former Pan African Students" (Ph.D. dissertation, Atlanta University, 1981). He looked at alternative schools.

19. Langston, *Political Socialization*, pp. 5-20.

20. Charles V. Hamilton, *The Black Preacher in America*, (New York: William Morrow, 1972), pp. 127-138.

21. Ibid., pp. 110-126.

22. Benjamin Mays and Joseph Nicholson, *The Negro's Church*, (New York: Arno Press, 1969), pp. 198-229.

23. See Vincent Harding, "Religion and Resistance Among Antebellum Negroes, 1800-1860," in A. Meier and E. Redwick (ed.), *The Making of Black America*, Vol. II, (New York: Antheneum, 1969). See also Hart M. Nelson and Anne K. Nelson, *The Black Church in the Sixties*, (Lexington: University Press of Kentucky, 1975), and Joe R. Feagin, "The Black Church: Inspiration or Opiate," *Journal of Negro History*, Vol. 60 (October, 1975), pp. 536-540.

24. Lee Rainwater and William Yancey (ed.), *The Moynihan Report: The Politics of Controvery*, (Cambridge: M.I.T. Press, 1967), pp. 369-479.

25. Brisbane, *Black Activism*, p. 592. See also Hanes Walton, Jr., "Black Culture in Films: A Book Review Essay," *Phylon* Vol. 42 (June, 1981), pp. 194-203.

26. See Hanes Walton, Jr., Review of Andrew Buni, "Robert L. Vann of the Pittsburg Courier: Politics and Black Journalism," *American Historical Review*, (December, 1975), p. 1409. See also Edwina Mitchell, *The Crusading Black Journalist: Joseph Everett Mitchell*, (St. Louis: Farmer Press, 1972).

27. James H. Brewer, "The Futile Trumpet: The Wars of the Richmond Planet Against Disenfranchisement and Jim JCrow, 1900-1904." (MS Virginia State College, 1959).

28. See the Civil Rights Record of the *Savannah Tribune* on deposit at Savannah State College, Vol. 1-10.

29. Martin Dann (ed.), *The Black Press: 1827-1890*, (New York : Capricorn Books, 1972).

30. For an excellent discussion of this see: James Harvey, *Civil Rights During the Kennedy Administration*, (Mississippi: University & College Press of Mississippi, 1971), and his *Black Civil Rights During the Johnson Administration*, (Mississippi: University & College Press of Mississippi, 1973).

31. See also Doris Yvonne Wilkinson, "Racial Socialization Through Children's Toys: A Sociohistorical Examination," *Journal of Black Studies*, vol. 5, (September, 1974), pp. 94-100.

Notes to Chapter Four

1. Paul A. Palmer, "The Concept of Public Opinion in Political Theory," in Bernard Berelson and Morris Janowitz (ed.), *Reader in Public Opinion and Communication*, Second Edition, (Illinois: Free Press, 1953), pp. 3-13.

2. Leonard W. Dobb, *Public Opinion and Propaganda*, (Connecticut: Archon Books, 1966), p. 201.

3. V. O. Key, Jr., *Public Opinion and American Democracy*, (New York: Knopf, 1968), p. 205.

4. Ibid., pp. 97-98.

5. Dan Nimmo and Charles Bonjean (eds.) *Political Attitudes and Public Opinion* (New York: David McKay, 1972), p. 381.

6. Key, *Public Opinion and American Democracy*, p. 14.

7. See Bernard C. Hennessy, *Public Opinion*, Second Edition, (California: Duxbury Press, 1970), and Susan Welch and John Comer (eds.), *Public Opinion*, (California: Mayfield Publishing Company, 1975).

8. See Hadley Cantril, *Public Opinion, 1935-1946*, (Princeton: Princeton University Press, 1951), and George Gallup, *The Gallup Poll—1935-1971*, (New York: Random House, 1972).

9. While articles and essays in this category dominate the literature, the leading books are: (1) *The Negro Revolution in America*, (2) *Black and White*, (3) and the two, Brink and Harris works are based on the 1961 *Newsweek* magazine study. In addition to the last two volumes, see Paul B. Sheatsley, "White Attitudes Toward the Negro," in T. Parson and Kenneth Clark, (eds.) *The Negro American*, (Cambridge: Houghton Mifflin, 1966), pp. 303-324.

10. Joel Aberach and Jack Walker, *Race in the City*, (Boston: Little, Brown and Company, 1973). See David Sears and John McConahay, *The Politics of Violence: The Urban Blacks and the Watts Riots*, (New York: Houghton Mifflin, 1973). Again articles dominated this trend but two important books in this area are: (1) *Race in the City*, and (2) *The Politics of Violence*.

11. An excellent example here is the work *Black Political Attitudes*, which is essentially a work on black socialization, in short, an equating of black political opinion with black socialization and alienation. The data on alienation, anomie, and hopelessness is still scattered throughout the literature. This has become a trend in the field: see Bernard Hennessy, "Public Opinion and Opinion Change," in James Robinson (ed.), *Political Science Annual*, (New York: Bobbs-Merrill Company, 1966), pp. 244-248. A good summary can be found in John Jackson, "Alienation and Black Political Participation," *Journal of Politics*, Vol. 35 (November, 1973), pp. 850-859.

12. See *The Urban Coalition, One Year Later*, (New York: Praeger, 1969).

13. Richard Bardolph (ed.), *The Civil Rights Record: Black Americans and the Law: 1849-1970*, (New York: Thomas Y. Crowell, 1970), p. 313.

14. For a discussion of the numerous social science theories surrounding this quest see James S. Geachwender, "Explorations in the Theory of Social Movement and jRevolutions," in his *The Black Revolt*, (New Jersey: Prentice Hall, 1971), pp. 6-18.

15. Eric Hoffer, *The True Believer*, (New York: Harper & Row, 1951), p. 129.

16. Ibid., p. 130.

17. See Jack L. Walker, "A Critique of the Elitist Interpretation of

Government," in Peter Bachrach (ed.), *Political Elites in a Democracy*, (New York: Atherton Press, 1971), pp. 83-86; and Theodore Lowi, *The Politics of Disorder*, (New York: Basic Books, 1973).

18. See Hanes Walton, Jr., *The Political Philosophy of Martin Luther King, Jr.*, (Westport: Greenwood, 1971).

19. See Karl Deutsch, et al., *Political Community and the North Atlantic Area*, (Princeton: Princeton University Press, 1957); his *Nationalism and Social Communication*, (New York: Wiley, 1953), and G. Almond and James Coleman (eds.), *The Politics of Developing Areas*, (Princeton: Princeton University Press, 1960).

20. Richard L. Merritt, *Symbols of American Community 1735-1775*, (New Haven: Yale University Press, 1966), pp. 142-182.

21. Ibid., p. 59. See also his "Nation-Building in America: The Colonial Years" in K. Deutsch and W. Foltz (eds.), *Nation Building*, (New York: Atherton Press, 1966), pp. 73-83.

22. Dann *TheBlack Press: 1827-1890* p. 13.

23. Ibid.

24. Dorothy Porter (ed.), *Early Negro Writing 1760-1831*, (Boston: Beacon Press, 1971), pp. 1-2.

25. Dorothy Porter (ed.), *Negro Protest Pamphlets*, (New York: Arno Press, 1969), pp. iii-vii.

26. Ibid., pp. iii-iv.

27. Robert T. Kerlin, *The Voice of the Negro 1919*, (New York: E. P. Dutton, 1920), p. x.

28. Maxwell R. Brooks, *The Negro Press Reexamined*, (Boston : Christopher Publishing House, 1959), p. 58.

29. Roland E. Wolseley, *The Black Press U.S.A.*, (Ames: Iowa State University Press, 1972), p. 292.

30. See Addison Gayle, *The Black Aesthetic*, (New York: Anchor Books, 1972), p. xxii; and Mercer Cook and Stephen Henderson, *The Militant Black Writer in Africa and the United States*, (Madison: University of Wisconsin Press, 1969).

31. Brisbane, *Black Activism*, p. 278.

32. Porter, *Early Writings*, pp. 1 and 5-430.

33. Arthur L. Smith and Stephen Robb (ed.), *The Voice of Black Rhetoric*, (Boston: Allyn and Bacon, 1971), p. 5.

34. See Paula Giddings, "From Black Perspective: The Poetry of Don L. Lee," *Amistad*, (New York: Random House, 1971), pp. 297-318.

35. Quoted in Kerlin, *The Voice of the Negro 1919*, p. 25.

36. Ibid., p.27.

37. Ibid.

38. For an excellent beginning, see Jacqueline Covo, "Henry Jackson Lewis and Moses L. Tucker: 19th Century Cartoonists: The Indianapolis Freeman," (paper presented at the 61st Annual Meeting of the Study of Afro-American Life and History, Chicago, Illimois, October 27-31, 1976). I would also like to thank the author for sharing with me additional materials in her possession. She has made a major advance into the area of black political cartooning.

39. Kenneth B. Clark, "The Present Dilemma of the Negroes," *Journal of Negro History*, Vol. 53 (January, 1968), p. 8.

40. Robert J. Pranger, *Action, Symbolism and Order*, (Nashville: Vanderbilt University Press, 1968), pp. 145-150.

41. Ibid., p. 186. See also Thurmond Arnold, *The Symbols of Government*, (New Haven: Yale University Press, 1935).

42. Ibid., p. 147.

43. Ibid., p. 147.

44. Allan Morrison, "The Crusading Press," in *The Negro Handbook*, (Chicago: Johnson Publishing Company, 1966), p. 380.

45. See Marie D. Brown, "Cable TV and the Black Community," *The Black Politician*, Vol. 1 (April, 1971), pp. 4-7.

46. See M.L. King, Jr., *Stride Toward Freedom*, (New York: Harper, 1957).

47. See Chapter 6, the subsection on Black Campaign Behavior for further data. See also Julian Bond, *Southern Black Campaign Experiences*, (Atlanta: Souther Regional Council, 1969). See also, Conyers and Wallace, op. cit., pp. 103-120. *Black Elected Officials*

48. See Richard R. Fagen, *Politics and Communication*, (Boston: Little, Brown 1966), Chapter I, II. Karl Deutsch, *The Analysis of International Relations, (New Jersey: Prentice-Hall, 1968), pp. 101-110.*

49. *Carl T. Rowan, Just Between Us Blacks*, (New York: Random House, 1974), p. 49.

50. See F. Chris Garcia (ed.), *La Causa Politica*, (Notre Dame: University of Notre Dame Press, 1974).

Notes to Chapter Five

1. Ralph Bunche, *The Political Status of the Negro in the Age of FDR*, Edited by Dewey W. Grantham, (Chicago: University of Chicago Press, 1973), p. 88.

2. See David Campbell and Joe R. Feagin, "Black Politics in the South: A Descriptive Analysis," *Journal of Politics*, Vol. 37 (February, 1975), pp. 129 159.

3. Bunche, *The Negro in the Age of FDR*, p. 87.

4. Matthews and Prothro, *Negroes and the New Southern Politics*, p. 12.

5. Ibid.

6. See Lester M. Salamon and Stephen Van Evera, "Fear, Apathy and Discrimination: A Test of Three Explanations of Political Participation,"*American Political Science Review*, Vol. 67 (December, 1973), pp. 1288-1306, 1326-1326.)

7. Sam Kernell, "Comment: A Re-evaluation of Black Voting in Mississippi," Ibid., pp. 1307-1318.

8. Sidney Verba and Norman Nie, *Participation in America: Political Democracy and Social Equality*, (New York: Harper and Row, 1972), p. 157.

9. Ibid., p. 150.

10. See Hanes Walton, Jr., *Black Republicans: The Politics of the Black Tan,* (New York: Scarecrow Press, 1975), See also Hanes Walton, Jr., "Perry Howard," *Dictionary of American Negro Biography* (ed.), Rayford Logan and M. Winston, (New York: W. W. Norton, 1983).

11. Ibid.

12. Henry Abraham, *Freedom and the Court,* (New York: Oxford University Press 1967), pp. 292-293.

13. William H. Flannigan, *Political Behavior of the American Electorate,* Second Edition. (Boston: Allyn and Bacon, 1973), p. 24.

14. Johnnie Daniel, "Changes in Negro Political Mobilization and its Relationship to Community Socioeconomic Structure," *Journal of Social and Behavioral Sciences,* Vol. 14 (Fall, 1968), p. 46; See also his "Negro Political Behavior and Community Political and Socioeconomic Structural Factors," *Social Forces,* Vol. 47 (March, 1968), pp. 274-280.

15. Ibid., p. 43.

16. Wirt, *Politics of Southern Equality* p. 163.

17. Douglas Rae, *The Political Consequences of Election Law,* Second Edition (New Haven: Yale University Press, 1963), pp. 3-4.

18. Ibid., p. 134.

19. See Peter Rossi, "Four Landmarks in Voting Research," in Burdick and Broadbeck, *American Voting Behavior* pp. 5-54.

20. Paul Lazarsfeld et al.,*The People's Choice, Second Edition, (New York: Columbia University Press, 1948), p. 13.*

21. *Bernard Berelson, Voting,*(Chicago: University of Chicago Press, 1954), p. 9.

22. Ibid., p. 63.

23. Verba and Nie, *Participation in America* p. 349.

24. Nie, Verba & Petrocik, *The Changing American Voter,* pp. 228-268.

25. See Lyman Kellstedt, "Race and Political Participation: A reexamination" Paper presented at the annual meeting of the Southern Political Science Association, New Orleans, Louisianna, (November 7-9, 1974), Table 3, pp. 9, 10.

26. Richard Niemi and Herbert Weisberg (eds.), *Controversies in American Voting Behavior,* (San Francisco: W. H. Freeman & Company, 1976), pp. 10-11.

27. Ibid., p. 11, note 2.

28. For an attempt to calculate the percent of sampling error as the number of blacks in the survey drops below the thousand mark, see Matthew and Prothro, *Negroes and the New Southern Politics,* pp. 492-494. And E. Terrence Jones, *Conduction Political Research,* (New York: Harper & Row, 1971), pp. 64-66.

29. For a good collection of the articles, see Harry Bailey, Jr. (ed.) *Negro Politics in America,* (Cleveland: Charles Merrill, 1968).

30. See C. A. Bacote, "The Negro in Atlanta Politics," *Phylon,* (Fourth Quarter, 1955).

31. For an early study see Hamann, "A Study of Voting Participation, 1945-1954, in an All-Negro Precinct in Atlanta, Georgia," pp. 26-54

32. Margaret L Dobbins, "Analysis of Negro Voter Registration and Voter Participation in the 1957-1961 Atlanta Mayoralty Elections," (Unpublished M.S. thesis, Atlanta University, 1963), pp. 75-76.

33. Bacote, "The Negro in Atlanta Politics," and his "The Negro in Georgia Politics, Today," *Journal of Negro Education*, (Summer, 1957),pp. 307-318.

34. Jack Walker, "Negro Voting in Atlanta: 1953-1961," *Phylon* vol. 25 (Winter, 1964), p. 382. For continuation of the story from 1961-1973, see Alton Hornsby, Jr., "The Negro in Atlanta Politics, 1961-1973, " *The Atlanta Historical Bulletin*, vol. 23 (Spring, 1977), pp. 7-33.

35. Charles Rook, *The Atlanta Elections of 1969*, (Atlanta: Voter Education Project, 1970), p. 6.

36. Bartley *From Thurmond to Wallace: Political Tendencies in Georgia: 1948-1968 (Baltimore: John Hopkins Press, 1970, pp. 40; 41-55; 67-101.*

37 .*See* Harold Gosnell, *Negro Politicians*, (Chicago: University of Chicago Press, 1935), and his *Machine Politics: Chicago Model*, (Chicago: University of Chicago Press, 1937).

38. For a list of the various black presidential candidates and the votes they received, See Hanes Walton, Jr., and Ronald Clark, "Black Presidential Candidates: Past and Present," *New South*, vol. 27 (Spring, 1972), pp. 14-22.

39. Ibid., pp. 15-16.

40. Shirley Chisholm, *The Good Fight*, (New York: Harper & Row, 1973), p. 38.

41. John H. Britton, "Black Voter Turnout Low in Primaries: Carter and Ford Big in Black Wards," *Joint Center for Political Studies—News Release* (March 19, 1976), pp. 1-2.

42. Ibid.

43. See Ron Bailey et al., *Black Power in Chicago: A Documentary Survey of the 1983 Mayoral democratic Primary (Chicago: People College Press, 1983).*

44. *Milton Coleman, "Blacks Consider Fielding a Democratic Candidate for President" Washington Post* (March 6, 1983), p. A-2.

45. William Brashler, "Dr. J." *The New Republic* (October 17, 1983), p. 14. See also Barbara A. Reynolds, "The Reynolds Washington Report: Run Jesse?' *Dollar & Sense Magazine* (October/November, 1983) p. 13.

46. Maruerite Ross Barnett, "The Strategic Debate over a Black Presidential Candidacy," *PS* (Summer, 1983), p. 490-91.

47. Ibid.

48. Robert G. Kaiser, "Will Jesse Do in the Democrats," *Washington Post* (April 22, 1984), p. D-2.

49. Rhodes Cook, "Mondale and Hart: Even in All But Delegates," *Congressional Quarterly Weekly Report* (March 31, 1984), pp. 712.

50. See NORC, *General Social Surveys, 1972-1982: Cumulative Codebook* (July, 1982) p. 362 Footnote 114. Tom Smith & Glenn R. Dempsey—"The Polls: Ethnic Social Distance and Prejudice." *Public Opinion Quarterly* (Winter, 1983), p. 586-87.

51. Rober H. Brisbane, *Black Activism* (Valley Forge: Judson Press, 1974),pp. 11, 289-93.

52. There were hundreds of these types of comments, See James J. Kilpatrick, "Jackson Due Big Reward in San Francisco," *Savannah Morning News* (April 10, 1984) p. A-4: Mark Shields, "Jackson's Bad Idea," *Washington Post* (March 22, 1984), p. A-3: For a Black Reply see Henton Thomas, "Letter to Editor: Jackson's 'Ominous' Role" *Savannah Morning News* (March 27, 1984), p. 4-A.

53. See Milton Coleman, "Jackson Keeps Getting in Way of Mondale Race Against Hart," *Washington Post* (March 24, 1984), p. A-2; and Milton Coleman and Eric Pianin, "Blacks For Mondale Face Jackson Factor" Ibid (April 20, 1984), pp. A-1, A-4.

54. Paul Taylor, "Don't Write Off Black Vote, Southern Supporters Advise Mondale" Ibid. (April 21, 1984).

55. Kaiser, "Will Jesse Do in the Democrats," p. D-2.   56. Matthew Holden, *The Politics of the Black "Nation"* (New York: Chandler, 1973), pp. 42-95.

57. Interview, Otis Johnson, April 16, 1984, 2 p.m.

58. Interview, Attorney Clarence Martin April 16, 1984, 8 p.m.

59. Kaiser, "Will Jesse Do in the Democrats" p. D-2.

60. David Broder, "The Incomplete Candidates," *Washington Post* (March 25, 1984), p. C-7.

61. For data on Johnson see Stephen Lesher, "Leroy Johnson Outslicks Mister Charlie," *New York Times Magazine*, (November 8, 1970), pp. 34-54.

62. For data on Bond see Julian Bond, *A Time to Speak, A Time to Act*, (New York: Simon & Schuster, 1972), and John Neary, *Julian Bond: Black Rebel*, (New York: William Morrow, 1971).

63. The problem facing black Republicans are not only the lack of local organization and popular political personalities, but closed party organizational structures and national party disinterestedness, see Walton, *Black Republicans*, Chapter 4.

64. For the number of black independents reported in SRC data from 1960 to 1972, see Gerald Pomper, *Voters Choice*, (New York: Dodd Mead, 1975), pp. 28-29, Table 2.3.

65 .Key was able to get the survey data for secondary analysis and check for those who changed. His data were analyzed in holistic form. Herbert Hyman, *Secondary Analysis of Sample Surveys*, (New York: Wiley, 1972), pp. 196-200.

66. In none of the black precincts did the Wallace vote exceed the number of white registered voters, making it highly probable that all of the Wallace votes in these predominantly black precincts were cast by whites.

67. Pomper *Voters Choice*, pp. 137-140.

68. See Angus Campbell and W. E. Miller, "The Motivational Basis of Straight and Split Ticket Voting," *American Political Science Review*, Vol. 51 (June, 1957), pp. 293-312.

69. Walton *Black Politics*, pp. 104-115.

70. See Charles Merriam and Harold Gosnell, *Non-Voting: Causes and Methods of Control*, (Chicago: University of Chicago Press, 1924), p. 37.

71. Penn Kimball, *The Disconnected*, (New York: Columbia University Press, 1972), p. 4.

72. Kurt Lang and Gladys Long, *Voting and Non-Voting*, (Mass: Blaisdell, 1968), p. 79.

73. Jerrold Rusk, "Comment: The American Electoral Universe: Speculations and Evidence," *American Political Science Review*, Vol. 68, (September, 1974), p. 1043.

74. National Urban League, *Abiding the Right to Vote: A Study of State Restrictions and Black Political Participation*, (New York: National Urban League, 1972),p. 8.

75. See the data in David H. Hunter, *Federal Review of Voting Changes*, (Washington, D.C., Joint Center for Political Studies, 1974), and his *Federal Review of Voting Changes* Second Edition, pp. 52, 67-74. Ibid. pp. 52, 67-74. And the Washington Research Project, *The Shameful Blight: The Survival of Racial Discrimination in Voting in the South*, (Washington, D.C., Washington Research Project, 1972).

76. For similar findings an earlier study, see Hamann "A Study of Voting Participation, 1945-1954, in an All-Negro Precinct in Atlanta Georgia," pp. 31-35.

77. Kimball, *The Disconnected*, pp. 13,17.

78. See E. E. Schattschneider, *The Semi-Sovereign People*, (New York: Holt, Rhinehart, and Winston, 1960), p. iii.

79. For one example of how the extension of material incentives to the masses of black increased black voter turnout by more than twenty percent see, Paul W. Valentine, "Heavy Turnout by Black Voters Credited for Upset in Baltimore," *Washington Post*, September 20, 1982, p. A-25.

Notes to Chapter Six

1. U.S. Senate, *Hearing before the Subcommittee on Constitutional Rights of The Committe on the Judiciary, Part I*, (Washington, D.C.: Government Printing Office, 1959), p. 561.

2. Ibid., pp. 560-561.

3. U.S. Commission on Civil Rights, *Hearing before the U.S. Commission on Civil Rights: Hearing Held in Montgomery, Alabama, April 27-May 2, 1968*, (Washinton D.C.: Government Printing Office, 1969), pp. 602-603.

4. Ibid., p. 596.

5. Walton, *Black Political Parties*, pp. 181-187; for data on SCPDP and LCFO, pp. 69-77, 138-140.

6. Gerald B. Finch, "Physical Change and Parisan Change: The Emergence of a New Electorate, 1952-1972," in Louis Maise & Paul Sacks (ed.) *The Future of Political Parties*, (Beverly Hills: Sage Publications, 1975), p. 53.

7. See Chuck Stone, *Black Political Power in America*, (Indianapolis: Bobbs Merrill, 1964).

8. Kay Lawson, *The Comparative Study of Political Parties*, (New York: St. Martins Press, 1976), p. 8.

9. Ibid., p. 9.

10. Ibid., p. 10.

11. For a study of Party Activist see, Samuel Eldersveld, *Political Parties: A Behavioral Analysis,* (Chicago: Rand McNally, 1964).

12. See Oscar Glantz, "The Negro Voter in Northern Industrial Cities," Bailey, *Negro Politics in America,* pp. 338-352; Henry Lee Moon, "The Negro Vote in the Presidential Election of 1956," Ibid., pp. 353-365; William J. McKenna, "The Negro Vote in Philadelphia," Ibid., pp. 366-375; and Oscar Glatz, "Recent Negro Ballots in Philadelphia," *Journal of Negro Education,* Vol. 28 (1959), pp. 430-438.

13. Matthews and Prothro, *Negros and the New Southern Politics,* p. 391.

14. Wasby, *Political Science: The Discipline and its Dimensions,* p. 309.

15. Samuel Lubell, *Revolt of the Moderates,* (New York: Harper & Row, 1956), pp. 107-125.

16. Campbell, *The American Voter,* p. 241.

17. Heinz Eulau, "Perceptions of Class and Party in Voting Behavior: 1952," *Political Behavior,* pp.295-296. See also his, *Class and Party in the Eisenhower Years, (New York: Free Press, 1962).*

18. Bowen Political Behavior of the American Public, p. 51

19. Fred I. Greenstein, "The Significance of Party Identification," in Leroy Rieselback and George Black (eds.), *Psychology and Politics,* (New York: Holt Rinehart and Winston, 1969), p. 190.

20. Ibid., p. 154.

21. I. A. Lewis and William Schneider, "Black Voting, and the Democrats," *Public Opinion* (Oct./Nov. 1983) pp. 12-15, 57.

22. Pomper,*Voters Choice,* p. 7.

23. Eldersveld, *Political Parties: A Behavioral Analysis,* (Chicago: Rand McNally, 1964),p. 504.

24. Ibid., p. 538.

25. Dan Day, "Claiborne Sought it Vote Plot," *Afro-American,* (November 14, 1964), p. 1.

26. Ibid., p. 2.

27. Ibid.

28. See "Ford Aide Notified 400 Black Clerics," *The New York Times,* (November 2, 1976), p. 19, and "Comment by Ford Aide," Ibid.

29. Ibid.

30. Wayne King, "Carter's Church May Dismiss Pastor for his Role Dispute Over Blacks," Ibid.

31. Ibid. See also "Ford Vote Aide Disavows Wire to Black Ministers: Call it 'Terrible Taste',Ibid., (November 3, 1976), p.21.

32. Pearl T. Robinson, "Whither the Future of Blacks in the Republican Party?" *Political Science Quarterly,* Vol. 97 (Summer, 1982), p. 217.

33. Ibid.

34. Ibid.

35. Jaun Williams, "Blacks Written off For 1984 Campaign, Reagan Aides Assert, *Washington Post* (May 13, 1983), p. A-2.

36. Hanes Walton, Jr., "Black Politics in the Centennial Year: 1876," *National Scene Magazine Supplement—New York Amsterdam News* (July-August, 1977) pp. 3-10.

37. Ibid.

38. On the proposals for a southern strategy for the democratic party see, Hamilton Jordan, "Is Chicago Really so Important,"*Washinton Post* (April 12, 1983), p. A-17; Art Harris, "Redemption: Bert Lance Returns to Limelight in Georgia," *Washington Post (May 13, 1983), p. A-4.*

39. Walton, *The Negro in Third Party Politics*, p. 28.

40. See Samuel W. Williams, "The People's Progressive Party of Georgia," *Phylon*, Vol. 10 (Third Quarter, 1949) pp. 226-230.

41. "The South Gets Rough with Wallace," *Life*, (September 13, 1948), pp. 33-35.

42. Ralph Matthews, "How New Jerseymen Polled 23,000 Votes for Govenor: Politicians Puzzled Over Score," *Baltimore Afro-American*, (June 19, 1965), p. 13.

43. Benjamin Davis, *Communist Councilman from Harlem*, (New York: International Publishers, 1969), pp. 101-117.

44. Leslie McLemore, "Mississippi Freedom Democratic Party," *Black Politician*, (October, 1971), pp. 19-23; and his "The Effect of Political Participation Upon a Closed Society—A State in Transition: The Changing Political Climate in Mississippi," *The Negro Educational Review*, Vol. 23 (January, 1972), pp. 3-12.

45. Hanes Walton, Jr., and William H. Boone, "Black Political Parties: A Demographic Analysis, *Journal of Black Studies*, Vol. 5 (September, 1974), p. 91.

46. Ibid., p. 94.

47. See Willie Yancey, "Levels of Support Among Black Partisans for a Black Political Party in an Urban Area: 1974," (Unpublished manuscript) for more data on this point see Johnnie Daniel, "The Development of an Independent Black Political Party: Structural and Socio-Psychological Considerations," Paper presented at the Annual meeting of the Association of Social and Behavioral Sciences, pp. 1-3. Daniel analyzed survey data found in works on black opinions and attitudes.

48. For data on the League and its impact, see Hanes Walton, Jr., "Focus on Georgia: Black Visibility—the Political Arena," *Black Politician*, (October, 1971), pp. 6-9.

49. For an overview see Julian Bond, *Southern Black Campaign Experiences*, (Atlanta: Souther Regional Council, 1968). For black congressional and presidential campaign experiences see Shirley Chisholm, *The Good Fight*, (New York: Harper & Row, 1973), and her *Unbossed and Unbought*, (New York: houghton Mifflin, 1970). For mayoral experiences see John Dean, *The Making of a Black Mayor*, (Washinton, D.C.: Joint Center for Political Studies, 1973). And Mtanya D. Tryman, "Black Mayoralty Campaigns: Running the Race," *Phylon*, Vol. 35 (December, 1974) pp. 346-358. For a broad coverage see, L. H. Whittmore, *Together: A Reporter's Journey into the New Black Politics*, (New York: William Morrow, 1971).

50. Mervyn Dymally, "The Rise of Black Political Leadership in California," in Nathan Wright, Jr. (ed.), *What Black Politicians are Saying*, (New York: Hawthorn Books, 1972), p.39. For a continuation of this type of argument by Dymally and other black elected officials, see his *The Black Politician: His Struggle for Power*, (Belmont, California: Duxbury Press, 1971).

51. Fannie Lou Hamer, "If the Name of the Game is Survive, Survive," Ibid. *The Black Politician*, p. 47.

52. See Charles Bullock, "The Election of Blacks in the South: Pre-conditions and Consequences," *American Journal of Political Science*, Vol. 19 (Nov. 1975) pp. 727-739. And Mack Jones, "Voters and Officeholders: Some Notes on the Black Political Condition in the U.S. South, 1974," (Atlanta: W. E. B. Du Bois Institute, Atlanta University, 1974), pp. 6-12.

53. Hanes Walton, Jr., and Leslie McLemore, "Portraits of Black Political Styles," *Black Politician*, (October, 1970), pp. 9-14.

54. Alexander Heard, *The Cost of Democracy*, (New York: Anchor Books 1960).

55. See: Lieutenant Governor, *Campaign Contribution Letter*, (August 18, 1976), sent to Author, p. 1.

56. Margaret Shapiro, "Jackson's Personal Pleas for Funds Fuel His Shoestring Campaign," Washington Post (April 23, 1984), p. A-3; See also Thomas E. Cavanagh, Race and Political Strategy, (Washington, DC: Joint Center for Political Studies, 1983).

57. Interview with Attorney Clarence L. Martin, (Law Office—Savannah, Georgia), April 16, 1984, 8 p.m.

58. For the traditional attitudinal approach with a few black delegates who responded to a single survey see Jean Kirkpatrick, *The New Presidential Elite: Men and Women in National Politics* (New York: Russell Sage, 1976). Comments about the black delegates to the 1972 national conventions are scattered throughout the book. The portrait is a sketchy one based on individual perceptions and attitudes. The book misses the structural problems. To get at this problem, the Ford Foundation gave Professor Ronald Walters a grant to study black delegates to the 1976 and 1980 national conventions. Although Ford is not providing any funds for the 1984 year, the project will still be carried out. The project was carried out under the direction of Dr. Lawrence Gary, the Head of the Institute for Urban Affairs and Research at Howard University. Dr. Diane Brown, one of the Senior Research Associate at the Institute, helped professor Walters and is still helping him finish the study. The study is currently incomplete but the authors, Walters and Brown provided the author with a typewritten draft of the 1976 study. One of their tentative conclusions is that there is "a systematic relationship between the delegate mix or composition, delegate perception on issues and candidates, and inferences concerning delegate behavior." In short, environmental forces in the black community operating through a socialization process impacts the delgates in such a manner that these delgates seeks to exercise influence in the process of presidential selection to achieve black objectives. See Ronald Walters & Diane Brown, *Black Presidential Politics in 1976: A Study of Black Delegates to the Democratic and Republican National Convention in 1976* (Washington, D.C.: Institute For Urban Affairs and Researchd, no date), pp. 64-69.

59. Lucius Barker and Jesse J. McCorry, *Black Americans and the Political System*, (Massachusetts: Winthrop Publishers, 1976), p. 248.

60. Ibid., pp. 249-250.

61. Ibid. See also Jeames Lengle and Byran Shafer, "Primary Rules, Political Power and Social Change," *American Political Science Review*, Vol.

70 (March, 1976), p. 70. And William Cavala, "Changing the Rules Changes the Game: Party Reform and the 1972 California Delegation to the Democratic National Convention," Ibid., Vol. 68 (March, 1974), pp. 27-42.

62. See Oliver W. Cromwell, "Black Delegate Representation," *Focus*, (June, 1976), p. 3. And The Joint Center for Political Studies, *Guide to Black Politics 1976: Part I—Democratic National Convention*, and their *Guide to Black Politics 1976: Part II—Republican National Convention*, (Washington, D.C.: Joint Center for Political Studies, 1976).

63. Rep. Yvonne Burke, "Democratic Platform: Black Input," (July, 1976), pp. 4-5, and "Analysis of Caucus of Black Democrats Issues in the Democratic Party Platform," *For the People*,(June/July, 1976), pp. 3-4.

64. See C. Vernon Gray and Hanes Walton, Jr., "Black Politics at National Republican and Democratic Cnoventions, 1868-1972," *Phylon*, (September, 1975), pp. 269-278.

65. Robert C. Smith and Joseph P. McCormick II, "The Challenge of a Black Presidential Candidacy," *New Directions: The Howard University Magazine*, (April, 1984), pp. 42-43.

66. Thomas E. Cavanagh, *The Impact of the Black Electorate* (Washington, DC: Joint Center for Political Studies, 1984), p. 7.

67. Margaret Shapiro, "Jackson Asks Manatt for 'Stolen' Delegates," *Washington Post*, (April 24, 1984), p. A-3.

68. Frank Riper and H. Rainie, "Game of the Rules," *The New Republic*, (January 9 and 16, 1984), pp. 10-18.

69. Shapiro, "Jackson Asks Manatt for 'Stolen' Delegates," p. A-3.

70. Smith and McCormick, "The Challenge of a Black Presidential Candidacy," pp. 42-43.

71. William Raspberry, "Hatcher's Warning to His Party," *Washington Post* (April 12, 1984), p. A-13.

72. Nie, Verba, Petrocik, *The Changing American Voter*, p. 214.

73. Barker & McCorry, *Black Americans and the Political System*,p. 31.

74. For an excellent study of how blacks in St. Louis tried to bypass the regular political organizational structure see, Ernest Patterson, *Black City Politics*, (New York: Dodd, Mead, 1974), pp. 30-86.

Notes to Chapter Seven

1. For a bibliography see Robert T. Perry, *Black Legislators*, (San Francisco: R. & E. Associates, 1975).

2. See Norman Meller, "Legislative Behavior Research," *Western Political Quarterly*, (1960), p. 152.

3. Heinz Eulau and Katherine Hinckley, "Legislative Institutions and Processes," in James Robinson (ed.), *Political Science Annual*, (New York: Bobbs-Merrill, 1966), p. 85.

4. Quoted in Ibid., p. 87.

5. Ibid.

6. Ibid.

7. Ibid.

8. Ibid., pp. 115, 150-151.

9. Ibid., pp. 151-179.

10. Rieselbach, *Congressional Politics*, p. 56.

11. See J. A. Moseley, *Sixty Years in Cnogress and Twenty-Eight Out*, (New York: Vantage Press, 1960); Mary Meyer "Black Congressmen and How They Grew." *Black Politician*, Vol. 1 (April, 1970), pp. 3-11; Samuel D. Smith, *The Negro in Congress* 1870-1901, (Chapel Hill: University of North Carolina, 1960).

12. James Q. Wilson, "Two Negro Politicans: An Interpretation," *Midwest Journal of Political Science*, Vol. 5 (1960), pp. 365-69.

13. For some different analyses of Powell's Legislative Behavior, see Mervyn M. Dymally, "The Legislative Record of Adam Clayton Powell," *Black Politician*, Vol. 2 (January, 1971), pp. 16-18.

14. See Hazel C. Smalley, "Black Women Legislators Answers Questions," *Black Politican*, (April, 1971), pp. 40-47; Judy Ann Miller, "California's Black Lady Legislator," Ibid., (October, 1970), pp. 14-18; Richard Harris, "Black Legislators and Their White Colleagues," Ibid., pp. 15-16; and Judy Ann Miller's, "The Representative is a Lady," Ibid., (October, 1969), pp. 17-19.

15. Maurine Christopher, *America's Black Congressmen*, Revised Edition (New York: Thomas Y. Crowell, 1975).

16. Alvin D. Sokolow, "Black Members—White Legislators," *Black Politican*, (Fall, 1971), pp. 23-30.

17. Maurice Woodard, "Legislative Record of Adam Clayton Powell, Revisited", *The Black Politican*, (July, 1971), pp. 36-39.

18. See Jewel L. Prestage, "Black Women State Legislators: A Profile," Paper presented at the 1974 meeting of the Southern Political Science Association, New Orleans, November, 1974.

19. The Black Legislative Clearinghouse arose out of the Black Legislators Association in Illinois in July, 1969. And many of its activities were copied by the Black Legislative groups, which would follow in its wake, at the various levels of government.

20. See Freddie Charles Colston, "The Influence of the Black Legislators in the Ohio House of Representatives," Ph.D. Dissertation, Ohio State University, 1972.

21. Another one is Robert T. Perry's, "The Black Legislator: A Case Study of the House of Representatives of the Missouri 75th General Assembly," Ph.D. Dissertation, University ofMissouri, 1972.

22. Colston, Influence of Black Legislators in Ohio.

23. Ibid., pp. 15, 193.

24. Ibid., p. 187; for an excellent state study for another time period see Charles Vincent, *Black Legislators in Louisiana During Reconstruction*, (Baton Rouge: Louisiana State University Press, 1976).

25. Ibid., p. 203.

26. *Gray* v. *Saunders*, 372 U.S. 368, (1963). Brett W. Hawkins, "Consequences of Reapportionment in Georgia," in Richard Hofferbert & Ira Sharkansky (eds.), *State and Urban Politics* (Boston: Little, Brown and Company, 1971), pp. 275-279. He writes: "Perhaps the most striking change accompanying reapportionment was the increase in the number of Negroes in

the legislature...No Negro ever served in the House until reapportionment, when 8 were elected in 1966." p. 278.

27. Colston, "Influence of Black Legislators", p. 197.

28. See Robert C. Smith, "The Black Congressional Delegation," *Western Political Quarterly*, Vol. 34 (June, 1981), p. 210.

29. The dissertations used are: Freddie Colston, *The Influence of the Black Legislators in Ohio House of Representatives* (Michigan: University Microfilms, 1972); Robert Perry, *The Black Legislator: A Case Study of the House of Representatives of the 75th Missouri General Assembly* (Michigan: University Microfilms, 1972); Lee McGriggs, *Black Legislative Politics in Illinois: A Theoretical and Structural Analysis* (Washington, D.C.: University Press of America, 1977); The other material used was: Secretary of State, *Member of the General Assembly of Georgia: House & Senate* 1972-73 term and 1983-84 term.

30. For the situation in Mississippi see Lester Salamon, "Leadership and Modernization: The Emerging Black Political Elite in the American South," *Journal of Politics*, Vol. 35 (August, 1973), pp. 630, 634.

31. Mack Jones, "Black Officeholders in Local Governments of the South: An Overview," *Politics 71*, Vol. 1 (March 1971), p. 65.

32. It should be mentioned at this point that 1982 was not a presidential election year like 1972 and traditionally voter turnout is smaller in off-year congressional elections.

33. Rieselback, *Congressional Politics*, p. 160.

34. See Marguerite Ross Barnett, "The Congressional Black Caucus: Illusions and Realities of Power," In Michael Preston, Lenneal J. Henderson, Jr. and Paul Puryer (eds.), *The New Black Politics: The Search for Political Power* (New York: Longman, 1982), pp. 28-54.

35. My interviews with some of the participants in these specific conferences noted immediately that they acquired knowledge useful to them in a functional manner and in their capacity as representatives of the black community.

36. See Elmer Lammi, "Black Caucus Seen in Quandary Over White Applicant," *Atlanta Daily World*, (May 27, 1975), pp. 1, 6; and "Black Caucus Turns Down White Membership Bid," *Jet Magazine*, (July 10, 1975), p. 19.

37. Barnett, "The Congressional Black Caucus," p. 53.

38. Ibid., p. 52.

39. Interview, State Representative Bobby L. Hill, at his Savannah Law Firm, May 1974.

40. The estimates are State Representative Hill's.

41. Interview, State Representative Robert "Bob" Holmes, GABEO Meeting, (May 7, 1975) and (March 24, 1983).

42. Black Caucus of Georgia General Assembly, *New Release*, (March 24, 1975), p. 1.

43. Interview, Alderman Roy Jackson, Savannah, Georgia, (July 10, 1975).

44. Ibid.

45. For similar arguments from other BEO's, see Conyers and Wallace, *Black Elected Officials*, pp. 139-140.

46. Interview, Alderman Otis Johnson, April 25, 1983 at his office at Savannah State College.

47. Interview, John Merritt, Thunderbolt, Georgia, (May 29, 1975) and June 21, 1981.

48. Diane Smith, "Thunderbolt Alderman Upset by Pro Tem Pick," *Savannah Morning News* (June 16, 1981), p. 1B, 5B.

49. Donnie Bellamy, "Whites Sue for Desegregation in Georgia: The Fort Valley State College Case," *Journal of Negro History*, Vol. 64 (Fall, 1979), pp. 316-336.

50. Letter from Alderman Marvin Arrington to Author, (May 30, 1975), p. 1.

51. Ibid., p. 2.

52. Letter from Honorable Maynard Jackson to Atlanta City Council, June 10, 1975, pp. 1, 2. In the letter he explains his veto.

53. Letter from Alderman Marvin Arrington to Author, (June 12, 1975), pp. 1, 2.

54. Robin Toner, "Young Says his Travels Promotes Atlanta's Image," *The Atlanta Journal-Atlanta Constitution* (April 3, 1983), p. 5E.

55. Ibid.

56. Black Alderman Ed Turner of Athens, Georgia, made the same point in his interview at the Georgia Municipal Association Meeting held in Savannah on June 24, 1975 and August 20, 1984.

57. Jeffrey Elliot, "The Dynamics of Black Local Politics: An Interview with Gilbert Lindsay," *Negro History Bulletin*, Vol. 40 (July-August, 1977), p. 720.

58. Ibid.

59. Ibid., p. 719-720.

60. Ibid., p. 720.

61. Malcolm E. Jewell and Samuel C. Patterson, *The Legislative Process in the United States*, (New York: Random House, 1966), p. 206.

62. M. Barone, G. Ujifusa, D. Matthews, *The Almanac of American Politics* (Boston: Gambit, 1973), p. 856.

63. Smith, "The Black Congressional Delegate," p. 217.

64. Ibid., p. 215.

65. Perry, op. cit., p. 141.

66. Ibid., p. 151.

67. Colston, op. cit., p. 83. "The Influence of Black Legislators in the Ohio House of Representatives"

68. C. Vernon Gray, "Black Politics & the Idea of Power," (Unpublished Paper).

69. See Jonathan Lyons, "Black Firefighters seek support" *The Columbia Flier* (March 31, 1983), p. 14; and His, "Klan Fires Up Station" Ibid., (March 24, 1983) p. 14.: Patricia Thompson "Klan recruiting Flier surfaces in Savage Fire House," *The Evening Sun* (March 22, 1983), p. D-2.; Gail A. Campbell, "Klan Leaflets in Howard fire station prompt call for inquiry," *The Sun* (March 22, 1983), p. D-12.: For a copy of the proposed resolution see, County council of Howard County Maryland, 1983 Legislative session, #7-5-2-83.

70. Telephone Interview with County Councilman C. Vernon Gray, April 23, 1984.

71. Interview, Chatham County Commissioner Willie Brown, Savannah, Georgia, 1975.

72. Jewell Prestage, "Black Women State Legislators: A Profile," (Paper presented at 1974 Southern Political Science Association, New Orleans, November 1974). See also Marianne Githens and Jewel Prestage (eds.), *A Portrait of Marginality*, (New York: David McKay & Co., 1977). See also Joseph Brown, "An Analysis of the Policy Priorities of Black Women State Legislators," paper presented at the 1984 Conference of Black Political Scientists, Washington, DC, April, 18-21, 1984.

73. Ibid., p. 10. Prestage, "Black Women State Legislators.

74. See also, Marjorie Lansing, "The Voting Patterns of American Black Women," (Paper presented at 1973 Annual Meeting of the American Political Science Association, New Orleans, Louisiana, Sept. 4-8; and Herrington Bryce and Allan Warrick, "Black Women in Elected Politics," *Focus*, (August, 1973).

75. Inez Smith Reid, *"Together" Black Women*, (New York: Third Press, 1975), p. 182. The percentage data offered in Table 5 on the political affiliations of black women are slightly incorrect.

76. Clinton B. Jones, "Structural and Demographic Correlates of Black Membership in City Councils," (Paper presented at the 1974 Annual Meeting of the National Conference of Black Political Scientists, Atlanta, Georgia, May 2, 1974), pp. 1-25. See also his "The Impact of Local Election Systems on Black Political Representation," *Urban Affairs Quarterly*, Vol. II (March, 1976), pp. 345-356.

77. Jones. Black Membership in City Councils, p. 3.

77. Ibid., p. 4.

78. Ibid., p. 6.

79. Ibid., p. 6

80. Ibid., p. 8.

81. Ibid., p. 19.

83. Karnig and Welch, *Black Representation and Urban Policy*, p. 95-96.

84. Richard L. Engstrom and Michael D. McDonald, "The Underrepresentation of Blacks on City Councils: Comparing the Structural and Socioeconomic Explanations for South/Non-South Differences," *Journal of Politics*, Vol. 44 (November, 1982), p. 1098. This essay has an excellent bibliography on the sundry literature.

85. See Alvin D. Sokolow, "Black Member—White Legislature," *Black Politician*, vol. 2 (Fall, 1971), pp. 23-29.

86. See "Black House Members From Shadow Cabinet on Civil Rights," *Congressional Quarterly*, (1970), p. 783 and Norman C. Miller, "Negroes in the House of Representatives Join Forces to Speak for Black Interest," *Wall Street Journal*, (March 31, 1970), p. 1.

87. Arthur B. Levy and Susan Stoundinger, "Sources of Voting Cues for the Congressional Black Caucus," *Journal of Black Studies*, Vol. 7 (September, 1976), pp. 29-46.

88. See Ralph Nader's *Project on Congress, the Black Congressman*, (New York: Grossman, 1974).

89. Sokolow, Black Member—White Legislature. *Black Politician*. Vol. 2, p. 23.

90. Ibid.

91. Ibid., p. 24.

92. Ibid., p. 27.

93. See Colston, "The Influence of Black Legislators in the Ohio House of Representatives," pp. 80-111; Perry, "The Black Legislator," pp. 161-213; and the publications of the Black Legislative Clearinghouse in Illinois, organized by Senator Richard Newhouse.

94. Cole, *Blacks in Power*, pp. 146-147.

95. Ibid., pp. 147-218.

Notes to Chapter Eight

1. See Stuart Nagel, *The Legal Process From a Behavioral Perspective*, (Homewood: Dorsey Press, 1969). This book has a rather comprehensive overview of the literature through 1969, and it gives a fair reading to those who are supportive of the behavioral approach as well as to its critics.

2. Another excellent overview of the literature and the different trends is C. Herman Pritchett, "Public Law and Judicial Behavior," *Journal of Politics*, Vol. 30 (May, 1968), pp. 480-509.

3. J. Woodford Howard, Jr., "Judicial Biography and the Behavioral Persuasion," *American Political Science Review*, Vol. 65 (September, 1971), pp. 704-705.

4. Ibid.

5. Helen Edmonds, *Black Faces in High Places: Negroes in Government*, (New York: Harcourt, Brace and Jovanovich, 1971), p. 121.

6. Ibid., pp. 159-160.

7. Charles L. Sanders, "Detroit's Rebel Judge Crockett," in *The Black Revolution*, (Chicago: Johnson Publishing Co., 1970), pp. 137-148.

8. Randall W. Black, *Private Pressure on Public Law: The Legal Career of Justice Thurgood Marshall*, (New York: Kennikat Press, 1973).

9. Sanders, *The Black Revolution*, pp. 137-148. See also William Raspberry, "Judge...and Judgment," *Washington Post*, (November 29, 1971).

10. Michael D. Smith, "Social Background and Role Perception of Black Judges," Paper delivered at the 1973 Annual Meeting of the American Poilitical Science Association, (Jung Hotel, New Orleans, Louisiana, September, 4-8).

11. Ibid., p. 2.

12. Ibid., p. 3.

13. Ibid., p. 6.

14. Ibid., p. 11.

15. Ibid., p. 11.

16. Gilbert Ware (ed.), *From the Black Bar: Voices for Equal Justice*, (New York: G. G. Putnam, 1976). See also his "Black Lawyers Lead Struggle for Freedom," *Dawn Magazine*, (August, 1977), pp. 8-12, 17.

17. Ibid., *From the Black Bar*, p. XXXIII. For a look at how the race of a Judge affects "justice" in one city, see Thomas M. Uhlman, *Racial Justice: Black Judges and Defendants in an Urban Trial Court* (MASS: Lexington Books, 1979).

18. Joint Center for Political Studies, *National Poster of Black Elected Officials—1981*, (Washington, D.C.: Joint Center for Political Studies, 1981).

19. Edmonds, *Negroes in Government,* p. 144.

20. Ibid., p. 161.

21. Ware, *From the Black Bar,* pp. XXVI-XXXVI; and Beverly Blair Cook, "Black Representation in the Third Branch," *The Black Law Journal,* Vol 1 (Winter, 1971), pp. 260-79.

22. *From the Black Bar,* p. XXX.

23. Ibid., and see "The Black Judge in America: A Statistical Profile," *Judicature,* Vol. 51 (June-July, 1973), pp. 18-20.

24. For a careful analysis of how each state selects its judges on each judicial level see LEAA, *National Survey of Court Organization,* (Washington, Government Printing Office: 1973).

25. Ware, *From the Black Bar,* XXI; and his "Proceedings: Founding Convention of the Judicial Council of the National Bar Association," *Journal of Public Law,* (1971), pp. 371-442.

26. Bruce Fein, *Significant Decisions of the Supreme Court, 1978-1979 Term* (Washington, D.C.: American Enterprise Institute, 1980), p. 22.

27. Ibid., p. 23.

28. The titles of the entire series are as follows: Eugene L. Meyer and Joseph D. Whitaker, "Blacks Moving into Key Legal Post," *Washington Post,* (April 11, 1976), p. A1; Joseph D. Whitaker, "Amos N' Andy Set an Image," Ibid., p. A18; Eugene Meyer "The only Colored Man at Justice," Ibid., p. A18; Eugene Meyer and Joseph Whitaker, "D.C. Forms a 'School' for Black Jurists," Ibid., (April 12, 1976), p. A1; Eugene Meyer and Joseph Whitaker, "Black Firms Moving into Civil Law," Ibid., (APril 13, 1976), p. A1; Joseph Whitaker, "Black Lawyer and Uptown Firms: Crisis of Indentity," Ibid., (April 14, 1976), p. A1; and their "Black Lawyer and Uptown Firms: Some Cite Difficulties," Ibid., p. A1; Joseph Whitaker and Eugene Meyer, "Moving up to the Bench," Ibid., (APril 15, 1976), p. A1; Eugene Myer, "Free Rides and Hard Work: Black Judge Recalls Party of D.C. Superior Court," Ibid., p. A14; J. Whitaker, "Judge Bryant Struggled to Reach his High Post; Jurist to Become First Black Chief Judge of U.S. District Court Race," Ibid.

29. Meyer, "The Only Colored Man at Justice," p. A18.

30. Meyer and Whitaker, "D.C. Forms a 'School' for Black Jurist," pp. A1, A21.

31. See Meyer and Whitaker, "Black Firms Moving into Civil Law," p. A1, A8; Whitaker, "Black Lawyers and Uptown Firms: Crisis of Identity," p. A1; and Meyer and Whitaker, "Black Lawyers and Uptown Firms: Some Cite Difficulties," p. A1, A5.

32. Whitaker and Meyer, "Moving up to the Bench," pp. A1, A14; see also "Presidential Appointments of Black Federal Judges and Presidential Appointment of Black Judges to District of Columbia Court," *National Bar Bulletin,* Vol. 5 (April, May, June, 1973), p. 6.

33. Ibid.

34. Whitaker, "Judge Bryant Struggled to Reach his High Post: Jurist to Become First Black Chief Judge of U.S. District Court Here," p. A14.

35. See M;yer, "Free Rides and Hard Work: Black Judge Recalls Path to D.C. Superior Court," p. A14.

36. On the matter of how the court uses other data to determine more than

individual influences see Abraham L. Davis, *The United States Supreme Court and the Uses of Social Science Data*, (New York: MSS Corporation, 1973).

Notes to Chapter Nine

1. See Harold Lasswell, *Psychopathology and Politics*, (Chicago: University of Chicago Press, 1930), and his *Power and Personality*, (New York: W. W. Norton, 1948).

2. Lasswell, "Power and Personality," in H. Eulau, et al. (ed.), *Political Behavior*, pp. 98-101.

3. Gordon Allport, *Becoming: Basic Considerations for a Psychology of Personality*, (New Haven: Yale University Press, 1955).

4. Lasswell, *Psycholopathology & Politics*, p. 183.

5. Alex Gottfried, "The Use of Socio-Psychologicla Categories in a study of Political Personality," in Eulau, *Political Behavior*, pp. 125-128; See also Gottfriend's *Boss Cermak of Chicago: A Study of Political Leadership*, (Seattle: University of Washington Press, 1962).

6. *Political Beahvior*, p. 130.

7. Ibid., p. 131.

8. Ibid., p. 130.

9. See Harold Zink, "A Case Study of a Political Boss," *Psychiatry*, Vol. 1, (1938) pp. 527-533.

10. Robert Lane, *Political Life*, (Glencoe, Ill.: The Free Press, 1959), p. 102.

11. Gerald Sorin, *The New York Abolitionists: A Case Study of Political Radicalism*, (Westport: Greewood: 1971), p. 4.

12. Ibid.

13. Seymour Martin Lipset, "Sources of the Radical Irving" in Daniel Bell (ed.), *New American Right*, (New York: Criterion Books, 1955), pp. 167-68.

14. Herbert McClosky, "Conservatism and Personality," *American Political Science Review*, Vol. 52 (March, 1958), pp. 37-38.

15. Seymour Lispet and Earl Raab, *The Politics of Unreason: Right-wing Estremism in America, 1790-1970*, (New York: Harper & Row, 1970). For a keen critical analysis of this type of literature see R. William Holland, "White Researchers in Black America: The Epistemological Boondoggle," *Public Policy*, Vol. 22 (Winter, 1974), pp. 84-85, 89-90.

16. Robert Cole, "What Segregation Means to a Segregationist," in James David Barber (ed.), *Readings in Citizen Politics*, (Chicago: Markham Publishing Co., 1969), pp. 127-140.

17. See Alexander George and Juliette George, *Woodrow Wison & Colonel House*, (New York: John Day, 1956), and Sigmund Frued & William Bullitt, *Thomas Woodrow Wilson: A Psychological Study*, (Boston: Houghton Mifflin, 1967).

18. Wendell Bell, et al., *Public Leadership*, (San Francisco: Chandler, 1961), p. 163.

19. Rudolf Heberle, *Social Movements*, (New York: Appleton-Century Crofts, 1959), p. 104.

20. Erich Fromm, *The Sane Society*, (New York: Holt, Rinehart & Winston, 1960). p.8.

21. See Martin Duberman, "Abolitionists and Psychology," in his (ed.) *Antislavery Vanguard*, (Princeton: Princeton University Press, 1965); and Bertram Wyatt-Brown, "Abolitionism: Its Meaning for Contemporary American Reform," *Midwest Quarterly*, Vol. 8 (October, 1966), pp. 41-55.

22. See Erik Erikson, *Young Man Luther*, (New York: Norton, 1969), his *Childhood and Society*, (New York: Norton, 1963); and his *Gandhi's Truth*, (New York: Norton, 1969).

23. E. Victor Wolfenstein, *Personality and Politics*, (Belmount: Dickerson Publishing Co., 1969), p. 103.

24. Ibid., p. 7.

25. Erickson, *Childhood and Society*, p. 12.

26. See Fred I. Greenstein, "The Impact of Personality on Politics: An Attempt to Clear Away Underbrush," *American Political Science Review*, Vol 66 (1972), pp. 629-41; and his *Personality and Politics*, (Chicago: Markham, 1969), and his and Michael Lerner, *A Source Book for the Study of Personality and Politics*, (Chicago: Markham, 1971).

27. E. Victor Wolfenstein, *The Revolutionary Personality*, (Princeton: Princeton University Press, 1967), p. 318.

28. Wolfenstein, *The Revolutionary Personality*, p. 99, emphasis added.

29. Ibid., p. 100.

30. Ibid., pp. 4-5.

31. Ibid., pp. 4-5.

32. Wolfensteinin, *Personality and Politics*, p. 100.

33. Glenn D. Paige, The Scientific Study of Political Leadership (New York: Free Press, 1977), and Betty Glad, *Jimmy Carter* (W.W. Norton, 1980), pp. 487-507.

34. Lester Seligaman, "The Study of Political Leadership," in H. Eulau, *Political Behavior*, pp. 178-180.

35. See K. C. Morrison, "A Survey of Literature on Black Politics: 1962-1972," (Paper presented at the Ford Foundation Conference on Public Policy, 1972), p. 19.

36. For a partial history, see M. Elaine Burgess, *Negro Leadership in a Southern City*, Chapel Hill: University of North Carolina Press, 1962); James Q. Wilson, *Negro Politics: The Search for Leadership Class*, (Englewood Cliffs; Prentice Hall, 1963); Daniel Thompson, *The Negro Leadership Class*, (Englewood Cliffs: Prentice Hall, 1963); John R. Larkins, *Patterns of Leadership Among Negroes in North Carolina*, (Raleigh: Irving-Swain Press, 1959); Guy B. Johnson, "Negro Racial Movements and Leadership in the United States," *American Journal of Sociology*, Vol 43. (July, 1937), pp. 56-72; and Gunnar Myrdal, *An American Dilemma*, (New York: Harper & Row, 1944), p. 720.

37. See Everett C. Ladd, *Negro Political Leadership in the South*,(Ithaca, New York: Cornell University Press, 1966).

38. Ibid., p. 150.

39. See Cedric Robinson, "Malcolm Little as a Charismatic Leader," (paper presented at the Sixty-sixth Annual Meeting of the American Political

Science Association, Los Angeles, California, September 8-12, 1970).

40. Wolfenstein, *Personality and Politics,* p. 100.

41. Ibid., p. 66.

42. Eugene Wolfenstein, *The Victims of Democracy: Malcolm X and the Black Revolution,* (Lost Angeles: University of California Press, 1981)

43. Lerone Bennett, "Of Time, Space, and Revolution," in Charles Hamilton, (New York: G.P. Putnam's Sons, 1973), p. 304.

44. For the most recent attempt to improve on the typologies and include the activities of the sixties, see Charles Hamilton, "Conflict, Race and System-Transformation in theUnited States," in L. Shaw and J. Pierce (eds.), *Readings on the American Political System,* (Mass.: D.C. Heath & Co., 1970), pp. 609-18, and Donald L. Tryman, "A Typology of Black Leadership," *The Western Journal of Black Studies* Vol. 1 (Mrach, 1977), pp. 18-22. See also, Nathan Huggins, "Afro-Americans," in John Higham (ed.), *Ethnic Leadership in America* (Baltimore: Johns Hopkins University Press, 1978), pp. 91-118.

45. Robert C. Smith, *Black Leadership: A Survey of Theory and Research* (Washington: D.C.: Institute for Urban Affairs and Research—Howard University, 1984), pp. 95-96.

46. Harold Cruse, *Rebellion or Revolution,* (New York: William Morrow, 1969), pp. 193-258.

47. Harold Cruse, *The Crisis of the Negro Intellectual,* (New York: William Morrow, 1967).

48. Cruse, *Rebellion or Revolution,* p. 246.

49. Ibid., p. 247.

50. See Amiri Baraka, "Why I Changed My Ideology: Black Nationalism and Socialist Revolution," *Black World,* Vol 22 (July, 1975), pp. 31-36.

51. See Walton, *The Political Philosophy of Martin Luther King, Jr.,* Chapter 3.

52. E. Franklin Frazier, *The Negro in the United States,* (New York: MacMillan, 1957), pp. 547-549; and his "The American Negro's New Leaders," *Current History,* Vol 36 (April, 1928), pp. 56-59.

53. Frazier, *The Negro in the United States.* p. 548.

54. Interview, W. W. Law, Savannah NAACP Office, (August 16, 1975), 6:00 p.m. In Mid-1976, Mr. Law stepped down from the presidency of the organization but continued to serve as a member of the NAACP's National Board of Directors until 1979—for 30 years of service. On March 19, 1977, a multi-racial citizen committee gave a testimonial dinner to the champion of human rights, where a letter from President Carter was read, resolution from the Georgia House and remarks from both of Georgia Senators and local Congressmen. See Tom Puckett, "W. W. Law: Career of Achievement," *Savannah Morning News,* (March 19, 1977), pp. 1B, 12B.

55. See Charles V. Hamilton, *The Black Preacher in America,* (New York: William Morrow, 1972), for a clear-cut discussion of ministers in politics. For another kind of analysis see William Berenson, Kirk Elifson and Tandy Tollerson III, "Preachers in Politics: A Study of Political Activism Among the Black Ministry," *Journal of Black Studies,* Vol 7 (June, 1976), pp. 373-392. For an excellent study see Peter Paris, *Black Leaders in Conflict,* (New York: Pilgrim Press, 1978).

56. Interview, Reverend Matthew Southall Brown, Pastor's Study, Saint John Baptist Church, Savannah, Georgia, (September 27, 1975).

57. Interview, Thomas H. Byers, Savannah, Georgia, (October 28, 1975).

58. For information on this study, which was conducted by a Black sociologist, Otis Johnson, and which ran in serialization in the local newspaper; See Ann Marshall, "Hill, Law Lead List of Blacks," *Savannah Morning News*, (December 5, 1973), p. 1D; "Black Power Structure Identified in Survey," Ibid., (December 7, 1973).

59. For data on this see Mack Jones, "Introduction: 1984 Minus Nine Equals Police Terror in U.S. 1975 or the Early Arrival of Big Brother," *Journal of Political Repression*, Vol. 1 (June, 1975), pp. 4-11.

60. See also Susan Johnson, "Fannie Lou Hamer: Mississippi Grassroots Organizer," *The Black Law Journal*, Vol. 2 (Summer, 1972), pp. 155-164.

61. Interview, Jimmy Bennett, Savannah State College Library, (October 4, 1975).

62. Gregory Gouteau, "Black Leadership Vacuum Discussed," *The Diamond Back*, (Study Newspaper, University of Maryland, College Park: interview Charles V. Hamilton), (July 3, 1975), p. 8.

63. James E. Mock, "The Black Vote Output: Black Political Executives, 1961-1980," paper delivered at the 1982 Annual Meeting of Midwest Political Science Association, Milwaukee, Wisconsin (April 28-May 1, 1982), p. 1.

64. Hanes Walton, Jr., "Black Political Payoffs: Used and Unused Strategies *Political Science Review* Vol. 20. (July-September, 1981), p. 292.

65. Robert C. Smith, "Black Appointed Officials: A Neglected Area of Research in Black Political Participation," *Journal of Black Studies* Vol. 14 (March, 1984), p. 369.

66. Robert H. Brisbane, *The Black Vanguard* (Valley Forge: Judson Press, 1970), p. 161.

67. Chuck Stone, Black Political Power in America (New York: Dell, 1968), p. 69.

68. James D. King and James W. Riddlesperger, Jr. "Presidential Cabinet Appointments: The Partisan Factor," *Presidential Studies Quarterly* Vol. 14 (Spring, 1984), p. 234.

69. Smith, "Black Appointed Officials," p. 378.

71. King and Riddlesperger, Presidential Cabinet Appointments, p. 234.

72. Ibid.

73. Ibid., p. 235. See also Lenneal J. Henderson, "Administrative Advocacy and Black Urban Administrators," *In* John Howard & Robert C. Smith (eds.), *Urban Black Politics The Annals* Vol. 439 (September, 1978), p. 68-75.

74. Robert C. Smith, "The Political Behavior of Black Presidential Appointees 1960-1980, Paper at Howard University November, 1983, p. 8.

75. Robert C. Smith, "Race and Administration: The Council of Black Appointee (Forthcoming Western Journal of Black Studies), p. 4.

76. Ibid., p. 20.

77. Smith, "The Political Behavior...", p. 9-10.

78. Lenneal J. Henderson, *Administrative Advocacy: Black Administrator in Urban Bureaucracy* (California: R & E Research Associates, 1979), p. 106.

79. Holden, *The Politics of the Black 'Nation'*, p. 43. Emphasis his.

80. Ibid., p. 47-52.

81. Ibid., p. 49.

82. David Garrow, *"The FBI and Martin Luther King, Jr. From Solo to Memphis.* (New York: W.W. Norton, 1981), p. 106.

83. Thomas Sowell, "Are Quotas Good for Blacks?" in Ellen F. Paul and Philip A. Russo, Jr. (eds.), *Public Policy: Issues, Analysis and Ideology* (New Jersey: Chatham House, 1982). pp. 272-73.

84. For a discussiopn of "how" black leaders of this ideological position have arisen to leadership positions in the black community in this era see, Christopher Jencks, "Discrimination and Thomas Sowell," *The New York Review of Books* (March 3, 1983), pp. 33-34 and his "Special Treatment for Blacks?" Ibid. (March 17, 1983), pp. 12-19. For a clear cut discussion on how current black conservatives were deliberately drawn into the Republican party see John S. Saloma III, *Ominous Politics: The New Conservation Labyrinth* (New York: Hill and Wang, 1984). He writes: "The conservatives and the Republican Party, as part of their effort to form a new political majority, have solicited the support of racial and ethnic minority groups. Their largest and to date most successful achievement has been the building of a distinctly conservative black political movement." All of chapter 12 is devoted to this effort. pp. 130-37.

85. See Hanes Walton, Jr., Blacks and Conservative Political Movements, in Lenneal Henderson (ed.), *Black Political Life in the United States* (Calif: Chandler, 1972), pp. 56-65. See also, Lee Daniels, "The New Black Conservatives, *New York Times Sunday Magazine* (October 4, 1981), pp. 20-24; and Walter Williams, *The State Against Blacks* (New York: McGraw-Hill, 1983).

86. Val J. Washington, "Freedom's Fight from Abe to Ike," *Phylon* Vol 16. (Fourth Quarter, 1955), p. 359.

87. Pearl T. Robinson, "Whither the Future of Blacks in the Republican Party" *Political Science Quarterly*, (Summer, 1982), p. 229-230.

Notes to Chapter Ten

1. Herbert C. Kelman (ed.), *International Behavior: A Social-Psychological Analysis*, (New York: Holt, Rinehart and Winston, 1965); see also R. Fisher (ed.), *International Conflict and Behavioral Science*, (New York: Basic Books, 1964); see also J. D. Singer (ed.), *Human Behavior and International Politics*, (Chicago: Rand-McNally, 1965).

2. Ibid., p. 29.

3. Ibid., p. 565.

4. Ibid., p. 566.

5. Ibid., p. 579.

6. Ibid.

7. Ibid.

8. Ibid., p. 601.

9. Ibid.

10. H. Grietzkow, et al., *Simulation in International Relations*, (Englewood Cliffs, N.J.: Prentice-Hall, 1963).

11. John Gillespie and Betty Nesvold (eds.), *Marco-Quantitative Analysis*, (California: Sage, 1971), and J. D. Singer (ed.), *Quantitative International Politics*, (New York: Free Press, 1968).

12. See Hayward Alker, Jr., Karl Deutsch, and Antonine Stoetzel, *Mathematical Approaches to Politics*, (San Francisco: Jossey-Bass, 1973).

13. David Bobrow and Judith Schwartz (eds.), *Computers and the Policy-Making Community: Applications to International Relations*, (Englewood Cliffs, N.J.: Prentice-Hall, 1968).

14. See Richard C. Synder, "Some Recent Trends in International Relations Theory and Research," in A. Ranney (ed.), *Essays on the Behavioral Study of Politics*, (Urbana: University of Illinois Press, 1962), pp. 1-3-171; and Harry Howe Ranson, "International Relations," *Journal of Politics*, Vol. 30 (May, 1968), pp. 345-371.

15. James N. Rosenau (ed.), *Linkage Politics*, (New York: Free Press, 1969).

16. Ibid., p. 45.

17. Ibid.

18. Ibid., p. 56; see also his *The Scientific Study of Foreign Policy*, (New York: Free Press, 1971).

19. Alfred O. Hero, Jr., *The Southerner and World Affairs*, (Baton Rouge: Louisiana State University Press, 1965), pp. 506-507.

20. Ibid., p. 509.

21. Ibid., p. 511.

22. Ibid., p. 513.

23. Ibid., p. 513.

24. Ibid., p. 515.

25. Ibid., p. 517.

26. Ibid., p. 520.

27. Ibid., p. 522.

28. Ibid., pp. 523-524.

29. Ibid., p. 527.

30. Ibid.

31. See George Shepard (ed.), *Racial Influences on American Foreign Policy*, (New York: Basic Books, 1971); and G. Shepard and Tilden LeMelle, *Race Among Nations: A Conceptual Approach*, (Lexington: B. C. Heath, 1970).

32. George Shephard and Tilden LeMelle, "Race in the Future of International Relations," paper presented at the Sixty-sixth Annual Meeting of the American Political Science Association, Los Angeles, California, (September, 8-12, 1970), p. 1.

33. Rosenau, *The Scientific Study of Foreign Policy*, p. 341.

34. See William P. Robinson, Sr., "The Impact of Discrimination upon American Foreign Policy—The Problem," *Negro History Bulletin*, Vol. 20 (Oct., 1957), pp. 19-21; and Charles Johnson, "American Politics: Race and Foreign Relations," *Negro Digest*, (August, 1950), p. 82. See also Rubin F. Weston, *Racism in U.S. Imperialism*, (Columbia: University of South Carolina Press, 1972).

35. Hero, *The Southerner and World Affairs,* pp. 527-540.

36. John A. Davis, "Black American and United States Policy Toward Africa," *Journal of International Affairs,* vol. 23 (1969), pp. 231-249.

37. Victor C. Ferkiss, *Africa's Search for Identity,* (New York: Meridian Books, 1970), pp. 291-292.

38. Ibid., p. 294.

39. Ibid., p. 295.

40. Ibid., p. 296.

41. Ibid., p. 314.

42. Ibid.

43. Alain Locke, "Appropos of Africa," *Opportunity,* vol. 2 (Feb., 1924), p. 37.

44. Ibid.

45. Adelaide Hill and Martin Kilson (ed.), *Appropos of Africa: Sentiments of Negro American Leaders on Africa from the 1880's to the 1950's,* (London: Frank Cass and Company, 1969), p. xiii.

46. Ibid., p. xiv.

47. Ibid., pp. 3-6.

48. W. E. Ward, *The Royald Navy and the Salvers,* (New York: Pantheon Books, 1969).

49. "Prospect of War," *The Liberator,* (April 1, 1842).

50. Read Douglass's editorial on the matter in his paper, "Peace! Peace! Peace!" *The North Star,* (March 17, 1848).

51. See M. R. Delany and Robert Campbell, *Search for a Place: Black Separatism,* Edited by Howard Bell, (Ann Arbor: University of Michigan Press, 1972).

52. George T. Dowing, "May Hungary be Free," in Philip S. Foner (ed.), *The Voice of Black America,* Vol. I. (New York: Capricorn Books, 1975), p. 125.

53. Ibid.

54. Willard B. Gatewood, Jr. (ed.), *"Smoked Yankees" and the Struggle for Empire: Letters from Negro Soldiers, 1898-1902,*(Urbana: University of Illinois Press, 1971), pp. 4-5.

55. Hanes Walton, Jr., "The South West African Mandate," *Faculty Research jBulletin,* Vol. 26, (December, 1972), pp. 94-96.

56. See Richard Wright, *Black Power,* (New York: Harper and Row, 1954).

57. Imamu A. Baraka (ed.), *African Congress: A Document of the First Modern Pan African Congress,* (New York: William Morrow, 1972).

58. Grayson Mitchell, "Kissinger Assures Black Caucus of Better Relations," *Jet Magazine,* (September 4, 1975), pp. 8-9.

59. "A Handshake—Between Brothers," *Ebony Magazine,* (September, 1975), pp. 162-168.

60. Jody Powell, *The Other Side of the Story,* (New York, 1984), pp. 158-167.

61. See TransAfrican Forum Symposium of Black American Ambassadors: "The Limitations of a Cold War Approach to the Third World," Cambridge, Mass. (Feb. 5, 1983). Contains comments of most Black Diplomats from 1948-present. TransAfrica was founded in 1977. See Henry F. Jackson,

From the Congo to Soweto: U.S. Foreign Policy Toward Africa Since 1960 (NewYork: Morrow, 1982), pp. 123-26.

62. See TransAfrica, *Namibia: The Crisis in United States Policy Toward Southern Africa* (Washington, DC: TransAfrica, 1983).

63. The transcript of this symposium will appear shortly in an issue of the *TransAfrica Journal*.

64. James E. Sulton, Jr. (ed.), "Abomination in Grenada", *TransAfrica News*, Vol. 2, No. 7, pp. 1, 6.

65. Interview, Ms. Cherri D. Waters, March 26, 1984 at the TransAfrica Office, 545 8th Street, NE, Washington, DC. The author would like to thank Ms. Waters for the wonderful assistance in providing me with all the published materials of TransAfrica on a moment's notice and then permitted xeroxing of very rare items. Her assistance was simply outstanding.

66. Hill and Kilson, Sentiments of Negro American Leaders on Africa., p. 3.

67. Morris, *The Politics of Black America* (New York: Harper & Row, 1975), p. 289; see also his "Black Americans and the Foreign Policy Process: The Case of Africa," *Western Political Quarterly* Vol. 25 (September, 1972), pp. 451-463; then see Alfred Hero, Jr., "American Negroes and United States Foreign Policy: 1937-1967," *Journal of Conflict Resolution*, (June, 1969), pp. 220-251, the parallels are striking.

68. Alex Poinsett, "Where are the Revolutionaries," *Ebony Magazine*, (February, 1976), pp. 84-86.

69. For an explanation why he returned, see Eldridge Clever, "Fidel Castro's African Gambit," *Newsweek*, (May 3, 1976), p. 13.

70. On Williams see Robert F. Williams, *Negroes with Guns*, (New York: Marzani & Mansell, 1962); and see John Clytus, *Black Man in Red Cuba*, (Coral Gables: University of Miami Press, 1970).

71. On the difficulty Cleaver might have in revitalizing his domestic base in certain quarters (because while in America, he favored one segment, the white left as opposed to certain blacks), see Pearl Cleage Lomax, "Clever Cleavage," *Atlanta Gazette*, (September 8, 1976), p. 7. This article is a rarity, one of the very few articles which notes how Cleaver performed before white left audiences and then an all black audience in the same day. See also Bayard Rustin, "Eldridge Cleaver and the Democratic Idea," *The Humanist*, (Sept.-Oct., 1976), pp. 20-21 for another point of view.

72. Wayne Lee, "Eldridge Cleaver: The American Way," *Washington Times*, (April 20, 1984), p. 1B-2B.

73. Ibid. For an earlier critique see Alex Willingham, "California Dreaming: Eldridge Cleaver's Epithet to the Activism of the Sixties." *Endarchia Journal of Social Theory* (Winter, 1976), pp. 1-23.

Notes to Chapter Eleven

1. Gerald Pomper, *Voters' Choice: Varieties of American Electoral Behavior*, (New York: Dodd-Mead, 1975), pp. 1-12.

2. Ibid., p. 6.

3. Ibid., p. xiv.

4. V. O. Key, Jr., and Frank Munger, "Social Determination and Electoral Decision," in Eugene Burdick and Arthur Brodbeck (ed.), *American Voting Behavior*, (Glencoe, Ill.: Free Press, 1959), p. 281, emphasis supplied.

5. Ibid., p. 299.

6. Robert H. Black, "Socio-economic Determinism of Voting Turnout: A Challenge," *Journal of Politics*, Vol. 36 (August, 1974), p. 732.

7. Ibid.

8. Ibid., p. 752.

9. Stanley Kelly, Jr., Richard Ayers, and William C. Bowen, "Registration and Voting: Putting First Things First," *American Political Science Review*, Vol. 61 (June, 1976), pp. 357-377.

10. Jae-On Kim, John Petrocik, Stephen N. Erickson, "Voter Turnout Among the American States: Systemic and Individual Components," *American Political Science Review*, Vol. 69 (March, 1975) pp. 107-123 and Douglas Rose, "Comment on Kim, Petrocik, and Erickson: The American States' Impact on Voter Turnout," Ibid., pp. 124-131.

11. See Steven Rosenstein and Raymond E. Wolfinger, "The Effect of Registration Laws on Voter Turnout," paper delivered at the 1976 Annual Metting of the American Political Science Association, The Palmer House, Chicago, Illinois, September 2-5, 1976.

12. For voices outside political science see Jacques Barzun, *Clio and the Doctors*, (Chicago: University of Chicago Press, 1974), pp. 148-150.

13. For another discussion of the interplay of individual and systemic variables see Jerrold G. Rusk, "Comment: The American Electoral Universe," *The American Political Science Review*, Vol. 68 (Sept. 1975).

14. James Q. Wilson and Edward C. Banfield, "Public-Regardingness as a Value Premise in Voting Behavior," *American Political Science Review*, Vol. 58 (Dec. 1974), pp. 876-887. See also their "Political Ethos Revisited," Ibid., Vol. 65 (Dec. 1981), pp. 1048-1062.

15. See Harold Baronville, "Negro and White Voter Participation in the 1963 Atlanta Bond Issue Referendum: A Comparative Analysis," (Unpublished M. A. Thesis, 1964), pp. 35-37.

16. Raymond Wolfinger and John Field, "Political Ethos and the Structure of City Government," *American Political Science Review*, Vol. 50 (June, 1966), pp. 306-326; and Charles Ekstrom and Thomas Keil, "Political Attachment in Black Philadelphia: Does 'Public Regardingness' Apply," *Urban Affairs Quartery*, Vol. 8 (June, 1973), pp. 489-506.

17. William Ryan, *Blaming the Victim*, (New York: Vintage Books, 1971), p. 11.

18. Ibid., p. 7.

19. Ibid., pp. 3-4.

20. Ibid., p. 7.

21. Ibid., p. 29.

22. Theodore H. White, "New Powers, New Politics," *The New York Times Magazine* (February 5, 1984), p. 26.

23. Ibid.

24. George Gallup, *The Gallup Poll*, Vol. 3, 1959-1971, (New York: Random House, 1972), p. 1788.

25. For a discussion of the centrality of political attitudes in studying political behavior see Jarol B. Manheim, *The Politics Within: A Primer in Political Attitudes and Behavior* 2nd Edition (New York: Longman, 1982), pp. 8-32. See also Edmund Ions, *Against Behavioralism* (New Jersey: Rowman and Littlefield, 1977), p. 25.

35. See Dean Jaros and Lawrence Grant, *Poltiical Behavior: Choices and Perspectives* (New York: St. Martin's Press, 1974), pp. 353-358 for a discussion of theoretical, substantive, procedural, philosophical and conceptual limitations of the behavioral approach. See also, John C. Wahlke, "Pre-Behavioralism in Political Science," *American Political Science Review* (March, 1979) pp. 9-31.

Notes to Appendix A

1. See Hanes Walton, Jr. and Clarence Martin, "The Black Electorate and the Maddox Administration," *The Negro Educational Review* Vol. 22 (April, 1971), pp. 114-122; and also in *The Black Politician*, Vol. 1 (April, 1971), pp. 31-33. Due to printers errors, pages in the last article are out of sequence and scattered throughout the periodical.

2. On this point see, Apter and Andrain, *Contemporary Analytical Theory*, pp. 14-17.

3. For the black turnout in presidential races, all of the black precincts in the city were used and not just those in the five House districts and two Senate districts.

Index